Praise for The New Human Rights Movement

"Peter Joseph is one of the great visionaries of our time. If there's a beautiful future—and I think there will be—then his fingerprints will be all over it."

—MARIANNE WILLIAMSON,
#1 *NEW YORK TIMES* BESTSELLING AUTHOR

THE NEW
HUMAN
RIGHTS
MOVEMENT

THE NEW HUMAN RIGHTS MOVEMENT

REINVENTING the ECONOMY to END OPPRESSION

PETER JOSEPH

BenBella Books, Inc.
Dallas, TX

BenBella Books, Inc.
10440 N. Central Expressway, Suite 800
Dallas, TX 75231
www.benbellabooks.com
Send feedback to feedback@benbellabooks.com

Printed in the United States of America
10 9 8 7 6 5 4 3 2 1

Library of Congress Cataloging-in-Publication Data
Names: Peter Joseph, 1978- author.
Title: The new human rights movement : reinventing the economy to end
   oppression / Peter Joseph.
Description: Dallas, TX : BenBella Books, 2017.
Identifiers: LCCN 2016043997 (print) | LCCN 2016059808 (ebook) | ISBN
   9781942952657 (hardback) | ISBN 9781942952664 (electronic)
Subjects: LCSH: Human rights movements. | Human rights—Economic aspects. |
   Business and politics. | BISAC: POLITICAL SCIENCE / Political Freedom &
   Security / Human Rights. | POLITICAL SCIENCE / Economic Conditions. |
   SOCIAL SCIENCE / Poverty & Homelessness. | PHILOSOPHY / Social.
Classification: LCC JC571 .P47 2017 (print) | LCC JC571 (ebook) | DDC
   330—dc23
LC record available at https://lccn.loc.gov/2016043997

Editing by Vince Hyman
Copyediting by Brian Buchanan
Cover design by Pete Garceau
Jacket design by Sarah Dombrowsky
Text design and composition by Publishers' Design and Production Services, Inc.
Proofreading by Amy Zarkos and Lisa Story
Printed by Lake Book Manufacturing

Distributed by Perseus Distribution
www.perseusdistribution.com

To place orders through Perseus Distribution:
Tel: (800) 343-4499
Fax: (800) 351-5073
E-mail: orderentry@perseusbooks.com

To the unpersons,
those who embody the evidence of our grand social failures

Contents

Acknowledgments

· ·

A FEW BLOCKS FROM MY PRODUCTION STUDIO in downtown Los Angeles rests the historic central public library. Built in 1926, it is one of the largest library systems in the world, a gateway to about 6 million volumes. It was here I set up shop to compose this book over the course of 15 months. As an institution, the very idea of a library is quite interesting. In a world dominated by property rights and general economic restriction, the library has been a rare source of sharing for many centuries. In fact, not only does the library signify an intuition that knowledge should be free, given its critical role in societal development, but it also serves as a poetic metaphor for human consciousness itself. Astronomer Carl Sagan, referencing the destruction of perhaps the grandest library in human history, the Library of Alexandria, some 1,800 years ago, wrote: "It was as if the entire civilization had undergone some self-inflicted brain surgery, and most of its memories, discoveries, ideas and passions were extinguished irrevocably."[1]

I find great solace in such a socially connected perspective. It hints at the truth of the human condition. Understanding the social nature of human development, a dynamic interplay of what could be called our "group mind," makes a healthy mockery of the egoism and proprietary neurosis all too common in modern culture. Fueled by a socioeconomic condition that financially and through accolades of "success" rewards individual action while ignoring the social process that led to that action, we remain stuck in a very immature place. The fact is, world society as we know it is a purely social consequence, ultimately cultivated by a process of sharing. The library, in all its ancient glory and hidden intuition, signifies this deeper wisdom. As such, and as clichéd as it may sound, it is to this process I acknowledge credit of this text. This is not to dismiss the many people past and present who have had a direct influence on this work's creation, but to embrace them all in their proper context. I, like them, am just a link in a chain.

Moreover, as inspiring and helpful as the downtown Los Angeles library has been while this work was formed, there was another feature of relevance present—a feature I doubt comes to mind when most consider this institution: the homeless. With about 80,000 homeless on the street each night in Los Angeles County, the libraries have served as a common refuge. It is here where the homeless can escape summer heat, use a bathroom, drink from a water fountain, and even use a computer. It took me some time to gain perspective of just how many homeless and poverty-stricken people there were on any given day, but their presence was overwhelming. Yet, at the same time, in an eerie way, they also didn't exist at all. They moved like shadows or ghosts that the general public and workers simply ignored. As it is on the street, where the more fortunate glide along with barely a passive acknowledgment of these fixtures of human dispossession, the homeless and destitute exist in a rather dismissed, ignored, and forgotten universe. To invoke George Orwell, they are a type of the *unpersons*.

As I sat each day surrounded by people who effectively don't exist in the eyes of society at large, I began to understand that the homeless and poor are really walking threats to the way most wish to think about the world. They are threats to the way most wish to think about themselves. They are society's black mirrors, reflecting the vast denial of our human incompetence. To acknowledge them is to admit a tragic fault. Consequently, people go out of their way to pretend those ghosts lurking about them really don't exist at all. And so it is to these people that I extend my acknowledgment. The homeless in that library served as a daily reminder of what is at stake, further inspiring my need to help understand and fix what continues to go horribly wrong in this world.

Preface

···

A S PLAYWRIGHT GEORGE BERNARD SHAW eloquently put it, "The single biggest problem in communication is the illusion that it has taken place." The depth of this statement took a while for me to understand. Over the course of the past decade, my professional work in film, television, and online media has, to my humble amazement, been experienced by roughly a quarter of a billion people and translated into more than 130 languages. I have spoken in a dozen countries, given hundreds of hours of interviews and expositions via radio shows and podcasts, and answered literally thousands of questions from people concerned about the state of society.

Yet, in my various attempts, effective communication is still something of an ongoing experiment, especially when it comes to the content presented here. Naturally, any idea, theory, or proposal is only as valuable as how well it is relayed. Each individual is a complex mix of rational thoughts and convoluted biases. There is a threshold of rationality when it comes to the human condition and I state this not from a paternalistic standpoint but from the standpoint of just another flawed, emotional mind. True intelligence is self-awareness—including a sense of just how wrong you likely are most of the time as a result of your biases. As with any educational content, the more controversial the subject matter, the more difficult the communicative challenge. And there isn't anything more controversial than questioning culture itself. Being the social creatures we are, our very identity is linked to the values and traditions that surround us. This gravitation is largely out of our control. Hence, questioning culture and its norms invariably turns the question to one's self. This is delicate territory, no doubt.

Contemplating this problem led me to the context of this work, as inspired by the writings of Frederick Douglass. Frederick Douglass was born into chattel slavery in the American South in the early nineteenth century. After escaping to freedom in the North, he became one of the most outspoken and effective leaders of the American abolitionist movement. His work led me to recontextualize my activist focus under the umbrella of civil or human rights. Douglass's literary style itself was also influential. His writing is deliberate, incisive, and motivating. There is idealism and yet pragmatism existing at once. So, not only do I hope the core argument of this work will be properly embraced as an extension of the *global abolitionist movement*, I also hope it will be as efficient in form and tonality as I found Douglass's literary expression to be.

As for detail, much here has been necessarily generalized in an attempt to be concise and accessible. The caveat, of course, is that I have made assumptions about what readers may or may not already be familiar with. While I have done my best to avoid unnecessary complexity, tedious clarifications, and fringe terminology, there is only so far one can go before generalizations become self-defeating. Given this, the reader is encouraged to review the source material in the endnotes. A great deal of care has been taken to anticipate unfamiliar subjects, providing rather extensive references to help further exploration and justification. A glossary has also been added to help with custom concepts and general clarity. In most cases, terms presented in italics are included in this glossary.

Regarding form, the style here is a combination. Publishing interests originally requested not only a treatment on social justice, but also something of a memoir. This approach did not strike me as productive initially. First, it seems confusing to mix a serious treatment about socioeconomics with personal anecdotes. Second, in the past I have deliberately not talked about my life history or myself in any real way, as I generally find it inhibiting to an audience's judgment. My goal is not to impose conclusions from the position of authority but to show the reasoning or train of thought that arrives at those conclusions. Yet, because I am not credentialed in any particular way, coming from a self-educated perspective, it has been difficult to crack the vault of mainstream dialogue.

While I have certainly done my homework over the past decade, exploring hundreds of texts on social theory, history, and economics,

I have no plaques or honorary degrees to impress you with. Given the emphasis our society places on perceived authority, the cynicism I often sense is not surprising. It is also natural that in our fast-paced, time-deficient world, most people simply want someone to "tell them what to think." Yet there is a serious problem here, as there is a tendency by modern academia to perpetuate existing normative assumptions—especially when it comes to socioeconomic theory. Most people who rise through the ranks of orthodox higher education experience an almost inevitable process of indoctrination. As with many cultural matters, so much has been presupposed about our way of life over time, people tend to assume the social institutions around them are all there is and ever was. Values become entrenched, identities become locked, and dogma is cultivated. The prevailing intelligentsia is far from exempt from this "normalizing" process and sometimes one needs to exist far outside the box to make a difference.

That stated, I decided I would let down my guard on this issue and try the experiment of explaining a little about where I came from and why I have the focus I do. This humanizing aspect will also, I hope, trigger associations within the reader that make the subjects more relatable. Surprisingly, it wasn't until I began to compile these stories that I came to understand just how predictable my life's unfolding has been. Many seemingly mundane events in my history have actually had profound implications hidden within. I simply didn't have the vocabulary at the time to understand them. However, I do wish to stress that these stories are not to be construed as actual evidence in defense of the conclusions argued. The technical scholarship of this work stands on its own and the anecdotes are merely supplemental in the hope of sparking a better sense of connection to the reader.

Finally, I want to point out that there is some repetition throughout the work. Due to certain topics existing in multiple contexts at once, the chapters often cross-reference one another, weaving in and out. This is mostly done to bypass anticipated confusion or incompleteness. By far the biggest challenge in writing this text has been keeping things connected, properly supporting the larger arguments. As abstract as the following comment may seem, the kind of thinking required here is actually not linear, but systemic. What I mean by that will become clear as you move forward. At the same time, I find that it doesn't hurt to periodically remind the reader of critical themes, especially given how unfamiliar some of this content and overall train of thought may be to some. While this text has been designed for people who have not been exposed to socioeconomic theory before, I admit there is a certain level of complexity that I hope will be tolerated and appreciated.

Introduction

We are all one. And if we don't know it, we will find out the hard way.[1]

—BAYARD RUSTIN

A CENTRAL MESSAGE OF THIS BOOK is that solutions to modern social problems are less about the moral aptitude of society and more about how society is technically organized. If I had to reduce the idea to a singular term, I would say the perspective is *structuralist*. Structuralism simply means we are accounting for larger-order relationships when thinking about social affairs. It is a derivation of a more generalized concept called *systems theory* (chapter one).

In terms of structuralism, if we had to locate the most influential man-made force affecting the human condition, there is no doubt that a society's *social system* would be most prominent. A social system is defined as the means by which a society organizes itself to facilitate survival, prosperity, and, ideally, peaceful coexistence. From networking the behavior of individuals and institutions, to characteristics such as security, medical access, resource management, political processes, and transport infrastructure, the defining features of a social system can vary.

Overall, a social system serves to maintain and improve *public health* (chapter four). Public health is an umbrella idea that embraces many factors and outcomes. As a broad measure, the quality of overall public health in a society ultimately reflects the quality of its social system. If it happens to be that a system is allowing or even facilitating unnecessary disease epidemics, pollution, starvation, violence, crime, deprivation, social oppression, bigotry, and other harmful features, then the integrity of that social system is brought into question.

However, any challenge to the integrity of the system is really a challenge to the integrity of its core foundation, and that core foundation is *economic*. How a society organizes its resources, labor, production, and distribution is by far the most defining and influential feature of culture. This is why when people discuss social systems in general they usually refer to them by their economic modes.

Capitalism, communism, socialism, feudalism, mercantilism, and so on, each have specific economic properties that temper the entire social construct. The economic foundation of society is what determines not only the kind of political and social institutions it has, but also its dominant cultural values (chapter two). An example of the latter is the cultivation of *consumerism*. Consumer culture reflects a sociological adaptation to the structural needs of our prevailing economic mode. The most optimized state of market capitalism is one of high product turnover. Without this, economic expansion would not be possible in technical terms. Therefore, a culture that is motivated to buy and sell as much as possible is one favorable to the structure of a market economy (chapter four).

I wish to clarify that throughout this work various terms will be used to reference our current economic mode. *Free market, capitalism, market, market system, market economy,* and *market capitalism* will be used in both a detailed and generalized context. To the chagrin of any traditional economic purists reading this, once this text establishes its core definition of a market economy, such terms become mostly interchangeable in use (chapter two). While direct clarification will still be made at times, the decision to use one term over another will be contextually subtle. For example, if the context pertains to class relationships, perhaps highlighting the historical wealth and power divide between "owners" and "workers," the term *capitalism* will likely be used. This is because inherent to that term is the structural distinction between the two labor classes. In contrast, if the context is about dynamics related to trade itself, such as general equilibrium theory, I will likely use the term *market economy* since it is more specific to the dynamics of exchange.

There is, however, one term that is very specific and will be used a great deal. That term is *socioeconomic*. This refers to economic activity that connects to social and personal outcomes. It can be used to describe a cause, or it can be used to describe an effect. A simple example is poverty. Modern poverty is actually not an inevitable byproduct of humans' sharing a planet that is supposedly deficient in resources. Rather, poverty today is a systemic consequence native to our current economic mode. In other words, its existence is artificial and contrived, not natural. Poverty is simply a negative externality of the market economy, just as industrial pollution often is (chapter three). However, while poverty is certainly an *effect* of the social system, it can also be separated as a cause. In modern sociological research, poverty is frequently referenced as a starting point, or precondition, that leads to a spectrum of socioeconomic problems. These include premature mortality, violence, social destabilization, epidemic disease, crime, suicide, mental illness, domestic abuse, and many other public-health concerns.

Yet, poverty is just one feature of the overall phenomenon of *socioeconomic inequality*. Socioeconomic inequality links to a range of detrimental social problems, many of which are quite surprising (chapter four). For example, as odd as it may seem, a person living in a generally wealthy nation, with a smaller income gap, may experience very different public-health outcomes than a person living in another generally wealthy country that has a larger income gap. This statistically occurs even if those people have the same absolute income. The more economic inequality, the unhealthier a country's people are on average.[2]

Put succinctly, socioeconomic inequality is the greatest detriment to human health and social stability in the world today. It is a systemic problem that has far-reaching consequences. *The New Human Rights Movement* is about ending it or coming as close as we possibly can. This is not to ignore other issues of social injustice such as racism, discrimination, or xenophobia; nor is it to bypass growing socioecological problems such as biodiversity loss, climate change, water pollution, and other problems that will harm the poor of the world long before the rich. Rather, *The New Human Rights Movement* serves to unify these issues.

While a fragmented focus has been required in pursuit of social and environmental justice historically, there is a dominant through-line that has consistently been missed or ignored. That through-line is that almost all forms of social oppression are rooted in *socioeconomic inequality*. And most forms of destructive environmental destabilization are rooted in the essential nature of our economic mode. These two issues are critical to understand.

Causality surrounding them may not always be direct or obvious. As will be discussed, our minds have a hard time understanding extended chain reactions. We tend to think in a very proximal sense rather than a systemic one (chapter one). This means when we see, for example, a company polluting a water supply, hurting a local population, we tend to blame the company, ignoring the larger structural pressures that may be occurring beyond that company, motivating or even coercing its decision to pollute.

The bottom line is that when we trace the systemic chain reactions of our most detrimental social problems, we almost invariably end up at the doorstep of the economy. If we expect to achieve new levels of prosperity, peace, and social justice on this planet, while also stopping or reversing many detrimental trends currently on pace, then it is about time we started to expand our sense of possibility. While the future has yet to be seen, it is safe to say that a "business-as-usual" scenario can only lead to increasing social problems at this stage of social evolution. While we have seen great strides over the past 200 years, the value of those strides is only as good as our ability to maintain them. Social and ecological trends now show not a path toward further prosperity, but a path toward social destabilization and an overall public-health crisis (chapter five).

I wish to reiterate that the real issue of concern today isn't moral; it is structural. It has little to do with people's general, day-to-day intent and everything to do with the organizing framework of global society. All the best intentions in the world are not going to stop the existing and emerging problems as long as the current socioeconomic framework remains unaltered. What we have today is an increasingly incompatible social system, clashing with a world very different than the one it evolved out of. While it is convenient to assume that we humans, as smart as we are, will naturally adapt society to new requirements, given current trends this very well might not be the case. In the same way the abolition of abject slavery or apartheid didn't occur through polite, rational conversation, at no time has the march toward social equality and rational societal adjustment been fluid.

As will be detailed, the character of our social system favors preservation and elitism (chapter three). *Social dominance* and the facilitation of social control and oppression is structurally codified in the system; a normative function born from its inherently competitive, scarcity-driven ethic. Given this, the odds of any kind of easy transition are slim. That is because those with great power and wealth, those who have been rewarded greatly by the system, naturally find cognitive dissonance with the idea of altering the very mechanism that has rewarded them so disproportionately. In the words of Frederick Douglass: "Power concedes nothing without a demand. It never did and it never will. Find out just what any people will quietly submit to and you have found out the exact measure of injustice and wrong which will be imposed upon them . . ."[3]

Therefore, the need for social movement on the global scale, with very specific and strategic plans to shift the social architecture, is now critical to progress. These needed adjustments have already been made clear by both modern trends in economic or productive means and the sociological and ecological revelations presented by contemporary science. The train of thought as to what socioeconomic preconditions will allow for a highly sustainable and socially just world is virtually self-evident. How we get there—and if we get there in time—is the ultimate question.

Chapter One

SYSTEM-BOUND: REALIZING RELATIONSHIPS

Whatever affects one directly affects all indirectly. For some strange reason, I can never be what I ought to be until you are what you ought to be. You can never be what you ought to be until I am what I ought to be. This is the interrelated structure of reality.[1]

—DR. MARTIN LUTHER KING JR.

W HEN I WAS ELEVEN YEARS OLD, I was assaulted by a young black teenager who stole the expensive new bike my mother had recently bought for me. The gift was fairly rare, likely provided out of guilt from my parents' recent divorce. At that time, I was living with my father in a poor urban area of Winston-Salem, North Carolina, having moved there from a more rural setting years before. The region was a strange mix of subsidized housing projects and large, circa-WWI Victorian homes in bad repair. It was basically the outcome of what some have termed "white flight" from the decades prior.[2] During more racially turbulent times in America, Caucasians migrated en masse from the cities to the suburbs. The end result was economic stagnation in the regions left behind. While the demographic in the area varied, my Italian-German family was certainly in the minority.

Running home after the attack, bruised and traumatized, I was relieved to find my older brother. In my emotional state I explained the situation. Furiously, protective of his younger sibling, he grabbed a golf club and dragged me out the door and into the car. Speeding around the neighborhood, we ended up in a crowded mall parking lot. Near the top of a hill, I noticed the silhouettes of a couple of young kids, working their way up on their bikes against the setting sun. One of the bikes appeared to have the same spoke structure as mine but I wasn't sure. In my delirium, I really wasn't able to make much sense of anything.

"Is that him?!" my brother demanded. I didn't know and shied away from any further pursuit. I just wanted it all to end.

When my father came home from work, I could sense his outrage as he examined me. As a second-generation Italian immigrant raised in New York poverty, he had a deep culture of family protection and honor ingrained in him. As in the clichés of Italian vengeance popularized in Hollywood Mafia films, I could sense his overwhelming need to "do something" about what had happened to me. This sense of retribution was gestural. After all, it was just a kid and no one was going to hunt him down and harm him. The police were notified and a general lookout for the young man went on for a few weeks. Though he was a minor, his being arrested, prosecuted, and penalized would have been the common path of what we call *criminal justice* in the United States. He was never caught, however.

As I will explain in a moment, I'm glad he wasn't.

SYSTEMS THEORY

I have set up this childhood story to contextualize a series of observations. Before I begin, however, let's review a tool needed to frame this assessment—something called *systems theory.*

Systems theory was made popular by biologist Ludwig von Bertalanffy in the late 1960s. It is a nonreductionist approach to understanding complex phenomenon, focusing attention on larger-order relationships rather than smaller parts.[3] There has been a tendency throughout the evolution of science to fragment fields, examining them independently. In school, we study biology, mathematics, psychology, sociology, physics, and other areas generally in isolation. This reductionism is logical in a preliminary phase of investigation. However, it becomes limiting if those

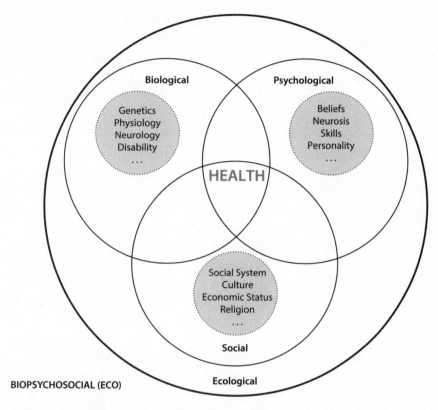

FIGURE 1A. While incomplete, this conceptual graphic represents the biological, psychological, and social (biopsychosocial) influences that intersect to define the health and character of a human being. The larger context of ecology has been included to emphasize the total influence habitat has on all factors.

fields are not eventually viewed in connection with each other, as they are in the real world. Systems theory highlights this need for inclusive comprehension in the search for causality in nature.

As is the case with the study of the human body, understanding the singular properties of parts only, such as cells or organs, is incomplete. We need to understand how all those parts work together, producing the human being as a single system. Yet at the same time the human body itself is not an island. It is also a falsely detached construct, as much as we are inclined to separate ourselves in consciousness. A human being is inclusive to the larger-order ecosystem or habitat from which it evolved and upon which it relies for survival and health. It is also inclusive to our manmade social structures and institutions, such as political, legal, and economic traditions.

The term *biopsychosocial* is commonly used in the public-health community to embrace such mixed influences.[4] As conceptualized in Figure 1a, our biology, our psychology, and the social conditions in which we live interconnect to define us as individuals. Who we are, what we think, and the quality of our health is a consequence of these influences. The figure includes a few listed examples. This attempt to delineate specifics is very general and incomplete. For instance, while genetics as a field of study is considered unique within biology, the broader notion of physiology can be used to embrace both biology and genetics together. Any attempts at hierarchies of this nature are rather ambiguous, as there is always overlap when we are trying to isolate attributes. Noted at the bottom of the figure, *ecology* has been added as a macro influence overall, basically extending the social component to the habitat.

As will be explored further, our habitat and its dynamics influence our social and personal lives in complex ways. For instance, any large-scale environmental disaster could deeply affect our biopsychosocial condition. An earthquake that creates a water shortage in a city is an example. This could trigger social disorder, reducing public safety in terms of both poor sanitation and stress-induced crime. Those suffering from dehydration could suffer serious physiological harm. Likewise, a person genetically predisposed to anxiety disorder might have behavioral reactions that in turn negatively affect others. Some may become so desperate that they end up drinking unsanitary water, triggering the spread of disease. This would further increase negative social stress and other chain reactions.

As expressed by this example, while the general idea of extended causality and interacting systems may be simple in theory, the technical, real-world dynamics are overwhelmingly complex. The main focus here is systems theory as related to sociology. Niklas Luhmann is a notable historical figure in this field and worth referencing. Luhmann basically reduces all social-system phenomena to processes of communication.[5] This makes sense since most all societal features, such as economy, law, politics, religion, and the like, are ultimately about human interaction. Each of these subsystems or institutions interconnect to define the larger-order social system and its dynamics.

This overlap between subsystems, such as how an economy can affect the well-being of a family, is termed an "intersection" by Luhmann. In this example, the intersection is between the needs of a family and the tradition of economic organization. He refers to everything outside of such interacting (or unifying) systems as the "environment," with this environment housing the delineated, intersecting systems perceived. A simple analogy is to consider Earth in the void of space. Given the vast distances between celestial bodies, we experience the Earth as a "closed" system, composed of endless subsystems, such as oceans, forests, and even the human species. In this analogy, space would be the environment, assuming we ignore the sun and other factors actually affecting Earth in an even larger relationship. Necessarily, the study of systems is a process of isolating them on some level, even though the intent of systems theory is the daunting task of comprehending the widest range of intersections, seeking as much unification as possible.

How the human being intersects with his or her environment, whether social or ecological, is fundamental to all human sciences. A core observation is that we appear to be built with certain biopsychosocial propensities and expectations. In other words, we have hard-wired aspects linking our biological and psychological selves to the social condition. We have evolved not only basic physiological needs but also psychological ones built around our social nature. Just as we completely depend on adults for survival in the first years of life, evolution has wired us for social connection and bonding in deep and profound ways throughout the life cycle.[6]

Youth development in general is no doubt the most critical phase of life. For example, in the thirteenth century, King Frederick II of Sicily conducted a wildly primitive experiment. Curious what the "natural language" of human beings may be, he commandeered some children from his kingdom and had them raised in complete isolation for years. Each child was given its own room and all the needs assumed required for survival, such as food, clothes, warmth, etc. However, no one was allowed to talk or communicate with them in any meaningful way. In the meantime, the king and his associates speculated on what language the children would eventually speak. Would it be Greek? Would it be Italian? Unfortunately, the experiment was inconclusive as all the children died of what is called stress or psychosocial dwarfism.[7] Also known as Kaspar Hauser Syndrome, this is the phenomenon in which extreme emotional deprivation leads to endocrinological disturbances that harm development and can even lead to death.[8] The same phenomenon has been witnessed with feral children, who are often abused through social isolation. Some of these children can never learn to speak, in fact, because the critical learning period for language attainment was also never utilized.[9]

In order to achieve healthy outcomes, there are things that should occur during child development and things that simply should not.[10] If a child is severely abused or traumatized, there is an increased likelihood that that child will develop destructive tendencies as an adult or suffer health complications.[11] In contrast, supportive emotional bonds can have powerful, long-term positive effects on children, even in infancy. For instance, caring for infants in very deliberate and physical ways has been linked to stronger immune systems.[12] A prominent study conducted by Tiffany Field of the University of Miami School of Medicine found that simply touching premature infants each day in neonatology wards sparked growth-hormone reactions that increased development rates by almost 50 percent, along with a host of other positive outcomes.[13] Such findings coincide with a large body of research demonstrating the biological importance of positive human (or social) connection.

Extending this logic, if aspects of adult well-being and behavior can be linked to childhood treatment, the question then becomes what factors or conditions set the stage for childhood mistreatment. Given the intersecting nature of things, both children and those responsible for them are subject to larger-order socioeconomic conditions. If those conditions aren't supportive to such nurturing, then we have a problem. For example, if a family lives in extreme poverty, the kind of social and material support needed to raise children properly simply may not be possible. It is here where the term *precondition* is worth introducing.

A precondition is defined as something that comes before or is necessary to a subsequent result. For example, a precondition to driving a car would be obtaining a driver's license. Medically, the term is used to denote factors that may lead to a statistically probable result, such as smoking tobacco leading to lung cancer. Sociologically, the term is used the same way. As opposed to individual health, however, the context is public health: health outcomes occurring on a population level. For example, as will be discussed in detail in chapter four, poverty is highly determinant of many negative outcomes, including child abuse and neglect. While society tends to view parents as the starting point of these problems, as does the legal system, this inclusion of social preconditions extends the chain of causality. For example, researchers at the American Academy of Pediatrics directly linked an increased unemployment rate to child maltreatment.[14] In this case, this precondition, unemployment, is being correlated to child abuse or neglect. Unemployment does not literally cause child maltreatment, but rather there is a statistical correlation between the condition of unemployment and chain reactions linked to it. Extending the example, the precondition of unemployment has actually been shown to correlate to a wide array of problems. In the United States, between 1991 and 2000 the annual unemployment rate went from 6.8 percent to 4.8 percent. According to a study by the Uniform Crime Report (UCR), that same period produced a 42.9 percent reduction in murder, a 33.6 percent decline in violent crime, and a 28.8 percent reduction in property crime.[15] A 2015 study focusing on sixty-three countries found that about 46,000 suicides were associated with unemployment in 2008, marking a dramatic rise related to the global financial crisis.[16] These people were stressed to the point of mental illness, predisposed or not.

In academic literature the terms *rational* and *structural* are often used, with the former referencing isolated human decisions and the latter referencing decisions manipulated by larger-order influences. Such structuralist correlations linking environmental preconditions to behavior and health are also replete throughout modern sociological and epidemiological literature. Yet policy makers have mostly ignored such informative research on how social conditions lead to detrimental public-health outcomes. There are some exceptions where attempts to limit negative social preconditions exist, such as the public-welfare systems of Nordic countries; however, the world generally neglects the concept. As will be explored throughout this work, our social system, despite any positive intentions and degree of supportive success, is at the same time the driver of extreme and unnecessary negative public-health outcomes. But the dominant political, legal, and economic institutions of society largely ignore or are oblivious to the depth of such problems. Overall, I find that there are two reasons for this.

First, regardless of the science, this kind of thinking is very counter-intuitive. We tend to perceive in very linear and superficial ways, as opposed to broader, more thorough ways. This contrast could be termed localized perception vs. systems perception. *Localized perception* is what you see directly around you, drawing conclusions and building associations from the incomplete sensory data coming through your five-sense reality. *Systems perception* or systems thinking is about understanding intersecting processes and chain reactions. Unfortunately, such thinking does not come naturally to us. We tend to see the world as a façade, perpetuating illusions of reality.

In fact, I would argue that this perceptual flaw is at the root of most all superstitions and false theories of the past. For example, ancient societies would look up at the sky and watch the sun, moon, and stars appear to "circle" the "flat" Earth. Why? No other reason than that it simply looked that way. Likewise, as we gaze outward it is also easy to forget that the light we see is only a tiny portion of the electromagnetic spectrum. It took the creation of advanced tools and more-scientific approaches for us to witness and better understand these once-hidden features. Even the most commonsense perception you have of yourself is largely an illusion. We experience our bodies as closed, free-moving systems. Our minds have a powerful sense of individuality and free agency. Yet the air we breathe, the gravity that defines our movement, the sun that powers life itself, and the culture that orients our values are just as much a part of us as the arms we extend. Our biopsychosocial nature primes and alters our thoughts, reasoning, and reactions, putting into question the degree of free will we think we have.[17]

Likewise, research shows how difficult it is for us to think in terms of probabilities. Probabilistic assessment is a critical mechanism of scientific evaluation and the understanding of complex, real-world interactions.[18] Today, we have firm understandings about social preconditions that lead to probable outcomes such as terrorism, violence, property crime, family abuse, mental disorders, sexual perversion, conflict, drug addiction, and a host of other behaviors once relegated to the realm of free will entirely. Without statistical study at the population level over time, many such connections would remain invisible, just as the link between smoking and lung cancer was once hidden. Similarly, we also tend to operate with *heuristics* in our everyday lives, using quick means to make decisions based on personal experience rather than through detailed analysis.[19]

All of this is to say that our minds naturally gravitate toward very narrow and superficial thinking. Only with the advent of science has our comprehension become more refined. Socially, we have come a long way from simply declaring a person evil because of an offensive act. Today, we have a better understanding of the systemic preconditions that create aberrant human behavior as a chain reaction.[20] As time has moved forward, we have continued to improve our tools and models, refining our understandings, just like we finally realized that the Earth was not flat and the sun did not orbit around it.

The second reason society tends to ignore the relationship between social conditions and public well-being is because this knowledge clashes with the nature of the established political, social, and economic order. This order includes the major philosophies and belief systems that underscore such dominant traditions, including theistic religion. Religious thinking is fundamentally nonsystemic, as it tends to separate humans from the natural world, focusing on individual behavior and human privilege. It implicitly assumes people have total free will and are isolated and responsible in their actions without any connective nuance. This makes sense since at the time most fundamental religious texts were written there was no real understanding of these systemic or scientific relationships. This kind of thinking is yet again a flaw of localized perception, as is the case with the overall idea of theism in general. To see ourselves as connected to and the same as everything else in the world, as science has shown, is a very unromantic detour from ancient belief systems determined to convince us that we are special. Hence, systems thinking puts into doubt the major foundations of religious belief, eliminating the idea that human beings have a privileged position in the universe.

Secularly, the established socioeconomic-political system has been built upon similar archaic and superficial assessments. For example, our economy is premised on a very early stage of civilization. As will be expanded upon in chapter two, the economy narrowly focuses on individual behaviors, without any real consideration of larger-order or aggregate consequences of such behaviors combined. For example, when people buy and sell in the market, they generally do so on the basis of their personal, short-term preferences. The collective result of these actions can create negative outcomes or chain reactions such as industrial pollution or resource overshoot that have nothing do to with the intent of individuals acting in the market. This lack of comprehension, rooted in a truncated or incomplete understanding of systemic economic outcomes, creates constant socioeconomic disorder, as we continue to see throughout the modern world. The same goes for our political and legal methods. These practices were also born from periods that had very little scientific foundation, assuming highly localized or truncated ideas about the human condition. Today, intellectual progress has literally left the socioeconomic-political system behind. A massive sociological cultural lag has been occurring for about a century now, wherein modern understandings that can dramatically improve human life go utterly unincorporated.

This is not hard to understand since power systems inherently fight interfering change, as noted earlier. After all, large changes to the social system could mean disturbance to those who benefit disproportionately, along with those in political control. The truth is that if the potential for positive change were truly realized, the entire architecture of society would be forced to shift dramatically. As such, there should be little wonder as to why modern sociological revelations have gone mostly ignored by policy makers.

FALSE CAUSALITY

With this systems framework in mind, let's now return to my story. As stated, from the standpoint of the criminal justice system, my assailant's being arrested, prosecuted, and penalized would have been the traditional path. As a minor, he likely would have landed in juvenile detention for the aggravated theft of that $200 bike. The United States not only incarcerates more of its citizens than any country in the world, it incarcerates more of its youth than any other country in the world.[21] Racism is literally built into the entire system, as almost half of those incarcerated are of African descent, with black youths six times more likely to be incarcerated than white youths for the same offenses.[22] As civil rights lawyer Michelle Alexander notes: "[Y]outh of color are more likely to be arrested, detained, formally charged, transferred to adult court, and confined to secure residential facilities than their white counterparts."[23]

The result of this highly punitive and bigoted system is the destruction of children's lives, especially black and minority children, since statistics show that youth incarceration actually increases the likelihood of future offenses, on average. A 2013 study produced by Massachusetts Institute of Technology found that: "Estimates based on over 35,000 juvenile offenders over a ten-year period from a large urban county in the US suggest that juvenile incarceration results in large decreases in the likelihood of high school completion and large increases in the likelihood of adult incarceration."[24] When you statistically examine the punitive outcome affecting black males in America, combining recidivism rates among both juveniles and adults, you begin see that the US criminal justice system is a machine that harms anyone subject to it, and specifically chews up and spits out blacks and minorities, ruining countless lives. The system also doesn't end at incarceration. Federal convictions as adults can remove possibilities for future employment, remove the right to vote, generate housing discrimination, lead to the denial of educational opportunities and loans, and remove access to social welfare benefits, along with other legal forms of what can only be called oppression.[25]

In light of these statistics, coupled with how the peak of this highly punitive approach was occurring in the early 1990s as far as juvenile arrest and incarceration are concerned, I can honestly say I'm glad my offender wasn't caught. While I certainly didn't enjoy his pummeling or the loss of my bike, the probability that his life could have been set on a path of destruction through a barbaric and structurally racist criminal justice system is much more offensive to me. Kids make mistakes and a great deal of compassion is needed to correct them. The US criminal justice system has proven not to be a means of reform but rather a mech-anism to exacerbate many problems. Also, since the system has been shown to actually breed violence, as will be touched upon in a moment, it's possible that other people could have been victimized as a result of his exposure to such punitive conditions.

All this begs the question of how such a distorted penal system came to be and why the black and minority population have been so dispro-portionately victimized by it. What cultural, socioeconomic, and histori-cal influences have intersected to produce such an institution? At this time of writing, not only have the US criminal justice system and its systemic racism been under attack by activists, but there is great outcry over repeated acts of police brutality against blacks and minorities as well. Organic grassroots organizations such as the Black Lives Matter movement, coupled with older, more established rights groups such as the ACLU (American Civil Liberties Union) and NAACP (National Associa-tion for the Advancement of Colored People), have made these concerns a top priority in public appeal. Of course, the efficacy of any policy propos-als can only be as good as the cause and effect understood. To consider this further, let's first review the basic premise of criminal justice itself.

While approaches vary from country to country, the idea that oper-ant negative conditioning will deter unwanted behavior is the central theme. In other words, punishment or the threat of punishment is the assumed means of control. While the term "rehabilitation" is often used in regard to incarceration or parole, it's hard to take that term seriously when the mechanism is mostly punishment. While it is true that operant conditioning works to a degree, as in the case of a child who learns not to touch a hot stove after being burned, the approach is incomplete.[26] It is once again localized, not systemic. The justice system generally ignores the social preconditions that lead a person to commit crime. The consideration of how economic and societal pressures distort human behavior, or perhaps even make an entire minority demographic vulner-able to legal persecution, is virtually nonexistent. Instead, a superficial process of individual judgment occurs, with no consideration for one's life experience or social condition.

While removing behavioral threats from society may be required, just as the need arises to quarantine a person with a highly contagious disease to prevent its spread, the overall premise of legal judgment is fundamentally shortsighted. In the words of Bertrand Russell:

> When a man is suffering from an infectious disease he is a danger to the community, and it is necessary to restrict his liberty of movement. But no one associates any idea of guilt with such a situation. On the contrary, he is an object of commiseration to his friends. Such steps as science recommends are taken to cure him of his disease, and he submits as a rule without reluctance to the curtailment of liberty involved meanwhile. The same method in spirit ought to be shown in the treatment of what is called "crime."[27]

Such a medical or public-health perspective is mostly missing in legal practice, especially in the United States. There are a few nations that have worked to incorporate a more humane approach, such as the Nordic countries. Sweden has one of lowest incarceration and recidivism rates in the world, being less punitive and more therapeutic in its methods. In fact, as of 2015, Sweden has actually been closing prisons, in stark contrast to the United States.[28] With 65 per 100,000 Swedish citizens incarcerated vs. 700 per 100,000 in the US, there is a clear difference at work.[29] However, that difference is not simply how criminal justice or rehabilitation is administered. The Nordic counties have also adjusted their market economies to include vast social-welfare safeguards, reducing socioeconomic stress. The social condition there is very different than in America, which has perhaps the weakest social-welfare system of any industrialized nation.

While effective rehabilitation is important, real success lies in preventing a criminal violation to begin with. This means the proper social preconditions that help ensure human well-being and the avoidance of criminal or offensive behavior must be in place. Hence, if the goal of society is to stop such behavior, the main focus can only be socioeconomic reform, not punitive threat. As research has shown, reducing negative social stress is critical, for such pressures can alter one's self-control.

Consider an unemployed American minority male living in a poor area with a felony on his record and a bad credit rating. His circumstances make it difficult to find a decent job, get a loan, or generally take care of himself or his family. Backed into a corner, examining the options in his region, he may resort to selling illicit drugs. He may dislike it. He may morally disagree with it. Ultimately, though, the instinct to survive will trump ideology and ethics when stress becomes high enough.[30] Put another way, moral principles, as will be discussed in the next chapter, are really only useful when pressures to violate such principles are low.

That understood, let's now home in on the highly punitive US criminal justice system, including its disproportionate focus on blacks and minorities. As stated, the US maintains the most punitive attitude in the world when it comes to criminal prosecution and incarceration.[31] This includes juveniles as well as adults.[32] It has indeed been found that these harsh practices actually *increase* recidivism as compared to other nations.[33] The harsh nature of incarceration takes a traumatic psychological toll and effectively the opposite of rehabilitation appears to be occurring overall. Dr. James Gilligan, prison psychiatrist and former director of the Center for the Study of Violence at Harvard Medical School, actually refers to US prisons as "graduate schools for crime." He stated:

> Prisons have often been called "schools for crime," I'd call them graduate schools for crime. People often have to become violent in order to survive in them. Or, even if they're not attacked by others, they are subjected to conditions of degradation and humiliation and intimidation and threats that I think might drive the most saintliest of people . . . to become violent in response.[34]

The US has a disproportionate prevalence of overall criminal behavior as compared to other developed countries. In 2011, there were 12,408,899 arrests.[35] This is the highest in the world; the second highest, Germany, had 2,112,843.[36] That translates to about 4,000 per 100,000 in the US vs. 2,300 per 100,000 in Germany, almost twice the rate. Some argue that America's signature draconian drug laws alone account for this spread, but this is incomplete.[37] Yet, if we remove drug arrests (1,531,251) entirely, it only brings the total down to 10,877,648. This makes the ratio 3,500 per 100,000, only a mild difference on the whole. Today, nearly one out of every 100 adults is in prison or jail in the US, five to ten times more than in Western Europe and other democracies.[38] This particular feature of imprisonment indeed blossomed with the application of highly punitive and intolerant judicial practices peculiar to the "tough on drugs" laws that burgeoned from the 1970s onward.

I wish to point out that while the punitive attitude is a serious policy problem, it doesn't change the fact that America still produces more overall crime than any other First World nation. There is some speculation as to why this is, but evidence points in part to the lack of social welfare, as touched upon before. Another reason appears to be inequality itself, something the US also leads the way in. As will be addressed later in this text, socioeconomic inequality is a powerful social destabilizer—and the more inequality in a society, the more problems, including violent crime, tend to occur.

As for how black and minority culture have been disproportionately affected, there is a systemic problem at work. Today, one out of every three black men will find himself in prison at some point in his life.[39] An extensive 2014 report on discrimination in the criminal justice system, *Falling Further Behind: Combating Racial Discrimination in America*, stated:

> Discrimination and racial disparities persist at every stage of the U.S. criminal justice system, from policing to trial to sentencing. The United States is the world's leading jailer with 2.2 million people behind bars. Perhaps no single factor has contributed more to racial disparities in the criminal justice system than the "War on Drugs." Even though racial/ethnic groups use and sell drugs at roughly the same rate, Blacks and Hispanics comprise 62 percent of those in state prisons for drug offenses, and 72.1 percent of all persons sentenced for federal drug trafficking offenses were either Black (25.9 percent) or Hispanic (46.2 percent), many of whom often face harsh mandatory sentences.[40]

Generally, racism and discrimination are observed as fairly straightforward phenomena. We understand them as something of deliberate intent by clearly bigoted mentalities and actions. But what is occurring in the

US criminal justice system is different. The intersection of historical, socioeconomic, legal, and cultural factors has created a dynamic that generates racist outcomes without directly racist intentions. In other words, it isn't the outcome of a sea of overtly bigoted police officers, lawyers, judges, parole officers, and other personnel. Rather, it is a confluence of America's racist historical baggage, the primitive legal logic of the justice system itself, and cultural bias that is subconsciously generated by the repetition of disproportionate minority arrests, along with the socioeconomic reality of minority poverty and inequality. These four preconditions ensure destructive and punitive outcomes against blacks and minorities throughout the system.

The 1960s civil rights activist Stokely Carmichael was perhaps the first to popularize this kind of systemic observation. Coining the term *institutional racism*, he stated: "Racism is both overt and covert. It takes two, closely related forms: individual whites acting against individual blacks [and] in the operation of established and respected forces in the society [that] receives far less public condemnation than the first."[41] He continues: "This is not to say that every single American consciously oppresses black people. He does not need to. Institutional racism has been maintained deliberately by the power structure and through indifference, inertia and lack of courage on the part of white masses as well as petty officials."[42]

The concept of institutional racism is an application of systems theory to express how racist outcomes occur without directly racist intentions. While Carmichael's stated context is a bit more narrow in focus, the same structuralist logic is critical to understanding not only the bigotry built into the US criminal justice system, but also the overall phenomenon of group oppression in the world today.

SYSTEMIC RACISM

As will be discussed further in chapter three, there is a kind of structural bigotry in society that links to our economic system. As in the prior case study, trying to understand the systemic factors that have culminated in a bigoted criminal justice system in America, the economic attribute is to be found as powerfully influential. The other factors mentioned—legal, historical, and cultural—actually all link back to political economy as well, both in the present and in the past.

As for the historical relationship specifically, while many countries employed abject slavery long ago, the focus on race-based slavery, with the condition of servitude even passed from parent to child, was fairly unique to the emerging US of the seventeenth century.[43] This set in motion a cultural divide that differs from such divides in other nations. The long-term result is a turbulent process of societal integration. From abject slavery to segregation to the spectrum of civil rights abuses, the racist baggage of US history is visceral and entrenched. And as much as many assume or demand a "color-blind" society in the twenty-first century, the truth is that American culture is still trapped in a systemic unfolding that goes back centuries.

Yet seldom does one ask how race-based slavery came to be. The prevailing view often taught in elementary school is that white Europeans enslaved black Africans because they simply thought Africans were inferior. While the idea of white superiority is certainly documented, especially during the late nineteenth and early twentieth century with blacks deemed "natural slaves" through what is now termed "scientific racism," this isn't the real origin of American slavery.[44] Rather, American slavery was a market-based economic decision to secure cheap labor and profitable investments. In the words of sociologist Robin M. Williams Jr.:

> In a very basic sense, "race relations" are the direct outgrowth of the long wave of European expansion, beginning with the discovery of America . . . [T]he resulting so-called race relations had very little to do with "race"—initially it was historical accident that the peoples encountered in the European expansion differed in shared physical characteristics of an obvious kind. But once the racial ideologies had been formed and widely disseminated, they constituted a powerful means of justifying political hegemony and economic control.[45]

While eons of slavery have been common by way of war, conquest, or debt, justification by physical appearance alone was little practiced until the time of the American colonies. Upon settlement, white European indentured servants were mostly used. However, they had fairly short multiyear terms and became limited in number as time went on. Eventually, African slaves were sought when it was obvious they were better business investments than the indentured Europeans. As explained by professor of sociology William Julius Wilson:

> The conversion to slavery was not only prompted by the heightened concern over a cheap labor shortage in the face of the rapid development of tobacco farming as a commercial enterprise and the declining number of white indentured servants entering the colonies, but also by the fact that the slave had become a better investment than the servant. As life expectancy increased, resulting from the significant decline in the mortality rate from disease, planters were willing to finance the extra cost of slaves. Indeed, during the first half of the 17th century, indentured labor was actually more advantageous than slave labor.[46]

During the initial stages of African slavery in the colonies, racial bias wasn't much of an issue. Black slaves worked alongside white indentured servants as equals. They even intermarried and had common social distinctions. This was before the artificial construct of "race" was legally created. As detailed by civil rights professor Carter A. Wilson:

> Color prejudice against Africans was rare in the first two-thirds of the 17th century. Legal distinctions between black slaves and white servants did not appear until the 1660s. At first, the plantation owners relied more on European indentured servants than African slaves . . . Initially, attitudes and behavior toward the African slave differed little from those toward the European servant, except that the servant served only a short-term, usually seven years, and the slave generally, but not always, served for life . . . Interracial marriages were common in the first half of the 17th century and . . . at this time they provoked little or no reaction. Christian status and Christian morals were important. Race was not.[47]

The true dawn of American racism was not slavery itself but how the framework of slavery was eventually supported and justified. The full transition from temporary white servants to lifetime-bound black slaves started around the last half of the seventeenth century, with enormous population increases by way of the global African slave trade. Expanded commercial agriculture in the Southern states specifically created demand.[48] Around this time, public policy started to change with the specific interest to create division between existing white servants or poor whites and black slaves. Historian Edmund S. Morgan notes that Indians were also being enslaved and alienated in the same way, referencing the actions of a government assembly in Virginia. He stated:

> [T]he assembly deliberately did what it could to foster contempt of whites for blacks and Indians . . . In 1680 it prescribed 30 lashes . . . 'if any Negro or other slave shall presume to lift up his hand in opposition against any Christian'. This was a particularly effective provision that allowed servants to bully slaves without fear of retaliation, thus placing them psychologically on par with masters.[49]

It was this tactic of social division, separating black slaves from poor whites, that served as a form of security through hierarchical dominance, stabilizing the economic practice. Over time, various excuses for black inferiority were concocted. These ranged from being non-Christian heathens to being "beasts of burden." This reorientation slowly generated a culture of bigotry and dominance that echoes to this day. So, in a sense, racism has effectively been a system reinforcer to optimize slave labor by way of sociological manipulation.

Moving on to the legal relationship, the evolution of legal statutes in America has obviously included very racist decrees linking back to slavery once again. The interest in controlling the black population as conditions moved away from slavery has been obvious. By the time of Jim Crow laws in the late nineteenth century, segregation served this means, locking black society into certain areas, bound to grinding poverty and consistent political and economic oppression. Such communities were easily and routinely victimized by a judicial system, controlled by whites, that allowed blacks very few truly recognized rights. By the time activists were able to force alleviation of direct legal oppression by the mid-twentieth century, the sociological damage already done was substantial.

Here you had a large, poverty-stricken minority population, isolated in poor regions with limited economic opportunities. Not only was the cultural baggage from generations of white oppression lingering, but the black community was faced also with internal destabilization due to a lack of basic means. By the 1970s, there was strong outrage and general disorder. Sensing this, a paranoid white political establishment gravitated toward policies to further control the black community. Richard Nixon's chief of staff, H. R. Haldeman, noted in his diary that Nixon held highly racist views. He wrote that Nixon "emphasized that you have to face the fact that the whole problem is really the blacks. The key is to devise a system that recognizes this while not appearing to."[50] Nixon is famous for starting the War on Drugs in 1971, which was eventually escalated by Ronald Reagan in the 1980s and then Bill Clinton in the 1990s, resulting in an enormous, disproportionate increase in black arrests and overall lower-class minority incarceration.[51]

Most serious researchers today are hard-pressed to view the origins of the American drug war as anything but a war, covertly rooted in policy, fought against the black community, the lower class, and subversive counterculture youth in general. This isn't to say the drug war was entirely deliberate in its targeting. But it is easy to see how policy makers could find ways to justify such actions in euphemistic ways, with the thought of social control and systemic oppression clearly in the back of their minds. After all, during the time of the drug war's conception, the two great forces proving they could alter the political establishment were youth and minority culture. The 1960s had some of the most effective social and civil rights movements in history. It is not out of the question for the political establishment to see this subculture as a threat, seeking means to deflate its power. As will also be discussed in chapter two, such dominance patterns have been constant throughout social evolution for a long time.

In sum, the legal system morphed from direct racial oppression to indirect by targeting the *outcomes* of historical and present socioeconomic inequality, rather than any specific group. Between the draconian drug laws and the effects of destabilizing poverty and deprivation in the black community, law enforcement could easily fill its arrest quotas. Racial profiling doesn't need to be police policy when all police see, day in and day out, is minority crime. They have been conditioned by superficial experience to associate black culture with criminal behavior. This association can be largely unconscious, in the same way the white community has grown to associate the young black male with crime due to decades of biased portrayals in the news media.[52]

Then we have cultural relationships. Returning to my story, after my attack I found myself reacting nervously when I would see a man of color walk toward me on the street. It was an irrational fear, emotionally triggered, as I had understood even at my young age that race wasn't real. Before my attack, this irrational fear wasn't an issue. Something snapped in my brain because of the trauma. While the effect went away after a few years, particularly when I attended a mixed-race, international art school from the age of thirteen on, I realized later that it wasn't just the traumatizing attack that created the effect. It was the overall social climate of paranoia and racism in the American South that primed me for the reaction, specifically the highly negative stereotyping of the young black male.

For instance, there was a popular television show in my youth called *COPS*. This show featured white police arresting poor black men constantly. At the same time, news footage I would see of American prisons always showed a sea of dark-skinned people, while depictions of crime in drug-infested black ghettos painted a primitive, uncivilized picture of black society. Even in my elementary school, there was a subtle segregation, with black youths often undergoing more scrutiny and accusation than white youths. These children were also likely to underperform on tests. Such outcomes are troubling because they again reinforce superficial and bigoted assumptions. If people see statistics such as black children performing worse on academic tests, black adults arrested and incarcerated more, or higher black unemployment, they may superficially gravitate toward assuming it is "just the way they are," having no other information. Our localized perception fails us in this way. Rather than looking at the condition the culture finds itself in as cultivated over time by such former pressures as abject slavery and Jim Crow segregation, compounded by ongoing economic deprivation and poverty, it isn't difficult to see how a culture of misguided bias can be created and perpetuated, even without malicious intent.

Now, returning to the issue of economy, the central argument here is that the economic foundation of our society is at the root of the problem. The early economic decision to exploit Africans for labor and profit helped give birth to the nature of our modern criminal justice system, resulting in a self-perpetuating machine of bias and bigotry. It is not just the generational tradition of racism in the white legal community that has created this pattern, but the ongoing socioeconomic inequality that has been common to the black community ever since. This has created a feedback loop that condemns the natural outcomes of socioeconomic deprivation (i.e., crime, lack of education), further securing systemic oppression of the black (and minority) community by law enforcement and even society at large.

A culture of aberrancy has also been groomed, such as the modern epidemic of black-on-black gang behavior in inner cities. While superficial assumptions condemn gang behavior, blaming the people involved, the reality is that this behavior has been the culmination of intersecting socioeconomic pressures over generations. In short, the consequences of systemic racism are now producing preconditions that ensure the future preservation of systemic racism. It is a cycle, and this cycle can't be broken in a real way without the removal of poverty and low socio-economic status.

Dr. Martin Luther King Jr. understood this. While remembered mostly for his help in enforcing black voting rights, ending segregation, and promoting the Gandhian vision of nonviolent civil dissent, he also led an antipoverty movement few seem to be aware of. Before his death, King was working on an Economic Bill of Rights to basically end poverty in the United States.[53] He knew that all the prior civil rights successes to help black culture prosper would not be as effective if the perpetuation of poverty continued. The systemic consequences of poverty were too strong, preserving bigoted reactions and oppression. To put it another way, the black community, no matter what legal or civil rights it obtained, was still locked into a tragic cycle of discrimination, and poverty was the binding factor. King made his position clear in his final book, *Where Do We Go From Here: Chaos or Community?* He wrote:

We have come a long way in our understanding of human motivation and of the blind operation of our economic system. Now
we realize that dislocations in the market operation of our economy and the prevalence of discrimination thrust people into
idleness and bind them in constant or frequent unemployment
against their will. The poor are less often dismissed from our
conscience today by being branded as inferior and incompetent.
We also know that no matter how dynamically the economy
develops and expands it does not eliminate all poverty.[54]

His solution was direct. Since the market system will unfold as it does,
perpetuating its signature feature of economic inequality, the simplest
approach was to install a universal minimum guaranteed income to
counter it. He stated: "I am now convinced that the simplest approach
will prove to be the most effective—the solution to poverty is to abolish
it directly by a now widely discussed measure: the guaranteed income."[55]
He also added in the same spirit: "For years I labored with the idea of
reforming the existing institutions of society . . . a little change here
and a little change there, but now I feel differently. You have to have a
reconstruction of the entire society, a revolution of values."[56] Universal
minimum guaranteed income means each citizen gets paid to live, with
no job requirement. Whatever the poverty line may be, each person is
supplied with that income directly, ending poverty.

While King's solution was not systemic in the sense of seeking to
change the actual mechanisms creating poverty itself, his understanding of the consequences of poverty certainly were. However, as this text
will argue in later chapters, while patches such as universal minimum
guaranteed income are just as relevant and needed today as they were in
King's time, they are still only one step in the right direction, seeking,
as he put it, "a reconstruction of the entire society."

PRECONDITIONS

Now, with the framework of systems theory in place, coupled with this
background knowledge of the historical, cultural, and economic roots of

institutional racism, and along with our understanding of how poverty and socioeconomic inequality are fueling the residual oppressive condition today, I will return to my story. Let's put ourselves in my assailant's shoes as a young black teenager existing as an extension of historical African American oppression. I would like to consider possible preconditions that may have guided him to commit the assault and theft.

The first and most obvious precondition is poverty itself, a characteristic inherent to the neighborhood and, judging by his torn and dirty clothes, likely his economic state. Perhaps he needed the bike for transport or wished to sell it for money. These are fairly obvious and common considerations, so I won't belabor them.

A second, less obvious possibility could be an interest in social status. It was clear that the bike was of high value and, as we all know, appearances are given great weight in modern culture. Social status has become synonymous with material wealth while the appearance of poverty implies personal failure.

Interesting studies conducted on class inequality found that high-status (or high-priced) goods are of more interest in places with larger wealth gaps between the rich and poor.[57] Such research also notes how people in a more unequal region, closely witnessing material wealth outside their reach, are more prone to risky behavior to fit in or try to match others' status symbols. Psychologists have referred to this as "wealth signaling" or *conspicuous consumption*.[58] On one end, we see strained purchases of high-status goods that have little to do with real human need by those who simply cannot afford them, including people going into debt simply to keep up appearances. On the other end, we see violent crimes of material lust, such as a teenager killing another for a pair of high-dollar sneakers or an expensive designer jacket.[59]

Underlying this tendency, as touched upon earlier, is our deeply *social nature*. Generally feeling connected, respected, and accepted by others to some degree is not a subjective preference; it is a hard-wired emotional requirement for good health.[60] How this expresses itself may be tempered by an individual's characteristics, but it is generally a universal phenomenon. Being without a sense of social inclusion, humans can become neurotic, just as our nonhuman primate brethren have also been shown to do in controlled experiments.[61] As independent as we may feel, social connection is a deep need, built directly into our evolutionary psychology. If connection is not obtained, imbalance and biopsycho (biological–psychological) distortion can occur.[62] The effects of exclusion, disrespect, and overall social-class hierarchy can produce a spectrum of negative outcomes. Feelings of being marginalized or of having lesser value than others have been correlated with mental illness, violence, crime, heart disease, and a host of other public-health issues.[63] It is just as much physical as it is psychological, meaning people can be in social settings but still feel excluded owing to status perception and other influences.

The materially obsessed consumer behavior we see today is really less about a given item's purpose and more about what that item means in terms of societal bonding. In effect, mere wants have been artificially turned into emotionally demanded needs by the drive for social inclusion. While many economists have argued that this insatiable desire is simply part of our shared human nature, it appears this tendency is only human nature in the sense of a shared social reflex, not some uncontrollable compulsion for material gain. As will be further explored later in this text, such materialism is really a byproduct of the nature of our economy itself, structurally induced.

At the same time, this pattern also produces a kind of perpetual human dissatisfaction.[64] In the words of psychologist David G. Myers, "Compared with their grandparents, today's young adults have grown up with much more affluence, slightly less happiness and much greater risk of depression and assorted social pathology . . . Our becoming much better off over the last four decades has not been accompanied by one iota of increased subjective well-being."[65] Because social connection and self-worth has been partly relegated to relative material success, people find themselves on what some social psychologists label the *hedonic treadmill*.[66] The more wealth people generate in this environment, the more they tend to expect things, thus reducing their capacity to be happy with less. The effect also trickles down in a socioeconomically stratified society from the public perception of the opulent, creating a reduced sense of inclusion. It has been exacerbated in more recent times by the accelerated rise of modern consumerism.

Avner Offer, professor of economic history at Oxford University, details this evolution in his book, *The Challenge of Affluence*. He states regarding the effects in Britain and the US: "The goods in question, how-ever dispensable in other cultures, were truly vital for social participation . . ."[67] As the twentieth century unfolded, newly created conveniences and material goods became looked upon as essential, and to "be without them was to be poor," he wrote.[68] The rise of consumerism will be discussed more in chapter four.

Returning to my story, given this cultural climate, there is the pos-sibility that the visually stimulating, high-dollar bike was less a means of utility or a source of monetary value than a status symbol—something he could show off to his friends.

A third and perhaps even less-considered possibility is that of my assailant's feeling power and control in the act of dominating another. Poverty, while often talked about only in terms of material deprivation, is also about a lack of control, lack of respect, and feelings of shame and helplessness. Dr. James Gilligan, again the former head of Harvard's Center for the Study of Violence, had this to say about the relevance of power and respect in such acts:

> I used to think that people committed armed robberies in order to get money; and indeed, that is the superficial explanation that they would often prefer to give, to themselves and to us. But when I actually sat down and spoke at length with men who had repeatedly committed such crimes, I would start to hear comments like "I never got so much respect before in my life as I did when I pointed a gun at some dude's face."[69]

Psychological research shows that feelings of shame, inferiority, and being disrespected are foundational preconditions for violence and crime.[70] If you have seen a bar fight in which the cause was merely one stranger uttering an insult to another, you have witnessed the reactive need for social respect. Because status is linked to material success in modern society, growing income disparity translates into a self-worth disparity. Therefore, it is no mystery that feelings of inferiority, shame, and humiliation are staples of modern culture. There is strong epide-miological evidence that correlates the amount of violence in a region to the amount of class inequality.[71] Gilligan and others have concluded that the broadest predictor of violent behavior is socioeconomic inequality itself. This is due not only to the material deprivation of poverty, but the stressful feeling of shame related to simply being lower in perceived status than other people.[72]

Studies also show this pattern with our nonhuman primate brethren. In strict hierarchical baboon troops of Africa, chain reactions of upper to lower status abuse have been observed. First, a dominant baboon strikes and humiliates a subordinate. The subordinate, knowing he cannot strike back, turns to strike his own subordinate to release the angst or save face, and on down the line it goes.[73] These primate dominance reactions, often termed *displaced aggression*, mirror patterns in the human population, such as domestic abuse.[74] Studies of husbands beating wives and children often find triggers related to job problems or other sources of emotional stress, ego loss, and feelings of inferiority. Sourcing a range of studies, domestic violence researchers Van Wormer and Roberts state: "Low economic status of men and the inherent stress of trying to eke out a living can also be a factor associated with violence, most likely in the form of displaced aggression by the husband onto the wife . . . Investigation of correlates of domestic violence found that the strongest contextual risk factor for intimate partner homicide is an abuser's lack of employment."[75] This overall line of thinking has led Gilligan to conclude: "If we wish to prevent violence, then, our agenda is political and economic reform."[76]

As for my assailant, one could speculate on a range of such possible influences, specifically related to his African American history. Perhaps I was a symbol of white oppression or elitist wealth given the race-class tensions common to the American South at that time. Perhaps his family upbringing had clear victimization by white forces, part of a tradition of bias. Perhaps a perceived injustice occurred that very day that offended the young man, who then felt the need to take it out on me. In other words, his targeting me may have had a deeper, even subconscious basis, seeking to elevate his sense of control, power, and integrity.

More broadly, the same kind of analysis can be applied to impulsive group violence such as "race riots," where people assault each other for no other reason than symbolic differences. For example, the Los Angeles riots of 1992 had many such characteristics. The poor, centralized black and minority population exploded in rage, ostensibly because of the acquittal of abusive police in a high-profile court case involving the beating of an unarmed black man. Yet many sociologists today source this rage to the poverty and oppressed socioeconomic conditions inherent in the community, with the acquittal of the white police merely a trigger for pent-up anger.[77] In the words of sociologist Joel Kotkin, "This wasn't a race riot, it was a class riot."[78]

PROBLEM SOLVING

Mohandas Gandhi was clearly aware of the influence societal structures have in shaping values and outcomes. He is famous for saying: "Poverty is the worst form of violence . . . It little matters to me whether you shoot a man or starve him to death by inches."[79] This implicitly criticizes the existence of class inequality and its systemic effects. His view is unique as it alludes to a subject that will be discussed in detail later—something called *structural violence*. Structural violence, meaning "preventable violence resulting from human-generated institutions," is an all-encompassing kind of indirect harm. In our localized sense of experience, we tend to think of violence as a direct, human-to-human affair, not a systemic outcome that tends to mask its original source.

Stokely Carmichael also alludes to this systems-based view in the context of institutional racism. He wrote in 1967:

> When white terrorists bomb a black church and kill five black children, that is an act of individual racism, widely deplored by most segments of the society. When in the same city— Birmingham, Alabama—five hundred black babies die each year because of the lack of proper food, shelter, and medical facilities, and thousands more are destroyed and maimed physically, emotionally and intellectually because of conditions of poverty and discrimination in the black community, that is a function of institutional racism.[80]

Norwegian sociologist and mathematician Johan Galtung, who was highly influenced by Gandhi, formally introduced the term "structural violence" in 1969 and has written extensively about it since.[81] In his work, he defined Gandhi as a "structuralist," stating:

> [Gandhi saw] conflict in the deeper sense as something that was built into social structures, not into the persons . . . Colonialism was a structure and caste was a structure; both of them filled with persons performing their duties according to their roles or statuses . . . The evil was in the structure, not in the person who carried out his obligations . . . Exploitation is violence, but it is quite clear that Gandhi sees it as a structural relation more than as the intended evil inflicted upon innocent victims by evil men.[82]

As mentioned in the introduction of this book, this structuralist, systems-based worldview is deemed critical to effective problem solving. This fact applies not only to human behavior, but the spectrum of public-health and ecological problems occurring in the world today. Any given problem, irrespective of its nature, will have systemic roots that facilitate or support it in some way. The question is, Can those roots be changed to stop the negative chain reactions? This is not to argue that all negative outcomes can be eliminated or controlled by this approach. There are limitations, just as we cannot today stop the everyday spread of the common flu. Yet we can strategically limit our exposure to the flu and ensure the best conditions in our environment to lower the odds of its occurring.

I doubt many reading this would decide to re-plaster a ceiling that keeps leaking every time it rains, knowing the real leak is on the roof of the building. Yet our localized view of the human condition is still plastering away. To stop the leak, we need to seek out and resolve root causes that continue to lead to social oppression, ecological disregard, and other influences that reduce human well-being. It has only been in the modern age that sociological research has provided powerful evidence of what's needed to resolve these problems. These new frameworks or models for understanding society must be applied if we expect to see true social progress.

Chapter Two

BEYOND THE PALE: OUR
SOCIAL MYTHOLOGY

This tendency prevails from the Continental Rationalists on. Leibniz, Spinoza, Descartes, Berkeley, Kant, and Hegel, for example, more or less entirely presuppose the social regime of their day and its constituent forms as in some way the expression of a divine Mind, which they see it as their rational duty only to accept or to justify.[1]

—JOHN MCMURTRY

WORLD HISTORY IS INTERWOVEN with an endless thread of unique myths about the origin of life, powerful deities, heroic quests, afterlife, the end of the world, destiny, and various other sacred ideas and narratives inspired by existence. From Greek mythology, with its twelve pantheon deities staged to demand obedience from us mere mortals, to Cavillace, the virgin goddess of the Incas who ate fruit that impregnated her, only to then throw herself and her newborn into the ocean to be turned into rocks, humanity's depth of creativity and capacity for invention is quite fascinating.

Underlying these stories and symbols are attempts to make sense out of a chaotic, daunting world. The drama of the human condition certainly creates a need to believe something in an attempt to organize reality and better understand our own lives. It is no wonder then why moral dilemmas, dualities of good and evil, astrological determinism, destiny, controlling gods, judgment, and a litany of other common mythological attributes are replete in almost every historical culture on Earth. Since myths are culturally shared beliefs by definition, regardless of their truth, we can also understand the importance they have had in creating social cohesion, group mobilization, trust, and deep spiritual and philosophical bonds between people.

It is in this framework that I would like to turn attention to *secular* mythology. As opposed to the traditional or sacred types just touched upon, secular mythology comes in the form of social, ideological, or political narratives.[2] These narratives include a spectrum of ideas that effectively serve to bond people around normative societal traditions, structures, and methods. Social psychologists have categorized aspects of this tendency in the term *legitimizing myths*—meaning myths that serve to protect the status quo and assist social control.[3] Whether dealing with nationalist, political, or economic loyalties, prevailing moral codes, underlying philosophies, or other dominant characteristics of society, there are numerous supportive myths that form a protective barrier around traditional values and practices.

OUR TRIBE

When it comes to secular mythology, there is perhaps no better case study than the nation state and its tribal politics. Loyalty to a country, its people, and its methods, and shared opposition to its decreed enemies, is facilitated by a catalog of symbols, stories, ceremonies, revisionist history, and other elements that serve the interests of social cohesion and status quo support. If you've ever had that looming feeling of being brainwashed when singing your country's national anthem or pledging allegiance as a child, you are familiar with such ceremonial reinforcement reminiscent of religion itself.

Nation states also tend to employ sacred symbols, another signature of religious culture. A nation's flag is one such example. Virtually all states, present and modern, have superimposed their sanctity onto flags, even including severe punishment if the flag is ever desecrated or disrespected. This patriotic protectionism reflects just how serious keeping national respect is, especially during times of war. In fact, perhaps the highest utility of such national mythology is to ensure that a citizenry willfully sanctions acts of state power, with any opposition considered "sacrilegious" or unsupportive of the national tribe.

This tradition of unquestioningly holding military forces in high public esteem, psychologically buttressed by ubiquitous ceremonialism including medals, parades, and other adornments, has been a historical constant across the world. The taboo against criticism is even extended to where questioning any aspect of the war apparatus is condemned as showing disrespect for the sacrifice of the honored, noble soldiers. In modern-day America, the current global empire, gestural yet irrational slogans such as "I am against the war but for the troops" are common, creating a form of Orwellian *doublethink* that limits critical judgment.[4]

Likewise, a vast array of euphemistic language and rhetoric is common to war politics, specifically on the side of an aggressor nation. American journalist Walter Lippmann, famous for his concept of "manufacturing of consent," a euphemism itself for how state power often uses propaganda and myth rather than direct force as a means of social control, sarcastically stated, "we must remember that in time of war what is said on the enemy's side of the front is always propaganda, and what is said on our side of the front is truth and righteousness, the cause of humanity and a crusade for peace."[5] As George Orwell wrote in his classic 1964 essay "Politics and the English Language":

> In our time, political speech and writing are largely the defense of the indefensible. Things like the continuance of British rule in India, the Russian purges and deportations, the dropping of the atom bombs on Japan, can indeed be defended, but only by arguments which are too brutal for most people to face, and which do not square with the professed aims of political parties. Thus political language has to consist largely of euphemism, question-begging and sheer cloudy vagueness.[6]

Social critic and comedian George Carlin satirized this phenomenon by coining the term "humanitarian bombing."[7]

Since we effectively think in language, cultural associations made to specific terms outside of their clinical meaning can often bias one's reasoning in an irrational way. For instance, stigmatizing labels can deter examination of issues simply by a kind of branding. Derisive use of the term "communist" in the early-to-mid twentieth century is an example. This label was often imposed upon anyone with anti-capitalist sympathies, even when the accused might have had no other interest than to see a more egalitarian and equitable society.[8] The term "conspiracy theorist" is another, more modern label, which serves to deter people from inquiring into any dishonest acts on the part of government or business.[9] This term has become synonymous with "irrational," used mockingly by politicians and the media.

Likewise, the term "terrorism" has become the preferred politicized imperial symbol to incite fear and insecurity in a population. It can be viewed as a more modern version of the term "communism" in this sense. This insecurity helps open the door to various power abuses, as seen in the past with the spying and intimidation that occurred during McCarthyism in the 1950s. Today, the "threat of terrorism" is used similarly, justifying power abuses on the part of the government and allowing for acts of civil oppression and military aggression that otherwise would have no justi-fication. As political theorist Carl Schmitt often argued, without a per-ceived enemy of a given society, something the majority feels threatened by in a unifying way, social cohesion and control may be jeopardized.[10]

Overall, political language by its very nature imposes an associa-tive mental framework that, if reinforced properly, can narrow one's thoughts about social issues. Through this process, people lose focus on other possible factors or viewpoints. Political language also exploits our innate tendency to be superficial, shortsighted, and fragmented, as explored in chapter one. Language, therefore, beyond being our main tool to learn and communicate, can also function as a tool for social control by strategically imposing or restricting ideas, values, and biases through associative influence.[11]

Historically, the use or threat of violent force has been the general route to ensure public compliance by state power. We still see this extrem-ism in societies such as Saudi Arabia's that engage in stoning, beheading, limb removal, crucifixion, and other barbaric practices for fairly modest crimes.[12] Highly controlled state media, propagandized education, and concentrated political power have also contributed to ensuring social uniformity and compliance. However, the past half century has seen a rapid rise in demand for "democracy and freedom." I place these terms in quotes since how they are defined is highly subjective, as this text will explore in future chapters. Regardless, the Arab Spring event triggered in 2010 is a modern example of this general growing global interest in moving away from overt dictatorship, monarchy, regimentation, and other echoes of older methods of state oppression and elitism.[13]

This long-term trend toward democracy, to whatever degree of definition or application, has challenged the nature of how national loyalty and status quo preservation is to be maintained. In other words, with populations becoming increasingly intolerant of overt oppression, other methods of social control by the establishment have been required, effectively cloaking the dominance effect. These newer techniques are perhaps best thought about as similar to those used in mass-media persuasion or commercial advertising. It is increasingly about cultural manipulation rather than direct violent force. Interestingly, as shadowy as all this may seem, such control theory is far from obscure, despite the contradictory mythology assumed by most living in the self-proclaimed "free societies" of today.

There has been consistent discourse among the intelligentsia that people simply need to be controlled. This has been viewed as a social imperative, not a nefarious act. One prestigious advocate of this view was Edward Bernays, who wrote a classic text appropriately titled *Propaganda* in 1928.[14] As will be addressed later in this book, Bernays's work also strongly shaped American advertising, helping to engineer a culture of material dissatisfaction to boost an economy driven by consumption. However, his ideas have also been applied to political persuasion. In fact, Nazi propagandist Joseph Goebbels is noted to have regarded Bernays's work quite highly in this context.[15] Yet Bernays was not malicious and simply saw this kind of need for social control as natural and necessary. He casually described the use of dishonesty and influence as though he was talking about an academic, anthropological reality. In *Propaganda*, Bernays writes:

> The conscious and intelligent manipulation of the organized habits and opinions of the masses is an important element in

democratic society. Those who manipulate this unseen mechanism of society constitute an invisible government which is the
true ruling power of our country. We are governed, our minds
are molded, our tastes formed, our ideas suggested, largely by
men we have never heard of. This is a logical result of the way
in which our democratic society is organized. Vast numbers of
human beings must cooperate in this manner if they are to live
together as a smoothly functioning society.[16]

Within this context of propaganda, we find consistent mythological patterns that tend to exist in all nations. Revisionist history, or the sanitiz-
ing of a nation's past to control perception, is a classic example. Most
nations tend to build great statues of their historical heroes as though
the actions taken by those people were with the intention of the current
population's well-being. Like most Americans, I was taught that the
"great explorer" Christopher Columbus "discovered" America, setting
the stage for the creation of the "land of the free and home of the brave."
I was taught the settlers worked to "civilize" the stubborn Native Indian
savages, bringing advanced knowledge and tools to help them "evolve."
I was also taught that the founding fathers preached how "all men are
created equal," and every American shall be granted the right to "life,
liberty, and the pursuit of happiness."

Of course, none of those things are true. Millions were living in
North America before Columbus's arrival, settlers systematically closed
in on the Native cultures with genocidal techniques, the founding fathers
omitted those of African descent from any form of equality to justify
slavery, and the right to the pursuit of happiness could only have been
directed toward the property-owning, white male elite who were the
ones originally granted political privilege. At the time of the first major
presidential election in 1789, only 6 percent of the population (white male
property owners) was eligible to vote.[17]

From Genghis Khan, to Napoleon, to Alexander the Great, to Francisco Pizarro González, we see regional homage still given to these
"great conquerors" today. The rhetoric is as though their actions were
of a benevolent loyalty to "their people." Of course, if the true acts of
any of these figures were witnessed in the modern day, they would be

seen as intolerant, xenophobic monsters.[18] Modern variations on this theme range from the suggested worship of political leaders via noble portraits hanging in civic areas, as made famous by more totalitarian regimes, to the soft idolatry of naming libraries or airports after past US presidents. These are echoes of a long tradition of power worship, harking back to such doctrines as the notorious "divine right of kings" of seventeenth-century Europe, which declared the monarch was subject to no earthly authority, deriving the right to rule and act directly from the will of God.[19]

This general pattern of codified or implied group superiority represents perhaps the most common and effective dominance myth in history. The view that one nation, religion, race, or whatever group is fundamentally superior to another has been at the root of vast historical injustices and atrocities. Of the numerous wars conducted over the past couple of centuries, very few have been publicly justified in terms of stealing something from another group of people or seeking strategic advantage over them, even though that has indisputably been the case overall. Arguably, all acts of war are foundationally acts of dominance, conquest, colonialism, or imperialism.[20] Yet, this aggression is generally cloaked with the claim of defense or a humanitarian act of help. Today, this syndrome is best exemplified by the now-clichéd Western imperial ruse of seeking to spread "freedom and democracy."[21] Similar to the exploited claim of "fighting communism" in the early twentieth century, this paternalistic position suggests that the current political condition of a targeted nation is simply too corrupt or inhumane. Therefore, intervention to "free" its citizens or stop the spread of ill thought becomes a moral obligation of the invading power (as the rhetoric goes).

This pattern of justification is also paralleled with the centuries of religious warfare and military evangelism common to the spread of Christianity, Islam, and other religions. The excuse to "civilize" a population with ostensibly more appropriate ethical or moral values has been common. From the Spanish conquistadores to the Crusades to the persecution of Native Americans in the pre-United States, paternalistic excuses abound. For example, with respect to the latter, James Knowles, an early nineteenth-century pastoral professor out of New England, famously argued that it was a religious mission to convert the

Native Americans to Christianity. If they refused, it was morally acceptable to destroy them, as they were simply not respecting God's will.[22]

It is also worth noting that while many view the Crusades and
other "religious wars" as purely ideological, evidence shows that material interests and trade expansion generally underscored these wars,
as well.[23] Religion often serves to help galvanize and justify aggression
or defense. This can be said about the modern Israeli-Palestinian conflict, too, where religious differences are really secondary to the dispute
over land, security, and resources. This isn't to deny the existence of
intolerant religious extremism. However, it will be found that regions
with the most religious conflict or insurgent terrorism tend also to be
regions with the greatest destabilization, insecurity, and history of foreign exploitation, scarcity, and deprivation.[24] The process is systemic,
with increased bigotry, racism, and xenophobia in themselves natural
consequences of social and economic insecurity overall, even if disconnected in perception over time.[25]

As a final historical example of this cloaked ideological justification for war, the same rationale for eventually justifying the enslavement and inferiority of Africans in the early United States also led a
pseudo-scientific charge to justify a colonial war to annex the Philippines
at the turn of the twentieth century. Fulfilling the emerging ideal of
America's Manifest Destiny, this war was blatantly characterized in US
media as battling a "primitive," backward people, even prompting the
1904 World's Fair to have on display imported villagers from the Philippines. Believe it or not, they were featured in the context of "early man"
and "stages of evolution."[26] This display clearly reinforced the American
public's sense of superiority and the illusion that the US invasion was
"for the better" in some paternalistic way.

President Theodore Roosevelt did not mince words on the elitist
view, stating in his 1902 Memorial Day address: "Just at this moment
the Army of the United States . . . is carrying to completion a . . . war
in which is involved not only the honor of the flag but the triumph of
civilization over forces which stand for the black chaos of savagery and
barbarism . . . The warfare that has extended the boundaries of civilization at the expense of barbarism and savagery has been for centuries one
of the most potent factors in the progress of humanity."[27]

This claim of cultural superiority also paves the way for other degrees of exceptionalism, invariably influencing the views of citizens almost subconsciously due to repeated media persuasion. Today, for instance, when American citizens hear about US-led international drone airstrikes that assassinate people deemed a threat to US interests, there is great public outcry when apparent mistakes are made. For example, in Pakistan, US drones have killed hundreds of innocent civilians in recent years.[28] Yet little is said about why the US is somehow exempt from international law and can send drones into almost any country, killing people with robots. That the US has not been at war with Pakistan, and Pakistan certainly does not approve of the drones' being sent into their region, makes it illegal.[29] Yet the Western population has been so indoctrinated into this assumed exceptionalism, currently under the guise of "anti-terrorism," that it barely raises an issue with the overt criminal behavior in and of itself, only questioning the apparent mistakes.

DOMINANCE THEORY

Building on the phenomenon of cultural exceptionalism, the study of social dominance has been a long-standing interest of sociologists. Whether we are dealing with international dominance between countries, or socioeconomic dominance between domestic classes, certain features and dynamics are consistent, leading to various theories attempting to explain why. One highly influential model is termed *social dominance theory* (SDT), established by psychologists Jim Sidanius and Felicia Pratto.[30] This theory attempts to explain the origin and consequences of social hierarchy and its related oppression.

They state: "Prompted by the ubiquitous nature of group-based prejudice and oppression, we developed social dominance theory. The theory postulates that societies minimize group conflict by creating consensus on ideologies that promote the superiority of one group over others. Ideologies that promote or maintain group inequality are the tools that legitimize discrimination."[31] "The theory views all of the familiar forms of group-based oppression (e.g., group-based discrimination, racism, ethnocentrism, classism, sexism, etc.) as special cases of a more general tendency for humans to form and maintain group-based hierarchy."[32]

In short, the theory claims humans are predisposed to group-based social hierarchies by nature. Strategic oppression through personal, social, and institutional means is hence deemed an immutable consequence of human nature.[33] The theory also observes and catalogs various characteristics of social-dominance hierarchies, notably *hierarchy-enhancing* and *hierarchy-attenuating* attributes. An example of a hierarchy-enhancing attribute is the police. They are designed, in part, to react against any insurrection that may arise from the lower-class "have-nots" against the upper-class "haves." This is not an issue of conscious police bias per se; it is simply the structural reality of their position. On the other hand, civil rights movements are hierarchy-attenuating, for they work against forces of disproportionate power and oppression.[34]

This theory also implies that without this structural oppression and elite-preserving controls, society would be unstable. The authors state: "Social dominance theory (SDT) does echo elite theories stating that, without a culturally normative and institutionalized control of power, social instability can devolve into extremely violent civil warfare."[35] While proponents of SDT are quick to condemn any use of their theory as blanket political justification for social oppression, along with a rather vague denial of promoting any absolute biological determinism, the overall observations and hypotheses made undeniably gravitate toward those implications.[36]

Sidanius and Pratto state: "[Social Dominance] theory views group conflict as having less to do with 'structural' features of the economy or culture than as being primarily driven by a ubiquitous human drive towards domination and group-based hierarchical social organization."[37] The theory argues that a human predisposition termed *social dominance orientation* (SDO) drives this group-based hierarchy phenomenon. This is implied as an evolutionary trait in human psychology, generating a tendency toward favoring domination of others and other nonegalitarian interests. Surveys designed for this apparently measure the degree of SDO people have on a sliding scale, as utilized by SDT researchers.[38]

Social dominance theory goes on to distinguish three forms of dominance hierarchies. One relates to age hierarchy, such as children dominated by parents; another relates to gender, observing the historical pattern of women dominated by men; and the final distinction is termed "arbitrary-set" group hierarchies, which is basically all other types.[39] While the first two distinctions are arguably worth debating, the arbitrary-set hierarchies will be focused on here as they are the most relevant to the discussion. The authors state, "The arbitrary-set system is filled with socially constructed and highly salient groups based on characteristics such as clan, ethnicity, estate, nation, race, caste, social class, religious sect, regional grouping, or any other socially relevant group distinction that the human imagination is capable of constructing."[40]

Furthermore, while not directly stated in such terms by the researchers, there is effectively an environmental *precondition* that triggers the SDO personality trait, driving the creation of these group-based hierarchies. This has to do with the introduction of an "economic surplus," according to the authors of the theory. When a society has sustained an economic surplus or excess of resources, people are theorized to have a predisposition to then create uneven distributions, manifesting social hierarchies. The authors write: "Even though there are temporal and intersocietal differences in the 'degree' of group-based social hierarchy, the sad fact of the matter is that all known surplus-producing social systems are, in fact, organized as group-based social hierarchies. There are no known exceptions."[41]

Superficially, this idea of an existing "economic surplus" leading to the development of hierarchy is interesting, given how other social theories tend to link *scarcity*, not *surplus*, to hierarchy-generating conflict overall. In much of the historical scholarship regarding factors that create and increase the propensity for most social conflict, resource scarcity, unequal wealth distribution, and deprivation are consistent preconditions.[42]

Naturally, many intersecting factors contribute to social destabilization and the push for increased hierarchical oppression. However, while a society's political system, religious values, and overall culture are important influences, the relevance of economic survival by way of needed resource access is no doubt the most critical. Any society, confronted with a severe survival risk, will likely become more divisive, aggressive, and competitive.[43] The consistent emergence of property crime, inner-city gangs, sectarian violence, and even terrorism in areas plagued by insecurity and limited means shows how deprivation, along with the consequential feeling of injustice, sets the stage for not only appropriative competition, violence, and war, but also jingoism, racism, and bigotry.[44]

In fact, the effects of scarcity and related environmental conditions can be recognized both on a micro and macro scale as well as short-term and long-term. Aside from the micro focus just mentioned, which can occur in a single generation, broad *socio-environmental* conditions experienced over long periods of time also appear to have powerful cultural effects. This field of study has been termed "cultural anthropology" and was notably made famous by Stanford anthropologist Robert Textor in his epic work, *A Cross-Cultural Summary*.[45] It has been found that cultures spawned from resource-scarce desert regions are more prone to monotheism, conflict, stratification, male dominance, and female oppression, while cultures originating from lush, abundant forest regions tend to be more prone to polytheism, egalitarianism, fewer sexual taboos, improved women's rights, and less conflict.[46] Naturally, these are broad, averaged, long-term observations with exceptions, but the consistency is nevertheless striking.

Even nonhuman primates exhibit this broad geographical influence. Anthropologists have compared chimpanzees to bonobos, two species of apes that are the closest living genetic relatives to humans.[47] Scientists found that due to their different environments, each ape culture has dramatically different social behaviors. Bonobo troops, living in lush, abundant rainforests, with females in alpha roles, have very little conflict relative to chimpanzees. In contrast, chimpanzee troops, living in raw, resource-scarce desert landscapes, with males in the alpha roles, have consistent conflict both in and out of a troop.[48] Yet these two species are genetically almost identical.[49] Of course, such primate analogs are never declaratory in and of themselves. Humans are simply not chimps or bonobos. Nevertheless, the correlations do have merit, given our evolutionary relationship.

Overall, the evidence shows that higher relative abundance, coupled with equitable distribution, correlates with a less stressful, more tolerant, and more peaceful society.[50] Of course, this certainly doesn't mean a simple reduction of relative scarcity and inequality would immediately change culturally ingrained behaviors. Assuming a culture had already adapted to a life of scarcity and inequality, it would take adjustment away from the customs and values cultivated by that scarcity-based condition. Economist Herschel Grossman talked about the "paradox of anticipated abundance," where groups who are expecting more resources will actually fortify protectionist activity and prepare for future conflict rather than simply ease such activity.[51] In other words, economic surplus can create an immediate fear of future loss in this context, not a sense of ease. This makes sense given thousands of years of psychological, sociological, and structural patterns reinforcing the existence of conflict and dominance. In effect, we have generated a *culture of conflict* based on fear. This is not to deny evolutionary psychology as a factor but to point out the extensive power that cultural tradition has over human behavior and social institutions.

SDT OMISSIONS

While social dominance theory (SDT) offers insight into certain dynamics of how group-based human hierarchies interact, its view of causality is highly suspect. Social dominance orientation (SDO), the deterministic "ubiquitous drive" that is said to lead to these hierarchies, generally omits the role culture plays in influencing behavior. Again, the basic logic is that once an "economic surplus" is introduced into a society, the SDO is triggered via people's evolutionary psychology and groups then divide into hierarchies. As convenient as this theory is and as empirical as the evidence may appear—environmental, social, and cultural factors are profoundly downplayed, as will be argued.

The aforementioned statement, "the sad fact of the matter is that all known surplus-producing social systems are, in fact, organized as group-based social hierarchies [and] [t]here are no known exceptions," is interesting because the distinction made is clearly in reference to hunter-gatherer societies, which (according to anthropologists) were generally *without* social hierarchy and did not have an "economic surplus" according to the definition of SDT proponents. I submit that when we contrast the relatively egalitarian hunter-gatherer cultures with more recent hierarchical societies, the relevance of socio-environmental influence and culture becomes quite strong. In other words, there is more to it than simply the introduction of "economic surplus." To explore this further, let's go back in time.

Roughly 12,000 years ago the human species transitioned from nomadic hunter-gatherer societies, tribes foraging and hunting with no agricultural skills, to farm-cultivating, settled societies. This transition has been termed the *Neolithic Revolution* and set the stage for civilization as we know it today.[52] This change marked a kind of technological shift. Like the advent of *mechanization* in the Industrial Revolution of the late eighteenth century, the discovery of agriculture was also the application of new economic technology. I point this out because it will be found that the most influential characteristic of a civilization is the kind of technological means it has and how it is applied. When very large changes in applied technology occur, human culture and behavior tend to change as well.[53]

It is interesting to think that for roughly 99 percent of our existence, *Homo sapiens* lived as hunter-gatherers, very few of which remain today. The different characteristics in social behavior between hunter-gatherer societies and modern settled societies are quite informative. Apart from being generally egalitarian with no real dominance hierarchy, it has been well argued by anthropologists that they also had much less violence and no large-scale organized warfare.[54] They generally thrived in areas with a rich bounty of cereal grains and wild livestock. Their subsistence-level existence created a unique kind of minimalistic affluence, where scarcity was not an overarching sociological pressure.[55] Such conclusions have been drawn partially from archaeological evidence from the pre-Neolithic period, but mostly from analysis of the few hunter-gatherer tribes that have existed in remote regions of the world over the past few centuries.

Contrasting the hunter-gatherer society with modern society, anthropologist Marshall Sahlins states:

> Hunter-gatherers consume less energy per capita per year than any other group of human beings . . . [yet] all the people's material wants were easily satisfied. To accept that hunters are affluent

is therefore to recognize that the present human condition of man slaving to bridge the gap between his unlimited wants and his insufficient means is a tragedy of modern times . . . Modern capitalist societies, however richly endowed, dedicate themselves to the proposition of scarcity. Inadequacy of economic means is the first principle of the world's wealthiest peoples. The market-industrial system institutes scarcity, in a manner completely without parallel. Where production and distribution are arranged through the behavior of prices, and all livelihoods depend on getting and spending, insufficiency of material means becomes the explicit, calculable starting point of all economic activity.[56]

In terms of sustainability, the economic simplicity of life made living beyond one's means virtually impossible. Unlike today, with the high technology to both create and destroy, there was a primitive natural balance with nature. At the same time, the inherent characteristics of nomadic life resulted in a very different sociology and culture from what we have today. For instance, since mobility was essential, hoarding property or basing identity on material possessions would have been impractical. The very idea of "property rights," which underscores modern economics and in many ways our society itself, really didn't exist in hunter-gatherer culture.[57]

If we were to put these concepts in modern terms, hunter-gatherers had a *gift economy* in their communities, where they shared with no expectation of reciprocation. In fact, there are stories of outsiders being given handcrafts from existing tribes, only to feel the need to give something in return, as many in modern culture do. This reciprocal behavior was considered offensive by the tribe, as they felt the "exchange" was a refusal of friendship.[58] British anthropologist Tim Ingold highlights the idea that the difference between "giving" and "exchange" has to do with social perception based around autonomous companionship vs. involuntary obligation. He states: "Clearly, both hunter-gatherers and [agricultural] cultivators depend on their environments. But whereas for cultivators this dependency is framed within a structure of reciprocal obligation, for hunter-gatherers it rests on the recognition of personal autonomy . . . the contrast is between relationships based on *trust* and those based on *domination*."[59]

The Neolithic Revolution set in motion a chain reaction, moving society toward very different social structures and values. The central mechanism of this change was the increased dependence on those geographical features required for economic success in the new paradigm of agriculture and settlement. In what has been called *geographical determinism*, it has been established that certain societal characteristics of a particular culture are historically shaped by geographic conditions. Similar to the aforementioned work in cultural anthropology, with unique differences developing between desert and forest societies over long periods of time, these ancient environmental preconditions set in motion trajectories for development that tend to become separated from their origins. In other words, over generations, people lose touch with why their traditions and practices exist, perpetuating them regardless.

As extensively argued by researcher Jared Diamond, the developmental path of human society, specifically the modern reality of socioeconomic and national inequalities, has been linked to different geographic exposures since the Neolithic Revolution.[60] From the standpoint of farming, animal domestication, resource extraction, and other practices common to the new post-Neolithic era, the surface of the Earth was certainly not uniform in capacity. Some regions were more favorable than others, with more ideal climates, terrains, conditions, and resources. Keep in mind, thousands of years ago our ancestors lacked advanced technology such as trains, synthetic fertilizers, and other modern realities that help level the economic playing field. There was no chance of farming arid zones or building cities in the desert, as we now have in places like Las Vegas.

These early differences have had a dramatic effect on the evolution of human civilization since the geographical advantages and disadvantages inherent resulted in some regions developing technology and improved means faster than others. This unequal development set the stage for material inequality and disproportionate power in terms of a region's capacity for conflict and war.[61] For example, if one regional group discovered how to make guns while another regional group was still using only swords, the latter region would clearly be at a disadvantage in times of war. This unequal regional advancement in technology throughout history has strongly affected the state of the modern world.

At the same time, these new environmental pressures and dynamics of the agricultural mode of production became the framework for a new *culture*. A natural logic based on the emerging requirements of survival guided development into predictable patterns of psychological and sociological thought, molding institutional practices. Expanding vocations and specialization is one such pattern, since division of labor generally improves overall productive efficiency. A specific person in the community is tasked to create a tool the community can use, developing a disproportional skill over time. Suddenly that skilled person has a differential value compared to those who lack that specific skill, but maintain other skills that may also be helpful. This then logically leads to barter, credit systems, and other means of trade, slowly evolving economic exchange networks between and within communities.

Furthermore, the practice of expanding trade naturally stimulates the formal institution of property and the need for rights and protection to help ensure some security and fairness. After all, creating a basic tool in early history could be very time-consuming and resource-intensive. Growing a field of corn, only to have it rot or be stolen, was certainly something to protect against. From this emergence of property, we get the root foundation of state regulation and institutional force. We also get the formation of a culture whose people begin to perceive life through a kind of scarcity-and-protectionist worldview. Again, this is something that really didn't exist in prior hunter-gatherer reality. Given disproportionate production skills and the unequal benefits of certain geographical features (geographical determinism), the outcomes of inequality, competition, and conflict were inevitable.

As such, it isn't difficult to understand how the requisites of the new agricultural mode of production and its related dynamics would create ever-hardening values around protectionism and competitive self-interest. This self-interest generates a psychological gravitation that then extends into a sociological one, in turn forming social structures, institutions, and customs derived from the scarcity, competitive, and protectionist worldview. From there, it is also easy to see how the offensive and defensive tendencies of dominance, war, and appropriative conflict would materialize in an institutionalized or normative way. Once established, this then solidifies an overall culture based upon competition, inevitably fostering inequality and insecurity in a vicious, self-perpetuating cycle of fear and dominance.

Worse, this worldview was compounded by the fact that the new mode of production (agriculture) was proving inefficient as population tried to grow, specifically with regard to a phenomenon and time period now termed the *Malthusian Trap*.[62] The Malthusian Trap refers to the eon-long inability to substantially increase the income (or resource consumption) of the overall population, resulting in little expansion in overall human well-being or population growth before the nineteenth century. Population could only expand so far, due to insurmountable scarcity and lack of means inherent to the new economic mode, causing die-offs. After the die-offs, things would even out a little, only to have the process repeat over and over again. This locked income and population growth into a cycle of expansion and contraction. The term is named after eighteenth-century economist Thomas Malthus, who insisted this pattern was a "law of nature," with human population and income unable to expand in any real way due to the natural state of the world itself.[63] Malthus even suggested that helping the poor was more or less pointless and that their suffering and death should be looked upon as a welcomed, natural process.[64] He was proven wrong by the Industrial Revolution, which dramatically increased economic efficiency through advancing technology. This efficiency sparked an exponential increase in incomes and population growth, as we see today (this important shift will be discussed further in chapter five). In the words of economic historian Gregory Clark:

> Indeed, in 1800 the bulk of the world's population was poorer than their remote ancestors. The lucky denizens of wealthy societies such as eighteenth century England . . . managed a material lifestyle equivalent to that of the Stone Age. But the vast swath of humanity in East and South Asia . . . eked out a living under conditions probably significantly poorer than those of cavemen . . . The average [hunter-gatherer] . . . had a diet and a work life, much more varied than the typical English worker of 1800 . . .

[H]unter-gatherer societies are egalitarian . . . [and] [m]aterial consumption varies little across [their] members. In contrast, inequality was pervasive in the agrarian economies that dominated the world in 1800.[65]

Broadly, the emergence of class inequality or socioeconomic stratification is a consequence of the Neolithic Revolution. Since that time, people have been divided into two groups: those who toil for little reward and have little social or political power and those who maintain vastly disproportionate wealth, social influence, and political power, generally at the expense of those toiling.[66] We see this broad socioeconomic duality across all historical social systems, such as abject slaves and ruling monarch-deities in ancient Egypt; vassals and lords in medieval *feudal* societies; handicraft merchants and state monopolists of *mercantilism*; and workers and owners in contemporary *capitalism*. Regardless of the era, economic and social inequality has persisted for millennia. While terms for the privileged or elite "in-group" have changed over time, from god-kings to aristocracy to bourgeoisie to today's ownership or investment class, the systemic framework that has assured one group will be superior to another has not changed.

Given this, some researchers have even referred to the Neolithic Revolution as an inevitable mistake, separating man from a primitive yet unique balance with nature. In the words of Stanford neurologist Robert Sapolsky: "Hunter-gatherers [had] thousands of wild sources of food to subsist on. Agriculture changed all that, generating an overwhelming reliance on a few dozen food sources . . . Agriculture allowed for the stockpiling of surplus resources and thus, inevitably, the unequal stockpiling of them—stratification of society and the invention of classes. Thus it has allowed for the invention of poverty."[67] This perspective is certainly not to argue that humanity should revert back to such primitive times, as though that would even be possible. Rather, it serves to give a sense of how the introduction of new means for survival can create complex and even negative trajectories as social evolution plows forward. In fact, how we define progress itself in society becomes equally complex, for what may seem like a logical step in the right direction at one time may very well prove problematic in certain ways as time goes on.

Now, to put this overall development concisely: Since the Neolithic Revolution, we've had a process of economically driven cultural adaptation built around the survival requisites of the relatively new, settled agrarian paradigm. This evolution of post-Neolithic culture was self-guided by systemic environmental pressures and survival inferences common to the natural dynamics of the new mode of production. This gave birth to dominance-oriented incentives, values, and protections, evolving patterns of conflict, hierarchy, and disproportional allocation of physical and social resources. Over time, these incentives, values, and protections became accepted as "just the way it is" and what most consider "normality" today has been the result.

That understood, let's return now to the idea, promoted by social dominance theory (SDT), that "economic surplus" is the precondition that triggers the noted social dominance orientation (SDO) trait—the trait that, in turn, leads to group-based hierarchy. It seems clear that this idea is grossly oversimplified, if not fundamentally wrong. Conflict and group-based hierarchy was inevitable to the new mode of production, regardless of any assumptions related to human nature. It was a geographically determined recipe for social inequality and the institutionalization of competition, conflict, and dominance. Saying that it could go another way would be to assume early cultures would choose to misalign with what was going to serve their advantage for survival. In short, as stated by Tim Ingold prior, the culture went from one of "gift giving" *trust* (of hunter-gatherer culture) to one of "trade strategizing" *dominance* (of the newly settled cultivating culture).

As SDT also implies, hunter-gatherers are claimed to not have expressed this SDO trait for hierarchy because they simply didn't have the "economic surplus" precondition. This is again a very weak assumption because it ignores all aforementioned issues regarding *sociogeographical* influence and the structural pressures inherent to the new mode of production. However, to further challenge the suppositions underlying SDT, there is good reason to assume that a sustained surplus of resources would not disrupt hunter-gatherer life, forcing the emergence of hierarchy in and of itself. In fact, many hunter-gatherer groups already had quite abundant resources by nature in the lush regions where they flourished. More important, hunter-gatherers are known to have generated a culture based upon cooperation, interdependence, sharing, and equality.[68] They actively created a *culture of egalitarianism*. They were conscious of the interest in equality and if others attempted to "rise up" or assume control, the tribe as a whole would correct the behavior though various strategies, something anthropologist Christopher Boehm termed *reverse dominance hierarchy*.[69] Evolutionary psychologist Peter Gray theorizes other cultural factors that preserved the egalitarian ethos, including the playful nature of their socialization and the customary manner of childbearing.[70]

So, the power of culture being what it is, there is little reason to assume such established social norms would be changed into group-based hierarchy by members consistently bringing back a "surplus" to store. In truth, we can't even really know what constitutes a "surplus" when the mode of production is hunting and foraging as opposed to agriculture. One wonders if the notion of economic surplus, meaning stored goods in excess of current needs, was even possible in the pre-Neolithic time to the same degree as in the post-Neolithic time. Assuming it was, is there still any reason to think the egalitarian nature of hunter-gatherer culture would then be disturbed into group-based hierarchies, without the additional influence of settled agriculture and its extensive social ramifications, as noted before? From a historical, sociological perspective, the evidence and logic supports a synergy of influences linking back to the structure of the new economic mode and the incentives it creates. Economic surplus can hence only be relevant in the context of other determining features and pressures inherent to the post-Neolithic world, as discussed.

As summarily rebuked by Turner and Reynolds in the *British Journal of Social Psychology*:

> SDT is both reductionist and philosophically idealist in that it seeks to derive all political ideologies, intergroup relations and indeed the whole social structure from one psychological drive . . . abstracted, reified and distorted to stand for some hard-wired original sin of biology ("the beast within"). Whereas, in fact, intergroup attitudes are not prior to but follow from social structure; they follow from the beliefs, theories and ideologies

which groups develop to make sense of their place in the social structure and the nature of their relationships with other groups. SDO is a product of social life rather than an underlying cause.[71]

SCARCITY CULTURE

SDT aside, we further see the power of this socioeconomic development in the evolution of intellectual culture. With the advent of writing around 3200 BCE, this scarcity- and conflict-based worldview slowly became formalized in educational awareness. Recorded history is replete with conclusions similar to those that Malthus reached with his theory, further supporting the perpetuation of inequality, hierarchy, and dominance. For example, a century prior to Malthus, Thomas Hobbes, considered the father of political philosophy, famously proposed that humanity's natural state was "one of war." Therefore, a dictatorial sovereign power to oversee society and keep control was required to keep stability.[72] When Charles Darwin came along with his theory of evolution, the "survival of the fittest" notion was quickly bastardized to mean "survival of the dominant class" in support of the Malthusian worldview. It was haphazardly called "social Darwinism," furthering intellectual speculation that dominance and inequality must not only be a fact of life, but being aggressive and "winning" also means you are doing a just service to the natural order itself.[73]

As to be expected, these prevailing assumptions became codified in the very architecture of society; its systems, structures, institutions, and traditions, with the most notable and powerful manifestation arguably being the *market system of economics*. This system is premised in the Malthusian period. Its root dynamics are based upon the observation of universal scarcity and the need for strategic dominance for survival, with its mantra being "not enough to go around." The very foundation of market theory and practice reinforces a social view that makes any notion of equality or abundance almost inconceivable and the gravitation toward dominance and exploitation virtually inevitable.

Anything contrary to those assumptions simply doesn't exist in the lexicon of market theory or the behavior it incentivizes. This is why, for example, profit is directly tied to scarcity and the scarcer an item in demand is, the higher its exchange value will be. Therefore, the incentive system of the market actually prefers a general condition of scarcity, since it translates into more short-term gain for producers of an in-demand good or resource. Abundance, on the other hand, has no value in this kind of economic logic. In other words, abundance has no structural function or reward. Creating or preserving abundance doesn't help income, job creation, or economic growth. If you think about it, preservation, abundance, and even sustainability are problematic for the market economy, as they remove instruments of exchange. As a mechanism, the market is based entirely upon the need for real or assumed deficiency and insecurity. In fact, not only is a threshold of resource or goods scarcity ideal to keep prices higher, increasing profits, but an insecure culture conditioned to want more and more material possessions is also ideal. Emotional insecurity, groomed to be rectified by material gain, neurotically becomes a positive feature of culture as it helps the market system work via increased demand.

Pick up any introductory textbook on market theory and you'll notice the rationale of the market's very existence starts with one basic premise—*resources and means are scarce.*[74] From that premise, the architecture of not only the economy but of society itself has been derived, again rooting back to trajectories set in motion from the Neolithic Revolution onward. This *root socioeconomic orientation* then justifies competition, self-interest, hierarchy, inequality, and oppression. It is important to make clear that the economy is not some secondary institution that is only engaged when needed. Rather, economic decisions permeate virtually everything we do.

From the stability of personal relationships, to the focus of vocation, to one's sense of security, to our perspectives on violence, crime, and competition, to the very vocabulary of political and social action, the prevailing economic method and its institutions are the strongest root sociological influence there is. One could argue that this economic orientation is perhaps second only to established religion; however, the retributive, polarized, and fear-based worldview rooted in most established religions actually shares the same stamp of economic scarcity and resulting xenophobia. This makes sense since the two dominant religions in the world today, Christianity and Islam, are desert-derived. As noted prior, they are rooted in a socio-geographical precondition that, among other things, distinctly highlights similar competitive and hierarchical worldviews.[75]

The main point here is that there is constant operant conditioning occurring, reinforcing behavior that narrowly serves a person's or group's economic success. This creates value systems and justifications that perpetuate a culture oriented around fear, self-interest, competition, and inevitably oppression and dominance. Put another way, a *thought syntax* is created in which people narrowly navigate life, focused on a contrived game of economic survival. This tunnel vision can blind us to the relevance of other issues, such as long-term social and ecological repercussions of our economic actions. The sustainability and pollution crises we see abundant today have been driven mostly by narrowly focused economic behavior, for example.

And it isn't just the procedural incentives of market behavior that are the problem. Over time our brains literally become *wired* to this dominant worldview, as has been confirmed by research in social cognitive neuroscience.[76] Given this, it isn't difficult to see how patterns such as what we call "greed" can become second nature. One would rationally expect a person to ease his or her sense of self-interest once he reaches a higher degree of wealth. Yet the very wealthy often conduct their business with the same self-maximizing, strategically competitive logic regardless of their current financial security and lack of need. The fact that they may have a billion dollars in the bank has no relevance. They only see the game, as oriented by this *root socioeconomic orientation* that is based upon scarcity, competition, and self-interest. As such, they are able to rationalize walking over homeless people in the street without a second thought. That reality has been accepted as "just the way it is," as per the thought syntax, expressing the win-lose gaming mentality.

To conclude this section, let's now examine the ramifications of competition itself, which is the basic driver of resulting dominance hierarchies. I'm sure we have all been in a social setting where the subject of war or conflict is being discussed, and somebody inevitably interjects, "Well, humans are just competitive and warlike." End of story. Such an intuitive diagnosis certainly seems to make sense from a superficial view of recorded history. Under the surface however, we see a complex mixture of collaborative and competitive behavior throughout time. Social science finds that we have the option to be competitive or collaborative, peaceful or warlike—both of which arise given the circumstance or environment in which we find ourselves.[77] We are adaptive to circumstance and culture and will generally conform to "what is working." As noted earlier, one of the great misinterpretations that has led to confusion surrounding competition was the introduction of the term "survival of the fittest" (in relation to Darwin's concept of natural selection[78]). This phrase has been abused for over a century as meaning "survival of the strongest, fastest, and most aggressive." Yet, "fittest" actually refers to what best suits the environment. This could be a range of behaviors including collaboration, tolerance, patience, and so forth. Survival of the fittest is about adaptation to a given environment, not the reign of the most dominant.

Unfortunately, such fatalistic views of competition have been part of a long-standing hierarchy-enhancing mythology, with endless historical claims invoking the idea that competition is an insurmountable impulse of human nature. In 1937, anthropologist Margaret Mead published a book called *Cooperation and Competition among Primitive Peoples*.[79] This work profiled thirteen indigenous cultures, finding that the variability among cultures could only mean "being cooperative, competitive and individualistic is the result of the culture they live in, and is a habit, a taken-for-granted daily activity, learned from parents and other members of the society."[80]

More recently, human and nonhuman primate anthropological research, coupled with work in behavioral neuroscience, has suggested the more-radical argument that humans are, by nature, actually more prone to cooperative, altruistic, and prosocial behvaiors as opposed to competitive ones.[81] It appears competition, aggression, and violence are natural reactions to *stress*, tempered by cultural influence. Anthropologist Douglas P. Fry's monumental work, *War, Peace, and Human Nature: The Convergence of Evolutionary and Cultural Views*, summarized the issue with respect to the myth of universal war:

> The grand conclusion . . . from archaeological, nomadic forager studies, primatology, and evolutionary theory, as applied afresh

to aggression, is that in humans, war is recent, not ancient and war is a capacity, not an evolved adaptation. In short, war was rare to nonexistent under the conditions in which our species evolved but obviously prevalent in more recent times that are dramatically different ecological and cultural circumstances.[82]

Therefore, we must look for the roots of aggression, conflict, and competition within our modern social structure and the culture of stress it has created. The global economy, which presents competition as a virtue, pushes an "earn a living," in-group/out-group ethic that basically says you either compete and win or you suffer and lose. We have nations competing against other nations for physical resources and power. We have corporations competing for profit and market share and we have average workers competing for survival itself. We also have employers competing against workers and unions for lower wages. We have companies competing against government for lower taxes and we have the upper class competing against the lower class to ensure its place in the hierarchy. While the term "war" is often used in the context of military or armed conflict, it is accurate to say that the entire society is basically founded upon a general war ethic. It is built right into the very architecture and belief systems of culture as we know it.

And while some good may come from competition in the context of business, such as a degree of technological innovation, society tends to overlook resulting problems like human exploitation, violence, and abuse. Numerous sociological and psychological studies have been done to reveal that the romanticism that ennobled the competitive ethos in modern life is almost entirely a myth. Competition is a mechanism for destabilizing conflict and weakening public health, not a virtuous source of collective human progress. In her paper *Competition as a Public Health Problem*, Pauline V. Rosenau exposes the mythology of competition as being some benign mechanism that drives social progress and health. She states:

Certain forms of competition may have quite serious negative effects on human health and productivity. The dynamic by which they do so are known and have been extensively studied—for example, they increase stress at the individual level. Destructive competition may also exacerbate already existing inequality among individuals, within societies, and between countries. Increased inequality is one of several social determinants of health. While commonly assumed to generate incentives for increased productivity, scholars in several academic disciplines have called the evidence for such an effect into question . . . There is little evidence that the current forms of unrestricted global competition maximize the health of populations or improve productivity.[83]

Furthermore, we should also reflect on how this ever-reinforced competitive fetish has generated a culture obsessed with war and conflict in entertainment and play. Competition and violence is not only a featured plot of almost every film, TV show, and video game, but it also underscores the extreme popularity of competitive sports. I am not saying that such themes shouldn't be of interest in general, but the tendency or obsession appears extreme. The belief in a competitive society preys on our natural gravitation toward group inclusion, exacerbating our divisive propensity to seek "in" and "out" groups, setting the stage for "winners and losers" and ultimately bigotry. Moreover, our competitive orientation also implicitly justifies the state of the world as it is, including ongoing imperialism, poverty, inequality, and other social injustices.[84] It is no wonder that the US Pentagon actually spent almost $7 million between 2012 and 2015 to fund "patriotic displays" at football and other games in an effort to boost military recruitment and support for national defense.[85]

In effect, these popular sporting rituals help assist social control. Ironically, this is also the same kind of confused thinking that has conditioned many in poverty to fawn over billionaires. Many admire the rich as though they are beacons of social success to which all should aspire. Yet, it is statistically impossible for the vast majority ever to achieve this position, since the structure of capitalism is provably slanted in favor of certain interests, as will be further discussed in chapter three.[86] Theorist Antonio Gramsci, who formed the concept of *cultural hegemony*, perhaps best expressed the idea of social domination by influencing the thoughts, behavior, and expectations of general society, thus conditioning them to support the worldview of the ruling class. In doing so, they tend to support the mechanisms and institutions that actually oppress them.[87]

In ancient Rome, the horrific gladiator games served many roles in securing social acceptance of the Roman Empire's atrocities, in the same way boxing matches, football games, and other sports do today. In the words of Rome researcher Alison Futrell, "the amphitheater was a politicized temple that housed the mythic reenactment of the cult of the Roman statehood. The death of a gladiator served as a foundation sacrifice that answered the crisis of empire, validating the Roman struggle for power and offering a model for understanding the basis of Roman power."[88] Fueling this competitive spirit, coupled with constant reinvigoration of an irrational sense of loyalty to some team (or tribe), gives a foundational psychological pretense toward further supporting acts of state war, class war, conflict, and general out-group human indifference.

THE MARKET

Now, to restate a critical thesis of this chapter, the Neolithic Revolution set in motion agricultural-based economic practices that triggered the development of fixed settlements, labor specialization, and eventually trade. The disproportional layout of the Earth's surface in regard to climate, resources, and suitability to this new means of survival can be viewed as a structural imposition (geographical determinism) that effectively molded a certain kind of cultural thought and practice. Rather than forage and follow animal migrations, people of the post-Neolithic world became tied to the land in a more direct way, critically dependent on factors such as regional suitability for crops and availability of food for domestic animals. This adaptation then led to inevitable borders between settlements that also didn't exist in nomadic life. As such, emerging settlements were vulnerable, requiring protection of their location and economic productions. This then meant the need for increased organization through new social institutions.

To translate into terms of modern political economy, you thus have the basis for property (ownership); capital (means of production); labor specialization (jobs); regulation (government); and protection (law/

police/military). In other words, you have grounds for what is now the ultimate mechanism of survival once again: the market system of economics.

Now, I say "system" of economics as these attributes are indispensable to its real-life functionality. While trade in one form or another has been with humanity for thousands of years, it wasn't until the Enlightenment that a truly formalized conception of market behavior and economy was born. This is perhaps best categorized by the term *free-market theory*, which is the market economy's purest theoretical formula for economic behavior. In traditional education, a pure free market is idealized as self-regulating, without the need for outside interference, such as government regulation. A pure free market is said to feature unobstructed trade between "voluntary" parties, with the prices people pay determined through supply and demand. Supply and demand is the self-regulating mechanism of price determination, adjusted dynamically by the ongoing actions of buyers and sellers in the marketplace. While both buyers and sellers effectively compete to gain the most optimal price in exchange, sellers also compete against other sellers to ensure they get enough sales or market share from the consumer public. This competition is also considered self-regulating, with the assumption that ineffective marketing strategies or poor relative product quality on the part of a given seller will naturally lose buyers, while the opposite will attract buyers—reallocating market share to the best performer.

Of course, this "pure," fully autonomous, self-regulating market economy is actually not possible in real life, even though many are still convinced that it could be. Simply put, such self-regulatory market forces have a limited range of effect and once factors of fraud, desperation, irrationality, and the host of detrimental *externalities* come into play, the whole thing falls apart into disorder and abuse. As such, most of the world has accepted that some degree of intervention is needed, realizing that social welfare policies such as a minimum wage or institutional oversight are dire necessities to ensure some fairness and security in the arena of market warfare.[89]

Yet the issue continues to be controversial, with ongoing debate over just how much regulation or interference the government should impose. In fact, most of the major economic schools divide themselves along these lines. Terms such as "neoliberal," "laissez faire," "deregulation," or "nonintervention" are common to those who feel the market should be more "free" in order to be most economically efficient. Conversely, those who argue for increased regulation, state controls, unions, welfare, and increased legal safeguards tend to be categorized along an ever-slippery slope that leads to the derided, pejorative bowels of market "socialism" at the other extreme of thought. The bias, of course, is always toward the former side, not the latter, since free-market theory is foundationally based on the reduction of interference, as the term denotes.

Put another way, at the very epicenter of the debate is the degree of faith in *market self-regulation*. Adam Smith, the eighteenth-century philosopher largely considered the father of this worldview, coined the now famous term *invisible hand* to suggest that people, acting selfishly in their economic behavior, will paradoxically produce outcomes that improve society as a whole. Smith wrote:

> [E]very individual necessarily labors to render the annual revenue of the society as great as he can. He generally, indeed, neither intends to promote the public interest, nor knows how much he is promoting it . . . he intends only his own gain, and he is in this, as in many other cases, led by an invisible hand to promote an end which was no part of his intention . . . By pursuing his own interest he frequently promotes that of the society more effectually than when he really intends to promote it.[90]

Smith's concept of the invisible hand basically laid the foundation for *general equilibrium theory*.[91] This theory seeks to explain the functioning of the market as a whole in terms of the dynamics of supply, demand, and prices, generally arguing for a kind of inherent resulting balance. The theoretical ideal assumes that through this self-regulation, market forces should find "equilibrium" and be stable to an acceptable degree without institutional intervention. In other words, it is assumed that people rationally going about their self-interested economic pursuits will somehow create balance, preventing things like banking failures, extreme wage differentials, goods shortages, and other destabilizing imbalances that, as we know, have been constant in capitalist society for a long time. Given the popularity of Smith's proposal, numerous traditional economists set out to prove his theory both formally and empirically. Not surprisingly, they have all failed.[92] While some equilibrium is present, such as the ebb and flow between low product demand tending to trigger lower prices and high product demand tending to trigger higher prices, the whole economy quickly moves to disequilibrium or destabilization when left to its own devices.

A notable modern example was the 1999 financial deregulation of US banks through the repeal of the Glass-Steagall Act. This act was introduced after the Great Depression in 1933 to help ensure commercial banks would no longer get involved with investment banks, pursuing risky speculation with their customers' assets. However, once repealed after about $300 million in lobbying efforts, commercial banks turned around and engaged in credit-default swaps and other high-risk derivatives, paving the way for the 2008 global financial crisis.[93]

Needless to say, there was no equilibrium to be found in the deregulated environment, which serves as yet another historical case study illuminating the fact that markets simply are not inherently stable. In the words of Harvard researcher and author Jonathan Schlefer:

> Beginning in the 1870s, theorists sought to build a model of the invisible hand. They wanted to show how market trading among individuals, pursuing self-interest, and firms, maximizing profit, would lead an economy to a stable and optimal equilibrium. Those theorists never succeeded. Quite the contrary: in the early 1970s, after a century of work, they concluded that no mechanism can be shown to lead decentralized markets toward equilibrium, unless you make assumptions that they themselves regarded as utterly implausible.[94]

Again, while most people today generally understand that markets need regulation, it is interesting to see how little attention this destabilizing tendency gets. What it means is that markets are fundamentally unstable and have negative consequences that can hurt people. Not only did the 2008 financial crisis trigger millions of home foreclosures, but an estimated 10,000 suicides between 2008 and 2010 have also been linked to the related "Great Recession" across America and Europe, along with 500,000 deaths worldwide from cancer due to a lack of medical attention as a result of financial loss, unemployment, and/or loss of public health care benefits.[95]

The belief in the "free market," as it is still politically termed across the world, is a critically important myth to modern society. The public's faith in the market system, with all its claims of "freedom" and "empowerment," serves to protect the status quo, dominance hierarchy, and, most important, the vast social and economic privilege enjoyed by the elite minority. It is a system, as will be explained, that paints the illusion of a nontotalitarian social order that engages in no real coercion or violence against the population. Yet the truth is that the market is at best only a mild improvement in the development of historical social systems still based upon the *root socioeconomic orientation* noted earlier: scarcity, self-interest, competition, and dominance. Ancient slavery, feudalism, mercantilism, and all post-Neolithic social systems thus far have been foundationally elitist in their mechanisms and loyalties, sharing this common thread.

Even communism, as historically practiced, required large-scale social control with heavy propaganda and legitimizing myths to maintain a controlling elite, just as capitalism does. Communism (as practiced) was a form of authoritarianism that simply approached social dominance in a different way. While I do not condone the practice of communism as it unfolded in the twentieth century, the highly biased Western mythology surrounding it does a great disservice to better understanding world history. It is true that communism suffered great economic inefficiency and corruption that led to famines, civil wars, violent political oppression, and forced labor. Some historians have estimated a death toll of around 94 million across all major practicing countries, with this figure sourced from a text called *The Black Book of Communism* that has been widely criticized for bias and inflating death tolls.[96]

Regardless, for the sake of argument let's assume this death toll is correct. When you strip away the traditional manner of thinking about violence, capitalism is far from an improvement when it comes to the structural nature of its effects. The difference is in how one defines violence and oppression. As will be expanded upon in chapter four, capitalism is and has always been vastly inefficient in its allocation of resources across populations, with now virtually half of the world's wealth owned by 1 percent of the population. To put these figures into perspective, it is estimated that the annual income of the richest 100 people is enough to end extreme global poverty four times over.[97] Given this characteristic of the market to create inequality and relative poverty, researchers in the 1970s found that roughly 18 million people die every year due to these uneven distributions.[98] Extrapolated for the twentieth century, that is 1,800 *million* deaths due to perhaps the most fundamental social characteristic of capitalism: inequality. In less than six years, capitalism's inequality arguably kills as many people as communism is claimed to have killed during the entire twentieth century. While communism in its original Soviet-style form is now a thing of the past, millions continue to die unnecessarily every year in the now overwhelmingly capitalist world due to economic inequality.

When the end result is unnecessary death and suffering, what is the difference between people who are consciously executing mass genocide and those who participate in a game of commerce that systemically creates comparable group death tolls, even if not deliberately intended? To repeat the words of Gandhi: "It little matters to me whether you shoot a man or starve him to death by inches."[99] So, I would again argue that while there are indeed improved features of capitalism relative to prior systems, the main difference between its method of oppression and older systems is really the degree of public acceptance and identification with it. The beauty of this "free market" mythology is that, from the standpoint of elitism, it poetically cloaks the severe dominance implications, giving the public a shallow illusion of volition, social mobility, and freedom. In fact, this mythology has been so deeply politicized and moralized as some mechanism of human dignity, you will find "free markets" often associated with democracy itself in political and economic discourse. People are even said to "vote with their dollar," which is ironic since that is exactly the problem when it comes to most corruption in the world today. A person with a billion dollars can certainly "outvote" the vast majority of people in the world, as we know all too well from global corporate lobbying of governments.

And this brings us back to the polarized debate between free markets and government regulation. Again, how and to what extent should governments regulate markets or interfere is an endless debate when it comes to political economy. In principle, the ultimate issue is what condition creates the best economic efficiency and stability. Those on the political "left" tend to want more control and safeguards, while those on the political "right" tend to want more market "liberalization" or self-regulation. However, when you begin to think more deeply about the synergy of the market and government, noticing how blurred the lines really are when it comes to loyalties, these ideological debates appear increasingly less coherent. It isn't that regulatory actions taken by state power don't often have negative consequences on trade efficiency in specific circumstances. This is often quite true, to the credit of proponents of laissez faire. The problem is that people misunderstand why certain government actions are taken to begin with, missing the motivation.

A simple example is the tariff. A tariff is a tax placed on imported or exported goods by a government. Macroeconomic theorists have long argued that tariffs are inhibiting to broad economic efficiency as they hurt the flow of capital and goods while disturbing natural price relationships. So why is it done? Of all the forms of taxation a government can impose, why this one? Is it possible a tariff is actually a tool that helps to protect certain favored industries from the risk of outside competition? If so, what does that say about the focus of government itself when it imposes such things? Isn't government intervention in the market generally argued to help secure larger-order market efficiency for the greater good, without bias? The truth is that governments are really vested interests, just like the businesses they claim to regulate, and tariffs exist to restrict trade between regions, generally favoring internal domestic industries. In other words, government intervention can be just as much about securing competitive advantage for profit-seeking industries as it can be about trying to keep market operations stable.

Similarly, a notable advocate for laissez faire markets, Ayn Rand, is famous for arguing that the development of monopoly and cartel are actually the result of government collusion and that a pure free market could never allow for monopoly due to market self-regulation.[100] In theory, there are kernels of truth to that conclusion, if we were to consider only her myopic definitions. In reality, Rand, along with other orthodox free-market adherents, denies the relevance of the fact that idealized free markets are actually impossible given the basic requirement of governmental oversight to ensure, to whatever degree, respect of property rights and some general honesty in trade. Given this capacity and power, the belief that government would ever be neutral and without hidden agendas or vested interests is deeply naïve. Whether a monopoly is government-sanctioned, as in the case of a state-run utility company, or a huge corporation is favored in trade policy to be a virtual monopoly in their industry, there is little difference in the end. Governments are effectively defined and composed of the business industries that fund them.

Yet the mythology persists that collusion between market interests and state power is an anomaly to be dealt with as though a few "bad seeds" are being "corrupt." On the contrary, the market economy is and has always been one of direct and constant collusion with state power, because they are interlinked as one synergetic system. The mythological idea that markets are a system of "natural liberty" and that any "corruption" is a rare, "moral" problem simply serves establishment preservation by distracting attention from a deeper and much more troublesome reality. Now, since this line of thinking may be new to some readers, I have created a semi-satirical short story depicting what happens when the basic logic of "free-market trade" is taken to its final conclusion.

Tom wants an apple. John has an apple and offers it for $1. Tom counter-offers 50 cents. John re-counters at 75 cents. They agree. Sale. John decides this is a business he likes. But he notices other sellers are nearby. So, John needs to be competitive. One day John has some older apples that he normally doesn't sell. But he thinks they are still good and he really needs the income. Tom buys these apples—eats them—and gets sick. Tom returns to John and asks for his money back. John refuses, claiming Tom has no proof it was his apples that made him sick. Tom calls his lawyer and sues John to pay for his doctor's visit. John goes to court and loses. John learns a lesson about the power of the government.

Yet Tom wasn't alone in reporting bad apples. Besides John, others have also been selling bad goods, causing many lawsuits. So the government decides to set up an organization to regulate the production and distribution of apples. John, bothered now by costly new regulations that are threatening the profitability of his apple business, decides to befriend the regulators and offers money in exchange for leniency. They agree, albeit covertly, and suddenly John has even better profitability, with his competitors now at a disadvantage.

Over the next few years, John expands his apple business, buying up other shops in the region to limit competition. At a certain point, he is able to undercut just about everyone else around due to mass production, putting many small shops out of business. One of the people he put out of business goes to the government and complains that there is no way others can compete with John in the market. The official decides the man is correct and, under public pressure, forces John to break up his apple-shop monopoly. John, who has become quite wealthy by this point, does not like this and quietly arranges for his executive friends to take control of the now divided apple-shop monopoly. Then, in secret, the different shops work together to ensure they get maximum returns by keeping prices fixed overall, creating a cartel.

Over time, John's public stature in the community grows as he gives to charities, attends fundraisers, and makes friends with government officials. John is happy. That is until it comes to his attention that a new apple shop is working to import apples from another town, posing a competitive threat. So, John, who gave generously to financially help a government friend get re-elected to office, asks for a return of the favor—that being to increase the town tariff on apple imports, making the cost high enough to ensure the other shop would no longer be profitable. It works and John is happy again—but not for long. It appears John's apple farm has been employing illegal workers and paying them very little. A gaggle of annoying human rights activists then come to his farm, causing a stink. John claims he was unaware of the illegal hiring and fires some of his staff as scapegoats. He then rectifies the situation, assuring his regulator friends it was all just an honest mistake.

Unfortunately, one of John's former staff members, upset by being fired, then goes to the authorities with legal documents and memos proving not only that John gave orders to hire illegal workers but also revealing payments to the apple-shop regulators, the conspiracy to ensure cartel power, and the collusion with government officials for the tariff hike. After being found guilty on all counts, John stands up to face the judge in court:

JUDGE: Do you understand the crimes you have been proven guilty of?

JOHN: No, sir. I was only following the ethic of the free market.

JUDGE: Clearly you must have failed economics in school, as you have engaged in government collusion, conspiracy, price fixing, and illegal employment.

JOHN: No, sir. I have simply let supply meet demand and voluntary choice decide each action.

JUDGE: So something like price fixing is not against the theory of free-market practice? Last time I checked a free market was to be free of interference and collusion.

JOHN: No, sir. A free market is having the freedom to trade and compete as you see fit, buying and selling whatever you choose, with all parties voluntary in exchange.

JUDGE: That may be so, but your actions, such as conspiracy in tariff fraud, are clearly going against such principles, as you are using force to stifle your competitors.

JOHN: Your reasoning confuses me, sir. All acts of competition exist to stifle and outperform competitors. Only voluntary exchange binds how the act of competition unfolds in a free market. One does not make your claim when a company purchases advertising, disproportionately exposing consumers to an item over other competitors'. Using government to my advantage is the same thing.

JUDGE: So let me get this straight. You are telling me that the free market allows for buying and selling of the very mechanisms designed to *regulate* the free market?

JOHN: That is correct, sir. The free market includes the freedom to take away the market freedom of others through the act of competition.

JUDGE: Well, I'm sorry to break it to you, John, but not everything in this world can be bought and sold. Our society was not set up to benefit those with the most money. Your sentence is 15 years in jail or a $50 million fine.

The judge then drops his gavel in a bold sign of dignity and satisfaction. John pauses, grins in amusement, and pulls out his checkbook. He pays the full fine, gets in his Ferrari, and goes back to his mansion in time for a dinner party.

Welcome to the true free market.

I call this the *paradox of free trade*. This paradox points out that to decide what is and is not for sale in the market is entirely subjective. Who is to decide if buying an apple is any different from buying government policy? The truth rests in the contradiction. Either we have a real, pure free market that requires no respect for law, buying and selling anything and everything; or we don't have a free market and never possibly could, for the act of buying and selling the mechanisms used to regulate the free market or simply interfering in general through monetary means will always be a problem, voiding the logic of its idealized foundation. I would add that in my personal experience with debating this issue, proponents of free markets tend to dismiss this ever-present reality as "crony capitalism." They view the phenomenon as moral corruption rather than a natural gravitation of market strategy to seek advantage along a competitive continuum, hence creating a morally relativistic logical fallacy.

BUSINESS DEMOCRACY

In the words of famed nineteenth century–born economist and sociologist Thorstein Veblen: "Legislation, police surveillance, the administration of justice, the military and diplomatic service, all are chiefly concerned with business relations, pecuniary interests . . . [T]hey have little more than an incidental bearing on other human interests."[101]

The impression that our major civil institutions exist to help perpetuate the well-being of society as a whole is one of the more notorious social mythologies to be found because it is a half-truth. We are taught that the police are there to protect the individual; the military works to protect the nation; legislation exists to ensure fairness and safety; while self-proclaimed democratic government itself represents the interests of the majority, adapting the society for the betterment of everyone.

In reality, while the average person will find some modest protections and benefits from these institutions as per the traditional claims, government's underlying loyalty and priority is and has always been to protect dominant business and economic interests. This is not to say that the average employee involved in law enforcement or legal service willfully and consciously focuses his or her attention away from general public good. It isn't necessarily about conscious, personal intent. Rather, it is about the structural function those civil service positions serve within the social structure itself—a social structure that is built upon a foundation of hierarchical loyalty and dominance, driven by the mechanism of market economics.

For instance, while a policeman may come and get your cat out of a tree or chase down a purse-snatcher on the street, the police as an institution are there to preserve the existing status quo of a nation. As such, their loyalty will always generally be toward established interests. This is why the history of activism, civil rights, and social change is replete with violent entanglement with law enforcement, regardless of the merit of the activist pursuit. This is also why most arrests and prosecutions originate from the lower socioeconomic classes, as they are the most profiled by the police due to the constant backlash that emerges from economic deprivation and inequality—two features that (as I've shown) are inseparable from market capitalism.

The ethic and practice of business runs throughout governmental organization. While it is true that money can "buy" politicians and policy, as charged in common rhetoric and activist outcry, the reality is much starker. If monetary influence is considered something that can corrupt government, why would corporate lobbying be globally legal? The public seems to miss the implications of this exceptional fact. While the principle of lobbying is based on the idea of simply working to inform and persuade government on behalf of a social interest, such as a public petition to improve highways, that isn't the norm. Instead, lobbying is the route by which business uses government to its competitive advantage. This method of influence is so dominant today, I would further argue that governments are not merely vulnerable to business interests—they *are* business interests, even if our politicians have convinced themselves they are serving "the people" and not business. Again, there are structural roles in play that override individual intent. The economic orientation of any society precedes its government, dictating what the fundamental functions of government are to be. Consequently the greatest priority for protection are business interests, and the larger the interests, the more outstanding the protection.

Now, since America is the current reigning empire and general father figure for much of the world, especially in regard to economic influence, it serves as an excellent case study of how business interests dominate and benefit from governmental decisions. Please note that I do not view America as an exception. True, there are other countries with apparently less collusion, as in some of the social democracies of Europe, but they merely exist at different stages of the same maturing disease. America is at a much more advanced stage of the problem, exacerbated by its global economic dominance and geopolitical power.

As of 2015, more than half the members of the United States Congress are millionaires.[102] It has been estimated that the number of working lobbyists in the US is around 100,000 and that lobbying brings in $9 billion annually.[103] The infamous "revolving door" between big business and politics is an everyday, characteristic feature. It's now standard operating procedure for political figures to come from powerful business origins only to eventually leave office and either return to those prior vested interests or actually become lobbyists themselves. Thomas B. Edsall, researching for the *New York Times*, concluded:

> When Washington politicians leave office, many, if not most, no longer return home. Instead, they head straight to the lucrative world of K Street, the nation's lobbying corridor, which runs through the heart of Washington. A former member of the House or Senate with even modest seniority can now expect to walk into a job paying up to $1 million or more a year—and much more when bonuses are paid for bringing in new clients.[104]

Given this, it is no wonder that a detailed study in 2014 conducted by Professors Martin Gilens of Princeton and Benjamin Page of Northwestern University concluded that "the preferences of the average American appear to have only a minuscule, near-zero, statistically nonsignificant impact upon public policy." The researchers concluded that lawmakers' policy actions tend to support the interests of the wealthy, Wall Street, and big corporations.[105] Even American history reveals the governmental foundation to ensure disproportional favoritism for those of great wealth, regardless of the mythology surrounding the founding fathers' claimed quest for "a government for and by the people." The American constitutional model, while progressive for the time, was still based upon the European model of aristocracy, only this time the aristocracy was born from class, ownership, and wealth, not family bloodline.

James Madison, known as the father of the U.S. Constitution, made it very clear in the Federal Convention of 1787 why the Senate should be created. He stated, "They ought to be so constituted as to protect the minority of the opulent against the majority. The Senate, therefore, ought to be this body; and to answer these purposes, they ought to have permanency and stability."[106] The founding fathers of America really had no interest in the resolution of class differences, and ensured, as it remains today, that disproportionate support and power was to be given to the "opulent" minority. They knew that a true democracy would force a vast redistribution of wealth, since, of course, the vast majority historically have been poor. In fact, it should be a fairly obvious feature of all national governments in the world that this kind of protection of the rich is structurally secured through governmental policy.

I would like to restate this for emphasis: If a pure democracy ever occurred—meaning every individual is given an equal, active influence on policy and could work in the majority interest to adjust society to actually benefit itself—it would be impossible for the modern reality of 1 percent of the world's population to own almost 50 percent of the world's wealth. The poor majority would simply create policy to reallocate economic wealth directly, as James Madison understood.

Now, earlier in this section Thorstein Veblen was referenced. He is highlighted because his analysis of the nature of government in the capitalist system has been instrumental in understanding the obscured economic loyalty of state power. A notable scholar of Veblen is Australian economist John C. Wood. Since Veblen's work can be verbose, the following passage from Wood's analysis will serve to concisely explain Veblen's important perspective. Wood states:

Veblen wrote extensively and insightfully on the relation between capitalist government and the class struggle. For Veblen, the ultimate power in the capitalist system is in the hands of the owners because they control the government. The government is the institutionally legitimizing means of physical coercion in any society. As such, it exists to protect the existing social order and class structure. This means that the primary duty of government is to enforce private property laws and protect the privileges associated with ownership. Veblen repeatedly insisted that "modern politics is business politics . . . " The first principle of a capitalist government is that [to quote Veblen] "the natural freedom of the individual must not traverse the prescriptive rights of property. Property rights . . . have the indefeasibility which attached to natural rights." The principle freedom of capitalism is the freedom to buy and sell. The *laissez-faire* philosophy dictates that [to quote Veblen] "so long as there is no overt attempt on life . . . or liberty to buy and sell, the law cannot intervene, unless it be in a precautionary way to prevent prospective violation of . . . property rights." Thus above all else [to quote Veblen] a "constitutional government is a business government."[107]

Given all this, the very idea of any kind of effective democracy becomes increasingly illusory. The system simply isn't designed to cater to the well-being of the general public as a priority. Rather, it is designed to facilitate the affairs of business and most of all the protection of big business, which are naturally the dominant interests in the revolving door of government. In fact, if you look closely, the dominant political parties in the world today reflect not so much different social views held by the public, but different underlying business and economic views.

And if you are wondering why the average population is granted the liberties and degree of choice it does have, for its benefit, the answer can be found back in *social dominance theory*. As accurately observed by Sidanius and Pratto, "a certain level of oppression is assumed to increase the survivability of a social system, while 'too much' oppression will tend to decrease the survivability of a social system. Therefore, in social systems that are relatively stable, we expect . . . an oppression equilibrium."[108] Put another way, those at the top of the hierarchy, who are invariably the large business-political powers today, are often delicate in their acts of strategic self-interest and elite preservation since they know that too much imbalance, inequality, or oppression will result in social backlash that can put their positions at risk.

Now, I would like to conclude this section by emphasizing that people in government and business engaging in this preferential behavior at the expense of public well-being generally do not do so with malicious intent. It is rather their belief system that is the problem. They may very well be somewhat indifferent, but the socioeconomic belief system they subscribe to allows for the rationalization of such abuse and imbalance, in the same way religion can justify inhumane behaviors. It is simply part of a moral ethic, as per the supposed virtues of business and "freedom." In the words of Thorstein Veblen once again: "It is not that these captains of Big Business . . . are naughty. It is not that they aim to shorten human life or augment human discomfort by contriving an increase of privation among their fellow men . . . The question is not whether this traffic in privation is humane, but whether it is sound business management."[109]

As long as there is no "sin" in one's behavior, as dictated by the market faith, all resulting outcomes and atrocities can be dismissed, including global poverty, human trafficking, resource overshoot, climate change, sweatshop slavery, water pollution, and other externalities that the market god need not recognize or understand. I would argue un-metaphorically that money and markets now serve as the prevailing religious order of the modern world. The "free market," with its still-upheld religious invocation of the all-seeing and all-knowing invisible hand, is the center of the faith. This idea that one can navigate selfishly and then expect outcomes for the greater good is profoundly mystical. As such, why should money and business, in all of its all-knowing omnipotent glory, not be the force that drives public policy? At the time of writing there are many frustrated grassroots campaigns saying, "Get money out of politics!" As well-meaning as they are, this is equivalent to: "Get liquid out of soup!" We live in a world where everything is for sale and the act of sale is considered sacrosanct. Life has been commodified, packaged, and made available to the highest bidder. So why should the line be drawn with government when it is drawn virtually nowhere else?

MORAL ILLUSIONS

My first real introduction to the business world was a corporate desk job as an entry-level video editor and music composer for a small production company in midtown Manhattan. Within two years I found myself as a manager, overseeing the work of a small creative team. Everything was fine for a while, but slowly the company started to fall apart. Paychecks started to be delayed here and there. And then they stopped. The bosses promised the issue was due to pending client payments. We became used to the ebb and flow of inconsistency, working diligently as we were told with confidence that everything would work out in the end. Unfortunately, that end proved more and more distant and eventually the entire staff found itself almost half a year behind in payment.

I decided to go to city hall and look up the company to see if it was going bankrupt. It turned out it was, and if the company kept up appearances long enough, it would not only void its debts, but it wouldn't have to pay the employees, either. I certainly needed to move on, but losing the money the company owed me was not an option. I was now in substantial debt, living off credit cards to make ends meet. I thought about small-claims court, but if the bankruptcy went through, the company would not be held accountable either way.

It was a trying personal experience, not only for myself but also for the other desperate employees, many of whom had families and children to take care of. Talking to the bosses proved fruitless, as they were not going to level with us given what they had at stake. I think in the back of their minds they were honestly trying their best, seeing the bankruptcy as a proactive stopgap, hoping they would turn the ship around for the sake of everyone. Unfortunately, when the walls start closing in and risk takes hold, ensuring personal survival is often not conducive to social goodwill or honesty.

So, growing increasingly desperate, knowing there was value to the data and projects I had on my server, I transferred files I had been working with onto an external hard drive and held them hostage. Upon quitting, I explained I had the files and would not return them until I received the salary owed me. After a week, I was sent a check and I returned the data. As it turned out, I was the only one who ever received back payment, leaving about a dozen others with aggregate loses of almost $200,000 after being officially laid off.

This experience really made me think about not only the market economy's inherent ethical challenges, but also how long one's moral convictions to be respectful and honest can withstand increasing levels of financial stress. The bosses were a married couple and they had just given birth to a second child a month prior. From their perspective, I suspect the well-being of their employees was secondary to family, as would probably be the case with most people. Was their decision to cover up what was going on unethical? What about my behavior of holding their files for ransom? Was it unethical for me to have held those files and not demand payment for all the employees, rather than just myself? In an economic reality where it is expected that some companies will fail as a natural law of competitive-market dynamics, how are moral lines in behavior to be drawn when well-being or survival is constantly at risk?

To consider such questions (which will be returned to later), let's examine the general history of moral debate. While it's certainly a vast and complex subject, with a range of theories as to the nature of what it means to be "right" or "wrong," most traditional discourse revolves around the duality between *moral relativism* and *moral objectivism.*

Moral relativism means different people (or different cultures) can hold different moral views of the same situation. For example, a person with the conviction that eating meat is immoral, hence deciding to be a vegetarian, stands in contrast to a person who sees no moral issue with the harvesting of animals for food. Yet that same person who does eat meat might find certain kinds of meat appropriate while other kinds not so much. For example, a Western meat eater, accustomed to the traditional fare, along with a culture of dog domestication, might very well find it repulsive and immoral that in areas of Asia people eat dog. Such is the nature of moral relativism.

German anthropologist Franz Boas extended this theory to demonstrate the power of culture itself in determining core values and beliefs of people within it. Boas coined the term *cultural relativism*, a further distinction expressing the strong influence social tradition has when it comes to what individuals consider appropriate or not.[110] Cultural relativism is obvious from a historical perspective, with a vast spectrum of deemed moral behaviors common to some cultures standing in stark contrast to others. From accepted human sacrifice of the Aztecs, to the polygamy of Mormonism, to the endocannibalism of the Yanomami tribe of the Amazon, social variance across time and region is quite fascinating. It is also easy to see how one's acceptance of a given belief, moral or not, can become reinforced simply because it is shared by many in the same culture.

Moral objectivism, on the other hand, says moral truths must be universal; that is, they are "external" to the beliefs of an individual or culture, like a law of nature.[111] This view is where the debate really heats up, since moral relativism is more of an observation than a method for analysis. There is something to be learned from the phenomenon of relativism, such as the power of culture to shape people's beliefs, along with the day-to-day heuristic logic that leads individuals to come to moral conclusions, based on their personal experiences. However, most moral concerns gravitate toward an imposition on others. After all, anyone with a true moral conviction generally expects others to conform to that belief as a matter of general integrity. They tend not to just sit by and allow the seemingly immoral behavior of others to go unaddressed, especially if they deem it severe. I have yet to meet a person who holds a strong moral belief who isn't socially active on some level, seeing the need to try to persuade others to share his or her view as a moral obligation. Philosopher of science Michael Ruse argues that humans evolved to think of morality as objective to motivate us to act.[112] If we do not feel the need to act and influence others, it could even be argued that the very purpose of moral conviction (or morality in general) is useless.

Yet, moral objectivism as a theory has serious faults. The first is the reality of *conflicting moral dilemmas.* A man comes to your house and asks if you know where a friend of yours is, saying he is going to kill him. You do know where he is and you happen to have the moral conviction not to lie. Yet, if you tell the truth, your friend will be in danger. Since you also hold the conviction that murder is wrong, you have a conflict. What do you do? Well, as most would, sacrificing one conviction (truth telling) to uphold the other (no murder) is the rational compromise. One is simply deemed more important than another, given the context and severity of consequence.

The problem with objective moral assumptions is they are isolated or *localized*, ignoring the systemic nature of causality. Moral logic cannot simply be reduced to singular instances. What may seem like moral behavior in one instance can very well create a systemic chain reaction that leads to highly immoral outcomes. To the extent that negative consequences can be predicted, they become a critical part of the assessment of any decision. In fact, I would go so far as to argue that reductionist morality—meaning moral judgments isolated to a given moment only—can be immoral in and of themselves since they forgo consideration of larger-order effects.

Another associated problem is the *continuum fallacy*. A continuum fallacy occurs when two or more different states or distinctions are assumed, while those distinctions actually exist along a fluid continuum of states that cannot be differentiated. A common example would be the debate on abortion. The continuum is human life itself. The general moral view is that murder is wrong. Obviously, we have laws to deter murder in society, even though many societies do allow for murder when it comes to combat, capital punishment, or self-defense. Regardless, on the whole, murder of human beings is generally seen as "wrong" and the abortion debate asks, At what stage of pregnancy a fetus is to be protected as a "human being"? Pro-life moderates may say it is okay to abort a fetus before six-to-eight weeks, with various explanations as to why. But regardless of these attempts to create a distinction, there is really no defensible starting point for the initiation and development of singular human life other than conception itself. All arguments to draw lines through time principally fail as a continuum fallacy, since how life is to be defined cannot be objectively differentiated once fertilization has started. The human life cycle is a process that starts with conception and ends with death.

Is there a way to create differentiation that avoids the continuum fallacy? Yes, but only when external factors are weighed in, bypassing the localized view and moving into a systems view. What are the possible long-term outcomes of having a child, based on the social condition? Is the fetus healthy or will it have a severe, painful, lifelong disability? Is the family in a financial position to support the child, ensuring good-quality upbringing? Is the region or even society itself equipped to accommodate another human life? These are difficult yet relevant questions, for if it is predictable that that child's birth is to set in motion a life of abuse, deprivation, illness, and suffering, the notion of what is moral then takes on a different tone. It could very well be that the most immoral thing a parent could do is to bring a child into conditions unfavorable for development. If pro-life concerns secure the birth of a child into an unfavorable precondition, and that child grows up as an abberated adult who kills another human being due to such life distortion, is the initial moral righteousness to "save the baby" still preserved?

Of course, one could turn that around and argue that if the issue is poor development, personal suffering, or a statistical threat to others, then why not just kill anyone at any age with those deemed issues? This argument fails because social factors change when a child is born, along with where the child is in the life cycle. In our basic drive to survive, it is an act of conscious self-interest to see to it that murder and violence are not wholly sanctioned by society, given our most basic social goals of a peaceful and fruitful coexistence and reduced suffering.

First, there is the clear destabilization that occurs in societies that constantly fear violence. I am unaware of anyone who prefers a gangland society, where people can be killed at whim for differing beliefs or just for walking down the street. Second, people in society naturally connect with others and become larger than themselves. We are social creatures and our very existence depends on and is defined by others. This means one's death can be not only emotionally traumatizing for others, even affecting their long-term mental health, but it can also lead to retributive murders, generating destabilizing chain reactions. We strive for rules of tolerance and advocate general peace in communities, not only because we may have a moral conviction but also because if we didn't, we would personally be at risk, along with social integrity itself.

This socially connected experience is not the same for a fetus in utero since the social bond is almost exclusively between the mother and child. This is why the pro-choice view focuses on the mother, as she is the one who has the most to endure as far as immediate risk is concerned. It is the mother who can suffer direct complications from an abortion or childbirth and is most prone to having long-term trauma, both physically and emotionally, from either event. It is also the mother who, assuming no legally recognized father, is responsible for the child when born. While it is indeed difficult to consider the level of awareness of an unborn child in utero, especially at the later stages of pregnancy, we do know that the unborn have yet to experience social existence in a real way. That can only occur once born, locking in a range of social bonds between mother, father, and other members of the family or tribe.

The bottom line here is that there can be no singular "right or wrong" view of this issue or, in fact, any issue. Moral assessments can only be made in consideration of context, with extended variables and consequences factored in. Put another way, a systems-based assessment is needed to make the most appropriate judgment for a given circumstance.

Now, this is not to say general moral guidelines have no role. The cultural decision to generally value human life and its protection is a viable moral worldview because it translates into increased personal and social security. However, that doesn't make it objective in the sense of being universally applicable without exception. The complexity of life poses far too many circumstantial variations and conflicts in which the violation of general moral principles can be justified.

Of course, superficial perceptions of this kind of thinking tend to make people nervous, and with good reason. It could be countered that if everyone freely evaluates a situation to decide on the morally appropriate course of action, people could justify destructive or immoral actions by subjective, biased, or poor rationalizations. A classic example is the "greater good" claim regarding war crimes by leaders, as noted earlier in this chapter on cultural superiority. History is full of genocides and murders led by seemingly ethical people, claiming that their actions are morally right in an "end justifies the means" kind of logic. Still, as problematic as this is, it does not change the fact that judgment is invariably contextual and multidimensional. So, just because an apparent wrong judgment occurs does not suddenly mean the only solution is the objectivist view.

We see this mistake made by religious institutions, codifying moral laws such as the Ten Commandments. It is very easy to simply declare that some singular act should be right or wrong. Social establishments have attempted this for thousands of years, with great, hypocrisy-ridden failure. The old but still-common view that religious moral objectivity is required by society to have any hope of not producing rogue, murderous, raping cannibals has also been a long-standing myth of many faiths.[113] The truth is that moral reasoning is really no different from any other form of intellectual judgment in the interest of truth. As such, the proper context for moral evaluation is *epistemological*, which simply means there must be some kind of justifying and inferential framework for validating ideas and knowledge.

From this epistemological perspective, moral objectivism, as in the nature of religious moral codes, falls under the umbrella of what is termed philosophical *foundationalism*. Foundationalism is the view that all knowledge ultimately rests on a foundation of non-inferential understandings or pre-justified belief.[114] *Non-inferential* means that at some point a given idea or statement of fact requires no further justification. It's deemed a fact and that is that. In other words, it should no longer be questioned. To use a tree metaphor, the firmly rooted trunk is like an unquestioned, foundational belief, while the branches are derived beliefs, built upon (or inferred) from the foundational trunk. For example, "There is a God" is a foundational statement that, through *faith* in its truth, requires no further justification. From there, people can inferentially build or justify a host of other beliefs, as is common to theistic religious philosophies.

Foundationalism is partly a response to an intellectual phenomenon known as the *infinite regress*. Infinite regress is considered the central problem in fully understanding anything. It expresses the fact that logically, any proposition or statement of assumed fact requires a justification.[115] Yet all justifications must in turn be justified by something else. This means that any proposition or statement of assumed fact can be endlessly questioned to infinity. A classic example of this regress is in questioning the existence of God. Somebody says, "God created the universe," with the logical thinker next to him chiming in with, "OK, then, who created God?"

Aristotle was perplexed by this problem, as it makes trying to understand anything rather unstable. If every cause is also an effect in reason, then how do we find any universal truths? So Aristotle argued that there must be a stopping point where a proposition or belief no longer requires further justification.[116] He vaguely described a kind of innate knowledge related to our built-in sense perception where, like a hierarchy, knowledge is built upon a foundation of these "true facts." To date, I have yet to read a really clear treatment on the issue, despite its popularity. René Descartes is famous for saying, "I think, therefore I am," implying that one can at least be sure of one's own existence, hence also arguing there must be some kind of an unquestionable foundation to all knowledge.[117] Again, how this pragmatically relates to viable inference and decision making is never made clear. What seems to be argued by Aristotle appears related to what biologist Edward O. Wilson termed *sociobiology*, which links our basic biological and perceptual nature to certain propensities as a species.[118]

An example of a possible sociobiological link to moral thought could be *mirror neurons*. As studied in many primate species, these are neurons that fire when one observes an event endured by another, generating an empathic response.[119] This kind of response is physiological, not logical, meaning it occurs in most people as an automatic reaction to observing others' behavior or experiences. An example is a person in great emotional distress. On average, people sense the distress and can become sad themselves. We see this phenomenon in the effect of movies, as the viewer identifies with a character and feels his or her experience, even though the character may be fictional. Generally, if there was ever evidence for something of a human nature related to moral sensibilities, mirror neurons seem to be the closest evidence for it. These neurons, apart from also assisting learning, seem to be a means to bond people, creating a sense of connection and compassion.[120]

However, as relevant as this phenomenon may be to human society, it doesn't serve our purposes here. The point here is to establish intellectual, defendable reasons for moral conclusions. If the evidence of mirror neurons and sociobiology does hold weight, then empirical observations of the phenomenon can be measured and included in larger-order arguments, just like anything else. For now, we will focus on the purely intellectual issues since there is no clear way at the present time to understand how such sociobiological reactions translate into full, defendable moral ideologies.

Now, the archenemy of foundationalism is called *epistemological coherentism*. As with foundationalism, there are many subtle distinctions around this idea, with no shortage of tedious historical debate.[121] For the sake of simplicity, all we really need to understand about coherentism is that for a belief to be justified it must be consistent (or coherent) with other beliefs.[122] These coherent beliefs generally form a belief system, where each singular belief in the system is supported by all the other beliefs in the system. In stark contrast to foundationalism, there are no absolute foundational or "privileged" ideas that can go unquestioned. Coherentism rejects this absolutism on the grounds that the infinite regress is not that much of a problem to understanding reality. By inferentially associating belief in linear and nonlinear ways, we can realize a kind of averaged equilibrium of truth that serves a functional role.

Of course, just because a belief finds coherence with other beliefs doesn't mean anything is actually true. Just as with people voting to reach a consensus about something (social coherence), they could all very well be wrong, regardless of their agreement. So, coherentism is really a probabilistic model of intellectual validation. A classic real-world example is the case of Dr. Ignaz Semmelweis, who in 1847 realized that simply washing his hands was reducing infection-driven deaths of mothers after childbirth.[123] This was well before Louis Pasteur discovered the germ theory of disease. Unfortunately, Semmelweis's findings were rejected by the mainstream medical and scientific community at the time, for they did not fit the prevailing system of belief put forward. It wasn't coherent, even though correct, as many deaths continued for years after as a result.

So putting all of this together, it's easy to see how ideas about reality can form based upon a small number of core beliefs, as foundationalism suggests. Yet it is also easy to understand how those "core beliefs" can very well be wrong. And if the very foundation of any inferentially derived ideas is wrong, it is safe to assume that so are those inferentially derived ideas. This is why coherentism does not assume any "privileged" root beliefs, and why its theory rejects such absolutism outright. Rather, it "floats" the idea of truth, using inference to both consider the structure that supports an idea and compare seemingly disconnected ideas to find validating consistency.

Now, why is all of this important? If we look beyond the polarized simplicity of *moral relativism* and *moral objectivism*, focusing on epistemological structures common to the assessment of knowledge, we can create an improved model of moral evaluation. Aforementioned problems such as *conflicting moral dilemmas* or *continuums* can be better addressed within the framework of epistemology, as opposed to elevating human morality to something outside of rational thought. Regardless of our emotional reactions, one's morality is really a belief system like any other intellectual process. As such, epistemological coherentism appears to be the best framework of evaluation as it is systemic, without the baggage of ideological preconception we find with foundationalism.

With this in mind, let's now return to the four questions I posed regarding my experience with the company that stopped paying its employees as it secretly went bankrupt to avoid all liability. *Was the company's decision to cover up what was going on unethical?* Well, if the owners had explained to the employees that they had just filed for bankruptcy and there would be no paychecks for months more or possibly never, destabilization of the office would have been certain. Small-business bankruptcy is complex, with a range of protections and vulnerabilities at different stages depending on the type. Under some conditions, the employees could have sued for back payment. This would have meant what money the owners did have could have been taken. If they were honestly working to save or transform the company through bankruptcy, it isn't hard to see how they could have morally rationalized their dishonesty in not presenting the truth because they wished to avoid such destabilization, assuming the best interests of the employees in the end.

What about my behavior of taking their files and holding them for ransom? While certainly illegal, this action didn't trouble me given the state of desperation I was in financially, owing back rent and living off credit cards. Effectively mirroring the logic for the owners to file for bankruptcy as a fail-safe, knowing it would mean screwing the employees in the end, my self-interest was also in play, coupled with the sense that I had worked hard for the salary owed to me and that getting that payment was an ethical right. Such is the nature of living in a social system that's foundationally oriented around competition, generating winners and losers.

*Was it unethical for me to have held those files and not demand pay-
ment for all the employees, rather than just myself?* While common-good
interest has always been something I feel is morally important in general,
there was a good possibility that the large amount of money owed to the
whole workforce exceeded what the owners had in total. Attempting to
use the file-ransom tactic to help everyone reduced the possibility of
getting anything at all.

And finally and most important: *In an economic reality where it is
expected that some companies will fail as a natural law of competitive-
market dynamics, how are moral lines in behavior to be drawn when
well-being or survival is constantly at risk?* This question illuminates a
systems view of market economics—one that creates a coherent framework to better understand not only the other three questions, but the
entire sociological condition.

While we may look at isolated actions in this world and try to judge
their moral integrity one by one, the real moral evaluation occurs on the
systems level. Remember, modern society, with its basis in market capitalism, as derived from the root socioeconomic orientation of scarcity,
self-interest, and competition (as born out of the Neolithic Revolution),
functions like a game, except this competitive game is about survival
and well-being. As such, the game takes on a very different dynamic
than a game in which there is nothing to lose. Not only does this game
pose the threat of loss, but its very architecture actually makes loss and
suffering inevitable for a large percentage of players. Given this, society's
long-standing moral claims and ethical demands find limited expression in such a condition. If the moral goal of society is to try to create
the best condition of public health, happiness, and stability possible for
the world's population, seeking to prevent suffering, it must be realized
that the structural impositions of our economy actually work against
that goal.

Contrary to prevailing philosophical mythology, moral behavior
isn't just about people's individual nature, their education, parenting,
peers, social bonds, personal intentions, or other such factors commonly discussed concerning a person's character. This mythology—
that morality is only about individual behavior—ignores the incredible,
stress-inducing pressure placed upon a civilization that is based upon

its members fighting with each other to survive. In such a world, ethical behavior as we traditionally consider it is severely limited in its capacity for expression. It isn't that people aren't capable of more caring, compassionate, helpful, and socially respectful behavior—it is that the socio-economic system won't support it. In fact, I would argue that the more ethical you are, the more likely you will fail in the game of commerce. The system simply doesn't support real human compassion on the socio-logical level. It isn't designed to.

FREE WILL

Now, a great deal has been covered in this chapter thus far. Before we conclude with what is perhaps the most core and paradoxical of all secular social mythologies—*free will*—I would like to quickly re-contextualize some of what has already been addressed.

In this exploration, the structural importance of the Neolithic Revolution has been emphasized, along with its cultivation of trade, settlement, specialization, property, protectionism, and other characteristics that continue to define modern society. In contrast to the assumptions of social dominance theory, with its conclusion that humans are wired to group-based hierarchy by nature once an economic surplus is created, regardless of the social system, the adaptive capacity of humans appears far more flexible. This is not to argue a behaviorist view of human nature, which, in extreme interpretation, views the individual as infinitely malleable by culture. Rather, this is about the highly deterministic role of anthropological effects related to broad shifts in economic conditions.

In this, the term *root socioeconomic orientation* has been coined and defined. This specifically refers to the nature of a society based upon competition, self-interest, and ultimately, a sociology formed around scarcity, fear, and in-group/out-group bias. While many may counter by pointing out that the animal kingdom generally operates in this same primitive way and humans should therefore not be expected to be any different, this response misses the fact that most species have no option but survival through force and competition. In contrast, humans are not like any other species when it comes to intelligence, variability, and adaptation. The real problem is that we have blindly accepted as custom a society based upon competition and scarcity, regardless of our vast intellectual ingenuity and the growing scientific evidence that we could, indeed, live quite differently if proper structural adjustments were made. In other words, we are reacting within a social system we have grown to perpetuate and assume is final, not reacting to some immutable restrictions imposed by the earthly habitat, human nature, or some natural law.

It is also important to make clear that the current economic mode of capitalism, while touted as the most productive and "free" system humanity has ever known, is really a system of social control, like all prior systems post-Neolithic Revolution. Its trademark is socioeconomic inequality, a feature that artificially partitions human well-being and power in favor of a very small minority. The modern manifestation of this is called "business," which is the competitive mechanism that sets in motion the inevitable inequality we see, organized in lockstep around government power, defusing any attempts at meaningful democracy. Government, used as a means to create stability in commerce (since there is no true "invisible hand" to be found), is also used to secure competitive advantage by a select breed of large business powers. These business powers circumscribe government behavior overall, even though the myth that government exists as an extension of the general public (i.e., as "the will of the people") persists today. This is why the noted national or tribal mythology has been so critical for social compliance and order. The statues, symbols, language, taboos, and other means of cultural manipulation are constant since the needed cohesion to stifle any interfering social change depends on it.

In this, the use of moral impositions and the idea that the problems of the world exist on the individual level and not the structural level are very powerful in effect. As argued, there is a tendency to be objectivist with our moral views, with overly simplistic slogans such as "just say no" or "do the crime and do the time," etc. Yet, moral decisions cannot really be separated intellectually from overall reasoning and logic. In this, we are faced with a systems-based reorientation since everything is far more entrenched in causality than has ever been understood before. Science has opened these doors and each situation presents a new set of variables. Proper decisions are contingent on a range of considerations, not static moral declarations. And the ultimate moral conundrum today is this: *How can we expect highly moral or ethical decisions by a population submerged inside a social system that rewards the exact opposite behavior?* Market capitalism is simply not conducive to mutual human concern. It is a system based on social warfare, cultivated by its root socioeconomic orientation. Now, with that stated, the final subject of this chapter will extend this primitive moral mythology to the notion of free will.

Free will is the most reinforced and consistent ideological assumption in the world today. Not only does it rest on the foundation of the central moral and philosophical belief systems of modern civilization, but it also appears to validate itself at every turn in society's architecture and institutions. Every human action is generally assumed to be a conscious, willful, free decision by both others and ourselves. It is a powerful intuition we all share. Our minds are simply wired this way.[124] Yet, once a *systems* perspective is taken, accounting for statistical research showing the effects of larger-order environmental and social conditions, and coupled with modern understandings in cognitive neuroscience, the mythology of free will quickly begins to unravel.

Returning to the subject of *preconditions* from chapter one, it is easy to notice the power of regional culture in determining the language we learn as a child, the religion we are taught, or the customs we embrace. It is less easy to notice how people can develop predictable, long-term behavioral propensities as a result of childhood experiences. It has taken advanced scientific study to identify our bio-evolutionary requirements, whereby certain things generally need to happen in child development to ensure long-term mental and emotional well-being, while certain things should not happen for the same reason. Our biology has been preprogrammed by evolution to respond in certain ways to stimulus and stress, with predictable outcomes when certain experiences happen. As one's life progresses, the biopsychosocial synergies of life dramatically shape one's thoughts, beliefs, impulses, and actions. This shaping makes certain propensities highly probable, with others highly improbable, regardless of the "free will" of the person.

Drug addiction, as noted by neurologists and pharmacologists, is a kind of "hijacking" of the brain that subconsciously leads a person's behavior toward the reward of use.[125] The addict is often fully disgusted by his (or her) actions, but the addiction pattern continues as changes to brain chemistry drive changes to both thoughts and behavior, justifying the next use of a drug. One may indeed overcome an addiction by choice, willpower, and likely external help, but that single end does not discount the general loss of control found during the addiction period. Likewise, analysis that takes a biosocial view of the issue finds great evidence that child abuse, stress, and emotional loss can contribute to one's development of addiction as a form of self-medication.[126] In fact, an entire range of health and behavioral issues can arise later in life, since childhood abuse literally changes and damages the brain. Not only can abuse disturb the brain's neurochemistry, but it can also shrink and distort critical areas, such as the hippocampus.[127] This can lead to severe impairments in one's ability to make decisions and judgments, in the same way a person who has severe brain damage from head trauma in a car accident may no longer be able to speak. Do we judge a person's speech impairment in such a case as a problem of free will? No, we understand the impairment.

In 1966, Charles Whitman, an American with no prior history of mental instability, suddenly murdered his mother and wife. He then proceeded to the University of Texas, climbed inside a tower, and killed fourteen others with a gun before taking his own life. In his suicide note he talked about his feeling of going insane and not understanding his thoughts, and he even requested an autopsy. While the public stood in horror at this "monster" mass-murderer, doctors discovered that he had a brain tumor pushing against his amygdala, in the prefrontal cortex. This was, without a doubt, a major factor in his violent acts.[128] While this is a rare case, it raises the question of where along the continuum of body-mind influence we can draw the line and conclude that a person is 100 percent responsible for his or her behavior. In modern culture, most people draw very clear lines between decisions they feel are "free" and decisions they feel are not, often with unrelenting judgment and criticism of others who act in ways deemed unsavory. This moral high ground is ever-present, which makes perfect sociological sense because once again, mainstream society flaunts the ideas of independence, free will, volition, and human choice as the starting point of all personal success and human virtue.

There is a term in social psychology called the *fundamental attribution error*. This is an error of judgment people make when they experience a person's behavior as unethical, without knowing about other factors involved.[129] A simple example is a man who dines at a restaurant and, upon paying the check, exits without leaving a customary tip. From the standpoint of the wait staff, that person could be judged as inconsiderate. After the employees share a cathartic verbal bashing of the seemingly rude person, the man then reenters and puts down a tip. When asked about leaving, the man explains he had no more money on him and needed to get some out of his car.

This idea of mistaking a person's apparent behavior as being entirely representative of his or her character can be extended to one's life experience and biology. In a sense, the entire criminal justice system is predicated upon expressing the fundamental attribution error as a formalized method of evaluation. This is not to argue that all human actions can always be clearly traced to delineated preconditions, nor is it to absolve anyone of wrongdoing by default. It is to point out the general dismissal of such considerations in legal practice, focusing on the fragmented actions of the single person.[130] I would even argue that to exclude the biosocial condition of a person is really a crime in and of itself when one attempts to evaluate someone's actions. The myth of free will makes it easy, while helping to preserve the legal system's role as a means of social control, once again.

The same goes for the economy, which has a clear coherence with the legal view. If you happen to believe that every human being has absolute freedom in thought and decision making, with no biological or environmental preconditions that can influence behavior to make it uncontrollable, then you would conclude that any action taken is a person's moral responsibility entirely. Similarly, if you also happen to believe the common capitalist myth that economic prosperity is available to everyone who "works hard," disregarding any structural elements that may create insurmountable social immobility, then you will likely agree that everyone who becomes wealthy or poor simply deserves what they get.

It also isn't difficult to see how such root assumptions can then form a basis to infer more extended beliefs. For example, from the "you get what you work for" dogma, one could reason support for more right-wing or conservative politics, also leading to support for more "free trade" or neoliberal policies. This could also mean finding little rational motivation for, say, increasing state-funded social welfare to help the poor. Likewise, if market virtue rests on free, "democratic" exchange and the maximization of utility "for the greater good," then any intervention by government can only be sacrilegious. To throw one more *coherent* validation into the mix, if social dominance theory is assumed to be true, then the inequality and poverty in the world can really only be natural and even necessary to some degree to ensure the larger-order stability of society. Such shared social characteristics derived from this free-will foundation are enormous in modern culture.

In the realm of philosophy, the assumption of human choice is a bedrock of discussion since philosophy is just as much about principles of proper behavior as it is about the investigation of knowledge and reality. Perhaps the most dominant moral philosophy today is *utilitarianism*. This is the view that the correct moral choice in any given situation is the one that produces the greatest utility (usefulness) in terms of generating happiness and reducing suffering. It is basically hedonistic, viewing the individual as interested in maximizing his or her own utility (benefit) at all times, while at the same time trying to maximize utility for the largest number of people, making them happy too.[131] Sounds great, right? While poetically viable, the way this theory has unfolded in the context of market economics has deviated quite far from its original intentions.

Basic economic utilitarianism says that all market behavior is to be reduced to rational, strategic attempts to maximize gain and avoid loss. This reasoning occurs in the purchase of a consumable good, the hiring of labor, or the process of capital investment. It is basically a form of *game theory*. In a way it is the theory of how humans behave and how they ought to behave in the context of "rational" economic decisions. In this process of rational self-maximization, as per the ideal of Adam Smith's "invisible hand," the greater good is to be achieved.[132]

While much could be said on the issue, what this theory effectively does is reduce human beings to mere gaming agents, shifting focus away from the actual nature of economic production and of real-life and societal interaction. The theory focuses only on the abstraction of trade itself. In a way, it creates a false view of equality among everyone in the economy, reducing people to hedonistic exchangers. As such, it distracts attention from structural and imbalance problems, justifying the market's basis in competition and narrow self-interest.

One important idea found within this school of utilitarianism is that of *voluntarism*. Quite popular in modern libertarian circles, voluntarism is about action based solely on free will, without any force. In market behavior, the act of "voluntary" trade is considered the ultimate moral priority. So, a woman has a ring. She goes into a pawnshop and sells it. From this perspective, the exchange is considered to be mutually beneficial to both parties since the woman willfully sold the ring and the shop willfully bought it. This simple idea of exchange is held up by microeconomic theorists to argue that a trade always serves the best interests of both parties, and even does so equally, since they are both just "exchangers," maximizing their utility (or personal benefit).

The problem with this view is that it ignores all other pressures that distort the will of the individual making the trade. From a voluntary, utilitarianism perspective, it doesn't matter *why* the trade occurs, as long as it appears both parties are acting on free will in the exchange. But what if the ring being pawned was her dead husband's, who had recently been in a fatal accident, leaving his family with no income or means? In distress, with bills to pay and no social safety net, the wife sees no alternative but to sell off a highly sentimental personal item. Can we still call it voluntary? In abstraction, yes. But in reality that circumstance cannot be dismissed as simply voluntary, just as we can't view as simply voluntary the choice of an impoverished, drug-addicted, and mentally handicapped prostitute to exchange sex for more drugs. Life is a sea of complex coercive pressures and external forces, occurring both consciously and subconsciously. The snapshot of a "voluntary exchange" is a dangerous free-will illusion as it distorts social perception of causality, limiting more thorough understandings.

At the same time we are faced with the question of rationality itself. While we are naturally unaware of choices and factors outside of our education or experience, making those choices or factors unavailable for consideration, we also have common inhibitions that interfere with the information we do have. These are referred to as *cognitive biases*. Cognitive biases are errors and gravitations in thinking and judgment usually tied to our social condition. Being the social organisms we are, arguably defined by others and culture itself in terms of personal identity and self-worth, the power of our social nature often gets the best of us.

A notable theoretical framework to understand this is called *social identity theory*. In short, people have a propensity to identify with groups, drawing their identity and sense of status from them in many ways. It is observed that people often view their own group as "in," with other perceived groups as "out," as is characteristic of racism and other forms of group-based bigotry.[133] Consequently, this ubiquitous social tendency for inclusion and approval creates serious psychological problems when it comes to rational choice and critical thought.

One such problem is the tendency toward social conformity (or the bandwagon effect). A herd mentality often arises, such that people gravitate toward being consistent with their group's actions or beliefs, suspending critical thought.[134] One famous study conducted in the 1950s entailed asking a group of people to make simple decisions about visual images, such as which line on a screen was the longest of a set. However, all but one test subject was in on the study. These other participants were fakes, planted to purposely agree on the wrong answer and encourage the test subject to go along with their group decision about the correct match. The controlled study proved a strong effect of peer pressure, with more than 75 percent of the participants in the total of 12 repeated tests conforming at least once. This is in contrast to the control group (no pressure to conform) where less than 1 percent conformed.[135]

It is not difficult to imagine how this same effect can occur in groups with shared values, such as political parties. People also seem to prefer being on the "winning," majority side of a given situation, bypassing true critical thought. Bandwagon persuasion is everywhere in the world today and can rightfully be deemed a natural gravitation of our evolutionary psychology. From advertising slogans declaring "millions of satisfied customers can't be wrong," to the self-fulfilling prophecy of stock market bubbles in which rising prices driven by buyers simply encourage more buyers in a euphoric trend. Political persuasion is also similar. The media need do little more than present the idea that a candidate, concept, or policy already enjoys popular approval, and the herd will usually follow blindly.

There is also the tendency of group bias in general. This means the propensity to favor your group (in-group) while disfavoring others (out-group). This is most common when the groups have some relationship to each other, such as rival baseball teams, religions, or nations. The development of prejudice is predictable, with the history of bigotry largely a group-based phenomenon. An informal yet famous study on this phenomenon was done by an elementary school teacher named Jane Elliot, who divided her third-grade class into two groups based on whether the children had blue or brown eyes. She then explained to the kids that those with blue eyes were naturally smarter than those with brown eyes. Amazingly, this simple act rapidly created group tension and conflict, including name calling, shaming, and discrimination against the brown-eyed kids.[136]

Now, I wish to clarify that this is not about absolute determinism. It is about a general propensity, linked to our evolutionary psychology, for humans to gravitate toward group identification and to develop biases based upon that identification. As Charles Mackay wrote in his famous text, *Extraordinary Popular Delusions and the Madness of Crowds*, "Men, it has been well said, think in herds; it will be seen that they go mad in herds, while they only recover their senses slowly, and one by one."[137] Our social nature being what it is, this tendency clearly does not favor critical evaluation of information. It takes a great deal of self-awareness to notice the propensity when it is occurring.

As for causality, our nervous system seems to reflexively "want" to remain part of a group identity, falling victim to the power of its social influence. Neurobiologist and researcher Vasily Klucharev writes that "the deviation of individual opinion from the group behavior (opinions) is interpreted by the nervous system as behavioral error or 'reward prediction error', which starts the process of behavior change, based on the dopaminergic mechanism of reinforcement learning."[138] In other words, our very brains are somewhat trapped between rational thinking and impulsive counter reactions that seek to prefer in-group conclusions. These lower brain reactions make us vulnerable to numerous thoughtless behaviors triggered by brain chemistry and make us susceptible to external manipulation. The arenas of marketing and politics are perhaps where the greatest damage is done today.

In general advertising, for example, much work has been executed in the field of subliminal effects that create unconscious bias. This has even led to making the practice, called subliminal advertising, illegal in many countries. However, more recent research has shown that the influence of general advertising has a similar subconscious effect. In a 2010 article published in the journal *Science*, psychologists Custers and Aarts report how the "unconscious will" has a powerful role in decision making, without our being aware.[139] Custers and Aarts write that people "should be much more scared of commercials they can see, rather than those they can't see," for the effect of things like psychological *positive-reward* cues can create bias.

Using an example of a soda commercial, Custers and Aarts write, "If you are exposed to these advertisements over and over again, it does create an association in your mind, and your unconscious is more likely to suddenly decide you want a Coke."[140] It isn't enough to simply be critical when watching a commercial; the ad can affect your subconscious even when you think it has had no power. It does this simply by repetition and by the (usually) positive emotions associated with the product. The only way to avoid the possible influence is to completely avoid the ad. This understanding also brings up a powerful question of ethics, for if people are exposed to repeated ads promoting unhealthful behavior, their "unconscious will" may influence them, leading to sickness. In this sense, we can rightfully view advertising as a possible form of violence.

Now, to conclude this chapter I wish to clarify my basic position on free will. Taking determinism to its extreme, we could see all human behavior as involuntary, a biological clockwork affecting every thought and cell, driving every event, shaping all aspects of reality with its massive, singular motion. Such an extreme perspective accomplishes little. It is much more productive to view the individual and his or her surroundings as a dynamic synergy of cause and effect. As the evidence shows, due to biological, social, and other factors, one's capacity to make choices is inhibited—sometimes profoundly—at every moment of existence. Grasping this gives us a more comprehensive understanding of not only human behavior, but of reality itself. After all, to view yourself and others as partly self-propelled and partly vulnerable to biological and cultural influences forces a very different sense of how and why the world is the way it is.

It is also important to point out that no matter what the truth may be in terms of exactly how much free will we have, to believe we are in control is very important to our psychology. Research has shown that people who believe they have control over their lives are much happier and more motivated, which makes perfect sense.[141] After all, who wants to feel like one has no control over anything he or she is doing? Yet the cold reality is that on a certain level we are not free and we are not rational. There is a surprising kind of *automaticity* to our existence, meaning we are doing many complex things automatically.[142] In this, we are faced with a very uncomfortable sense of self and identity. We have to admit that on a certain level we are simply *out of control*. We are not in full control of our thoughts and behaviors and neither are the people around us. Yet, in recognizing this, we are then able to better understand human limitations and weaknesses, allowing for more-intelligent decisions on how to better adjust our society to improve well-being, public health, and social relations. This view, once again, rests on a system-based context of our existence.

While having some purpose in supporting our required sense of identity and sanity, the highly propagated, dogmatic, and institution-alized idea of free will and morality is also what keeps us from better understanding the causal factors paralyzing the world, perpetuating the same destructive patterns in public health, civil injustice, and environ-mental destruction. We are constantly judging people and their indi-vidual actions, rather than factoring in the structural roles, cultural pressures, modulating stressors, incentivizing influences, dominance mechanisms of control, human vulnerability to submission, cognitive biases, and the litany of other system-based factors that keep the vicious cycles of human disorder in motion. When this higher view is taken— one that positions the individual in a network of factors, bypassing the illusion of singular will and autonomy—a more holistic and effective sense of problem solving emerges.

As such, social activism must become a social science in and of itself. The synergetic, *biopsychosocial* nature of the human condition needs to be not only understood but also used as a strategy for instigating needed social change. We also need a firm grasp of history and its effects, knowing that our society's *root socioeconomic orientation*, as derived from the geographical determinism of the post-Neolithic Revolution, has evolved a condition based upon factors of competition, dominance, and scarcity. These factors have been fully absorbed into virtually every aspect of our lives, from the social system, to its institutions, to the prevailing psychology of the masses.

Without these foundational understandings, very little progress can be expected in the realm of human justice and equality as we move further into the twenty-first century. The negative forces preserving the status quo today are not substantially affected by street protest, public outcry, media exposure of corruption, or other traditional methods. It is fruitless for us to demand idealized or "more just" behaviors from our existing institutions, since they have been built around a value and incentive system that thrives on the very behaviors we wish to change. Only deep system changes will prove to have long-standing effects, as will be argued in future chapters.

Chapter Three

STRUCTURAL BIGOTRY: THE ECONOMICS OF OPPRESSION

Where justice is denied, where poverty is enforced, where igno-
rance prevails, and where any one class is made to feel that
society is an organized conspiracy to oppress, rob and degrade
them, neither persons nor property will be safe.[1]

—FREDERICK DOUGLASS

AFTER HIGH SCHOOL I moved to New York City to attend a music con-
servatory in pursuit of a degree in classical percussion performance.
As passionate as I was about music, the financial reality of my student
loans quickly polluted the circumstances. Combined with a growing
disillusionment with having to "monetize" an art form I considered
sacred—a tool for meditation and personal growth—I ended my college career at the age of twenty after a mere two years. Amazingly, the
interest-bearing loan schedule for this short time projected values of
over $40,000, a shocking sum for a young adult just entering the "earn
a living" reality. Of course, watching my friends graduate with master's
degrees from prestigious institutions such as the Juilliard School, only to
moonlight in coffee shops thereafter as they struggled with low-paying
gigs, wasn't very encouraging, either. While I was disappointed at the
time, the prudence of the decision is as clear to me today as it was then.

As expressed in the previous chapter, economic deregulation and
privatization are considered sacrosanct requirements of a supposedly
free world. Ironically, the "freedom" of markets means effectively *nothing*

should ever be free, and being $40,000 in debt certainly didn't give me a sense of liberation. I suspect I have not been alone in that feeling. As of 2015, American student loan debt was about $1.2 trillion, surpassing the GDP of Australia, New Zealand, and Ireland combined.[2] One may rightfully wonder why a society that ostensibly seeks to educate and prepare young people to be intelligent problem solvers and creators would perpetuate a system that shackles them with immobilizing debt the moment they enter the post-education workforce. One may also wonder why many other countries that subsidize higher education through strategic taxation, making sure young people are not inhibited by financial limitation or debt, consistently outperform the United States in global test comparisons.[3] Yet this is only curious if one is unaware of the dominant socioeconomic philosophy of the United States, along with its position as a global empire.

Today, the US leads the world in terms of both economic influence and military force, endlessly pushing the neoliberal values of "free trade" as a root priority. Like a philosophical crusade, it has been deemed an imperative of Western business-political leaders to ensure that people comply with what is in effect the new global religion—a religion that invariably prioritizes commerce over everything else, with human rights increasingly subordinated to *business rights*. When one understands how the rules of trade, property, and exchange have become the determining mechanisms of society, decoupling focus from actual life-supporting means and factors of social trust, the dehumanized, conflicted-ridden nature of the modern world begins to make a lot more sense. Given this ethic, education is simply another product to be bought and sold and little more. The US government allocates roughly 2 percent of its annual budget to education. This is in stark contrast to the 20 percent allocated to the military, suggesting war is more beneficial to the nation's leaders than an educated population.[4]

At any rate, with the minimum debt payments from my student loan mounting, I quickly sought whatever work I could find. Within a few weeks, I found myself in the glamorous field of work as a "cater waiter." In comparison to traditional restaurant service, this job consisted of being bused around New York City from one privileged upper-class event to another. We were an army of servants in tuxedos, following the wealthy 1 percent around the Big Apple. While certain traditional functions had endearing merit, such as weddings and birthdays, the majority were corporate, political events and superficial charity fundraisers. I say superficial because if the goal of charity is to help those in need, you certainly wouldn't know it based on the degree of waste and decadence present. There is something fundamentally wrong when people are eating extravagant meals, wearing $5,000 suits, and drinking $800 bottles of champagne while a guy on stage preaches about global starvation and poverty. This is particularly troubling in New York City, a place with about 60,000 homeless on the street each night.[5]

Nevertheless, it was certainly an education to be a fly on the wall. At one event executives from the Walt Disney Corporation were being honored for both their apparent philanthropy and record profits, explaining how they were bringing needed jobs to impoverished people in Bangladesh and Haiti. It wasn't long after I saw Disney exposed on the news for facilitating some of the worst human-rights abuses in sweatshop-labor history, paying as little as four cents an hour; denying basic labor rights and benefits; tolerating the beating of workers for failing to meet quotas; sexual harassment; using children as labor; and more.[6] It's a unique state of mind when a company moves operations to impoverished areas of the world, exploiting the vulnerable for cheap labor, only to then try to convince themselves and others they are doing the region a favor.

In the end, during this time as a cater waiter, I was able to see a side of society I think most do not. Coming from a lower middle-class upbringing, my father a postman and my mother a social worker, I had little exposure to such privilege. What I came to realize is that there is often a distinct detachment from reality in wealthy culture. It wasn't that these folks were overtly disrespectful or mean. Most were quite polite when "dealing with the help." Sometimes, I would end up at mansions and exotic penthouse apartments serving as a family's personal servant for the evening. These were generally kind people and clearly caring when it came to their home life. Still, a clear disconnect from general society was obvious—a kind of cultural alienation, if you will. Given the access the wealthy have to means and conveniences that most do not, coupled with different social atmospheres and other cultural nuances, this alienation isn't difficult to understand. In the same way we can understand why the Amish tend to isolate themselves as a community, the rich tend to do the same, losing touch with the plight of the normal world.

Rather than simply demonize the wealthy, it is important that we realize they are victims of circumstance and groomed into their characteristic worldviews and behaviors by larger-order forces like everyone else. They are only partially responsible for their actions, as expressed in this chapter. This fact is important, for viewing society through this system-oriented lens is needed to better understand the true nature of class conflict. It is also needed to establish a new level of compassion toward others. There is little value in "group vs. group" thinking, as the real problem is not the nature of any group but how that group manifested its values and biases to begin with. I view those whose values and worldview are distorted by power and wealth as little different from those suffering from any other biopsychosocial derangement of culture. In the same way that we can expect certain social preconditions to lead to problematic outcomes within the lower class such as street gangs, crime, and violence, similar sociological processes all too often lead the rich to develop selfish, apathetic, and power-hungry behaviors.

SOCIAL PSYCHOLOGY

As F. Scott Fitzgerald cogently wrote, "Let me tell you about the very rich. They are different from you and me . . . [t]hey think, deep in their hearts, that they are better than we are because we had to discover the compensations and refuges of life for ourselves. Even when they enter deep into our world or sink below us, they still think that they are better than we are. They are different."[7] Social status is not just about material access and social privilege. Our sense of rank has a deep impact on our self-identity. It doesn't have to be money that creates the difference, but in the world today this is by far the most defining cultural modulator. And the unsettling truth is that there are, on average, pronounced psychological differences between upper and lower classes.

Confidence and self-esteem is an example. As was touched upon in the preceding chapter with respect to in-group/out-group associations, our social nature is a feedback system and how we perceive ourselves is inexplicably linked to others. In a 2004 study focusing on two different ranking social castes (birth classes) in India, it was found that if the whole combined group did not know they were a mix of two castes, their performance on problem-solving tests was different from the results when they did know. When the caste was not announced, the two castes performed basically the same on the test. When the caste was announced, the lower caste did far worse.[8] This study is one of many confidence studies showing that if people feel inferior and lower in value, they very well may act that way, losing confidence. This is called the *golem effect* and it has been widely researched.[9]

There are also measurable neurobiological effects of perceived social status. In a 2002 study with macaque monkeys, it was found that those in lower ranks had less dopamine activity in the brain as compared with those in upper ranks. This effect would then change when the monkeys were strategically regrouped; when lower-status monkeys assumed higher-status positions, they had more dopamine activity, while the prior alphas had less.[10] This shows a direct correlation between perceived social rank and biological expression—a pretty damning link that reveals public-health ramifications to social status in a very clear way. Reduced dopamine activity can lead to serious psychological and emotional effects, including depression, loss of motivation, anxiety, attention problems, and other problems.[11]

What such studies also highlight is how psychological traits can be consequential to a social condition, as opposed to determinant. In other words, when people see the confidence, will, motivation, apparent intelligence, and other virtuous traits celebrated as characteristic of the rich and "successful," superficial reasoning suggests that they gained their financial success owing to those traits. While that may be true at times, the biopsychosocial reality is that those traits also arise from the mere privilege of simply being in a high-class, respected, and rewarded position to begin with. Hence, one's sense of status can become a self-fulfilling prophecy.

Perhaps more troubling are differences in empathy and compassion between upper and lower classes. A 2010 study found that higher-class individuals actually had a more difficult time recognizing emotions in others. It appears the lower class develops more perceptive social skills than the upper, including the ability to better recognize emotional details in others, making empathic connections. One of the study's researchers concluded, "Upper-class people, in spite of all their advantages, suffer empathy deficits . . . and there are enormous consequences."[12] Likewise, numerous studies examining differences in compassion suggest that the more one's bank account increases, the less compassionate he or she becomes. In a paper titled "Having Less, Giving More: The Influence of Social Class on Prosocial Behavior," the relative poor were found to give over twice as much to charity as the relative rich in percentage terms. The study also stated: "[L]ower class individuals proved to be more generous, charitable . . . trusting . . . and helpful . . . compared with their upper class counterparts. Mediator and moderator data showed that lower class individuals acted in a more prosocial fashion because of a greater commitment to egalitarian values and feelings of compassion."[13]

A similar study by the *Chronicle of Philanthropy* showed that households earning between $50,000 and $75,000 a year give an average of 7.6 percent of their discretionary income to charity, while those making more than $100,000 gave only 4.2 percent. In some of the wealthiest neighborhoods with the largest share of people making in excess of $200,000 a year, the average giving rate was only 2.8 percent.[14] In the words of Ken Stern, writing for *The Atlantic*:

> One of the most surprising, and perhaps confounding, facts of charity in America is that the people who can least afford to give are the ones who donate the greatest percentage of their income. In 2011, the wealthiest Americans—those with earnings in the top 20 percent—contributed on average 1.3 percent of their income to charity. By comparison, Americans at the base of the income pyramid—those in the bottom 20 percent—donated 3.2 percent of their income.[15]

Again, while these percentage numbers may seem small, 1.3 percent to 3.2 percent actually means the poor are giving well over twice the amount in percentage terms.

I remember going to work early one winter morning, riding the subway into Manhattan from Brooklyn. An older homeless man was making his way through the mostly empty train car, pausing in front of me as I scrounged for whatever change I had to put into his empty cup. After I dropped in two quarters, the man thanked me and moved on. At the other side of the train was a clearly poor woman, bundled up and appearing to try to sleep. The man shuffled along as though to pass her, only to stop and make eye contact. After a brief moment of interaction, he reached into his cup and took out one of the two quarters and gave it to her. I was stunned to see the compassion. While I did not know the man's circumstances, there is good reason to assume that with that act of charity, he actually gave away 50 percent of all the money he had in the world to a stranger. While today many fawn over the "billions" given by this or that wealthy icon, the real measure of compassion has to do with how giving affects you personally, and that is why the percentage people give is more telling than the absolute values.

Sociological research also suggests that something happens to people's ethics as they move up the economic ladder. While there are always exceptions, a general loss of social concern appears common. In a 2011 study from the University of California, Berkeley, it was found that:

> [U]pper-class individuals behave more unethically than lower-class individuals . . . upper-class individuals were more likely to break the law while driving, relative to lower-class individuals. In follow-up laboratory studies, upper-class individuals were more likely to exhibit unethical decision-making tendencies, take valued goods from others, lie in a negotiation, cheat to increase their chances of winning a prize, and endorse unethical behavior at work than were lower-class individuals. Mediator and moderator data demonstrated that upper-class individuals' unethical tendencies are accounted for, in part, by their more favorable attitudes toward greed.[16]

It has been something of a historical cliché that those who achieve great financial success in business tend to be ruthless or desensitized. It has even been said that the more caring and empathic you are, the less likely you are to succeed in capitalism. It appears the Ebenezer Scrooge phenomenon is not far off the mark as per modern social science. Given the self-interested focus required in economic competition, increasingly rewarded as one climbs the socioeconomic ladder, it makes sense that such disassociated values become dominant. Detached from the plight of the lower class, the rich begin to think the padded world they experience is the world everyone else experiences. In other words, people in the lower classes are more attuned to the common suffering and hence more compassionate.[17] Some call this the *empathy gap*, embracing both the lack of exposure the rich have to the plight of common folk and the psychological changes that reinforce social indifference.[18] Needless to say, it doesn't bode well for general society when those of great wealth and resulting power tend have a propensity to be indifferent and apathetic.

Another feature of this phenomenon is the relationship between the degree of apathy and selfishness and the prevailing socioeconomic climate. The United States is a unique case for observing this, given its status as a kind of "forbidden experiment" in class extremity and material culture. During the "Great Recession," it was found that those who made more than $200,000 a year donated 5 percent *less* than in prior years, while those who made $25,000 or less a year actually *increased* giving by 17 percent.[19] The *Proceedings of the National Academy of Sciences* found that as income inequality increases, the wealthy tend to give less.[20] The research suggests that elite wealth concentration tends to lead to "the belief that one is more important and deserving than others" and "that resources rightly belong to them" in an increased sense of entitlement. This tendency has also been verified by an extensive lab study led by psychologist Paul Piff, who found that in a rigged game of Monopoly, with one player given more turns, more initial money, and every advantage ensuring an inevitable win, those winning subjects actually acted as though it was their cunning and smarts that led to the outcome when interviewed afterward.[21] This finding has a clear parallel with the real world, where the social system, as will be further discussed in this chapter, provides great *structural* advantages to a small minority. People simply want to believe they are "getting what they deserve," ignoring the unearned advantages they happen to have over others. Put bluntly by Piff, "While having money doesn't necessarily make anybody anything . . . the rich are way more likely to prioritize their own self-interests above the interests of other people. It makes them more likely to exhibit characteristics that we would stereotypically associate with, say, assholes."[22]

There is also a correlation found between wealth status and what charitable causes donated money goes to. Unsurprisingly, the rich tend to give to elite schools, museums, symphonies, and other more "tasteful" interests on average, bypassing social-welfare programs such as homelessness or poverty. In 2012 "not one of the top 50 individual charitable gifts went to a social-service organization or to a charity that principally serves the poor and the dispossessed."[23] While it is true that in monetary terms the upper class gives more than the lower, even though substantially less in percentage terms, the fact that their focus tends to avoid core social-welfare interests, favoring more luxury interests such as higher education, arts, and research, is certainly troubling. It isn't that those interests are not important, but with almost a billion people failing to meet basic daily nutritional requirements, we need to question the sense of priority.[24]

PHILANTHROPY

It is interesting how the term *philanthropy*, defined as "the desire to promote the welfare of others," has become associated almost exclusively with the wealthy; a badge worn to show how they "give back" to the community. Yet, rarely is the question of *why* there is the need to give back considered from the standpoint of market dynamics itself. While there is indeed growing global concern about increasing inequality, existing poverty, and so on, little real effort is being made to counter the problem from the standpoint of altering the social structure to correct what are clearly systemic problems inherent in our society. In fact, philanthropy appears to be the *only* practice to redistribute wealth that isn't met head-on with great disdain by the prevailing intelligentsia, especially in America. Even quite basic traditional platforms, such as increased taxation of the rich, are routinely met with contempt by gatekeepers of the capitalist religion.

In the words of conservative *Forbes* contributor Jeffrey Dorfman, "once you admit that income redistribution is fair, there is no logical stopping point short of communism."[25] By this, Dorfman essentially implies that there is no stopping point short of everyone's simply getting "the exact same" distribution of income regardless of what job they perform. From there, of course, the gesture suggests this path can only lead to gulags, indifferent central planners, and the loss of individuality and liberty itself. This kind of anti-socialist dogma is nothing new, prominently set in motion in the early to mid-twentieth century when the threat of communism was putting capitalist hegemony at risk. The long-term consequence has been a reactionary Western culture that sees any direct government action toward economic equality, especially if it inconveniences the wealthy, as little more than a move toward bureaucratic tyranny.

Not only does this bias vindicate the idea of philanthropy as the only acceptable solution to inequality and its consequences, but it also ignores the simple fact that the market economy is a process of wealth redistribution in and of itself. That is what the market does. It redistributes, literally, existing wealth and materials, whether raw, produced, recycled, financial, intellectual, or otherwise. As such, market dynamics cannot be merely assumed to be untouchable simply because its mechanics are seen as an "objective" process. In other words, it is deemed sacrilegious to impose equality-targeting taxation since the market faith rests on the "invisible hand" of the market god to make everything OK. If this god is fallible, then the whole belief system becomes suspect. But there is nothing but evidence, formal and empirical, that the market god is horribly incompetent at best.

Thomas Piketty, a French economist who became famous in 2014 for his treatment *Capital in the Twenty-First Century*, makes a strong case, concluding that there is no way the growing global class divide can subside given the way capitalism is unfolding in its natural, "financially liberalized" state. The amount of money being made off existing wealth itself will continue to far exceed what normal people make through labor income. High-level capital investment in the form of financial instruments such as stocks and other means are producing returns far exceeding anything the public can generate without such existing levels of wealth to invest. The technical term is the "wealth to income ratio" and the higher it is, the worse off the general population. A 2015 Oxfam study found that by 2016, 1 percent of the global population will own more than the other 99 percent combined, with dire implications for related social problems.[26]

Piketty's proposal to stop this trend is the most expected one—a large progressive annual tax on wealth. Yet, even with this practical, commonplace attempt at a solution, the wealthy community quickly and expectedly condemned the idea. Most notable was the response by Bill Gates, the founder of Microsoft, who is worth almost $80 billion and the richest person in the world as of 2015. He partly contested the idea of capital taxation since, in his view, philanthropy by the rich should be considered a viable institution in itself.[27] He argues that those who choose to be philanthropic with their wealth should not be treated the same as wealthy folks who simply buy yachts and sports cars. While the gesture of this is respectable, given how Gates and his famous Bill and Melinda Gates Foundation have indeed performed positive charitable acts, we need to step back and examine what he, along with an entire culture of high-level, "big money" charities, are actually saying.

Naturally, the main focus of society should be to solve problems directly, addressing root origins. In fact, I would argue that a true philanthropic "desire to promote the welfare of others" could only seek to alter the preconditions creating social problems to begin with. The ongoing need for social-welfare charities is really a response to an inefficient economic system. It is a supplemental action to help those who are not as "fortunate." The idea of turning this supplemental act of charity into an established social institution, deemed inclusive to the system of capitalism itself, implies the society is no longer to view outcomes such as poverty and other interests common to philanthropy as a real problem. Rather, it is a tacit admission that the resulting deprivation must be necessary, expected, and effectively accepted as "just the way it is." Forget trying to change the preconditions leading to these problems—let's just focus on "giving back" after the fact. That is the message—and it is a terrible one, as it avoids examining the structure of the economy itself.

So, neither Piketty nor Gates offers actual solutions. Taxation, as suggested by Piketty, is only a "patch," as it doesn't address the structural and systemic mechanisms that converge to create inequality. As with a car engine constantly leaking oil, you do not cover up the problem by continuing to refill the oil tank, pretending everything is fine. You fix the engine or replace it to stop the leaking. Gates, however, takes things to a new level by arguing he and other people of great wealth should simply use their charitable foundations to affect the disadvantaged world directly. Forget government, public policy, democracy, transparency, or even account-ability—private foundations built by billionaires will now save the world.

While all charity is admirable, once it becomes institutionalized and funded to the extent seen by organizations such as the Gates Foundation, it turns into something different, with extended social ramifications.[28] These elite charities are true, large-scale institutions with power, engag-ing in lobbying, transnational partnerships, political policy alignments, and so on. Where and how the George Soroses and Bill Gateses of the world mobilize money can have powerful effects on industry, politics, culture, academia, scientific research, national policy, and the like. In the case of Gates, his foundation is "undeniably, the most powerful and influential global health charity in history," in the words of health-law professor Lawrence Gostin.[29] What critics rightfully point out is that, regardless of good intentions, unaccountable, singular private power in global health affairs poses serious problems, in the same way autocratic dictatorships pose serious problems for democracy and liberty. Any orga-nization with the power to actually affect the lives of millions of people needs transparency, accountability, and a democratic presence. These private institutions have little to none.[30]

So, what we have is the rise of a new breed of pseudo-egalitarian capitalists. They generate their great wealth by way of often ruthless competitive behavior in the private sector, arguably promoting the very mechanisms that have led to the vast structural violence and extensive poverty existing on Earth to begin with. They then turn around and offer their charity as the solution to the problems created by the very system that rewards them. Once again, this has nothing to do with intent. It is about an underlying hypocrisy that bypasses and obscures the real problem-solving focus desperately needed to further human-rights jus-tice. That focus can only be structural.

At the same time, this institutionalization of philanthropy also serves to placate the public, giving a caring face to those who have often extracted such great wealth at the cost of others' well-being. In the words of activist Slavoj Žižek, "Charity is the humanitarian mask hiding the face of economic exploitation."[31] As shown before with the research regarding how people tend to change as they gain more wealth and advantage, there is a deep psychological need in those of great wealth to feel that their exceptionalism is justified. They naturally wish not only to ensure everyone believes they deserve what they have, but also to justify it to themselves. An example of this is the "Giving Pledge," wherein a group of more than130 people, mostly billionaires, have promised to give half or more of their wealth to charity before or after their death.[32] This now globally recognized project has been met with great humanitarian accolades in the media, especially given its timely creation as public outcry against inequality grows. Yet it's very difficult not to view the entire project as a PR stunt for the upper 0.1 percent. As the organization states: "The pledge is a moral commitment to give, not a legal contract. It does not involve pooling money or supporting a particular set of causes or organizations."[33] In other words, it is first and foremost a gesture and no one signing the prestigious pledge has any obligation to do anything. There is also no transparency, so the public might never know whether a person gave or not.

For those who do follow through, there are prominent tax incentives, specifically in the United States. Since donations to charity and philanthropic foundations allow for reduced tax liability for the rich, giving money away often becomes an act of strategic self-interest. Very often, the rich simply set up their own foundations and move money through them via tax loopholes. For example, the infamous Walton family, five people with a combined net wealth of over $139 billion as of 2014, more than what the bottom 40 percent of Americans have combined, do some fantastic tax gymnastics through their foundation.[34] An independent audit of the Walton Family Foundation found that not only did only .04 percent of its wealth make it to charity in its generation's lifetime, but it also stated, "The Walmart heirs have built one of the largest and most powerful private foundations in the country—at almost no cost to themselves . . . In addition, the Waltons are exploiting complex loopholes in the tax code in order to avoid billions of dollars in estate taxes by funding their Foundation with special trusts."[35]

Estate taxes are interesting as they relate to the rich only. In the US when people with more than $5.43 million die, the tax is 40 percent as

of 2015.[36] The rich work around this tax in various ways, with charitable foundations forming the most common means. Billionaire Albert
Ueltschi signed the Giving Pledge in 2012, and died later that year. It was
reported that in his will, he made the condition that nothing would go
to charity if there was no US estate tax. Since there was one, he followed
through, moving that money to his own charities.[37] This is also interesting as a general correlation. A study done by the Tax Policy Center in
2003 found that "the estate tax encourages charitable giving at death by
allowing a deduction for charitable bequests" and "also encourages giving during life."[38] The center calculated that if the estate tax was removed,
there would be a *reduction* of charitable giving upon death of up to 37
percent, while the Congressional Budget Office corroborated this finding and added that during life, this same class would also reduce giving
by up to 11 percent.[39]

What this means first of all is that the giving doesn't appear to be
entirely genuine. We can understand a poor family donating to a charity,
knowing they can write the donation off their taxes if the deduction is
itemized. They might not be able to afford the donation otherwise. The
wealthy have no such excuse and sociologically that is quite interesting.
What they are really doing is bypassing state funding in favor of their
own interests. Moving money to charity foundations, effectively consolidating wealth in the hands of private interests rather than government,
is a logical method to better keep things "in the club" of private business power. Keep in mind the state is deeply flawed, as noted previously.
But at least the state has some basic formal responsibility to the public,
regardless of how corrupted it may be by vested interests. The Giving
Pledge is partly just another avenue for this anti-government and hence
antisocial behavior.

In the words of German multimillionaire Peter Krämer, an open
critic of the Giving Pledge, "It is all just a bad transfer of power from
the state to billionaires. So it's not the state that determines what is good
for the people, but rather the rich want to decide. That's a development
that I find really bad. What legitimacy do these people have to decide
where massive sums of money will flow? . . . That runs counter to the
democratically legitimate state."[40] Pablo Eisenberg, a senior fellow at the
Center for Public and Nonprofit Leadership, said regarding the pledge:

"What concerns me is that no one has said what the pledge is going to do, who it will serve and how it will be accountable . . . it will increase the number of mega-foundations, and I worry that will hurt our democracy because of the influence these institutions will exert."[41] These are legitimate social concerns given how such high-level, unaccountable private power is similar in effect to that of regulatory dictatorship.

This is something deeply obscured in prevailing views of capitalism. While the world still seems to associate markets with freedom and democracy, the very structure of private business is actually in direct opposition to both. In the words of political economist Robert Brady: "Within the corporation . . . all policies emanate from the control above. In the union of this power to determine policy with the execution thereof, all authority necessarily proceeds from the top to the bottom and all responsibility from the bottom to the top. This is, of course, the inverse of 'democratic' control; it follows the structural conditions of dictatorial power."[42] The accelerating rise of private charity foundations have the same flaw, as they can set their own public health and social standards, bypassing public participation in areas that require it.

INEQUALITY MACHINE

As expressed, the socioeconomic system produces predictable outcomes in social psychology, and better understanding the characteristics of the upper class is specifically important. After all, it is this class that indisputably dominates social affairs. Again, this has nothing to do with deliberate conspiracy or the like. It is simply a systemic result inherent to the logic, values, and structure of capitalism. The sense of superiority naturally cultivated by the upper class, coupled with measurable losses of empathy, compassion, and ethics, makes the condition of modern power highly troublesome. The more people become rewarded by market economics, the more they tend to identify with the market, assuming its integrity. Hence, the rewarded wealthy are naturally the last to be critical of the very system that allowed for their flourishing and they are certainly hesitant to change it. Such is the historical nature of class conflict itself.

Yet it goes deeper than elitist behavior or general policy administration. Mechanisms of social oppression come in many complex forms, some of which are built directly into the architecture of the social system—something referred to as *structural bigotry*. Building upon the idea of Stokely Carmichael's institutional racism, structural bigotry recognizes mechanisms in the social structure that create and reinforce social oppression indirectly. Unlike the aforementioned personality distortions and system loyalties of the upper class, guiding biased behavior almost subconsciously, these indirect mechanisms tend to go unnoticed. At least bad decisions and policies of biased politicians or corporate leaders can be exposed and (ideally) corrected within the realm of political or legal action. However, these more indirect mechanisms tend to go unnoticed or misunderstood.

By "indirect" I mean they are engaged in a procedural way, without deliberate intent to cause harm. This involves the interaction of essentially everyone in society. We are all pulling levers on a giant machine and the consequences of these actions go far beyond our localized perception, making our ability to comprehend the outcomes difficult. Structural bigotry is about relationships and reactions, not necessarily individual decisions or events. While one may argue that a government's tax policies are structurally oppressive if they favor the rich by allowing loopholes, reduced maximum rates, and so on, it isn't exactly structural by my definition, as tax policy is actually designed to change and commonly does.[43]

What I am referring to goes deeper and I will focus on two mechanisms. The first has to do with the incentive psychology inherent in market behavior itself and the structural interplay that naturally leads to highly unequal outcomes and ultimately injustice. The second mechanism is slightly more obvious than the first, addressing the nature of the monetary system itself—specifically the existence of and dynamics related to debt. These are both structural in that they are interactive frameworks engaged by everyone, with very little objection. You will likely not see voter referendums related to them, protests in the street, or official governmental meetings about altering them in root form. Rather, what you do see are constant protest movements and public outcry against the chain reactions created by these hidden structural mechanisms. Again, society is constantly battling symptoms, not causes.

For example, to revisit a subject from chapter one, at the time of writing there is a growing social movement in America called Black Lives Matter, which protests for justice and seeks solutions to a modern epidemic of racially charged American police brutality and general discrimination. The work is very much an extension of the 1960s civil rights movement in America, and eerily so. To really understand the origins of such problems as police brutality and discrimination, one must look beyond the current political environment, specific police department policies, or even the lone mentality of the individual perpetrators. The problem is sociological as opposed to political or moral. These sociological issues stem from early economic practices—namely abject African slavery. Like an infection that is constantly reinvigorated by contaminated conditions, racism between white and black culture has continued as a form of class conflict, long after abject slavery ended. In fact *classism* is really racism's father. In the words of Dr. King:

> Racial segregation as a way of life did not come about as a natural result of hatred between the races immediately after the Civil War. There were no laws segregating the races then . . . the segregation of the races was really a political stratagem employed by . . . the South to keep the southern masses divided and southern labor the cheapest in the land. You see, it was a simple thing to keep the poor white masses working for near-starvation wages in the years that followed the Civil War. Why, if the poor white plantation or mill worker became dissatisfied with his low wages, the plantation or mill owner would merely threaten to fire him and hire former Negro slaves and pay him even less. Thus, the southern wage level was kept almost unbearably low.[44]

As such, impoverished white society was forced into competition with the now semi-free impoverished black society. This sparked a complex reinforcement of "in-group/out-group" fear and exacerbating bigotry that has pushed racial tensions ever since. Coupled with the consolidation of poor blacks in urban areas after segregation, with reduced means and options, the focus of law enforcement has been disproportionately targeting blacks and minorities to help meet arrest quotas because it is easy given how vulnerable and often desperate those impoverished communities have been. From there, the racial profiling begins to take on a life of its own and suddenly a white cop, who likely has many black friends and doesn't think he is racist, still conditioned by his experiences, impulsively shoots a black man in a middle-class neighborhood with no viable provocation. The racism is ingrained in his mind through a web of influences, literally stretching back hundreds of years. Yet activist communities still tend to fragment things in a more localized way, missing deeper connections.

While we cannot go back in time to change the history of economic slavery to stop the toxic chain reactions that brought us to where we are today, we can, however, change the current conditions that continue to preserve and inflame those traditionally bigoted associations. This is something Dr. King knew well as he pushed his Poor People's Campaign of 1968. He understood that if we could just remove general poverty, easing desperation and labor fear, many of the pressures and associations creating racial bias would dissipate. It is not a complete solution, but it would help. As will be detailed in chapter four, racism, bigotry, and xenophobia, including resulting consequences such as minority-targeted police brutality, are ultimately linked to mechanisms of economic inequality and its consequences. Until economic inequality and its causes are reduced or stopped, bigotry and social injustice on many levels will continue as a systemic result. In fact, as I will also argue, positive social trends that have occurred have a good probability of *reversing* in certain ways as looming negative social and ecological pressures mount. I have little doubt that if our "business-as-usual" socioeconomic practice remains, the growth of bigotry, race-based or not, will continue to accelerate rather than decline.

"RATIONAL" CHOICE

Now, the first class-dividing structural mechanism to discuss has to do with the inherent gaming logic or so-called rational behavior demanded of the market economy to ensure survival. This is again about the shared-incentive psychology of the interacting masses. While the generally caustic nature of competition itself was already touched upon in the previous chapter, the issue here is specific to the actual dynamics of mass competitive behavior. What is to be found is that inequality and oppression are systemically reinforced through the market's most basic, trivial, incentivized gaming behaviors, regardless of the personal intentions of people.

In the prior chapter, utilitarianism was introduced. This idea of people seeking to "maximize their utility" (or self-interest) in economic decisions was further codified in microeconomics by *rational choice theory*. This is defined as an "economic principle that assumes individuals always make prudent and logical decisions that provide them with the greatest satisfaction and act in their highest self-interest."[45] This simplistic principle raises difficult philosophical questions about what exactly rational or prudent decisions are and to what degree they are rational and prudent. What exactly is "self-interest" in the long run?

For simplicity, let's divide market-decision considerations into two categories, primary and secondary. *Primary considerations* have to do with the root incentive logic of markets. This means reducing costs and maximizing income. Each one of us orients our economic behavior this way in general. From buying discount clothes, to selling off the old family car for the highest possible price, to running a company, we naturally seek to maximize our income and reduce our expenditures as best we can. In fact, most do not even think about this procedure today, as it is now so customary. Every day, our lives revolve around the abstraction of minimizing costs and maximizing gain.

Secondary considerations are actual real-life considerations, such as gauging how your actions may tangibly affect the well-being of others and the environment. These decisions enter the realm of morality or ethics. Do you buy slave-harvested chocolate or clothes made by children in sweatshop conditions because they are less expensive, even though your purchase is maintaining abusive labor demand? Should your company use a cheaper part in a product to save money and increase profits, even though it will prematurely break and contribute to waste and pollution? Should your company maximize the price of a scarce resource in a poor region to ensure optimized profits, even though it may further impoverish the locals?

Primary considerations are abstract considerations, made irrespective of real-world conditions. They are morally or ethically life-blind, which is why secondary considerations are needed. For example, a company could dump toxic waste into a local water supply to save money on disposal, while also cornering their market through cartel power to sell their product at many times the market value, exploiting consumer vulnerability. While considered unethical, the logic is in perfect accord with primary market rationalization. When the Bayer pharmaceutical company willfully and knowingly sold HIV-tainted drugs across the world in the 1980s, killing thousands, simply because "the financial investment in the product was considered too high to destroy the inventory," basic moral integrity was no doubt in question.[46] But where do we draw lines in more subtle cases, where people succumb to undertaking negative behaviors not because they are malicious, but because the pressures of their circumstances require acting for market survival? When it comes to ethical assessments in the market game, the real calculation very often comes down to how much "ethics" you can *afford*, not what you think is morally correct.

Once again, the *root socioeconomic orientation* of commerce is based upon scarcity. This means that regardless of the reality of the human condition, the market system looks for deficiency and seeks to capitalize off of it. This is built directly into the logic of every business decision by way of the primary incentive framework of "reducing costs and maximizing income." All players are seeking advantage in every circumstance, fundamentally denying the well-being of others by strategic default. Therefore, the moral continuum resulting from primary market logic is already structurally biased in an inhumane (or at best indifferent) way. This makes whatever extreme of perceived moral violation merely a matter of degree.

In other words, when it comes to primary rationale, there is no difference in principle between selling people HIV-tainted drugs to save money and increase profits and knowingly selling people cheap processed foods that contain sickness-causing additives to reduce production costs and make the product more "affordable" in the competitive market place. There is no difference in principle between exploiting the labor of an intern fresh out of college at minimum wage and exploiting the extreme poor in the Third World for two cents an hour. There is no difference in principle between dishonestly selling a used computer that has a major hidden defect to a person who isn't the wiser and a corporation selling factory-new computers that have inferior quality components in them so the corporation can save money in the short term and increase profits in the long term by repeat purchases.[47] In a system fundamentally based upon the exploitation of economic circumstances, morality becomes one massive grey area along a continuum of general social indifference.

That understood, let's now extend this primary rationale from individual actions to interactive or systemic actions. In other words, instead of thinking about one person making such decisions, let's consider many people making them, interacting and competing with one another, as is the case in reality. Related to the equilibrium ideal behind Adam Smith's "invisible hand," mass interaction based on primary market logic results is what can be called *competitive self-regulation*. Competitive self-regulation is about the dynamic of multiple, interactive parties in trade, producing mutually affecting systemic outcomes. It can be considered a sub-mechanism of *market self-regulation*, focusing specifically on competitive dynamics between agents. A simplified example is a storeowner who buys goods wholesale and sells them retail. The prices he ends up selling his goods for are not randomly decided at whim. They are semi-determined based upon market factors, such as the cost of inventory and the prices set by his competitors. This economic interaction helps determine the "market price" of his goods, based upon competitive self-regulation. This was already touched upon in chapter two.

However, determining prices is just one of many consequential outcomes of competitive self-regulation. Returning to the foundation of systems theory from chapter one, by definition systems produce consequences undetermined by the sum of their parts. The dynamics of competitive self-regulation are what link and turn individual human actions into collectively generated system-level outcomes. And these outcomes can arise with no direct intention on the part of the players. Again, this is very important to understand, as our world has been obsessed with ethical arguments to improve things, missing the system-level outcomes that have little to do with an individual's moral compass. The specific outcomes I would like to focus on here can be categorized as *negative externalities*.

An *externality* is generally defined as "a consequence of economic activity that is experienced by unrelated third parties, positive or negative." A common negative example is pollution. Oil businesses that pump, refine, and distribute oil products factor in only their internal financial costs of operation, generally basing their prices only on supply and demand. If pollution occurs, the costs associated with that problem, such as cleanup, are usually not factored in. They are external costs and they will need to be paid by someone. Yet, while from an economic standpoint external costs are to be measured in financial terms, these costs also far exceed something one could put a price tag on. In many cases damage caused is irreversible, posing serious threats to entire ecosystems and to public health. And while certain industries or even specific companies can be sourced to certain problems, with legal actions taken to get them to change their behavior or cover costs, the deeper problems are those that cannot be easily linked to any single company or industry. They are system-level problems and just about everyone is to blame to some extent for participating in the market economy itself.

When we consider overall pollution, inequality, poverty, resource depletion, species extinction, loss of biodiversity, reductions in public health, civil conflict, behavioral violence, overall structural violence, and other pervasive social and ecological problems, we are looking at consequences not of one person, one institution, or one industry. We are looking at problems literally produced by market behavior itself, like an old combustion engine constantly spewing caustic exhaust. These problems are really categories of problems, with one externality triggering many others. For example, imagine a company that over the course of years pollutes a water source to save money on proper disposal. That polluted water is linked to a town's water supply, leading some people to get cancer, not knowing why. In one family, this pollution leads to the sickness and death of a father. Since the father was the breadwinner, the widow is now trying to afford to take care of two kids. This financial strain increases their debt, with the oldest child then unable to attend college, as he needs to help support the family, etc. You can see how chain reactions spread in complexity and are difficult to track due to unforeseen consequences linked to negative externalities.

A defining characteristic of externalities is that they require actions outside of the market's primary logic for resolution. This is another reason why mainstream economists take such a positive view of charity. Since those who are homeless and poverty-stricken clearly have no money to buy things, charity is the only real option as a workaround. In fact, these system-level externalities explain why there are so many nongovernmental organizations (NGOs), charities, activist groups, and nonprofits in the world today. These groups are mostly trying to help clean up the constant mess the market leaves in its wake. In essence, these organizations represent the *secondary considerations* mentioned previously, trying to correct the real-world consequences constantly created by the primary ones. Unfortunately, as will be detailed, no matter what such groups do within the existing socioeconomic system to help, problems resulting from these negative external forces will remain to one degree or another.

Now the central point here is how these costs, both financial and in terms of real public health, unequivocally hurt the lower class. As phrased concisely by Charles M. Kelly, author of *Class War in America*, "negative externality is the fundamental reason we need regulations for every aspect of corporate activity that impacts the environment. However, the same thing can be said about all other corporate behaviors that transfer what should be their own costs onto workers, the economy, the taxpayers, or the community."[48] The socialization of external costs from big business to the general public happens through taxation or subsidization and *systemic servicing*. By systemic servicing I mean each related consequence has to be dealt with on a per-case basis, connected to a complex chain reaction, such as the example above with the father getting cancer. There is the financial cost of cleaning up the water source, medically treating the cancer, possible government income subsidization to help the family after the father's death, etc. These are difficult costs to track as they blend into the normal, everyday world of problems. However, they are not normal, and the literal costs of these externalities reach into the many trillions each year.

For example, a 2015 economic report by the International Monetary Fund put the external costs of fossil fuel alone at $5.3 *trillion* a year (6.5 percent of global GDP).[49] This report attempts to account for extended health and environmental costs associated with fossil-fuel use both on the side of the producer and the consumer, but not factored into its price. The economists stated, "The fiscal implications are mammoth: At $5.3 trillion, energy subsidies exceed the estimated public health spending for the entire globe."[50] Their general use of the term "subsidies" is not to be confused with direct government subsidizing of fossil fuels, which is about half a trillion a year.[51] Rather, it is about the collective costs (including systemic servicing) that have to be paid in general, distributed across the population. More dramatically, in a 2013 report on behalf of The Economics of Ecosystems and Biodiversity (TEEB) program sponsored by United Nations Environmental Program, it was found that, in effect, no major industries in the world could be considered profitable from the standpoint of external costs.[52] In other words, if our core industries actually had to pay for fixing the external problems they create, they simply would not be profitable. The major profits gained are occurring without regard for the long-term destruction they are creating.

How all this affects the poor disproportionately is twofold. The first is the direct financial burden. The direct tax subsidies come from public coffers that could be used to better help the poor, improve education, and expand other social-welfare programs. While one can argue the lower prices obtained by subsidization help the poor as well, such that in some regions an increase of $.25 per liter in fuel would reduce the purchasing power of a poor household by more than 5 percent, poor households actually account for only a *small portion* of total fuel use.[53] The stark reality is that households with incomes in the top 20 percent get the majority of the financial benefits.[54]

At the same time, real-world public-health and ecological problems fall predominantly upon the lower class. The most notable example is climate change, which is already affecting the poor across the world disproportionately.[55] As Kermal Dervis of the United Nations Development Programme concluded, "Ultimately, climate change is a threat to humanity as a whole. But it is the poor, a constituency with no responsibility for the ecological debt we are running up, who face the immediate and most severe human costs."[56] Water pollution, which is largely attributed to industrial behavior, has been estimated to account for 40 percent of all global deaths.[57] This negative externality and its consequences targets the poor overwhelmingly. On both a global and domestic level, such as in the US, the well-to-do have the option to avoid polluted water supplies for consumption. The poor generally cannot afford such options and rely on basic infrastructure such as tap water or local reservoirs. These types of examples go on and on. The point being, while in the long run pollution and other externalities can affect everyone on Earth, they will engulf the poor and lower classes first and foremost. This disadvantage furthers their individual economic inhibition and class suppression not only by way of an increased economic burden but by way of health and social problems as well.

And as a final variation of this analysis, externalities create economic imbalances that have chain reactions throughout the business network, due to *competitive self-regulation*. Like a trapped air bubble being pushed around poorly hung wallpaper, shifting but not really going away, an unexpected cost incurred by one agent can start a chain reaction of adjustment across many agents. For example, imagine a tuna company that has been profitable and stable for some time. One day it is found that the tuna it has been fishing is highly polluted with mercury. This mercury pollution is an externality coming from power plants nearby. People who have become sick bring lawsuits against the tuna company, and it loses business. The company cannot in turn sue the power plants for its resulting losses, as the tuna company is not directly in trade with the power plants and hence the pollution is legally seen as an "act of God." The tuna company is stuck with costly litigation, a need to shift its fishing to another region, and the loss of sales. So, bound by the law of competitive self-regulation, the company has to make adjustments in order to adapt and stay competitive with other tuna producers who are not weighed down by these external costs.

Hence, the tuna company is now highly disadvantaged and perhaps even desperate. And with desperation, the grey area of what constitutes moral behavior in business starts to widen. Up until this time, the tuna company was held in high social esteem. It had clean boats with no fuel leakage, cared for workers with extensive benefits, and was even careful not to overfish, to prevent depletion. However, with this new pressure, those high standards have to be lowered for the sake of company survival. So the company lays off some employees, extends the hours for others, and reduces medical benefits. It also curtails equipment inspections and mechanical updates, while raising fishing quotas so it has more tuna to sell. While these changes return the company to profitability, new external costs have been created that otherwise would never have occurred.

The employee layoffs have put more pressure on the city's unemployment-insurance program, increasing taxes on the general public. The extended work hours result in more employee injuries, while the loss of medical benefits puts them and their families in debt, injuring overall financial health. The reduced equipment inspections and mechanical updates lead to equipment decay, and some of the boats start to leak fuel, causing even more pollution. Meanwhile, the higher quotas hurt the ecosystem, reducing tuna fertility and increasing regional scarcity. This scenario has immeasurable downstream effects. The point is that once an externality is set in motion it can trigger many others as companies try to compensate for the disequilibrium.

As financial stress increases, companies become less "ethical" as they try to remain competitive and profitable. And who suffers disproportionately in these "corrective" circumstances? The workers and, in general, the lower class. In fact, all debilitating influences that reduce market efficiency, regardless of what they are or where they came from, will hurt and suppress the health, income, and options of the lower class more than the upper class. This unfolding in turn maintains downward negative pressure. Such reality becomes even more frustrating when one realizes that no matter what the market system does, these problems will arise over and over again because the market's function is constrained by its own "rational choice" mechanisms. It creates negative externalities not as an anomaly but as a constant predictable attribute of its system-level behavior.

All this is particularly alarming when we look at current large-scale negative externalities that are trending into more and more ominous territory. While this will be addressed in detail in chapter four, there is no doubt a sociological correlation between desperation and less-ethical behavior. Therefore, the more pressure put on the profitability of existing companies, the less ethical they will tend to become, no different from how perceived scarcity and desperation can affect one person's decisions. In fact, you might notice how consumers today are encouraged to be "socially conscious" with their purchases or to "vote with their dollar." Yet, the inconvenient fact is that being socially conscious is contingent upon one's financial flexibility. Many who would prefer to avoid items made in morally questionable circumstances such as sweatshops often still end up making those purchases because of the lower prices. A debt-strapped single mom working for minimum wage will be hard-pressed to be selective when buying her child shoes, even if those shoes were produced in an unethical way. People can only spend within their limits and there is no doubt that ethics are expensive. So, competitive self-regulation is not just a determinant of prices and other economic variables; it is also a determinant of ethical capacity. It comes down to what degree of morality can be *afforded*, depending on how badly profitability or survival is hindered by external pressures.

DEBT BONDAGE

Shifting gears here, the second mechanism of structural bigotry I wish to discuss is a little more straightforward than the winding road of negative externalities and competitive self-regulation. This mechanism deals with debt and its dynamics. Stretching back thousands of years, credit and debt practices can be found in virtually all societies with written records. In fact, it appears early civilizations actually used debt systems for trade even before they used money.[58] One could imagine how an early farmer, experiencing a bad crop season, might go to a neighbor to borrow some grain. The loan is made under the condition it will be paid back in a future return of grain or something deemed to be of similar value, with the lender also asking for an extra amount as a service charge—what we now call interest. Over time the practice of making loans and storing deposits has evolved into the powerful banking/financial system we know today—a system that effectively underscores the entire global market economy.

However, this seemingly innocuous practice has a very dark history. In fact, to track the history of debt is also to track the history of something else: *class conflict* and *slavery*. They are so interlinked throughout the evolution of human civilization that an entire college course should be dedicated to it. In the words of anthropologist David Graeber, "For thousands of years the struggle between rich and poor has largely taken the form of conflicts between creditors and debtors . . . the rights and wrongs of interest payments, debt peonage, amnesty, repossession, restitution, the sequestering of sheep, the seizing of vineyards, and the selling of debtors' children into slavery."[59] The practice of debt peonage, also called servitude or bondage, has been a formal institutional practice throughout the past 5,000 years, coupled with debtor prisons that existed up until the mid-nineteenth century.

Of course, most First World cultures today see *debt slavery* as a relic of the past, along with abject or chattel slavery. Unfortunately, the obscured reality is quite different. First, I would argue that the only real reason we do not have debtor prisons anymore is that people in prison are not generating any value. Unless it is a slave-labor prison, there is no real point since the creditors gain nothing. And the reason we have very little abject slavery anymore, meaning the complete ownership and control of people, is that time has eroded its feasibility and necessity.[60] During the post-Neolithic Malthusian Trap, abject slavery became "justified" partly because labor and survival were highly arduous. This climate led to serfdom and slavery as a social-dominance reaction by those who could assume such power and control, embracing the competitive nature of survival.

However, once the Malthusian Trap broke upon the Industrial Revolution, things started to change rapidly. Most countries moved to abolish chattel slavery in the early nineteenth century, starting with the British in 1833 and the United States in 1863. There is a seldom-talked-about correlation between applied mechanization in production and the reduction of abject slavery. With the rise of technology in farming and the slow shift from land to factory work, the nature of labor itself has changed, becoming more and more interactive with efficiency-improving technology. As generalized by *The Abolition Project*, "[A]s the Industrial Revolution took hold in the 18th century, Britain no longer needed slave-based goods. The country was more able to prosper from new systems."[61] From there, the ever-looming moral quandary grew more compelling to resolve, with each country further incorporating low-wage "free labor" upon the rise of modern industrial capitalism. Well, at least to a degree. European countries still specifically traded for America's slave-made cotton long after their abolitions since it was still the cheapest on Earth. By 1860, 80 percent of the cotton grown was exported across the Atlantic, much of it to Britain.[62] In fact, the American South's cotton production of the nineteenth century dominated global markets and was the cornerstone of the Industrial Revolution.

There is a long-standing economic myth that "free labor" proved to be more efficient than slave labor and the transition away was economically practical.[63] This is untrue and appears to be mere hopeful dogma; essentially, it's an attempt to avoid the reality that slavery is inherent in the true roots of capitalism. There is no empirical or statistical evidence that paid labor on its own was or is more profitable or productive than slave labor. US cotton production had reached a staggering four million bales a year in 1860, up twenty-two times the rate from 1790, meeting enormous global demand.[64] Cotton was the "oil" of the world in economic force, setting the stage for the emerging US empire. In Edward Baptist's work *The Half Has Never Been Told*, he explains how the real driving force that increased productive output by slaves was not just more slaves being brought over through the slave trade, but strategic torture. "What enslavers used was a system of measurement and negative incentive. Actually, one should avoid such euphemism. Enslavers used measurement to calibrate torture in order to force cotton pickers to figure out how to increase their own productivity."[65] While it may superficially seem that "free labor" was more efficient than slave labor due to the increase in productivity, once the Malthusian Trap broke, it was actually the cultivation of technology that set this trend. This trend very slowly eased stress on low-status labor roles, as machines assisted tasks, increasing efficiency.

That being noted, the main evolutionary link between modern capitalism and abject slavery rests with the practice of *debt slavery*, something still with us to this day. After the American Civil War, millions of slaves were suddenly free in the South. Quickly, a troubling yet not unexpected practice termed *convict leasing* arose. With the white Southern population in economic disarray, a very deliberate method of arresting and charging former black slaves with bogus crimes became common. Vague vagrancy laws and other fraudulent means to conduct an arrest sent enormous numbers into the courts. When inevitably found guilty, they would usually be charged a fine. They could either pay that fine, get a bondsman to pay the fine, or go to jail—except it wasn't jail. It was forced labor, then still legally allowed for criminal punishment by the Constitution.[66] So, if the person could pay the fine, which was rarely the case, then he would be free—at least until the next bogus arrest. If he couldn't pay, he would be sent off to forced labor by private contract to pay off the "debt."

Or, the person could get a bondsman, who was usually a former slave-plantation owner sitting in the corner of the courtroom. The bondsman would pay the debt for the person, then force him to sign a contract to work until the new debt was paid off. Since literacy was almost nonexistent for former slaves, rarely did they know what they were signing. Many were multiyear contracts, effectively putting them right back where they were before emancipation. The practice was so popular that by 1898 convict leasing constituted 73 percent of the state of Alabama's total revenue.[67] This brutal practice, which caused immense suffering and death since convict workers were considered easily replaceable, was very slowly shut down by the federal government over many decades. It really wasn't until 1951 that the government finally created comprehensive statutes against any form of "involuntary servitude," including such debt peonage.[68]

As an aside, what this convict-leasing version of debt slavery also reveals is a feature buried deep inside the American criminal justice system. The general practice of imprisoning people who cannot pay fines while employing private prisons that use prisoners to create goods for corporations is alive and well in the United States and elsewhere. In fact, just like convict leasing in the late nineteenth century, in which corrupt arrests were made based upon meeting labor-demand quotas, today private prisons actually have contracts with state and local governments that effectively encourage the same thing. These contractual agreements require a certain number of "occupants" to be sent by the courts to the prison. The state complies, agreeing to meet a prison-occupancy quota, and if the state doesn't, then it (or the taxpayers) must pay for the empty cells.[69] One may argue that this quota stipulation is a simple technicality for the service offered by the private prisons, but it actually encourages maximum occupancy of the prisons, regardless of the level of crime in a region. In fact, this incentive has manifested in predictable associated corruption, including the 2008 scandal known as "kids for cash," in which two judges in Pennsylvania were caught taking millions in bribes from a for-profit prison company to increase the number of inmates.[70]

As far as labor goes, numerous corporations exploit prison populations today.[71] Earning as little as twenty-three cents an hour in some cases, modern prisoners make things for the US military, McDonald's, Microsoft, and Starbucks, along with furniture, car parts, solar panels, and a host of other goods.[72] The façade is that convicts are "learning a trade" so they can be better prepared when they get out of prison. Convict leasing, which was an extremely violent, racially targeted practice to enrich the corporations of the postbellum South, is just a variation on the common theme of labor exploitation by whatever means businesses can get away with. Modern private prisons making money off of inmates, along with prisoners working for corporations, are principally the same thing. This pursuit of cost-efficiency is what notably defines market efficiency and hence profitability. This is simply the nature of capitalist logic, and the still-common idea that the rise of capitalism was somehow instrumental in the general ending of abject slavery on the structural level is little more than denialism.

That noted, what I find most interesting about debt slavery as a through-line of labor exploitation and coercion is how almost all the prior forms of its use—going back 5,000 years—*still* exist on Earth to one degree or another. As recognized by the United Nations, for two decades now, it has been estimated that there are roughly 27 million slaves in the world, more in absolute terms than ever before in human history.[73] However, these numbers have recently been challenged. In 2016, an organization called the Walk Free Foundation released new estimates, finding a startling total of 46 million slaves.[74] The vast majority of those slaves are bonded laborers (debt slaves) in India, Pakistan, Bangladesh, and Nepal, according to expert Kevin Bales.[75] Human trafficking is also a large part of the problem, moving coerced prostitutes, domestic servants, and other groups around the world. General debt bondage industries include brick making, mining, jewelry making, carpet weaving, and a vast amount of agricultural labor. As expected, the areas where people are most vulnerable to this exploitation are in extreme poverty. In the words of Bales,

"The question isn't 'Are they the right color to be slaves?' but 'Are they vulnerable enough to be enslaved?' The criteria of enslavement today do not concern color, tribe, or religion; they focus on weakness, gullibility, and deprivation."[76] Debt bondage is so strong in some areas today it can still actually be passed through generations, with children literally being born into slavery due to a parent's debt.[77]

MONETARY SYSTEM

Now, with all that in mind, let's examine where we are today. Credit, debt, interest, and money creation are deeply connected, with debt resting at the epicenter. While for a time in the modern period money was "backed" by precious metals such as gold and silver, its root association is and has always been based around credit and debt. Today, this relationship is even more apparent, since quite literally money is brought into existence by a process of inventing debt at the exact same time. As odd as it may seem, virtually all money is created out of debt by banks "extending credit" or giving loans. If all the debts of the world were paid off, there would be no money in circulation.

How does this occur? Allow me to oversimplify, starting with government. When a government needs money, it creates bonds. These bonds represent debt. It then exchanges these bonds with its central bank, an institution granted the ability to create money. Of course, governments can also sell the bonds to the general public and even foreign nations to raise money, but that doesn't actually create money—only banks can do that. Though considered investments, these bonds are really interest-bearing loans. If I buy a government bond for $1,000, I have actually loaned that amount to the government with the expectation that it will pay me back with interest accrued. Likewise, when the government sells bonds to its central bank, the central bank is technically loaning the newly created money, expecting interest payments. Bear in mind, both the government and the central bank are exchanging things invented out of thin air by essentially the transaction itself.

Of course, the central bank doesn't just create money to loan to government, it also has the power to create money and loan it to common commercial banks, effectively upon request. The commercial banks in turn make loans to the general public, setting in motion what is actually the most active money-creation process of the global economy. While most tend to believe governments create money and that money is simply put into circulation, that is not at all what happens. The government acts as another "debtor" of the banking system, albeit one with special privileges. The vast majority of the money supply is actually created by commercial banks through a process of deposits and loans. All that is really needed to create new money is, first, a demand for a loan, such as by a family who wants to buy a car, and second, a bank's meeting a required reserve percentage in existing deposits. This reserve requirement, which is usually 10 percent, simply means a bank can create new money by issuing loans of up to 90 percent of the value of its existing deposits. So, let's say a person is approved for a $9,000 automobile loan by his or her local bank. The loan will not come from existing stores of deposits in the bank, as is commonly assumed. Rather, the bank invents the money through credit, out of debt, assuming it has at least $10,000 (90 percent of $10,000 is $9,000) in existing deposits to "base it on." In other words, that $9,000 is literally created when the debtor party signs the loan contract.

Likewise, since most money in the system just moves between banks, if that $9,000 is indeed loaned out, it will likely end up as another deposit in another bank. So, let's say you borrowed $9,000 from a local bank to buy a car, giving a check for that amount to the car dealer upon purchase. The car dealer will then deposit that check into its own bank account. And with that deposit this money-creation process can repeat. Given the 10 percent "required reserve," that bank is now able to create/loan out $8,100 (90 percent of 9,000 is $8,100) in new credit money upon demand. If that new loan does occur, the $8,100 will then likely make it to another bank, becoming the basis for $7,290 in new loans . . . and so on. Taken to its mathematical extreme, an initial $10,000 deposit that is repeatedly used as a basis for new loans can create about $90,000 in new money.[78] Of course, each time a loan is paid back, that money disappears. So, like a financial monster breathing in and out, the money supply expands and contracts as loans are given and returned.

However, there is a severe problem with all of this. Since the business of banking needs profit like any other, each loan given is done with *interest* attached. So, if a person borrows $9,000 for a car loan at 6 percent interest, she will need to return $9,540. Yet, if all money comes into existence through loans, with the returning of those loans removing the money from the money supply, where does the money to pay the interest come from? To better understand the question, consider a small island with 100 inhabitants. They have a bank that creates and loans money. Let's assume each person gets a $100 loan. This means $10,000 has been created as the island's total money supply. Everyone then buys goods and services, exchanging this money with each other, generating economic activity. This $10,000 in loans could then technically be returned to the bank, fulfilling the society's loan obligations, removing all money from existence. However, if interest is charged, more money needs to be returned than actually exists. If each of those $100 loans required has a 10 percent interest fee, then while the total money supply is still $10,000, the actual value owed back to the bank is actually $11,000. So where does that extra $1,000 come from?

In modern society, with its enormous amount of economic activity, it is very easy to miss this reality. In theory, if the velocity or rate of money changing hands is quick enough, then society—paying back and loaning money at a certain simultaneous pace—could theoretically operate without experiencing shortages. But that is far from the case in reality. Rather, the entire world is producing debt by way of interest charges that are mathematically impossible to repay, and there are severe consequences. The proof of this is in plain sight. As of early 2015, there was $199 trillion in debt in the global economy, 286 percent of GDP.[79] So just how much money is in our global economy, you ask? About $81 trillion as valued in US dollars, well under half the amount of debt outstanding.[80] See the problem? The only outcomes that reconcile it are bankruptcy, defaults, property repossession, or more loans to extend the day of reckoning. It is like a game of musical chairs. At some point, certain people somewhere are not going to have the money to pay back their loans. As the world witnessed to an extreme in the 2007 US housing crisis, when defaults occur, the most common step is repossession. In this, the same banking system that created money out of nothing and loaned it at interest can now take ownership of *physical* assets, such as houses or cars.

It is bad enough that debtors can pay off 99 percent of a debt and still have 100 percent of the property repossessed if the final 1 percent isn't paid. But often the failure to repay is not even an issue of responsibility or personal choice—it is a mathematically inevitable result due to the amount of debt in the system. In this scenario, what we really have is a structurally induced transfer of wealth from the lower class to the upper class, for guess who owns the banks? The lucrative financial sector, including lending institutions, is the realm of the wealthy 1 percent. Now, a traditional economist hearing that would quickly object, noting how the bank will often take a loss on a loan when it sells off property at auction after repossession. This is true on paper. But remember, in real life the money for the loan was created out of thin air, whereas the property is real. Banks merely deal in bookkeeping ledgers.

At the same time, since money is debt and when it is moved or spent, the debt "separates" from the money, you can better understand why the people in the lower class are most injured. Consider the island example of 100 inhabitants again. Ignoring interest, if each takes a $100 loan, creating $10,000 in the money supply, and through capitalist gaming for profit $9,000 ends up in the hands of only *one* person; the other 99 percent still need to pay back $9,000 in debt, abstractly speaking. Yet they only have $1,000 among them. As of late 2015, US household consumer debt, which includes mortgages, student loans, credit cards, and the like, was over $12 trillion.[81] Once again, that is only consumer debt, with the total outstanding US money supply at about only $12.2 trillion (based on M2 data).[82] Needless to say, it is the lower class that takes on most consumer debt by a long shot, in effect creating $12 trillion. So where did all that money go? Why do 62 percent of Americans not even have $1,000 in savings, living paycheck to paycheck?[83]

Obviously, the loans creating the money supply are spent in the economy and, due to the magic of structural classism, much of that money trickles right up to the upper class. I liken it to taking out a loan to buy a house, and paying the mortgage, while another person lives there without you. The poor create the money and debt, while the upper class extracts the money, leaving them with the debt. In the words of Dimitri Papadimitriou of the Levy Economics Institute of Bard College: "The evidence demonstrates that the de-leveraging [debt reduction] of the very rich and the indebtedness of almost everyone else move in tandem; they follow the same trend line . . . there's a strong and continuous correlation between the rich getting richer, and the poor—make that the 90%—going deeper into debt."[84]

Likewise, this debt system that suppresses the lower classes further rewards the upper class by way of capital investment. While a lower-class person may take on the burden of common loans and interest payments, an upper-class person who has no need for such loans can simply invest in things like interest-bearing certificates of deposit (CDs) or other financial vehicles to create interest income. For instance, a person who puts $1 million into a CD at 5 percent interest will generate $50,000 a year merely for that investment alone. This situation relates back to the research of Thomas Piketty, showing that the wealth capital inherent to the upper class leads to highly disproportionate gains by the rich as compared to everyone else, increasing economic inequality. While interest income is one of many kinds of returns possible for the investment class, what is really happening is also a transfer of wealth. Although indirect, the interest payments from the lower, consumer class are effectively being funneled into the pockets of the upper, investment class.

Then we have inflation. Inflation is generally defined as "the rate at which the general level of prices for goods and services is rising, and, subsequently, purchasing power is falling."[85] While the causes of inflation are nuanced, devaluation of a currency by way of money supply increases is the most powerful.[86] The hyperinflationary period in Germany after the First World War—old photos show people loading billions of marks into stoves to burn for heat—is a classic example of what increasing the money supply too much can do.[87] Germany had massive deficits after the war and decided just to start printing money itself. By 1923, it took 200 billion marks just to buy a loaf of bread. With respect to debt, there is naturally a correlation since money is created out of debt; the more debt, the more money and the more inflation, generally speaking.[88]

In the US, $100 in 1950 is equivalent to almost $1,000 today in its power to purchase things, an almost 900 percent cumulative increase in sixty-five years.[89] So a $50 dinner today would have cost you $5 in 1950. Of course, while there is often great time lag in the relationship, economists rationalize "modest" inflation as acceptable since wages also tend to rise along with the price of goods. But what isn't talked about is how inflation functions as something of a hidden tax, strongly affecting people's savings and people with fixed incomes. While people are encouraged to counter inflation by putting money into interest-bearing savings accounts or the stock market, not everyone has or prefers those options. Eighty-three percent of all US stocks today are owned by 1 percent of the population.[90] Only the rich really have the risk threshold to take full advantage of the financial market's ability to offset inflation, not to mention most savings accounts as of 2015 offer a mere 0.06 percent annual interest on average. Meanwhile, annual inflation averages 3 to 5 percent, conservatively measured.[91] So, a person with a life savings of $30,000 will only have the purchasing power of $21,000 after ten years given a 3.5 percent rate of inflation. While this applies to any value, a person with $1 million in savings will clearly be better able to absorb or counter the devaluation than a person with only $30,000. More important, what the rich and poor tend to buy and the proportion of income spent on such things varies greatly. In other words, different income groups tend to have different consumption habits; for example, the poor generally spend a much higher percentage of their income on food.[92]

German economist Michael Grimm has studied these effects, concluding that inflation, especially in poorer countries, leads to crippling inequality and social disadvantages, such as children not being able to go to school.[93] In a global study titled "Inflation, Growth, and Income Distribution: A Cross-Country Study," it was found that "inflation worsens income distribution; increases the income share of the rich . . . and reduces the rate of economic growth."[94]

Now, short-term inflation and deflation usually relate to expansion and contraction in the economy, something commonly referred to as the *boom and bust cycle*. While there are many variables, generally speaking the more money in the system, the more it is "put to work" and the more goods and services are created and sold. GDP rises, employment increases, and so on. However, monetary expansion and economic growth can't go on forever, owing to a number of factors, namely the increasing parallel debt and eventual inflation. As a result, contraction has to occur at some point to reset the cycle.

Perhaps you have noticed how central banks often manipulate interest rates. This is a kind of acceleration and deceleration on the rate of money being created, as interest rates go up or down. When interests rates go up, borrowing becomes more expensive, leading to a reduction in loans given—meaning less money being created. Since this behavior is generally in an economy already saturated with debt after a period of credit expansion, the existing loans will start to be repaid faster than loans given, effectively removing money from the money supply. This means that debt that cannot be repaid is brought to the surface as the pool is drained. And it is the poor who are "holding the bag," suffering defaults and enduring unnecessary economic stress. Bear in mind that in 2003, 43 percent of American households spent more each year than they actually earned.[95] Now, we can argue that they are "living beyond their means"; however, it isn't that simple. The debt burden of mortgages, student loans, and credit cards, supported by average-paying jobs, often means that taking on more credit is the only option to keep up. And once the availability of jobs, wages, and loans starts to dry up, low- and middle-class households, with proportionally greater debt, suffer first and foremost.

While considered natural to capitalism, this boom-bust process is a vehicle of class war, highly destructive to those who hold most of the debt in society. Likewise, in times of recession, values of many assets and businesses diminish, making them more affordable to the wealthy. Business consolidation is very common during these periods as vulnerable small businesses can be wiped out, then absorbed by larger ones for pennies on the dollar. Recessions also help tame labor rights and reduce union expectations, benefiting owners. The creation of increased unemployment naturally works in favor of the upper classes as it increases labor power surplus, consequently lowering wages. When you add these factors together, not to forget the debt default-driven redistributions of wealth, you find a powerful, largely hidden systemic mechanism that moves wealth from the lower to the upper class, periodically over time.

The 2007 Great Recession, while extreme, is an excellent example of it all. In the US, a massive housing bubble was in play prior, peaking around 2006. Bubbles are characteristic of monetary expansion/economic growth and represent concentrated capital accumulation usually confined to one sector of the economy. Before the housing market bubble, we had the dot-com bubble, which crashed in 2000. After the dot-com bubble, the US central bank "primed the pump" by expanding credit, freeing money for more speculation. The housing bubble was also fueled by profit-seeking banks pushing risky loans. Many of these loans went to poor families that likely wouldn't have secured the loans if not for bubble fever. Regardless, when the housing bubble finally popped, these highly vulnerable communities, which were effectively preyed upon more than usual by lenders, quickly defaulted as housing values tanked.[96] And since the banks were at the same time and in large-scale "securitizing" those mortgages—meaning turning them into financial assets to hedge and gamble with—these post-bubble defaults caused a complex chain reaction that spread across not only the US but also the world financial system. It was the largest economic downturn since the Great Depression.

Since then, as of 2015, almost 7 million people have lost homes to foreclosure in the US alone.[97] As an aside, the ratio of empty homes to homeless people is troubling to think about. In Europe there are about 11 million empty homes and 4 million homeless—a ratio of just under three homes for every one homeless person—while in the US the ratio is six empty houses to one homeless person.[98] In the UK alone, there are ten empty houses for every homeless family.[99] This is no doubt a clear indication of serious structural inefficiencies in the economic system. Beyond that, while unemployment has been a notable problem since the end of the Great Recession, with the real US rate at about 10 percent as of 2015,[100] wages have also declined. As reported by the National Employment Law Project, since the recession, "most workers have failed to see improvements in their paychecks . . . taking into account cost-of-living increases since the recession officially ended in 2009, wages have actually declined for most U.S. workers." The report added that the trend was only really accelerating, stating, "The declines in real wages since the Great Recession continue a decades-long trend of wage stagnation for workers in the United States."[101] As far as related small US business failures are concerned, between 2008 and 2010 alone 170,000 were destroyed, subsequently causing countless jobs losses.[102]

Of course, the wealthy took a hit too upon the collapse, and naturally so. The housing bubble had deep ties to Wall Street and the financial sector. From late 2007 until its "official" end in 2009, the top 1 percent of America saw its income drop about 36 percent, while average family income dropped by about 17 percent. However, that was just a transition phrase. From 2009 to 2012, the 1 percent gained 31 percent while the 99 percent gained 0.4 percent. In effect, 1 percent captured 95 percent of the total wealth growth in the US recovery.[103] In fact, if you track the ebb and flow of expansion and contractions, there is a common theme. The rich do lose with everyone else during recessions, usually a bit more in percentage terms, but once the boom starts again, the rich gain substantially more than everyone else, while pushing inequality higher.[104] In 2012 the top 10 percent took 50 percent of all income, an amount unprecedented in US history. The moral of the story is that in the long run recessions simply help the rich overall, and it has been that way for a long time. There may be upper-class carnage with this or that mega-failure, but that is minor compared to the enriching power of adjustment and monetary "stimulus" that sets the stage for expansion and disproportionate upper-class wealth gain.

And this brings us to quantitative easing (QE). When things get really bad, beyond the economic failures of the lower class, more is needed than common monetary-expansion tactics through enticingly low interest rates. These methods include QE, an increasingly common practice of central banks. From 2008 to 2015 the US central bank, called the Federal Reserve, bought bonds in order to inject almost $4 trillion into the troubled economy.[105] With the bonds being bought from the holdings of financial institutions such as commercial banks, pension funds, and insurance companies, all that money was basically funneled right into Wall Street, not Main Street. While some "trickle down" helped create jobs and expand the general economy, the profit gained by the existing rich has been substantial. In the words of economist Anthony Randazzo, "[QE] is fundamentally a *regressive* redistribution program that has been boosting wealth for those already engaged in the financial sector or those who already own homes, but passing little along to the rest of the economy. It is a primary driver of income inequality."[106]

A report by the Bank of England stated that its QE program raised the value of stocks and bonds by 26 percent, or about $970 billion, with about 40 percent of those gains going to the richest 5 percent of British households.[107] In fact, in 2013 Andrew Huszar, a former US central bank employee, made a rather dramatic guilt-driven admission, as reported by the *Wall Street Journal*. He stated:

> I can only say: I'm sorry, America. As a former Federal Reserve official, I was responsible for executing the centerpiece program of the Fed's first plunge into the bond-buying experiment known as quantitative easing. The central bank continues to spin QE as a tool for helping Main Street. But I've come to recognize the program for what it really is: the greatest backdoor Wall Street bailout of all time.[108]

It is troubling to realize that the institutions most responsible for creating economic crises are actually the ones to gain disproportionately by attempts to fix them.

Now, very often in public talks and conversations on these issues the idea of simply removing debt and interest from the economy is brought up. But these features are predominantly structural. Debt goes back thousands of years and forms the root of capitalist exchange, since exchange is about mutual values being traded. In cases where a need is required but equal exchange cannot be satisfied at the moment, debt is created. The implications of this led to control and domination as a natural side effect, once again.[109] To simply get rid of debt from the economy, in the sense of a "policy shift," would effectively change the nature of things beyond the scope of what we could call capitalism. Debt is foundational to the market system. The same goes for interest, but to a lesser degree. Interest itself simply represents profit for the service of loaning money. Like the retail markup on any inventory, interest is principally just a fee. Could it be removed from the equation? Yes, it is possible. But it would first require that the entire banking system be turned into a nonprofit agency, funded directly by other means. However, as will be explained in the next section, the financial sector itself has now become the epicenter of the super-rich. As such, it is also the epicenter of political lobbying power and hence the cornerstone of the revolving door of plutocracy. Bank nationalization and other dramatic changes, therefore, would be met with fantastic resistance.

FINANCIALIZATION

As discussed, the Neolithic Revolution gave birth to the slowly evolving organism we know as market economics today. While the *root socio-economic orientation* has remained the same, unique mutations have occurred. If Adam Smith were alive today, he would likely be baffled at the incredible rate of technical advancement and how what was once a world marked by great scarcity and endless strife has transformed to one where machines are replacing jobs entirely, increasing technical efficiency exponentially. And while he might not be too surprised by how the colonialism of his day has merely morphed into a higher-tech version now termed *globalization*, he would still be shocked by how powerful transnational corporations have become. These operate with larger GDPs than many countries, have little loyalty to specific nations, have built global trade agreements that act like their own legislative authority, and effectively have transcended national sovereignty through a kind of financial "deterritorialization." In effect, big transnational businesses have been slowly morphing into a kind of sovereign entity network in and of themselves, making their own rules.[110]

However, I think the most shocking thing Smith would notice is the *financial* system, with its trillions in stocks, bonds, derivatives, and other assets, and how it increasingly overshadows in performance the tangible productive market. In effect, gambling and service fees are replacing real production, with the financial sector becoming proportionally the most profitable sector on the planet. Yet, it creates nothing of any tangible relevance and, in point of fact, has no true structural importance to meaningful economic production. I state that, of course, not from the standpoint of capitalist operations, but from the perspective of pure technical economic reality. I suspect that never in a million years did Adam Smith think the real-world market of handicraft, basic services, and physical trade would evolve into the abstraction of financialization, while giving birth to the mutant monster known as Wall Street.

I was first introduced to Wall Street and financial trading when I was about twenty-five. This was a few years after my cater-waiter days and that dubious first corporate job I spoke of previously. At this point I was working at an ad agency in lower Manhattan, doing audiovisual design work to sell high-end real estate. As in my cater-waiter days, the clients were super-rich and the focus was on luxury properties only they could afford. Basically, we would make "movies" to sell these overpriced places to people with money to burn. It was the ultimate vulture institution, as advertising companies generally are. At one point it was leaked that the bosses would ask for around $75,000 to produce a two-minute promo, paying my production team about $7,000 in salary to produce it. That is enough "surplus value" exploitation to give Karl Marx a stroke.[111] Of course, the rich clients simply had no concept of real production costs and hence could be milked for their ignorance, as they routinely were.

Needless to say, I was far from fulfilled in this job and tired of working ten hours a day with harsh deadlines and aggressive, stressed-out coworkers. However, I didn't just want out of that job and the industry, I wanted out of the entire top-down dictatorial structure inherent to business itself. So I looked around and eventually homed in on short-term, private stock trading. In hindsight, I'm not quite sure which I find more offensive—advertising or the financial markets—but from the standpoint of personal freedom, equity trading from a private account is the only job I know of that literally has no boss and no clients, and that is all that mattered to me at the time.

So, with the little savings I had, I shifted my ad work to part-time freelance and focused on equity trading in the morning markets. The learning curve was steep and I had expensive mentorships with various professional traders. These were people mostly like me in that they had just wanted to be outside the corporate structure. While I certainly have met some traders with truly distorted worldviews, the guys I learned from were not inhumane, soulless people. They were simply professional game players, not insiders, who understood risk management, macro-economics, and mass human psychology. It was through this training and related research, via reading literally hundreds of texts on economic theory and behavioral psychology, that I began to really understand the nature of capitalism, leading me to where I am today as an activist, interestingly enough.

Now, for those unfamiliar with the history of financial markets and where they came from, allow me to summarize. The global financial markets, including stocks, bonds, futures, currencies, options, and a host of other "derivatives," are an outcome of thousands of years of what I consider the "maturation" process of trade-based economics. While the *root socioeconomic orientation* of capitalism is built around scarcity, competition, and dominance, as noted in the previous chapter, the financial markets embrace the pure abstraction of capitalism's primary incentive structure—that being the art of reducing costs and maximizing income. This translates into buying an asset at one price and selling it at a higher price, making a profit. It doesn't matter what that asset is or even if it exists, just as long as one can reasonably assume it will gain value and can be sold back off, securing profit.

The evolution of this practice is in lockstep with the rise of *merchant capitalism*. Upon the advent of agriculture and settlement, labor specialization and good markets slowly emerged, along with mediums of exchange or money. A merchant class developed where producers would create goods and their merchants would take them to public market centers and sell them. This division of labor then led to more modern systems of distribution, where the merchants simply bought items in advance, selling them independently at higher prices. At this stage, you can begin to see how the idea of trade for the sake of trade started to take hold as an abstraction. It didn't matter what the merchants bought and sold, they simply made profit on the act of exchange.

By the late nineteenth century, the practice of raising capital to start new companies was common. In this, representative company shares or "stock" would be issued to those who invested, with that stock entitling them to a percentage of ownership and profits of the company. If there were ten investors, for example, there would be ten shares of stock and each would get a tenth of the profits. This practice evolved into the idea of public ownership, in which stocks would be offered and sold to the public to raise money, with the owning public then being paid dividends, which could be fixed or variable.

However, in the midst of all of this, the merchant mindset of simply trading for the sake of trading shifted focus. Stock exchanges allowed people to trade their shares of stock with other people they had never met. And while gaining dividends was once a major focus, trading the stock itself and speculating on its price moves emerged as the main interest for profit. Initial public offerings of company stock now grew to include millions or billions of shares depending on the interest and company size. Likewise, commodity markets (trading in staples such as wheat, cotton, steel, etc.) went from finding value based on real material supply and demand, to prices being pushed around by speculative traders through commodity futures (the speculated future cost of a commodity). Currency-exchange markets allowed people to literally make money off of money, gambling on how the value of one nation's currency would change relative to another's. Of course, this idea of speculation goes back hundreds of years, with the Tulip Mania of the seventeenth century a notable highlight. In Holland, people became obsessed with tulip bulbs and the bulbs skyrocketed in price as people paid more and more for them. Some even sold off their homes to buy the flowers, assuming the value would keep rising. [112]

Now, to correct a common misconception, the actual real-world performance of a publicly owned company is not directly related to its stock price. Rather, prices are driven by the perceptions of people as they buy and sell existing stock shares, moving share prices around by their collective actions. While the performance of the company is a factor, it is just information or news to the trader or investor. There is a predictable psychology that tends to move prices in certain ways on the basis of different performance metrics released by a company, but these metrics are still superficial. For example, it could very well be that the CEO of a company gets caught cheating on his wife, sending his company's stock lower because of emotional public reactions. Just as easily, a company could lie about record profits, sending the stock price upward. As one of my trading mentors used to always say: "We don't trade stocks. We trade people."

So, what we have is a kind of financial parallel universe. There are real producing companies and resources in one universe and these proxy, avatar-like financial representations of them in the other. A company such as Apple has a market capitalization of about $700 billion as of 2015. This number represents the total value of its more than 5 billion stock shares outstanding. Does this mean Apple is worth $700 billion as a "wealth creation" industry, turning raw materials and information into tools for people to improve their lives? No, the value is derived from mass speculation after an initial public offering of the stock (IPO) and little more. As of 2015, the US stock market itself was valued at about $25 trillion, with the global stock markets at about $70 trillion.[113] Total global financial securities value, meaning not only stocks but also bonds, options, and other such assets, was about $300 trillion.[114] Then we have *derivatives*, which are financial instruments that "link" to underlying assets created out of thin air once again. These are cartoonish proxy instruments that take anything from stocks, bonds currencies, interest rates, indices, options, commodities, credit, or just about anything two financial parties can agree upon, deriving a new instrument for gambling.

Of course, if you read mainstream views of derivatives, they are defended as "hedging," or a means of lowering risk for some party. While this may be true in the fantasyland of abstract investment, the argument defends nothing as to their root absurdity. Today, the total value of these derivatives has reached epic levels, with conservative estimates being about $700 trillion in notional value.[115] If we add common securities, we get an estimated global market value of more than $1 quadrillion. This number, which is about 1,300 percent of global 2015 GDP, would be almost funny if it didn't have such serious real-world implications, such as the 2007 global financial crisis that destroyed 45 percent of the entire planet's financial wealth in one swoop.[116]

Now, this abstract trading reality is only part of a larger trend termed *financialization*. Financialization can broadly be defined as a "pattern of accumulation in which profit making occurs increasingly through finan-cial channels rather than through trade and commodity production."[117] Generally, it has to do with the increase in the scope, power, and range of application of the world economy's financial sector. The financial sector is composed of financial services. These deal with the management and administration of whatever financial activities are in play, usually based around bank loans, stocks, investment services, insurance, and so on.

Financialization is an evolutionary outcome of market capitalism, prevalent in economically mature nations. It appears to be part of an increasingly common developmental path as countries' true productivity declines, pushing nonproducing mechanisms for income. Now emerg-ing as, indeed, the most profitable industry on the planet, this economic mutation from *merchant capitalism* into *financial capitalism* is further expanding the already problematic inequality and oppression-producing tendency inherent to the system. Like the growth of cancer in an organism, the global market economy is becoming increasingly more life-blind and polarized as financialization takes over and abstraction becomes reality.

From the broad view, given trends over the past forty years, it is difficult not to view the growing financial sector as little more than an upper-class money machine that does little for the normal economy. Its growth and profitability has eclipsed other sectors' growth, even though there is little evidence this disproportionate income has had any benefit for anyone in the world but the investment banks, brokers, and other financial players. In fact, if you compare the profit trends from the manufacturing sector to the financial sector, you will notice they are now inversely related.[118] The production of goods is becoming less profitable while immaterial financial services are becoming more so. This is particularly bothersome since the number of people employed in the financial sector has virtually stayed the same, while the amount of profit they extract has skyrocketed.

According to economist Michael Konczal, "Between 1980 and 2006, while [US] GDP increased five times, financial-sector profits increased *sixteen* times over. While financial and nonfinancial profits grew at roughly the same rate before 1980, between 1980 and 2006 nonfinancial profits grew seven times while financial profits grew [again] sixteen times."[119] In 1950, the US financial sector accounted for about 2 percent of GDP, growing to 9 percent by 2013.[120] In the 1980s, profits in this sector were about 10 percent of GDP, while thirty years later they are more than 30 percent.[121] Yet, the number of people employed in this US sector has been less than 5 percent since 1950.[122] That is a ton of money going to very few people. Again, we are talking about an industry that deals with intangible financial assets and fees, not true production. This radical income growth has been occurring during a time when wages for the rest of the American (and global) economy have been stagnating for decades.[123] In fact, research conducted on countries with large financial sectors has found that this trend is actually detrimental to overall economic expansion and prosperity. Admittedly, it is difficult to imagine how the growth of any given sector of a country's economy could be a negative pressure in general, but that is exactly what has been found.[124]

In fact, the correlation of financialization to inequality, counterproductive effects on general economic expansion, wage stagnation, and periodic crises such as the staggering 2007 derivative-triggered economic collapse invites the question of what this institution (and phenomenon) really means and why it is tolerated at all. Economist Gerald A. Epstein in his text *Financialization and the World Economy* states:

> Finance benefits handsomely from the same processes that create economic crises and injure so many others. Hence the costs of financial crises are paid by the bulk of the population, while large benefits accrue to finance . . . [F]inancial institutions and owners of financial assets . . . have been able to greatly increase their shares of national income in a variety of OECD [Organisation for Economic Co-operation and Development] countries since the early 1980s . . . [F]inancialization has had a profound and largely negative impact on the operations of US non-financial corporations.[125]

Epstein's research also explores how the growth of financial power is deeply related to *globalization* and *neoliberalism*. With globalization being the expansion of market networks across the world and neoliberalism being the view that deregulated "free trade" is the proper mode of markets, *financialization* is well-argued to be a natural development in this supposed "liberalization" of the world economy.

To complete this section, I would like to pause and consider the sociological ramifications of all this on the cultural level with regard to how we view ourselves. The rise of financialization is the rise of an economic abstraction that exacerbates the already dehumanizing, "commoditizing" nature of market capitalism. Like a large, suffocating tumor spawned from a long-existing underlying cancer, the life-blind nature of this development reveals where global society is heading. While financialization is contextualized here as a structural development furthering class separation and oppression, there is a deeper sickness in play—one of enormous moral hazard. I extend this definition of moral hazard to anything that encourages the disregard or injury of others, including apathy to other people's suffering. What we have is a kind of sociopathology born from commercial enterprise, compounded by the now ever-expanding financialization of the world.

From the creation of securitized slave mortgages in the early nineteenth century American South that allowed many "anti-slavery" countries to invest in slave labor while hedging financial risk on the part of slave owners,[126] to the modern practice of "dead peasants" life insurance, in which companies take out policies on their employees, wagering on their lives and making money when they die, the sickness is palpable.[127] This moral hazard is in lockstep with the reality that the financial industry is constructed around making money in "both directions." In the stock market, one can execute what is called a "short sale." This is the practice of "selling before you buy," which simply means you are gambling on the decline of a company's stock. This type of bet exists in virtually all financial trades, including complex "hedging" derivatives like credit-default swaps. In the case of mortgage swaps, investors are basically betting on whether people will lose their homes or not. And someone will make money if they do. Also, high-energy mass speculation in commodity markets can artificially raise the real exchange price of things like food and energy, deeply affecting the lower classes that rely on affordability. In fact, since the repeal of the Glass-Steagall Act and other adjustments, speculation in the commodity markets went from 12 percent to 60 percent, with a great deal of detrimental volatility ever since.[128]

While more extreme, let's not forget that financialization and the ability to profit directly off of social failure and human suffering is really just a variation on a long-standing theme. While Wall Street incentivizes human indifference in a more direct way, commoditizing destruction, Main Street also structurally requires general disregard for competitors, employees, and even consumers. When a competing business fails, it is in the best interest of other competitors. When employees are vulnerable and desperate, it is in the best interest of employers. When people are unsatisfied and even sick, it is in the best interest of industries catering to those needs, such as the medical community. However, at least on Main Street everyone is frequently reminded that we are all human beings, usually bringing out *some* basic moral, empathic sense. On Wall Street, however, the human aspect is removed, replaced by abstractions that are utterly detached from any sense of humanity. I call it "drone warfare" economics. The military people today who command remote-controlled drones into distant territories to kill others do so in the abstraction of a video game, losing a sense of reality. I consider the rise of financialization as a means for capital accumulation a cogent parallel.

CLASS WAR

To conclude this chapter, I would like to now step back and examine the overall state of class conflict. Perhaps best formalized by sociologists Karl Marx and Max Weber, class conflict or *class war* is defined as an antagonism between socioeconomic groups, with the dominant class minority disproportionately favored against the subservient class major-ity by a range of social factors. There are many intersecting mechanisms in play, including class-biased psychology, sociology, politics, legislation, economic policies, and so on.

Culturally, we have what historian Carl Becker called the *climate of opinion*. Commenting with respect to recorded history, Becker wrote, "the facts which historians include or omit, the interconnections between the facts given which they stress, depend in no small part upon the 'approach' which seems to them a meaningful one, and that approach which at any time will seem significant to the historian depends in no small part upon the social situation in which he finds himself—in short, upon the preconceptions and value judgments . . . of the age in which he lives."[129] In the age in which we live today, with all the media power to remind us of what we are supposed to agree with or not, the climate of opinion still overwhelmingly favors materialism, competition, self-ishness, dissatisfaction, war, and elitism. These are critical social values for maintaining the capitalist social order. Anything contrary to those values is fundamentally a threat.

Needless to say, there is nothing more important to modern class war than the widespread belief that capitalism is in the best interest of everyone and any alternative will only lead to social destruction. Any speculation that the market system may indeed function as a means of oppression and social control, or is perhaps just highly inefficient in its assumed purpose, must be actively countered and made to appear irrational. Such activity was notably ramped up in the late nineteenth and early twentieth century upon the first and only great mass global revolt against capitalism thus far. Fearful corporate and political power centers in the United States responded by unleashing an unprecedented public-relations campaign. It was not only a reaction to the growing spread of anti-capitalist ideas and socialism; it also directly targeted emerging *labor unions* that were demanding better circumstances.

The tactic was to associate organized labor with communism and tyranny, portraying it as un-American. Before this, American labor was literally embroiled in a bloody class war, resulting in a great deal of violence against workers trying to strike or formally organize.[130] From the machine-gunning of striking coal miners in Pennsylvania in 1897, to the Colorado labor wars of 1903, to the Ludlow Massacre of 1914, to the 1917 lynching of prominent American Labor leader Frank H. Little, to the far-reaching union-busting espionage and sabotage activities that became formalized near mid-century, the rise of "free labor" was far from free.[131] However, once the Wagner Act of the 1930s was passed as part of Roosevelt's New Deal, legally protecting union formation and collective bargaining, business owners realized force wasn't the best route. It was time for pro-capitalist psychological warfare.

The National Association of Manufacturers (NAM) conducted a massive media blitz, painting unions as anti-American and communistic, the New Deal as slavery, public ownership as totalitarian, and free-market capitalism as the only true savior of humanity. This propaganda was incorporated in schools, social events, and every major form of media. According to the Hagley Archive (a museum and library of business material), the NAM public relations team "circulated 2 million copies of cartoons, 4.5 million copies of newspaper columns written by pro-business economists, 2.4 million foreign language news pieces and 11 million employee leaflets. It also displayed 45,000 billboards, which were seen by an estimated 65 million Americans daily, while its film series was viewed by approximately 18 million."[132] In Elizabeth A. Fones-Wolf's *Selling Free Enterprise: The Business Assault on Labor and Liberalism, 1945–60*, she further details the vast extent of this campaign. She writes, sourcing primary materials:

The NAM was joined by several trade associations, including the American Petroleum Institute, the National Association of Electric Power Companies and the American Medical Association, in an effort to derail Fair Deal programs on such issues as natural resources, public power, and healthcare. J. Warren Kinsman, chairman of the NAM's Public Relations Advisory Committee and vice president of Du Pont, reminded businessmen that "in the everlasting battle for the minds of men" the tools of public relations are the only weapons "powerful enough to arouse public opinion sufficiently to check the steady, insidious and current drift towards Socialism." In 1950, the NAM turned to television, launching a weekly program, "Industry on Parade," which showcased companies, explained how products were made, and demonstrated what industry gave to individuals, communities, and the nation . . . In early 1952, Oklahoma City reported that the series ranked among the first five programs in popularity, and Milwaukee gave "Industry on Parade" a higher audience rating than "Meet the Press," telecast in the same segment.

She continues:

Corporations as well as the NAM saw advantages in movies and television . . . Ford, for example laced its "Ford Sunday Evening Hour" with attacks on New Deal programs and government interference in business . . . The Bohn Aluminum and Brass Corporation's NBC program, for instance, regularly warned the public about the dangers of "socialist schemes" that looked safe but in reality were "deadly poison" that limited "individual rights and freedom." Other firms dramatically expanded their production and distribution of movies into clubs, schools, churches, and theaters as well as to television. These movies range from simple company promotions to sophisticated attacks on what business viewed as a growing socialistic economy. By late 1951, business-sponsored movies reached an audience of 20 million people per week, more than one-third of the nation's weekly attendance at commercial movies.[133]

In short, it was perhaps the largest propaganda campaign in American history. While unions survived, the overall pro-capitalist climate this campaign established still lingers, to be sure.

As for the place unions have in this evolution, labor has always been at the heart of class struggle. And it is important to recognize that the world's labor movements are really extensions of abolitionism. From abject and debt slavery to "free labor" by wage, there is a continuum of exploitation in play that goes mostly unacknowledged by historians and social theorists. Again, from the standpoint of owners, laborers factor in as economic commodities, in the same way abject slaves were. I state this not to be sensational but to be principally factual. No matter how wealthy and happy a slave may be, it doesn't change that he or she is being coerced into labor for the disproportionate gain of an owner. The qualifying difference has to do with the degree of coercion or force perceived. Where in the continuum of coercion do you draw the line saying one form of labor is "free" while others are not?

In today's modern era, most would agree that chattel slavery, meaning direct human ownership through violent force, is incomprehensibly inhumane. But what about debt bondage? While humans are not technically owned, they are bound to contracts to work off debts, often in extremely inhumane circumstances. Again, tens of millions of people in the world today exist in this condition and even the UN refers to it as slavery. Then we have *wage slavery*. In this case, the coercion comes from various unrelated pressures that appear to exist outside of the labor role itself. There is no gun held to one's head and no debt contract looming. Instead, there are systemic forces that constantly put "free laborers" into vulnerable conditions such as the pressure of unresolvable debt, as noted, or the simple threat of poverty itself. While they may have some "choice" as to whom they work for, they have no choice but to submit. And it doesn't matter if one can select between two companies or two million companies, it does not change the structural, manmade coercion present.[134] Obviously, the majority of this chapter has been about such forces, ultimately keeping the working class vulnerable and submissive. The most cogent example to me is sweatshop slavery. The sheer destitution in poor, developing nations *forces* people to "volunteer" for grueling, low-wage jobs—and yet it's referred to as "free labor."

Overall, the general economic slavery of the majority has been well masked by the neoclassical, utilitarian euphemism of "mutual exchange," often condemning those who talk about structural coercion and exploitation as whiny, annoying "Marxists." This has also been a common aspect of the strategic *climate of opinion* that helps ensure docility, creating the illusion that people are as free as they ever could be. Today, many pro-market theorists actually deny the structural reality of labor exploitation outright, turning the tables to argue that everyone is simply "helping everyone else," networking specialization for mutual benefit through "voluntary" trade. While I certainly appreciate my dentist and will exchange money for the service, reciprocating in a mutually satisfactory way, this singular exchange is not even close to what defines capitalism as a structure or its systemic effects. This myopic, overly reductionist perspective simply avoids the nature of inevitable hierarchy and the primary logic of reducing costs and maximizing returns.

Moreover, laissez faire or neoliberal predominance in economic policy, specifically in the West, constantly refocuses attention on the importance of the ownership class rather than the wage-working majority. The mantra that the rich need more tax breaks since they are the "job creators," along with the vast exceptionalism big business experiences when problems arise, reduces any ambiguity as to who is deemed socially important. These laissez faire views were reinvigorated in the 1980s during the Reagan and Thatcher era, when further tax cuts for the rich, deregulation, and a move from public provision to private provision were seen as the only solutions to social woes. The long-term result has been an exacerbation of inequality and further loss of public and environmental health.

At the same time, the "free trade" or "market discipline" hypocrisy is palpable, as it most certainly doesn't apply to the rich and powerful. From "too big to fail" bailouts, to massive corporate subsidies and general international protections, the truth is that big business and the rich elite operate with direct, nonmarket, "socialized," top-down controls. As put succinctly by Dr. King with respect to America, "This country has socialism for the rich, rugged individualism for the poor."[135] It seems the lower class can battle it out in the "free market," fighting, failing, and suffering, while the rich tend to enjoy a general exceptionalism, unsusceptible to market forces when things get bad. Of course, as expressed in chapter two, I say "hypocrisy" only in gesture. It is only hypocritical if you were to believe the current system was actually supposed to respect true laissez faire principles, applied to everyone regardless. The truth, as I hope this text demonstrates, is that capitalism is a system of structural class oppression and social control, with only the naive illusion that these pure "free market" principles are universal, effective, or even possible.

One example is low-wage labor subsidization. At the time of this writing there are US protests demanding higher wages for lower-class jobs. Since the minimum wage is far from livable for many, welfare support from the state is needed for millions of people. Some of the most profitable companies such as McDonald's and Walmart are able to keep these low wages because the state is filling in the gap. In other words, the state is subsidizing the wages, effectively saving these big corporations responsibility and money by taking tax dollars from the public. One estimate put the value of this subsidization at $153 billion a year, as of 2015.[136] Meanwhile, while wages generally stagnate, CEO pay continues to grow globally. Naturally, the US leads the way, with CEOs earning about 354 times more than their average employee, while often-deemed "socialist" Canada trails with a modest 206:1 as of 2014.[137] In fact, in a study conducted by the Canadian Centre for Policy Alternatives, it was found that Canada's top CEOs make an average worker's yearly salary in just three hours.[138] Meanwhile, general corporate welfare practice is found throughout the industrialized world and in various forms, working in concert with strategic tax avoidance. The UN estimates about $200 billion is avoided in annual tax each year by corporations owing to offshore holdings alone.[139] In 2016, 11.5 million documents were leaked by an anonymous source, revealing the financial specifics of over 214,400 offshore entities sheltering in what would otherwise be known as tax havens.[140] Now called the "Panama Papers," this leak revealed the enormous amount of tax avoidance and other schemes practiced in the world today by the super rich, with reportedly an estimated $21 trillion to $32 trillion invested virtually tax-free as of 2010.[141]

We also can't ignore the legal exceptionalism inherent. As common to all historical royalty, those in power generally make the rules, not follow them. Of course, to ensure the appearance of democracy, examples must be made and every now and again a very powerful, rich figure will be prosecuted, with great fanfare, in lieu of addressing the modern epidemic of corporate crime. But generally, as author Glenn Greenwald would put it, most are "too big to jail." In his work *Liberty and Justice for Some: How the Law Is Used to Destroy Equality and Protect the Powerful*, Greenwald catalogs the modern history of white-collar and political crime. From hedge-fund managers getting away with hit-and-runs to banks absolved of rampant fraud, Greenwald concludes in regard to the US financial elite, "Worse still, the scope of these financial crimes is so vast, and the suffering they have caused so deep and enduring, that the refusal to impose any consequences on the culprits proves the near-absolute nature of this elite law breaking license. It is now clear that there are virtually no limits on the magnitude of the crimes that the nation's most powerful private actors can commit with impunity."[142]

At the same time, as touched upon in chapter one, the general US population experiences a legal punitiveness unmatched in the industrialized world, with much higher levels of incarceration, longer sentences, worse prison conditions, and other draconian attributes. While most politicians give lip service to an ideal society without crime or insurrection, a looming sense of public fear and a certain amount of crime actually assists the preservation of the ruling class. On the most basic level, criminal behavior consequential to the precondition of socioeconomic inequality within the lower class allows for a systemic targeting by legal forces. Again, it is within this lower-class demographic that society can expect the majority of common crime, along with political or economic disapproval. In other words, the subculture most likely motivated to change society, to alleviate their plight, are also these poor or lower-class demographics. So, keeping highly punitive attitudes in legal justice proceedings is a straightforward act of social oppression of this demographic, helping to keep sources of insurrection fragmented and at bay. Again, this is a systemic consequence, like a feedback loop that structurally favors the preservation of existing power.

Another level has to do with dependence. We again see this with the highly politicized use of "terrorism" as it makes the general population feel as though they must succumb to the whims of state power for some kind of alleviation. This has led to a general public sanction of arguably fascist social policies that have systemically reduced civil rights while allowing for numerous human rights violations on the whole. The phenomenon is really no different than the "war on drugs," only this "war on terrorism" extends what was mostly US class oppression into global nation-class oppression. Politicized or not, "terrorism" has become an excuse to inject social dominance both domestically and internationally, justifying war, theft, and violence against the global poor.

Regarding war, it is important to realize that when it comes to root cause, *all wars are class wars*. While the lower social classes tend to have limited options, partly serving as cogs in the wheel of upward wealth redistribution, the rise of national empires exploiting their vassal or tributary states is effectively the same thing. In other words, we can view the nations of the world as stratified in a power-and-wealth hierarchy in the same way a national population is. The United States empire, like Britain and many before them, has great geopolitical and economic power over the affairs of much of the world. With nearly 800 military bases across 70 countries, the US casts a wide shadow. Through what is the new colonialism, by way of globalization, neoliberalism, and financialization, the US and its parallel Western interests have been pulling the world into a tight web of international financial and transnational trade agreements that favor Western imperial business interests.

Over the past century, highly privatized, deregulated economic policies have spread globally, often by force. Many wars have resulted in the overthrow of old national regimes, giving way to this expansion, while the growth and power of international finance institutions has increased. These dominant global trade and banking institutions—the World Bank, World Trade Organization, and the International Monetary Fund, which are Western in origin—blatantly subscribe to these neoliberal views, constantly imposing welfare-removing *austerity* on poor countries in debt, leading policy shifts in favor of "free trade," "liberalization," and so forth. This process of conformity only strengthens the power of US transnational corporations, as the leverage they hold is already vast in the globalization game. This is not speculation. You can simply examine the growth and influence of these powerful corporate entities statistically as they have expanded via free-trade agreements and structural-adjustment policies.

Even the smaller, socially democratic Scandinavian countries that are often praised as examples of what capitalism "should be" since they have generally had less inequality and stronger social safeguards are systemically being dismantled with the spread of financialization, globalization, and neoliberalism.[143] In fact, all OECD (Organisation for Economic Co-operation and Development) countries are seeing inequality rise, as tracked by comparing Gini coefficients (which measure income inequality).[144] Government subsidies for education, transportation, health care, food, housing, and so on are continually being eroded, replaced by privatization. Understanding this as a global trend is important, as it has become very common for economists to assume what is going on in one country can simply be applied to another. Norway, Denmark, Sweden, and other countries have had low inequality, high relative standards of living, low crime, low unemployment, and fairly stable overall economies as compared with the erratic and elitist West. It is almost like they are two different worlds. Can't countries like the US just copy their policies?

While there is certainly good sociological information found in understanding how other nations are successful in specific ways, the mistake is to assume they are isolated from global dynamics, each existing in a vacuum. The rise of empires, a historical constant for thousands of years, reveals a systemic drive for dominance inherent in global affairs. This has become much more apparent with the rise of advanced weapons, communication, and transport technology, with the British Empire the first to really have the ability to control vast amounts of territory from a small plot of land. By 1922, it covered 13,000,000 square miles, dominating 20 percent of the world population and controlling 25 percent of the world's lands.[145] The resonance of European ideas and policy certainly made its mark as well, as is the case with the United States empire today. The dominance of American media and fashion alone demonstrates the power of its presence and the same goes for its social and economic views. In fact, we really cannot understand the state of the world crisis today without understanding the role of the United States' influence.

With the growth of technology in the twenty-first century, the power wielded by US-centered Western interests has also increased, enabling the American empire to extend its influence in ways once impossible. There is far less of a need for physical colonial invasion anymore, since the dynamics of trade agreements and financial negotiation can create the same subservience and exploitation of resources and labor. This isn't to say military power isn't apparent or utilized, as the world continues to impoverish itself by way of global military spending. However, it is now mostly an ominous backdrop to the highly strategic economic warfare constant at all times among and surrounding today's major industrial powers—the US, China, and Russia. All of this is to say that no country is an "island" and the interplay of global affairs creates outcomes across countries in the same way socioeconomic classes self-arrange in a given nation. In the world of nation-states, the Scandinavian countries play the same role as the fleeting "middle class" in American society, with security, fulfilling jobs, little debt, reliable transport, a good home, and overall balance. These countries are the resulting "global middle class" and exist only because of the extremes surrounding them. And, like domestic classes today, they are also slowly being eroded by the ongoing pressure of neoliberalism, which is again really the socioeconomic colonization of the modern era. Contrary to popular belief, this game of strategic international exploitation and geopolitical dominance has not declined in the past century, only morphed into new methods.

French colonial secretary of state Albert Sarraut stated bluntly in 1923 regarding African resource expropriation:

> What is the use of painting the truth? At the start colonization was not an act of civilization, nor was it a desire to civilize. It was an act of force motivated by interests. An episode in the vital competition which, from man to man, from group to group, has gone on ever increasing; the people who set out to seize colonies in distant lands were thinking primarily of themselves, and were working for their own profits, and conquering for their own power. The origin of colonization is nothing else than enterprise of individual interests, a one-sided and egotistical imposition of the strong upon the weak.[146]

This is as true today as it ever was, despite modern rhetoric. Only today, the profiting interests Sarraut speaks of operate in plain sight, with no shame. This pattern of dominance is facilitated by an increasingly fluid global infrastructure that, like a well-oiled machine, extracts wealth for the benefit of a small elite while ensuring resulting concentrations of power are protected from all sides.

Why? Because this is what the economic system is and what its structure creates. The social psychology it manifests, compounded by the historically self-generating culture and its customs, fueled by structurally consequential negative pressures that constantly reinforce the psychological need to fear and fight, brings out the worst of the human condition. The structural bigotry inherent only mutates, never changes. As will be discussed further in the next chapter, the gravity of this entire sociological predicament is and has been tearing the fabric of humanity apart, resulting in a schizophrenic culture that is quickly moving toward social and environmental oblivion.

Chapter Four

PUBLIC HEALTH: SPECTRUM OF DISORDER

Not only does structural violence kill more people than all the behavioral violence put together, structural violence is also the main cause of behavioral violence.[1]

—DR. JAMES GILLIGAN

W HAT IS POVERTY? Poverty is generally defined as "the economic condition where people are unable to meet their most basic needs." Yet there is natural ambiguity as to what defines a "basic need" after a certain standard of living is achieved. Generally, poverty takes on three forms. First, there is extreme or *absolute poverty.* This is where people are not meeting nutritional requirements and/or are vulnerable to debilitating environmental conditions. Today, nearly 1 billion people fit this criterion, the bulk of whom live in the Southern Hemisphere. The "Global South," as it is often referred to, houses most of the "developing" and Third World regions, such as Africa, Latin America, and parts of Asia. The prevalence of poverty, pollution, and communicable disease there is dramatically higher than in the wealthier North, meaning the US, Canada, Western Europe, etc. While absolute poverty is certainly present in the North and widely so, it doesn't compare in scale to the deprivation, destitution, and preventable disease epidemics found in the Global South. Forty-five percent of all child mortality under five years of age links to malnutrition, amounting to about 3.1 million deaths a year, most of which occur in sub-Saharan Africa.[2]

A second type of poverty is relative. Like absolute poverty, *relative poverty* is a socioeconomic condition that leads to a decrease in one's well-being; people in relative poverty are unable to rise to the most common, shared standard of living in a country or the world. While appearing almost trivial on the surface since it is relativistic, meaning it is based on comparisons and not absolutes, this inequality is a powerful driver of negative public-health outcomes. Only recently have social scientists come to realize the destructive nature of relative poverty, as the problems associated with it tend to blend into the general disorder of society. As will be explored further, the very existence of socioeconomic stratification or class generates a vast range of problems. It isn't just about inequity, with its lack of true life-supporting resources; it is also about the stress of social comparison and the sense that well-being is not shared fairly. The way society morally justifies unnecessary human suffering due to such inequality imposes some of the most profound existential questions about what it means to coexist.

Overall, modern social science shows that an economically stratified society is fundamentally destabilized, manifesting a range of public-health problems. While social dominance theory and other elitist views regarding group-based hierarchy see stratification as necessary for "social stability," as touched upon in chapter two, it is a fact that public health is directly inhibited in vast and complex ways. This phenomenon is a fairly new area of study that is increasingly being explored by epidemiologists.[3] From the prevalence of physical and mental health disease that targets the lower class, reducing life expectancy and well-being, to the *psychosocial* stress of social exclusion generating antisocial behaviors such as violence, relative poverty is caustic, unnecessary, and extremely inhumane.

The third form of poverty to introduce could poetically be termed *poverty of the spirit*. I first heard this phrase used by Dr. Martin Luther King Jr. in describing the maladjusted way society utilizes the material success it has gained through science and technology. He eloquently stated in his 1964 Nobel Peace Prize acceptance speech:

> Yet, in spite of these spectacular strides in science and technology, and still unlimited ones to come, something basic is missing. There is a sort of poverty of the spirit which stands in glaring

contrast to our scientific and technological abundance. The richer we have become materially, the poorer we have become morally and spiritually. We have learned to fly the air like birds and swim the sea like fish, but we have not learned the simple art of living together as brothers. Every man lives in two realms, the internal and the external. The internal is that realm of spiritual ends expressed in art, literature, morals, and religion. The external is that complex of devices, techniques, mechanisms, and instrumentalities by means of which we live. Our problem today is that we have allowed the internal to become lost in the external. We have allowed the means by which we live to outdistance the ends for which we live. So much of modern life can be summarized in that arresting dictum of the poet Thoreau: "Improved means to an unimproved end." This is the serious predicament, the deep and haunting problem confronting modern man. If we are to survive today, our moral and spiritual "lag" must be eliminated. Enlarged material powers spell enlarged peril if there is not proportionate growth of the soul. When the "without" of man's nature subjugates the "within," dark storm clouds begin to form in the world.[4]

Beautifully put, to be sure. However, if we were to technically reduce his poetry, this "poverty of the spirit" really signifies a *value-system disorder*. While Dr. King's views express it as a moral problem, which it is by extension, the root is still sociological. As such, these characteristics invariably link back to the structure of society and what is incentivized by the social system. As expressed, there is a *primary* market logic that leads people to operate in very shortsighted and ultimately neurotic ways. This is consequential of the overall *root socioeconomic orientation* of assumed scarcity and competition, also discussed before. This orientation continues to mold and reinforce a destructive kind of tunnel vision that guides human focus along a detrimental path, favoring values actually needed to perpetuate capitalism, not perpetuate sustainability, justice, or social well-being.

Many philosophers frequently imply that moral maturity is a solution to our poverty of the spirit. However, it is incomplete to argue for improved morality merely through personal growth and increased empathy. It is not enough to "change yourself." From a systems perspective we cannot rationally conclude that an ideal moral compass can be fostered or perpetuated in a socioeconomic condition that doesn't reward it. People typically can only walk against the current so long, no matter how strong their convictions. Humans are far too vulnerable to pressures in their environment. Without the social structure's changing to directly embrace our idealized moral strides, little progress can be expected. The fact is, no matter how moral we may think we are or how moral we think the world could be, the structural bigotry inherent in market logic will forever get the best of us, undermining integrity, fueling this poverty of the spirit relentlessly.

IMPOVERISHED VALUES

This value-system disorder, from in-group, upper-class dominance to the casual discrimination common to everyday competitive thinking, has already been touched on in various contexts. In the next two sections I will home in on two specific distortions: the first being a general incapacity to problem-solve accurately, given that overwhelming loyalty to market values blinds society to mechanisms of true improvement; and the second being the rise of consumerism, infinite wants, and the commodification of reality.

With respect to problem solving, almost all modern attempts to resolve existing social problems seek to use markets as the means. You may recall that we explored this some in the prior chapter in the context of the role charity plays in mitigating negative externalities. This market-based attempt at a solution is particularly troubling given that in most cases the very dynamics of markets are what have created the problems to begin with. Society pays great lip service to poverty resolution, increased equality, improved democracy, resource conservation, ecological sustainability, and the general hope for social and environmental justice. Yet regardless of the media fanfare, highly publicized conferences, the UN's "Millennium Development Goals," ubiquitous protest movements, and endless "green" rhetoric, we've effectively been running in place with only minor improvements for decades.

Of all the conceivable ways to approach socioecological problems, the most common solution proposed has merely been the pursuit of more "economic growth." Increased economic growth along with other market-based initiatives continues to be pitched as the solution for just about every social problem there is. Those areas where economic growth can't be at least gestured at as a solution are simply ignored outright, further adding to the endless frustration of the activist community. Given the very nature of the market economy, economic growth has, indeed, helped alleviate some poverty and some loss of opportunity, and so economists speak of it as though it is the only possible solution. Yet, economic growth is far from a universal positive in its dynamics. Economists tend to ignore its fundamentally problematic nature, forgetting that market-based economic growth is first and foremost a function of human and habitat exploitation.

The United States, which is home to 5 percent of the world's population, consumes 25 percent of the world's energy production and 50 percent of the world's production of raw materials, and produces 40 percent of the world's waste.[5] In fact, only 20 percent of the world's wealthier population consumes a massive 80 percent of the world's goods.[6] What this means is that the standard of living enjoyed by the United States and the Global North is largely built upon international trade, and that trade is highly incentivized to find and utilize cheaper resources and labor. The decision to globalize, moving industries and markets to developing regions, is not based upon goodwill or an interest in relieving poverty. It is done to exploit countries and improve profits, with any alleviation of social woes in the long run merely a side effect or afterthought.

There is no question that over the course of the last few centuries the fruits of the Global North have been built on the resources and labor of the Global South, exploited for the purposes of the North's economic growth.[7] This isn't to say that many poor nations of the world currently fill this subservient role, for many have already been effectively used, gutted, and tossed aside after decades of exploitation. As a result, these regions tend to fester vast internal corruption, regional fracturing, and destabilizing tribal warfare, as evidenced by areas such as sub-Saharan Africa, home to perhaps the greatest foreign exploitative abuse. Once one of the most resource-rich places on Earth, it is now largely a vast expanse of destitution and corruption. Many observers fail to see this chain of causality, sharing the view that these countries were "always corrupt" or "always poor." As described in what has been termed "postcolonial theory," the long-term socioeconomic and cultural effects of historical imperial abuses have proven highly caustic.[8]

In the words of Vandana Shiva of the *International Forum on Globalization*, responding to the myth that the poor of the world have simply not implemented proper market reforms and are the authors of their own poverty:

> This is a totally false history of poverty. The poor are not those who have been "left behind"; they are the ones who have been robbed. The riches accumulated by Europe are based on riches taken from Asia, Africa and Latin America. Without the destruction of India's rich textile industry, without the takeover of the spice trade, without the genocide of the Native American tribes, without Africa's slavery, the Industrial Revolution would not have led to new riches for Europe or the US. It was this violent takeover of Third World resources and markets that created wealth in the North and poverty in the South.[9]

Put mildly, economic growth or development results in inequality as a side effect. This is due to the inherently exploitative and imbalanced procedural dynamics of market economics. This inequality materializes both within nations and between nations in the same basic way, as we see with globalization. We have been told that "rising tides lift all boats" and while that idea may be somewhat true over time, it is a grossly misleading aphorism. The truth is that this "rise" only occurs in tandem with the creation of corrosive inequality, including many stages of adjustment and abuse before the possibility that those "drowning boats" find mild buoyancy. In the words of Gavin Kitching, professor of social science and international relations at the University of New South Wales: "[E]conomic development as a long-term process of structural change, as a historical process, poses awful and awesome moral and political dilemmas which, even to be confronted adequately, require hard and informed thinking . . . Development is an awful process. It varies only, and importantly, in its awfulness."[10]

Likewise, the positive outcomes of the growth process are limited to areas that have a certain degree of relative economic development already. In other words, the extreme poor are less affected by broad economic growth because their regions lack the proper infrastructure and resources to benefit. As concluded by Matilda Dahlquist in a detailed study of low-income countries, "Does Economic Growth Reduce Poverty?": "Economic growth does not appear to be sufficient a tool when the level of extreme poverty is high. This seems to indicate that poverty reduction must be triggered, the gears must be set in motion, especially in countries with a large portion of extremely poor . . . Accounting for this fact should, if something, be an initiative for governments across the world to invest in poverty reducing activities targeted strongly toward eradication of extreme poverty."[11] Africa has 75 percent of the world's poorest countries, with only nominal poverty reduction over the past few decades. The number of African people living on less than $1.25 a day has declined a mere 8 percent since 1990.[12] Not to mention that the $1.25 guideline put forward by the United Nations in its original *Millennium Goals* as the working threshold of global poverty is far from viable as a public-health measurement. Even with the recent 2015 elevation of the poverty line to $1.90 a day, it is still not enough. Arguably a more accurate measure, termed by some researchers as the *ethical poverty line*, puts the dollar value much higher, revealing a different picture of reality. As articulated by Jason Hickel of *The Guardian* in late 2015:

> If we want to stick with a single international line, we might use the "ethical poverty line" devised by Peter Edward of Newcastle University. He calculates that in order to achieve normal human life expectancy of just over 70 years, people need roughly 2.7 to 3.9 times the existing poverty line. In the past, that was $5 a day. Using the [World] bank's new calculations, it's about $7.40 a day. As it happens, this number is close to the average of national poverty lines in the global south. So what would happen if we were to measure global poverty at this more accurate level? We would see that about 4.2 billion people live in poverty today.

That's more than four times what the World Bank would have us believe, and more than 60% of humanity. And the number has risen sharply since 1980, *with nearly 1 billion people added to the ranks of the poor over the past 35 years.* The UN's sustainable development goals, launched in September, are set to use the $1.90 line to measure poverty. Why do they persist with this implausibly low threshold? Because it's the only one that shows any meaningful progress against poverty, and therefore lends a kind of happy justification to the existing economic order.[13]

This means that the effective use of market solutions and financial measures to address the problem of poverty, unemployment, and deprivation is limited and can often be misleading. This orientation simply continues to injure global society in the long run, regardless of minimal gains, distracting from the underlying economic problems inherent in the system itself. This issue becomes clearer when we consider economically rooted environmental problems.

Proposed solutions to resolve pollution, biodiversity loss, and resource overshoot have only recently brought the issue of capital accumulation and economic growth into question. Today, particularly with respect to climate change, the idea that capitalism in and of itself just might be detrimental to earthly sustainability is slowly entering the conversation, and inevitably so. However, all it has generated is confusion and cognitive dissonance since any talk of grand revisions to the economic system is still taboo. Society has persisted with the Malthusian view that our ecological problems are mostly inevitable, and only a proportional decline in human population or standards of living can result. Hence, "survival of the fittest" is deemed justified and the fortunate can go to bed at night thinking they "did what they had to do" and this is "just the way it is."

Once again, it is the poor who disproportionately suffer from environmental problems, making the issue less about "green activism" specifically and more about *social justice* itself. The fact of the matter is that the current state of ecological affairs is far from natural, with industrial inefficiency and the deliberate, system-specific creation of unnecessary waste to blame. As will be argued in chapter five, capitalism's industrial orientation, meaning how the actual processes of production and distribution are conducted, is arguably the most inefficient mode of economic behavior one could come up with in light of modern possibilities. It basically favors the opposite of what is needed to ensure environmental sustainability, perpetuating extremely inefficient resource allocation across the global population.

Classical market economics teaches us that supply and demand power the world. Yet it ignores the fact that *constant* supply and demand is actually required. Structurally, the market can basically be reduced to interaction between consumers and producers. The wheels of economic growth only turn when people produce, sell, and buy at an increasing rate. That is the root mechanism powering our economic survival, like a vehicle's gas pedal. The more people produce, sell, and buy, the better the "health" of the economy and supposedly the population. This means that in order for people to get work, they must be needed, according to existing demand. Where demand is low there is no need to employ and those who are unemployed cannot help the economy by spending money back into it, fueling it, since they have no income to spend.

So, the market economy is based on *cyclical consumption* and it really doesn't matter what is being produced, how it is being produced, or why. If demand or production slows, so too does the movement of money, and when this happens, the economy contracts, systemically reducing the standard of living for many. Ecologically, this means capitalism is structurally oblivious to humanity's existence on a finite planet. The system wants to produce, not conserve. In fact, if you think about it, you will discover an interesting paradox to market logic: the fact that capitalism is a scarcity-based economic system that actually seeks infinite consumption. In other words, it favors a threshold of goods scarcity to secure competitive profits, theorized as a model to properly manage scarcity, optimizing resource use and distribution. Yet, at the same time, the system demands more and more human dissatisfaction and "want" in order to function and grow. It rewards consumption, with no inherent incentive to conserve anything.

The consequence is an economic system that is environmentally unsustainable, increasingly leading to ecological problems and consequential social problems. Any attempt to slow industrial behavior, hence slowing economic growth, will be met with dramatic pushback by almost all economic actors, regardless of their sincere interest in seeing conditions improve. The quest to slow climate change, stop biodiversity loss, reverse resource overshoot, and the like are all being fought, advertently or inadvertently, by business interests trying to simply stay profitable. The working logic of market behavior is that the planet is nothing more than an *inventory* to be extracted from and exploited for financial turnover. That is all it knows. It has never been about coexistence with nature, but rather the exploitation of it.

As such, what we have is a schizophrenic reality where problem solving amounts to putting a round peg into a square hole. Or, perhaps as better put by Abraham Maslow, "If the only tool you have is a hammer, you treat everything as if it were a nail."[14] For example, what has the global community actually done to combat climate change and carbon dioxide (CO_2) emissions, a problem of possibly near-apocalyptic outcomes? Has there been a deliberate, well-organized, industry-specific shift of economic behavior, including perhaps a moratorium on hydrocarbon production where feasible, initiating a step-by-step, regulated move into renewable energies? Has industrial agriculture, also a major source of greenhouse gas emissions, been approached to initiate large-scale redesigns of its processes, shifting to lower-footprint, soilless methods or other proven sustainable means? Has the idea of subsidizing this kind of important transition by repurposing money from other expenditures (such as the world's vast military spending) that serve a lesser social role been given thought? Have any of these and other tangible prospects been realistically considered in mainstream circles? No. Procedural solutions to directly redesign and alter human industrial activity haven't been discussed at all, because that kind of thinking is antithetical to market logic and "economic freedom."

Instead, programs such as "carbon trading" have been applied. This *financialization* of the problem is quite interesting, for it actually turns the act of polluting into a tradable market asset. It fits market logic well, serving to create a new mechanism for profit, while masquerading as some kind of effective regulation of carbon emissions. Also known as "cap and trade," carbon trading allows companies to buy and sell carbon permits. In short, governments set an annual limit on emissions. They then create permits to pollute that can be traded between companies, like commodities. The logic is that a company will work to be innovative and reduce emissions, never reaching its annual limits and not needing to "spend" its store of "pollution permits." It can then sell its surplus permits to other companies that need more credits, knowing they will exceed their limits. In other words, they can buy these permits to pollute from companies that don't need them. The idea is that as long as the "cap" is respected, it doesn't matter who is polluting and who is innovating.

Amusingly, folks at Enron and Goldman Sachs developed this system. Enron, whose executives were later famously prosecuted for vast corporate fraud, could perhaps only be topped by Goldman Sachs, which was pivotal in the subprime-mortgage scheme that helped trigger the Great Recession. These shrewd companies have made a fortune off "cap and trade," while the value of the carbon permits, determined by demand in the "carbon market," move with little truth as to how they actually affect emissions. Beyond the obvious absurdity, there are also widely recognized loopholes, false reporting methods, and general hidden fraud throughout the entire system.[15] In other words, *business as usual*. Mostly utilized in Europe, cap and trade has shown only weak and ambiguous long-term effects in helping reduce carbon emissions. As reported by the *Wall Street Journal*:

> According to European Commission figures, emissions from the 27 member states increased by 1.9% in the first three years of the regime. Following criticism, the caps for the period to 2012 were reduced for the majority of member states, but only to a little lower than actual emissions in 2005, and the evidence is that the recession is having a much more direct impact on emissions than the trading scheme . . . Despite the system's questionable results, the costs are considerable.[16]

Since initiation of the Kyoto Protocol in 2005, with the stated objective being the "stabilization of greenhouse gas concentrations in the atmosphere at a level that would stop dangerous anthropogenic interference with the climate system," there has been only nominal progress.[17] The Kyoto Protocol excluded pivotal, large polluting nations such as China and India (and the US never ratified it), making what little progress was achieved virtually moot given the vast amount of greenhouse-gas pollution coming from the excluded nations. China and the United States are by far the largest polluters on the planet.[18] While legally binding in theory, the Kyoto Protocol could be opted out of. In 2011, Canada simply quit after its emissions doubled. Rather than paying the $14 billion in penalties, the government simply withdrew, saying it needed to favor its economy and oil production over environmental concerns.[19]

In 2015, a seemingly more-promising meeting was held in Paris, known as COP21. The $200 million, two-week event, attended by 40,000 participants representing 200 countries, sent positive publicity and shockwaves of hope across the world. Yet, when the dust settled, one wondered what exactly was accomplished. Not only was the global agreement reached nonbinding and full of promises with no real basis of enforcement, but there was also a near-complete lack of industry-specific technical goals. As Tom Switzer reports:

> The 196 nations only agreed to volunteer their carbon-cutting promises to the IPCC [Intergovernmental Panel on Climate Change] every five years. They don't have to set ambitious goals, not least because there are no common standards for measuring improvement. Nor are they required to meet their targets, largely because there is no penalty for noncompliance. Unlike 1997's Kyoto Protocol, Paris isn't a legally binding treaty. Nations can provide excuses for failure and pledge to do better next time. That hardly bodes well for verifiable and enforceable action to slash greenhouse gas emissions.[20]

As far as the issue of biodiversity loss goes, in 2002 representatives from 192 countries gathered at the Convention on Biological Diversity, making a public commitment to significantly reduce the loss of biodiversity and increase habitat preservation by the target date of 2010. Eight years later their results were published, stating: "None of the twenty-one subtargets accompanying the overall target of significantly reducing the rate of biodiversity loss by 2010 can be said definitively to have been achieved globally."[21] It continued:

There has been insufficient integration of biodiversity issues into broader policies, strategies and programmes, and the underlying drivers of biodiversity loss have not been addressed significantly. Actions to promote the conservation and sustainable use of bio-diversity *receive a tiny fraction of funding compared to activities aimed at promoting infrastructure and industrial developments.* [emphasis added] Moreover, biodiversity considerations are often ignored when such developments are designed, and opportuni-ties to plan in ways that minimize unnecessary negative impacts on biodiversity are missed. Actions to address the underlying drivers of biodiversity loss, including demographic, economic, technological, socio-political and cultural pressures, in mean-ingful ways, have also been limited. Most future scenarios proj-ect continuing high levels of extinctions and loss of habitats throughout this century, with associated decline of some eco-system services important to human well-being.[22]

Should we be surprised by any of this? Again, the entire ethic of conservation, efficiency, and, in effect, sustainability itself, moves against the structural nature of market economics. No matter what the long-term threat may be, people's most immediate sense of security comes from ensuring their next paycheck or next business opportunity. There will always be a seemingly rational justification to disregard larger-order eco-social factors. In other words, market logic has everyone "backed into a corner," forcing short-term preservation at the cost of long-term destruction. Of course, this isn't to argue that some improvements have not been made. For example, the Montreal Protocol, a global effort to stop ozone-layer depletion by reducing chlorofluorocarbon (CFC) emis-sions, is an example of a successful initiative. However, the financial pain that solution required of business pales in comparison to what is needed today. Today, unlike any other period in history, the ecological crises at hand present the greatest technical and existential problem humanity has ever faced.

Much like during the CFC crisis, the case for human-generated cli-mate change and the need for action are also being opposed by a highly funded public-relations and faux-science campaign working to diminish the argument. This is yet another level of the competitive *self-preservation* inherent to market logic, deeply distorting motivation and honesty. A study by Drexel University in 2013 traced the financial roots of what it terms the "climate change counter-movement" (CCCM).[23] It found that 91 CCCM organizations, consisting of think tanks, advocacy groups, and other industry-associated organizations, were funded by 140 different conservative foundations, the vast majority of which could be tied to vested corporate interests. Through lobbying, media campaigns, and political contributions, billions are spent to persuade the public that the science behind manmade climate change is wrong and that oil and other suspect industries should continue business as usual. The study says:

> The CCCM efforts focus on maintaining a field frame that justifies unlimited use of fossil fuels by attempting to delegitimate the science that supports the necessity of mandatory limits on carbon emissions. To accomplish this goal in the face of massive scientific evidence of anthropogenic climate change has meant the development of an active campaign to manipulate and mislead the public over the nature of climate science and the threat posed by climate change. This counter-movement involves a large number of organizations, including conservative think tanks, advocacy groups, trade associations, and conservative foundations, with strong links to sympathetic media outlets and conservative politicians.[24]

That noted, what makes this whole environmental situation even worse is that given the current rate of problems and this "business-as-usual" approach to problem solving, the poor developing nations have very little hope of ever pulling themselves out of destitution before near-irreversible, high-impact ecological problems truly surface. This isn't to say it can't happen—it means that *established* industrial and economic means are too archaic and destructive. For example, China has based its entire growth model on the early United States, meaning the use of fossil fuels and belligerent consumption to "lift all boats." In this process, with high growth and low environmental protections, China now has sixteen out of twenty of the world's most polluted cities.[25] In the words of sociology professor

Walden Bello, "This leads us to the dilemma of the South. Before the full extent of the ecological destabilization brought about by capitalism, the South was expected to simply follow the 'stages of growth' of the North. But now, the South can't do so without bringing about ecological Armageddon . . . yet the elite of China as well as those of India and other rapidly developing countries are intent on reproducing the American-type overconsumption-driven capitalism."[26] Based on current methods it would take literally numerous Earths and something of a giant pollution-removing vacuum cleaner to make the whole world a "first world."

The truth is that it is going to require a radically new form of orchestrated economic activity to alter these trends to increase standards of living without the extreme negative externalities. *Green capitalism*, as much as people enjoy its appeal, is a contradiction in terms. Dr. Lee-Anne Broadhead, professor of political science at Cape Breton University, puts it well:

> Economic growth in the organization of international society around the goals of efficient capital mobility and the profit margin its controllers seek are inherently anti-ecological. Any way it is looked at, the extraction of raw materials for the manufacturing of goods—the demand for which in many cases has been artificially created—does not lead to an ecologically sound existence. No amount of masking the reality with talk of environmentally friendly technologies will offset the destructiveness of the growth ethic when the resounding failure of the technological fix is taken into consideration.[27]

CONSUMERISM

Broadhead's preceding quote, regarding resource use and production to meet "demand . . . which in many cases has been artificially created," provides a good segue into the second issue I wish to address here—consumerism. I honestly used to think this term was a pejorative. I had no idea that economists of the past actually considered it a viable theory of economic behavior, idealizing a world of overt consumption, and the more the better. This is a truly stunning historical fact given its obvious irrationality with respect to a species living on a finite planet. In short, the ethic of consumerism is a public-health threat.

To frame this issue properly, it is important to understand that what separates our economic condition today from that of the past is that we simply didn't have the technological capacity to exploit and pollute in the past at the rate we do now. Two hundred years ago market behavior was simply incapable of approaching the limits of environmental sustainability. Back then people could try all they might to produce, sell, and pollute repeatedly, and it wouldn't have made a dent in the long run because the economic means were too low-tech, slow, and arduous. All that changed after the Industrial Revolution. While we can now produce exponentially faster than before, expanding the economy and elevating standards of living, we can also destroy, pollute, and use up resources just as fast because our methods and incentives are mostly wrong. Like the rise of financialization as an outcome of capitalism's maturity through time, our current predicament of grotesque material production and consumption, along with the mammoth amount of pollution and waste generated, is also a realization of the market's true character. Like a dormant cancer waiting for the right conditions to flourish and kill its host, the true face of the system is being revealed as our advanced technological capacity is enabling accelerated economic turnover to satisfy the market's need for constant economic growth, clashing with natural planetary limits.

Overall, the crux of the issue is centered between two incompatible processes: business and industry. In his famous work *The Engineers and the Price System*,[28] Thorstein Veblen (first referenced in chapter two) was perhaps the first to really express the root difference between these two orientations. In short, business and industry have contradictory views of what efficiency means. Business employs *market efficiency*, which is about maximizing extraction, production, distribution, turnover, and labor employment. Industry employs *technical efficiency*, which is about sustainable design, conservation, reduced turnover, per-case labor employment, optimization of resource use, reduced waste, and effectively being "economical" in the truest sense of the term.

Historically, the assumption has been that these two processes were complementary. It was assumed that money saved meant resources saved, and money earned or spent meant resources efficiently utilized. This is far from reality—a reality that has become more evident given the rapid rise in productivity over the past 200 years. What we find is that business efficiency disdains industrial efficiency. Being truly economical, accomplishing "more with less," maximizing longevity, and facilitating conservation is not what works for business. Rather, it needs technical inefficiency to ensure repeat purchases and a dissatisfied, generally unhappy culture that has endless, neurotic material desires.[29] Inefficiency and its partner, *planned obsolescence*, now largely drive economic growth in the twenty-first century, coming in the form of consumerism. Even more, since business is confined to money and trade only, the abundance capacity (and benefits) of modern industry only extends to those regions and classes where purchasing power exists. This fact explains why, in a world able to achieve such vast productivity, poverty is still rampant.

How did we get to this place? In the 1920s, increased industrial productivity translated into a loss of consumer demand in America and Europe. Extended periods of goods surpluses drove exchange values down. This resulted in diminished profits, slowing job and economic growth. This slowdown created pressure to find ways to increase consumer demand and get *cyclical consumption* moving faster. While the Protestant, puritanical ethic of American culture has been argued as favorable to capitalist development, a view famously promoted by sociologist Max Weber, the same ethic meant that flagrant, conspicuous consumption was not a virtue.[30] As such, commercial leaders and government knew something had to be done to change people's values. The Great Depression brought into global question not only the US economy, but the very integrity of capitalism itself. Yet even before this, the effects of mass production on a relatively conservative culture were a mounting concern. In 1927, Paul Mazer of Lehman Brothers famously wrote in the *Harvard Business Review*: "[W]e must shift America from a needs to a desires culture. People must be trained to desire, to want new things even before the old have been entirely consumed . . . We must shape a new mentality in America. Man's desires must overshadow his needs."[31]

Charles F. Kettering, the head of research at General Motors for almost three decades, wrote an article in the *Nation's Business* magazine in 1929 titled, "Keep the Consumer Dissatisfied." In this, he argued for the merit of consumer *dissatisfaction* as a force of social progress, stating:

Change, to a research engineer, is improvement. People though don't seem to think of it in that manner. When a change is suggested they hold back and say, "What we have is all right—it does the work . . . " We, as manufacturers, must offer those improvements after they have been found to be capable improvements. The public buys and disposes of what it has . . . If everyone were satisfied, no one would buy the new thing because no one would want it. The ore wouldn't be mined; timber wouldn't be cut. Almost immediately hard times would be upon us. You must accept this reasonable dissatisfaction with what you have and buy the new thing, or accept hard times. You can have your choice.[32]

Kettering's view became largely accepted after World War II, as consumerism was perceived as literally an obligation of the citizenry, something that would help "defeat the communists" and fuel the "American Dream."

Harvard historian Lizabeth Cohen, author of *A Consumers' Republic*, makes it clear that there was a highly concerted effort to guide the public toward seeking endless consumption. After World War II, the social climate in America was weary of the exceptional acceleration of material production. Why should people feel the need to alter their lifestyle if they were satisfied? Also, given the general relativity of what is or is not a "respectable" standard of living after certain core needs are met, it is clear that consumerism and materialism are contrived sociological phenomena. While some have argued that a culture of "infinite wants" is simply human nature, anthropological evidence shows otherwise. Many Native American cultures, for example, have or had a very deep value for balance with the environment, seeking to avoid material acquisition in favor of a spiritual sense of connection and responsibility.[33] Therefore, at least among some cultures and clearly in the US, the requisite insatiable values needed to be programmed in, manipulating our social nature so that we represent ourselves through what we own, rather than what we actually think and do. With great effort, social engineers accomplished this task through emotionally fueled advertising and various levels of marketing. Edward Bernays, who was mentioned in chapter two, was a highly pivotal figure in this transition. Cohen states:

> If encouraging a mass consumer economy seemed to make good
> economic sense for the nation, it still required extensive efforts
> to get Americans to cooperate . . . [B]eginning during the war
> and with great fervor after it, business leaders, labor unions, gov-
> ernment agencies, the mass media, advertisers, and many other
> purveyors of the new postwar order conveyed the message that
> mass consumption was not a personal indulgence. Rather, it was
> a civic responsibility designed to improve the living standards
> of all Americans.[34]

The persuasion was multidimensional. For example, this large influx
of productivity and goods driven by technology was touted as evidence
that capitalism was on pace toward a more egalitarian and democratic
society, with politicians using the fruits of mass industrial production
as psychological warfare to further condemn competing communist
nations. This was the dawn of the elusive "American Dream." However,
what people forget about the vast destruction of World War II is that most
major powers outside the US lay in shambles. The United States still had
its infrastructure intact. Hence, once the economic machine resumed
postwar, the US had all the advantages to eclipse the economic capacity
of other nations, not to mention having just terrorized the world with
its power play of dropping atomic bombs on Japan. Cohen continues,

> Wherever one looked in the aftermath of war, one found a vision
> of postwar America where the general good was best served not
> by frugality or even moderation, but by individuals pursuing
> personal wants in a flourishing mass consumption marketplace.
> Private consumption and public benefit, it was widely argued,
> went hand in hand. And what made this strategy all the more
> attractive was the way it promised a socially progressive end of
> social equality without requiring politically progressive means
> of redistributing existing wealth.[35]

This is a very convenient disposition for those in positions of political and commercial power since it implies that any lack of fortitude in
working and consuming on the part of the public is the problem, not

the power establishment or even the social system. Meanwhile, the profit obtained by commercial interests was elevated and the capitalist, "free market" system of social control could remain ideologically sound in public perception.

In the end, this poverty of the spirit, manifested in the form of mindless consumerism, has led not only America but also the world to embrace what is a profoundly unsustainable and dehumanizing ethic. It distracts society from the source of true happiness and satisfaction, which is cultivated through social bonds, task accomplishment, and the increase of knowledge and wisdom. It is no wonder that modern social research suggests that developed countries with the highest levels of wealth and ultimately consumerism are also often unhappy and stressed out.[36] Today, this grand conformity to the will of market dynamics, pushing cyclical consumption by way of constant human dissatisfaction and insecurity, illustrates the incredible susceptibility humans have to the demands of the social structure in which they find themselves. The system requirements of market economics have now been *encoded* into culture, if you will, turning human beings into mere cogs in the wheel of capitalism. From that pivotal point in the mid-twentieth century, when the theory of consumerism really took hold, the complementary practices of vast credit expansion, higher tolerances of debt, increased work hours, and new variations of classism, racism, and sexism were set in motion. The blending of "needs" and "wants," making them effectively the same thing, conformed human values to the utilitarian abstraction of market logic.

Today, this growing social pathology, central to the needs of the economic system, continues to further morph and expand. With the predictable erosion of Keynesian economics and the rise of neoliberalism, consumerism is now not only global, but the *marketization* of basically everything has also taken hold, with very little deemed sacred anymore. In his text *What Money Can't Buy: The Moral Limits of Markets*, author Michael Sandel highlights the profound spiritual impoverishment that the practice of putting dollar signs on everything has fostered. What we see is a growing commodification of life itself, from paying children to read for school, to purchasing the right to hunt endangered animals, to simply buying acceptance into prestigious universities.[37] People are also being paid to rent out ad space on their foreheads, to be human guinea pigs in experimental tests, to stand in line for others, to fight in wars as private contractors, and even to lose weight. I think even the most hardened free-market advocate would find something profoundly wrong when everyday life turns into a mere goods market. Yet this is the current trend, with money becoming the measure of value and incentive of human existence and action. Sandel states, "Without quite realizing it, over the past three decades, we have drifted from having a market economy to becoming a market society, a society where just about everything is up for sale."[38] He adds: "Today, the logic of buying and selling no longer applies to material goods alone but increasingly governs the whole of life. It is time to ask whether we want to live this way."[39]

PUBLIC HEALTH

Naturally, a socially just and sustainable society must have a culture with socially just and sustainable values. When we realize that the dominant values common today have been molded and reinforced by the social system, it follows that we must then design a socially just and sustainable social system if we expect such cultural change. The prior sections of this chapter have focused on the value-system disorder fueled by society's current framework—a framework that is very much opposed to social justice and sustainability. When you further consider the caustic sociology created, you realize that this market-biased mentality is not only problematic—it is dangerous. This means our normative social psychology—our mainstream values—are really public-health threats in and of themselves. To better understand this let's now review the general concept of *public health* in detail.

Public health is generally defined as "the science dealing with the protection and improvement of community health by organized effort."[40] It is usually associated with government policies that promote community health. This includes preventing disease and accidents; providing physical and mental health care; conducting research, educational, and social programs; and even improving infrastructure such as sewage treatment, sanitation, and water treatment. However, in its broadest form, public health is really a category of socially oriented cause and effect. In other words, you can refer to a condition as a public-health concern, such as the repeated occurrence of cancer in a community. Or you can refer to preconditions that create such an effect, like a water supply that has been polluted, causing cancer in a community. It is a "population level" phenomenon, where societal actions (or lack thereof) systemically lead to outcomes that affect significant numbers of people.

A notable modern example is diarrheal disease, a leading cause of death in children under five years old. Common to the Global South, diarrheal disease is fostered by poor water quality and improper sanitation, killing roughly 2,200 children each day.[41] From a public-health standpoint, the question becomes: what are the environmental, social, or economic factors creating this and how can they be altered or removed?

The same goes for other statistically recurring social phenomena, including suicide. Suicide, something our intuition would peg as a very personal, detached act of "free will," is very much a public-health problem because of its population-level predictability in reaction to certain social preconditions. While it is often difficult to determine why a given individual commits suicide, the socioeconomic correlations are undeniable. For example, suicides can be directly correlated with inevitable outcomes of the "boom and bust" cycle of economic growth and recession. As referenced earlier, a study produced by the London School of Hygiene & Tropical Medicine and University of Oxford, using data from Canada, the US, and twenty-four EU nations, found that an additional 10,000 suicides were linked to the global recession between 2008 and 2010.[42] The study found the biggest risk factors were job loss, home repossession, and debt. Coauthor David Stuckler stated with respect to the economic correlation, "Suicides are just the tip of the iceberg . . . these data reveal a looming mental health crisis in Europe and North America. In these hard economic times, this research suggests it is critical to look for ways of protecting those who are likely to be hardest hit."[43] This data is corroborated by a more dramatic 2015 study (also aforementioned), which found that about 46,000 suicides across sixty-three countries were associated with unemployment in 2008 alone, also due to the global financial crisis.[44]

Then there is behavioral violence. Also one of the more difficult areas to contextualize in terms of public health since it means one must factor in social preconditions rather than "free will" individual actions, behavioral violence is slowly being understood as a systemic problem. Dr. James Gilligan, a lifelong prison psychologist and former director of the Center for the Study of Violence at Harvard Medical School, has been at the forefront of describing violence as a public-health problem rather than a moral or legal one. While acknowledging the complexity of the issue, his research has concluded that socially specific negative emotions operate like pathogens, leading to behavioral violence in the same way a biological agent leads to general disease. He writes:

> A consensus on the causes and prevention of violence has been emerging over the past few decades among investigators of this subject from virtually every branch of the behavioral sciences. All specialties, independent of each other, have identified a pathogen that seems to be necessary but not sufficient cause of violent behavior, just as specifically as exposure to the tubercle bacillus is necessary but not sufficient for the development of tuberculosis. The difference is that in the case of violence, the pathogen is an emotion, not a microbe—namely, the experience of overwhelm-ing shame and humiliation. And just as people's vulnerability to tuberculosis is influenced by the state of their body's defense mechanisms, so their vulnerability to violence is influenced by the state of their psychological defense mechanisms.[45]

This is a radical departure from the free-will orientation of human agency common today, particularly in judicial practice. Once we view behavioral violence as a problem in public health, the entire social system becomes suspect. Gilligan makes it very clear what the most power-ful generator of shame and humiliation is in human culture, according to his extensive study. As corroborated by others in epidemiological research, *socioeconomic inequality* appears to be the greatest driver of behavioral violence in general. Gilligan states, "Worldwide, the most powerful predictor of the murder rate is the size of the gap in income and wealth between the rich and the poor. The most powerful predictor of the rate of national or collective violence—war, civil insurrection, and terrorism—is the size of the gap between income and wealth between the rich and poor nations."[46] This is a troubling finding as wealth inequity is a textbook characteristic of capitalism, effectively making capitalism itself a precondition for war and violence.

Such correlations between population level, statistically consistent negative health outcomes, and various socioeconomic preconditions are abundant. In the work *The Spirit Level—Why Equality Is Better for Everyone* by Wilkinson and Pickett, a large amount of epidemiological data is explored and correlated. As will be revisited later in this chapter, what is found is that many public-health and social problems are correlated to economic inequality. By comparing developed nations specifically, we can see clearly that the more equal a society is in terms of income, the more stable, healthy, and happy that society will be. On the other hand, societies with large income gaps, such as the United States, suffer disproportionately across a range of problems, including higher incidences of heart disease, obesity, infant mortality, homicides, imprisonment, teen birth, mental illness, poor education, and more.

Socioeconomic inequality is also correlated to a gradient of health and well-being such that those with higher socioeconomic status have better health than those with lower status. While this may seem like common sense due to differing lifestyle options, researchers have recently found that a critical component is actually stress. Both general survival insecurity and psychosocial stress have been found to take a powerful toll on people's health in the lower classes, in addition to their lifestyle choices regarding food, smoking, and the like. The stress of simply feeling poor and inferior, a direct socioeconomic consequence given how personal success is currently measured in material and class terms, has emerged as just as relevant a health detriment as a poor diet or polluted environment. In effect, social stratification is a mechanism of *structural violence*, as will be explored throughout the rest of this chapter.

STRUCTURAL VIOLENCE

As defined in chapter one, structural violence is about preventable violence, death, and suffering resulting from human institutions. The body of research on this complex idea has grown over the past few decades. In 1976, Gernot Köhler and Norman Alcock produced a defining paper titled, "An Empirical Table of Structural Violence." Building on related ideas by Johan Galtung, they refined a model of the idea that is just as viable today as it was then. They state, "Whenever persons are harmed, maimed, or killed by poverty and unjust social, political, and economic institutions, systems, or structures, we speak of structural violence. Structural violence, like armed violence, can have two effects—it either kills its victims or it harms them in various ways short of killing."[47]

Gilligan refines the definition to home in on its root socioeconomic relationship. While structural violence can theoretically occur in a purely political and social arrangement without economic influence, its main manifestation comes from social class by way of economic inequality. In fact, general economic factors actually precede sociopolitical ones, once again putting the nature of the economy at the very root of societal organization. Gilligan says:

> [I]ncreased rates of death and disability [are] suffered by those who occupy the bottom rungs of society, as contrasted with the relatively lower death rates experienced by those who are above them. Those excess deaths . . . are a function of class structure; and that structure is a product of [society's] collective human choices, concerning how to distribute the collective wealth of society.[48]

Gilligan's notion of "excess deaths" has to do with deciding what degree of suffering and death is avoidable or not. If it is plausibly avoidable, it is violence. Johan Galtung, in his original treatment on structural violence, stated that the difference rests "between what could have been and what is . . . Thus, if a person died of tuberculosis in the eighteenth century it would be hard to conceive of this as violence since it might have been quite unavoidable, but if he dies from it today, despite all the medical resources in the world, then violence is present according to our definition."[49]

Put another way, imagine a person pulls out of a gun and kills a thirty-year-old person. Given the modern average life expectancy of eighty-four, fifty-four years can be assumed to have been taken from that person. This is certainly violence, as everyone would agree. Now imagine the same person born into the toxic condition of poverty, in the midst of an overall affluent, abundant society, dying at the age of thirty from a disease linked to poverty. Is that also considered violence? It hasn't been until recent times that inequality has been seen as an umbrella condition for many public-health problems. Generally, we sense that inequality is socially corrosive and detrimental to those in abject poverty, but the true depth of that violence has gone widely ignored. Gilligan's expression, "increased rates of death and disability," conveys the general idea that poverty is a kind of violence, but that violence is expressed in countless ways, often too subtle to see. In fact, it is difficult for me to think about the issue without associating it with a unique period of my childhood.

My mother was a social worker in rural North Carolina for almost thirty years—an occupation that is a direct response to structural violence by way of socioeconomic class. Returning home each evening, she would often comment to me about her cases. Working in perhaps one of the most unpleasant jobs possible, she had to decide whether children should be taken away from their families to be placed in foster care. Given that even the most dysfunctional and abusive families still form deep bonds, the idea of government coming in and intervening in such sensitive affairs is quite controversial. Yet some of her cases involved neglect, sexual abuse, child prostitution, addiction, extreme criminality, incest, and various extremes of perversion that would convince even the most steadfast family preservationist to intervene.

Around the time of the North American Free Trade Agreement (NAFTA), she changed jurisdictions to an already poor region that was being hit with increased job losses. NAFTA, promoted as a "free-market" liberator between Canada, Mexico, and the United States, had the effect of job flight from the US, increased inequality, and human displacement.[50] In my mother's jurisdiction, the already low-wage factory and farming jobs dissolved as plants closed or moved, producing a sea of even poorer families with less opportunity. In this climate, social services did what they could. Still, she would be the first to tell you that most victories were small. A child taken from one abusive or neglectful family very often ended up in only a slightly better home. Foster care itself was incentivized by money, sought by already poor families in the same general region. The dark cloud of poverty and its violence was ever-present.

Though, not all of her cases were of an extreme nature. Many were slowly unfolding tragedies of well-meaning people who really tried, but lacked the means ever to gain traction or stability. This relentless stress often leads to despair, along with self-medication through alcohol and drugs. While we may look at a drug-addicted mother as being a terrible person, sacrificing the welfare of her child for her habit, we miss the back story of how she got to where she is. This is not to absolve people of responsibility, but to uncover the complexity. Humans can be frail creatures and enough stress and pain can break just about anyone.

Oftentimes my mother would be alerted by schools reporting something wrong. For example, children would come to school filthy, beaten, without shoes, or emaciated. Social services would investigate on such grounds, finding consistent patterns. A "snowball" effect was often clear, wherein already disadvantaged poor people, often with little education, end up with children they can't financially support. In many cases of assumed neglect, the circumstance was really not malicious. Parents were working long hours at low-wage jobs, unable to pay for day care, so child supervision simply wasn't possible. This resulted in accidents, such as children playing with their parents' guns, and also misguidance through a lack of familial presence and support. It isn't difficult to understand how such lack of structure, coupled with the dynamics of poverty in general, can mold a child in negative ways or difficult to see how those influences extend into adulthood. These habits were repeated when those adults had their own children, often in the same poor conditions, creating feedback loops of human distortion.

In the mid-1990s, I had a personal experience in which the abstraction of this world I had been passively hearing about through my mother's stories became a reality. Due to financial limitations and her need to work close to home, my mother moved into the very conditions that she so often tried to combat in her work. It was an area of rural white poverty consisting of an array of dilapidated mobile homes sprawled about in a generally wooded area. Old cars and industrial debris peppered the terrain. Attending school in the city where my father was, I visited during summers and weekends. The area and culture was in mild contrast to my father's neighborhood, which, while also poor, was instead urban and mostly occupied by nonwhite minorities.

In one of my first visits, after befriending some local children, I was guided to a parking lot up the street. Here I saw a couple of dozen teenagers and a few adults intently gathered in a semicircle. The focus was on two fourteen-year-old boys fighting. While young teens fighting is nothing new, what made this circumstance unique, as I came to learn, was that the fathers of the two boys were the ones enforcing the fight. It appeared the kids had gotten into a scuffle at school and the fathers took it upon themselves to teach their kids a lesson by having them fistfight in a public display. One kid was pummeled and humiliated by the other in front of his peers, and he ended the fight in a fetal position, crying in the back of a pickup truck. I glanced around to notice the primitive reactions of the locals as they praised the dominant figure and yelled obscenities at the defeated one. It appears this was how some adults in the community dealt with adolescent conflict. Needless to say, even at my young age, I was troubled by the situation, wondering how anything positive could have possibly come from such a scene. What does this teach impressionable kids about conflict resolution? What does it teach about parenting? This was a hint of the spectrum of social disorder inherent in this community, fomented by poverty.

Over the course of visiting, making friends, and getting to know other families, I found my sense of destabilization growing more visceral—an unnerving sense that anything could happen at any moment. As years went on, I came to recognize that the children my age who had been born and raised in those conditions really had little hope of breaking the cycle of racism, illiteracy, privation, violence, and drug addiction that surrounded them. They only knew what their cultural condition presented to them, compounded by the complex stress of limited options. In truth, they were victims. They were victims along with their parents before them, who, more often than not, were born into the same basic deprived socioeconomic condition. They were victims of socioeconomic circumstances that created feedback loops of negative stress and limitation. The loss of opportunity, lack of education, absence of status, and echoes of prior generations' bigotry and derangement are all outcomes of poverty and inequality itself, forming chain reactions and cycles that perpetuate a never-ending human tragedy.

From one acquaintance who was beaten by a gang to near-permanent disability, to the next-door neighbor who would crossbow stray dogs in his front yard, to the boy up the street who one day put a shotgun in his ex-girlfriend's vagina and pulled the trigger, this was a breeding ground of crime, violence, anger, and bigotry. While my experience was of an American variety, the correlation between poverty and this vast array of what are effectively public-health problems can be found in every country and across every culture. It is a pivotal example of the systemic, corrosive nature of inequality. These people were not authors of their own poverty; they were consequences of the structural violence resulting from the economic imbalance generated by the social system itself.

With that in mind, let's step back and consider the idea of economically driven structural violence in abstract principle. Imagine an island with 100 inhabitants. One person has managed to acquire, through customary trade methods, 99 percent of the resources of the island. The other ninety-nine are poor, sharing only 1 percent of the resources, and they are consequently suffering physically and psychologically. They are getting sick, fighting among themselves, and dying off prematurely for lack of economic means. The one wealthy person has more than enough to provide for everyone on the island without suffering any real loss of well-being, but chooses not to help. While intending no harm to anyone, the wealthy person simply thinks "everyone gets what they deserve" however unfortunate their plight.

Is this a condition of violence? When systemic social mechanisms result in a highly disproportionate benefit to one group while preventing another from meeting basic needs, logic demands the acknowledgment that the effect is, indeed, one of violence. While most recognize violence as a direct result of one person's or group's doing deliberate, clear harm to another, our society also recognizes the need for personal responsibility for public safety. When a person kills a pedestrian by accident while driving drunk, we view this incompetence and lack of external concern with contempt. While the harm was not intentional, it was unnecessarily consequential to poor judgment and hence inadvertently violent. Likewise, if a restaurant doesn't properly process its food, creating toxins that then poison and kill patrons, society also reacts in contempt since the harm done was caused by unnecessary neglect. There was no direct intent to do harm—it was consequential to other behavior or lack thereof. It is in this context of social responsibility and the avoidance of neglect that structural violence can be framed. The question is, To what extent are any or all of us responsible for the unnecessary suffering of others?

As discussed in the previous chapter regarding structural bigotry, the architecture of the market economy is such that no matter what the public does, economic inequality is going to occur, leading to social injustice. It can expand and contract, but it will never go away. That precondition of inequality then translates into structural violence when it results in harm—harm that is provably unnecessary. Yet, due to society's localized perception, such harm goes unregistered as actual violence since people haven't been taught to see the connection. Hence they feel no sense of responsibility. This is further compounded by the individualistic value disorder inherent in the system's social psychology, which effectively locks most people into assuming "everyone gets what they deserve," compounding the problem even further. Such has been the common perception for a long time. In the words of Nancy Scheper-Hughes, "Structural violence erases the history and consciousness of the social origins of poverty, sickness, hunger, and premature death, so that they are simply taken for granted and naturalized so that no one is held accountable except, perhaps, the poor themselves."[51] It has only been through modern statistical research in public health that the depth of structural violence and its systemic roots has come to light. Given this, I repeat the question: To what extent are any or all of us responsible for the unnecessary suffering of others? I assert that the same sense of social responsibility that obligates us to help protect public safety—whether it's driving safely and unimpaired by alcohol, properly preparing restaurant food, or protecting the environment from our pollutants—applies to our participation in and tolerance of socioeconomic inequality.

As mentioned earlier, the distinction to be made involves what suffering is necessary and what suffering is not. Is it necessary for almost 1 billion people to effectively starve during an age of advanced technology and mathematical proof that we can feed everyone?[52] Is it necessary to create a world where the top twenty-five billionaires could end world hunger, while millions of families like those I experienced in rural North

Carolina must endure debilitating poverty, leading to a vast spectrum of social disorder?[53] Is it necessary that sub-Saharan Africa alone has 69 percent of all the people with HIV, and 70 percent of all the deaths, when the Global North has been preventing and treating the disease effectively for many years now?[54] Such questions can go on and on as there are endless contexts—both macro and micro, both cause and effect—that to some degree probably wouldn't exist if proper structural changes were made. These problems include, but are far from limited to: psychological and physiological disease, the cultivation of racism and bigotry, underground economies such as drug trafficking and prostitution, gang violence, all forms of slavery and exploitation, suicide, behavioral violence, addiction, general crime, destructive elitism, debilitating inefficiency, child abuse, spousal abuse, terrorism, social destabilization, animal abuse, environmental pollution, biodiversity loss, and even war.

Put another way, structural violence is the mother of all negative economic externalities. If we define negative externalities as outcomes of economic behavior that lead to social harm, directly or indirectly, the proactive question again becomes, are they preventable? In an astounding number of cases, when we trace them back to their deepest origins within the dynamics of capitalism, we realize that the very social system is emanating such outcomes as a natural consequence of its basic functionality. And the overall outcome is devastating.

In the earlier-mentioned work "Empirical Table of Structural Violence," authors Köhler and Alcock conclude that up to 18 million unnecessary deaths occur annually—a number they obtain by comparing lifespans across different countries.[55] Ninety-five percent of those deaths occurred in the Global South, showing the incredible disparity between the two hemispheres. In a sense, this makes structural violence the leading cause of death in the world.[56] But then we have to ask, what is creating the structural violence? And that leads us to answer, inequality. If we then ask what the greatest driver of inequality is, we are led to the very foundation of market economics, as expressed in the prior chapter. Hence, it follows that market economics, in its now formal state of capitalism, is the world's leading cause of unnecessary death. As bluntly framed by Dr. James Gilligan: "[E]very single year, two to three times as many people die from poverty throughout the world as were killed by the Nazi genocide of the Jews over a six-year period. This is, in effect, the equivalent of an ongoing, unending, in fact accelerating, thermonuclear war, or genocide, perpetuated on the weak and poor every year of every decade, throughout the world."[57]

Of course, critics are quick to argue that Köhler and Alcock do not provide evidence that the world is technically able to bring everyone to the ideal life expectancy, implying Malthusian deficiencies in resources and means. As chapter five will investigate further, this is wildly false, especially in the twenty-first century. It is only through the highly inefficient distribution mechanism of markets that the current circumstances prevail, appearing normal. Even if we were to ignore actual technical potentials, thinking about things only in terms of money and purchasing power, the lost potential of financial reallocation alone translates into millions of deaths. There are about 1,800 billionaires in the world as of 2015, with more than $7 trillion between them.[58] The Food and Agriculture Organization of the United Nations (FAO) calculated that it would take roughly $30 billion a year to solve world hunger through mostly agricultural development in poor regions. These billionaires could provide this direct aid for 200 years and still have about $550 million each, on average. A fraction of US annual military spending alone would also suffice. In fact, since the FAO estimate was based on long-term development and not merely periodic aid, much less would be required over time as those poor regions' infrastructure improved. Recognizing this deeply impoverished value disorder, FAO Director Jacques Diouf said, "Against that backdrop, how can we explain to people of good sense and good faith that it was not possible to find US $30 billion a year to enable 862 million hungry people to enjoy the most fundamental of human rights: the right to food and thus the right to life?"[59]

Such comparisons of what we are doing and what we could be doing with a portion of this wealth if properly allocated are more than enough to highlight the violence inherent in the system and the culture it has created. In fact, Johan Galtung, one of the first to investigate structural violence in the 1960s, expanded the idea twenty years later to include what he called *cultural violence*. This has to do with those aspects of culture that normalize both direct and structural violence and their mechanisms, sanctifying it as natural.[60] It is in this line of thinking that Dr. King's "poverty of the spirit" really hits home. That a person can have a billion dollars in the bank and walk around as though that excess is OK in the midst of the vast suffering around him is an exceptional state of ethical and empathic impoverishment. But instead of looking at billionaires as a manifestation of both our problematic social system and disturbed human psychology, the public is lured into *cultural violence*, idolizing billionaires as heroes and beacons of success. As of 2015, sixty-two people have more wealth than the bottom 50 percent of the entire human population, some 3.5 billion people.[61] It is quite amazing that we don't view that reality as an expression of pure violence against the general population.

SOCIAL POLLUTION

As noted, while there are political, religious, and other social aspects to the broadest definition of structural violence, only those aspects that can be linked to the market economy's organization structure and its derived incentives are applicable here. This is not to diminish the relevance of other forms of institutional or political oppression, but to reinforce the importance of the socioeconomic one. It is the socioeconomic form of structural violence that correlates to millions of deaths a year through poverty. This is again about death that is arguably unnecessary, with the conclusion that this form of structural violence kills and harms more than all the wars, dictators, genocides, and other direct kinds of violence put together. In the words of scholar Joel Kovel, poetically encapsulating the procedural nature of this ongoing yet rather silent tragedy, "Never has a Holocaust been carried out so impersonally."[62]

In this section, an attempt will be made to organize some specific characteristics and outcomes related to this economically driven structural violence. This is tricky for there are so many simultaneous and overlapping contexts. As with the difficulty in trying to delineate economic externalities, the systemic nature of this kind of analysis can be confusing. For example, some observations are cause and effect at the same time. Detrimental personal stress, which is a measurable effect of low socioeconomic status, is also a cause, leading to physical and mental health problems, for instance.

Some observations also require an extended analysis of time, linking past life experiences to present effects. An example would be socioeconomic preconditions resulting in child abuse in early life, eventually leading to long-term adult disorders of the once-abused child. Emotional damage in youth correlates to adult neurosis, yet it is hard to pinpoint exact situational details in the chain reaction of one's life experience that inflame or reduce these propensities. Likewise the influences that interact to produce a negative public-health outcome can range in complexity from fairly obvious to nearly incomprehensible. For example, it is predictable—that is, fairly obvious—that a person who smokes cigarettes has a greater chance of developing lung cancer later in life. However, it is more complicated to show that a person who experiences the psychosocial stress of low socioeconomic status has an increased risk of heart disease. This latter correlation is more complex, apparent only through wide population analysis over long periods of time. The same goes for suicide, direct violence, terrorism, and other complex human actions that are also consequential to the social system.

Perhaps the most embracing way to think about how structural violence unfolds or metastasizes throughout society is as a form of social pollution. Just as air pollution common to cities has been linked to a spectrum of physical and mental health problems, one can think of market-induced inequality as a "toxic cloud" looming over society. While inequality isn't the only manifestation of socioeconomic structural violence, it is the central one of concern here, as it is the most prevalent and preventable.

In Figure 4a, a causality tree linking the market system to the end result of unnecessary human mortality, deprivation, and suffering is presented. This is necessarily general and incomplete, and each outcome is certainly not to be assumed as only related to market-driven economic inequality. The outline helps to organize, in a concise and semi-linear manner, what modern social science has been realizing, as discussed throughout this chapter. To explain the outline and flow of causality, I'll start by restating that a social system based on property, exchange, labor-for-income, competitive self-regulation, and the capacity to profit from scarcity and deprivation, sets in motion this predictable array of outcomes. The cyclical consumption needed to keep employment up, along with the need for economic growth to recover from previous contractions, powers the machine's structure. Earthly resources are inventory to be exploited, along with human labor. At the same time, negative externalities flourish, and increasingly so, as our technological capacity grows, often being used for the wrong purposes. This is all embodied in the market structure, like the tiny seed that sprouts a towering tree.

Again, it is often argued that capitalism is a specific mode of market behavior, separate from other forms of market economies. This is a false distinction. While economists often talk about true "free markets" or differentiate between "state capitalism," "merchant capitalism," and even "market socialism," these are all variations on a core, foundational theme. The tiny seed that grew to a towering tree may produce various fruits, but no matter how diverse they seem the genetics of that tree remain the same. To repeat my statement above, "a social system based on property, exchange, labor-for-income, competitive self-regulation, and

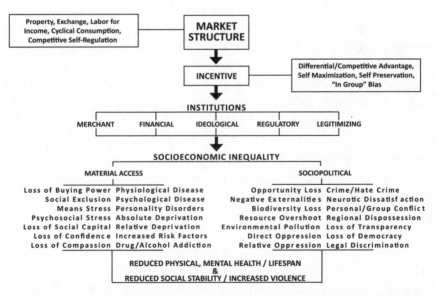

FIGURE 4A. The market structure produces behavioral incentives that are codified in both formal and conceptual social institutions that enforce and preserve the market structure. This leads to a host of socioeconomic inequalities, which, in turn, produce numerous negative public health outcomes. The figure is for from definitive and there is some contextual overlap between the listed examples.

the capacity to profit from scarcity and deprivation" can only produce a limited range of societal variation, along with a limited range of resulting social psychology. "Capitalism," as most know it, is simply a structurally mature form of market economics, rooted in the Neolithic Revolution. Its maturity over the past 200 years has been marked by its increasingly totalitarian nature, notably large commercial power hierarchies. While one can theorize a market with no hierarchy or dominance by an elite *capitalist ownership class*, that is not the natural gravitation at all.

Moving to the second tier in the figure down, there is incentive. The incentive system resulting from the market's structure has been described previously as the "primary logic" that guides human behavior in the quest for financial success in the market game. It is this incentive logic that simply cannot be avoided if a person or business expects to succeed, no matter what their moral or ethical views may be. This includes, as listed, the need to be competitive and differentially so in order to convince the consumer that a product is better than competitors'; the need to self-maximize when the opportunity arises to try to gain as much profit as possible; the need to protect the associated "in-group" related to the venture; and the need to self-preserve in the sense of ensuring that no matter what happens, any drawdown or loss will never jeopardize the business itself. This self-preservation need often results in highly offensive outcomes.

The history of tobacco and cigarette use is a classic example of such an outcome. Decades of lying, lobbying, and fraud to secure profits occurred once it was clear that smoking causes serious health problems. Currently we see this behavior in the energy industry, with hydrocarbon-based corporations slowing the desperately needed shift to renewables for the sake of maintaining profits.[63]

Returning to Figure 4a, we next have the institutions, third tier down. These are the formal and conceptual institutions that organize the market system in day-to-day reality. These include merchant institutions (goods-producing corporations), financial institutions (central banks or monetary policy), ideological institutions (neoliberalism or consumerism), regulatory institutions (property law or government), and legitimizing institutions (the market-favoring discourse of the intelligentsia, general state propaganda, and even the industry of commercial advertising itself). Advertising, while also a merchant institution, exists to promote cyclical consumption, supporting the ethic of consumerism and hence economic growth. I would like to clarify that ideological institutions and legitimizing institutions are similar as they both promote values and arguments in favor of the market system. The difference is that ideological institutions are long-standing and widespread, like a core religious belief. Legitimizing institutions are periodic and can vary, effectively existing to enforce or justify the core ideological institutions.

It is, then, from these institutions that socioeconomic inequality is born, bringing us to the fourth tier down in Figure 4a. Here there are two broad categories: inequality in economic access ("material"), meaning material needs including services, along with social and ultimately political inequality ("sociopolitical"). These two categories embrace the laundry list of social injustices noted. This is far from a complete list and there is overlap. On the left side, perhaps the most critical issues are the categories of psychological and physiological disease. These two issues resulting from socioeconomic inequality include a vast array of specific problems. However, stress, psychosocial stress, and addiction are also highly caustic. On the right side, perhaps the most critical issues are the categories of personal/group conflict and negative externalities. However, oppression and legal discrimination are also highly important. In the end, all of these injustices and detrimental pressures lead to the "final stage" manifestation of structural violence, as expressed in the two resulting categories at the bottom of Figure 4a.

EPIDEMIOLOGY

For the remainder of this chapter these two categories, listed as "reduced physical/mental health and life span," along with "reduced social stability and increased violence," will be explored. We will begin with the former—reduced health and life span. Epidemiological research into health disparities based around socioeconomic status (SES) predictably shows that being poor and lower class is devastating to health in ways many never consider. Putting aside for a moment the mortality and suffering produced by behavioral violence or broad physical detriments such as a city's air pollution, low socioeconomic status links to a spectrum of common physiological and psychological problems.

With respect to the macro, this distinction wouldn't be needed if socioeconomic classes were distributed uniformly across the world, such as we find in a single country like the United States. Because of the historical unfolding of competitive economic behavior, colonization, and the more modern rise of neoliberalism and globalization, the Global North and Global South have separated into two very different worlds.

For example, according to the World Health Organization (WHO) classifications and measures as of 2012, the top three leading causes of death in the "high-income" countries common to the North are heart disease, stroke, and cancers of the lung, ordered respectively. The top three leading causes of death in "low-income" countries common to the South are lower respiratory infections, HIV/AIDs, and diarrheal disease, ordered respectively.[64] This macro perspective shows a very different overall condition from the micro conditions seen within countries, especially in the North, which have substantially more development. All three of the leading causes of death in low-income countries are rarely present in the high-income countries. This is the tip of the iceberg in the case for structural violence, as these major killers in poor countries are highly preventable if economic means facilitating basic health care, education, and infrastructure revisions are provided. Infectious diseases kill 15 million people a year, with 75 percent of those occurring in Southeast Asia and sub-Saharan Africa.[65]

HIV/AIDS alone in sub-Saharan Africa is an excellent case study. In 2013, approximately 24.7 million people there were living with HIV. While there has been a decline in cases of HIV/AIDS over the prior decade, the epidemic is still of genocidal proportions due to a lack of economic means. Globally, sub-Saharan Africa accounts for 70 percent of all new HIV infections, with well over 1 million people dying every year.[66] Ninety-one percent of the world's HIV-infected children are also in Africa, with about 25.8 million infected.[67] Such an epidemic has far-reaching consequences, since such a plague can stifle economic development by reducing people's ability to work. This epidemic has also brought back a resurgence of tuberculosis and other diseases, generating a plethora of debilitating social problems. While there is debate surrounding the causes of the perpetuation of the crisis in Africa, the poverty of the region, compounded by neoliberal international policies and corporate indifference, is no doubt the central factor.

Since market logic sees no merit in bringing service to those who cannot pay for it, it isn't difficult to understand the destitution in Africa. Today, more money is being spent on treating male pattern baldness than finding better treatments for malaria.[68] New treatments have not been developed for tuberculosis (TB), a common side consequence of HIV infection, in fifty years.[69] Annually, TB kills 1.5 million people, 95 percent of whom are in the Global South, yet transnational pharmaceutical companies have actually been abandoning TB research. Regarding the lack of focus, Nesri Padayatchi from the Center for the AIDS Program of Research in South Africa states, "TB does not make enough profit."[70]

In the late 1990s, new and effective drugs to treat HIV were rapidly slowing infection and reducing death tolls in the United States and other First World nations. However, these drugs, strictly protected by legal patent rights and international trade agreements, were far too expensive for African and other nations. The average annual income for people in South Africa at the time was $2,600, while the imported brand-name treatment cost $1,000 a month or $12,000 a year.[71] In response, South Africa and other regions sought to produce generic versions themselves or import them from regions that already had permission to produce generics. While international trade agreements and the World Trade Organization had stipulations for this kind of "emergency" action, the South African decision was met with an appalling backlash from the pharmaceutical industry and Western power hubs such as Washington.

Sabin Russell reported in the *San Francisco Chronicle* in 1999 that "the quest to flood Africa with cheap AIDS drugs has run headlong into conflict with American trade policy. High level Clinton administration officials are blocking attempts to tamper with AIDS drug patents, saying that they undermine the entire system of intellectual property protection that encourages businesses to find new drugs."[72] In 2001, *Time* magazine reported:

> Despite years of evidence of AIDS' genocidal toll on poor countries, no one has brought these drugs within the reach of ordinary

> Africans . . . the . . . American and European multinational
> pharmaceutical corporations—and their home governments,
> notably Washington—have worked hard to keep prices up by
> limiting exports to the Third World and vigorously enforcing
> patent rights. They argue that drug firms legitimately need the
> profits to finance research on new wonder drugs. But at what
> point does the human benefit to desperate, destitute countries
> outweigh strict adherence to patents and profits?[73]

Fully indicative of self-maximizing market logic, with protections in
favor of a system process over human life, South Africa's decision to
import generic drugs was criticized as a violation of international law
(TRIPS agreement) by the United States. More than forty pharmaceutical
companies then sued the South African government, claiming a violation
of patent rights.[74] Fortunately, public outcry at the absurdity of the situation forced the US government and the pharmaceutical industry to back
down, but only after an agreement was reached in which discounts were
to be offered by the pharmaceutical industry rather than permission for
generic production or import. In other words, rather than allowing the
import of cheap generics, South Africa would now buy the brand-name
drugs for less. This may seem like a "win" for South Africa but, in the
words of journalist Garry Leech:

> The companies had simply realized that if they failed to provide
> discounted drugs then countries would follow the example set by
> South Africa . . . [seeking] domestic production, or the importa-
> tion, of cheaper generics. The companies responded to this threat
> to their market share and their ability to maximize profits by
> negotiating discounts only where they did not believe they can
> successfully prevent compulsory licensing [or generic use].[75]

One may wonder how large and highly profitable pharmaceutical companies can rationalize the restriction of independently produced versions of their drugs in poor regions suffering from catastrophic disease.
The most common reaction invokes the infamous word "greed." Greed,
however, is a relative qualification. Income self-maximization is part of

the market system's primary logic, once again. It is a strategic rule of the game, with limited rational flexibility. The actual amounts realized are irrelevant. It is very easy to rationalize the need for any amount of money or profit because it translates into "future security" or "future productivity." From those individuals who hoard billions under the pretense that they "need it" to help the world through philanthropy or even just "to help their children," to the large corporations that see their income as more fuel for research and development, there is no end to such "greedy" rationalization.

Unsurprisingly, in response to generic HIV drugs' being produced by poor countries, Merck pharmaceuticals stated, "Research and development based pharmaceutical companies like Merck simply cannot sustain a situation in which the developed countries alone are expected to bear the cost for essential drugs in both least-developed countries and emerging markets."[76] This would seem like a fair statement if one ignored the fact that research and development–based pharmaceutical companies like Merck have and continue to enjoy astronomical profits, far exceeding what would be needed to dramatically slow epidemic disease in the Third World. As of 2012, only 6 million of the 24 million infected were receiving HIV treatment in sub-Saharan Africa.[77] For the sake of abstract argument, let's assume the price for a year's treatment is the same as it was around 2001—$1,000 for a generic drug made in India.[78] If we take the number of people untreated, based on the 2012 estimate (18 million), the cost to cover all infected persons in sub-Saharan Africa per year would be $18 billion. Seems like a lot of money, right?

Well, it does, until you realize that in 2012 the pharmaceutical industry spent over $27 billion on marketing and advertising alone.[79] If 66 percent of that marketing budget were shifted, the HIV crisis in sub-Saharan Africa would be dramatically reduced, with millions of lives saved in the long-term. To add insult to injury, the eleven largest drug companies made $711 billion in profit between 2002 and 2012, eclipsing virtually all other sectors.[80] The structural violence of an industry unwilling to forgo a small percentage of industrial profits to save millions of lives adds an increasingly somber tone to Dr. Martin Luther King Jr.'s "poverty of the spirit." But once again, this is not so much an issue of greed or even character—it is an issue of system logic; of appropriate, self-maximizing, "business-as-usual" decision making. HIV/AIDS in Africa is just one example of the incredible degree of manifest human indifference today, when outrageous wealth and resource inequality on the global level, if equalized even slightly, would save millions of lives every year, reducing vast suffering and destabilization.

Moving on and returning to our larger-order context of physiological and psychological health issues resulting from low socioeconomic status, let's now explore the micro realm. While the consequences of inequality are extremely severe in the developing world given the degree of abject poverty, a more subtle and overshadowed level of structural violence is also ubiquitous. We can see this more clearly in the developed world, where across populations we find a clear socioeconomic distribution of disease and mortality. In short, the poorer and further down the socio-economic ladder you are, the more suffering you endure and the faster you will die. Statistical evidence of this is particularly clear in wealthy countries with larger income disparities. The United States makes an excellent study, since it has one of the largest income/wealth gaps in the world, along with a workable amount of reported public data.

A 2011 study by researchers at Columbia University's Mailman School of Public Health found that factors surrounding poverty, lack of education, and racial discrimination were linked to the death of approximately 874,000 Americans in 2000.[81] About 2.8 million Americans died in 2000, meaning 31 percent of the US population died because of these arguably preventable circumstances tied to income and loss of opportunity.[82] Dr. Sandro Galea, the chair of epidemiology at Columbia, states, "Social causes can be linked to death as readily as can pathophysiological and behavioral causes . . . These findings argue for a broader public health conceptualization of the causes of mortality and an expansive policy approach that considers how social factors can be addressed to improve the health of populations."[83]

A 2015 report from the National Academies of Sciences, Engineering, and Medicine found an average life-span difference of about thirteen to fourteen years between rich and poor in the US.[84] Even worse, the trends actually show stagnating and even declining life spans for the poor in the past thirty years, with the rich gaining years of life quite rapidly. For example, roughly six years have been gained by the richest class of women measured, while the poorest class measured *lost* about four years.[85] This research was corroborated by the Brookings Institute, with its report confirming, "Life expectancy is rising for those at the top of the distribution of individuals ranked by alternative measures of socioeconomic status, but it is stagnate or declining for those at the bottom."[86] A more extreme result exists in the city of London, where the London Health Observatory found a staggering twenty-five-year gap in life expectancy between the rich and poor overall.[87]

Today, there is no question that low socioeconomic status is a true risk factor for many mortality-producing diseases. Socioeconomic inequality directly links relative poverty to strokes, cancer, cardiovascular disease, and many other ailments. Dr. Samuel Broder, former director of the National Cancer Institute, declared that "poverty is a carcinogen," referring to it as a cancer-causing agent.[88] A 2013 study expanding previous stroke correlations to income confirmed:

> Poorer people within a population and poorer countries globally are most affected in terms of incidence and poor outcomes of stroke . . . Mortality rates and disability-adjusted life-years lost have been reported to be up to 3.5-fold higher in low-income compared with middle- and high-income countries. The number of deaths from stroke is projected to increase from 6.5 million in 2015 to 7.8 million in 2030 with a faster increase projected for LMIC [low-middle-income countries] compared with HIC [high-income countries].[89]

As for heart disease, the evidence is even stronger that social stratification causes increased mortality. As the leading cause of death on Earth overall, heart disease kills around 17 million people annually.[90] A 2011 study done by UC Davis found that people with lower socioeconomic status had a 50 percent greater chance of developing heart disease.[91] Using data from the United States, where more than 600,000 deaths occur each year, the lead author of the study concluded, "Low socioeconomic status is a heart disease risk factor on its own and needs to be regarded as such by the medical community."[92] This is an important observation; it essentially states that the intersecting problems common to the lower class are consistent enough for us to view class itself as a public-health detriment. When that view is taken, causality then links directly to the structure of the social system, as explained before.

How exactly does inequality translate into such health disparities? There are a range of notable influences. The combination of stress, lack of absolute resources, lack of options, and lifestyle choices are core factors. While it may seem to some that lifestyle and education are unlinked from poverty, the truth is that there is a direct correlation between low socioeconomic status and low educational attainment, along with negative lifestyle choices. Regarding education, ChildFund International, a nonprofit that compiles research on the effects of child poverty, stated:

> [O]ne of the most disturbing links between poverty and education we see is that low household income correlates closely with poor achievement in school. Children from lower-income families are more likely than students from wealthier backgrounds to have lower test scores, and they are at higher risk of dropping out of school. Those who complete high school are less likely to attend college than students from higher-income families. For some children, the effects of poverty on education present unique challenges in breaking the cycle of generational poverty and reduce their chances of leading rewarding, productive lives.[93]

A 2015 Columbia University study found that cognitive impairment correlates to poverty in the form of brain damage. It showed that the brain structure of children and teenagers in poverty actually differs from those in affluent conditions. The largest study of its kind, focusing on areas of the brain related to functions such as language, reading, and decision making, revealed that children in families earning less than $25,000 a year had 6 percent less development than in those earning $150,000 or more.[94] A similar study also found that poverty overall correlates to a reduction of cognitive capacities and subsequently an effective reduction in IQ. This study, which was done at the University of Warwick, concluded that the stress of worrying about money and survival, clearly common to the lower classes, can create a cognitive deficit equivalent to a loss of thirteen IQ points.[95] The researchers suggest that this stress explains why poorer people are more likely to make decisions that exacerbate their financial difficulties.

Poor nutrition also strongly correlates to poverty. A 2010 study confirmed the obvious, stating, "Many nutritional professionals believe that all Americans, regardless of income, have access to a nutritious diet . . . In reality, food prices pose a significant barrier for many consumers who are trying to balance good nutrition with affordability."[96] The nutritional deficits, obesity, and other physical and mental health consequences associated with poor nutrition are not simply "lifestyle choices" but, at least in part, a consequence of the limited access to nutrition available to people with little money living in low-income neighborhoods.

When I lived in Bushwick, Brooklyn, some years ago, I witnessed this phenomenon firsthand. I was residing in an illegally converted commercial loft, a common feature of West Brooklyn in those days. My neighborhood had a cliché, gangland feel reminiscent of a Charles Bronson movie. While it has improved a bit today, this pre-gentrified area was an echo of 1980s New York City poverty, with steel bars on everything and store clerks hiding behind bulletproof glass. My apartment building, a converted factory, was surrounded by a steel gate that rose thirty feet in the air, making it look more like a prison. Right next door was the local grocery store, which I frequented. As a glaring white anomaly roaming the aisles among the predominantly poor black and Hispanic customers, I came to realize that not only did many of my neighbors pay for their food with food stamps, but they also appeared to pretty much live on cheap ramen noodles, frozen pizzas, Coca-Cola, and other high-sugar, high-sodium, and high-fat processed foods.

In 2014, the nonprofit group Feeding America surveyed 60,000 people who used such food-subsidy programs, finding that 80 percent tended to buy "junk food" to further save money. They also found an expected yet startling disproportional occurrence of diabetes and high blood pressure.[97] This problem is compounded, they noted, by the larger-order problems such as how stores in poor neighborhoods tend to stock low-quality food over more-expensive, healthful food, further reducing choice. This is to be expected, since in a market economy product quality is associated with *purchasing demographic*. Just as a company will make a very expensive car to target the rich, food companies produce low-quality, unhealthful, preservative-polluted food to sell to the poor. However, when you have little purchasing power, the nutritional content of a food becomes secondary to the desperate interest in saving money, coupled with the aforementioned educational limitations inherent in poverty. People cannot be expected to purchase more healthful food that is also more expensive when they lack the means to afford it and when they may also be ignorant of the health problems that lower-quality food can cause. Regarding psychological stress, an interesting nutrition-related case study is the phenomenon of poverty-driven obesity in the First World. Astoundingly, it has been projected by the Centers for Disease Control and Prevention (CDC) that 42 percent of Americans will be obese by 2030.[98] In the work *Stress Science: Neuroendocrinology*, by neuroscience and mental health expert George Fink, powerful research on the adverse effects of emotional stress on the human body is explored in great detail. The work states:

> Many overweight people, particularly those with abnormal obesity, find that eating increases in situations of discomfort and also soothes their feelings of stress and anxiety. This phenomenon is usually called *stress-eating* or emotional-eating. While obese individuals may realize that in general they eat in response to stress/emotions, they are typically unable in the moment to stop themselves from eating . . . this type of stress-eating might be due to disruptions of central regulatory systems involved in the control of energy intake. In obese binge eaters, stress-eating occurs, and it is up to 100% specifically triggered by stress and negative moods (e.g., depression, anger, anxiety, etc.).[99]

As is also the case with compulsive drug or alcohol use, stress-eating as self-medication can find its root in immediate conditions, as a result of prior life trauma, or both. A 2014 Swedish study examining 112,000 participants found a well-defined link between child abuse and adult obesity.[100] It states, "The study clearly shows that difficult life events leave traces which can manifest as disease much later in life. The mechanisms behind this process include stress, negative patterns of thought and emotions, poor mental health, increased inflammation, as well as lowered immune function and metabolism." Now, one may counter-argue that incurred physical, emotional, and sexual abuse in childhood has nothing to do with the later adult's socioeconomic status and hence class cannot be blamed. However, this argument holds little ground since the *precondition* of poverty is arguably the largest broad predictor of physical, emotional, and sexual abuse in childhood.[101] When exactly this socioeconomically triggered causality occurs in life doesn't change its relevance.

There are also unique biological synergies that make matters worse, wherein stressed, possibly predisposed people not only eat too much, but also will naturally crave foods containing high levels of salts and sugars. When the brain is stressed, it releases certain stress hormones. These hormones push and pull on one's system, with the body often seeking alleviation. One outlet is an increase in dopamine. Dopamine, a powerful neurotransmitter, gives a sense of pleasure when released. Sugars, salts, and fats are known to trigger a dopamine response over other foods, which is why people gravitate toward "comfort foods," especially when stressed. A 2008 study undertaken with genetically altered mice also showed "that stress contributes to increased consumption of food high in fat and carbohydrates and could possibly increase the risk of obesity."[102]

Overall, in the developed world, the highest rates of obesity occur among population groups with the highest poverty rates and the least education.[103] However, it is worth pointing out that obesity is unique in its biopsychosocial causality, since body-image stigma, loss of confidence, and hence reduced perceived social status can create a vicious feedback loop. The depression and anxiety common to people already overweight or obese is exacerbated by the stress of poverty, lack of options, and feelings of low self-worth. This stress then triggers the biological urge to further overeat often unhealthful yet satisfying high risk–factor foods, repeating the cycle.

Now, while more specific mental health issues will be touched upon—notably psychiatric disorders and the psychology of behavioral violence—it's important to highlight that in the field of epidemiology, what used to appear as only "physiological" has come to be understood as often equally "psychological." The truth is there is actually no singularly physiological or singularly psychological phenomenon, just as there is no "nature" as separate from "nurture." Body and mind act in synergy. After all, regardless of its grand mystique, the brain is still an organ like the heart or liver. What has been discovered is that the effects of emotional stress are no longer mere agitators of already unhealthy states. Negative stress is actually a silent killer; it is a pathogen linked to social inequality, constituting a public-health epidemic in and of itself.

Psychosocial stress, meaning psychological stress coming from the social environment, links to brain damage, hormone problems, depression, anxiety, reproduction complications, sleep disorders, growth impairment, memory problems, diabetes, cardiovascular disease, gastrointestinal disorders, sexual disorders, and overall immune deficiencies that open the door to a host of other diseases and complications.[104] One of the more studied links is heart disease. Atherosclerosis, a condition in which plaque builds up in the arteries, leading to a heart attack or stroke, has been tied to stress hormones such as glucocorticoids, which trigger immune processes that lead to plaque deposits in the arteries.[105] Chronically stressed people slowly poison their arteries, ultimately reducing their life span.

A landmark study started in 1967 by Michael Marmot of the University College of London analyzed more than 17,000 British "civil servant" workers over ten years. These were middle-class people, representing a more narrow range of socioeconomic stratification. Oriented around job status specifically, or what the study called an employment "grade," the study found that the highest and lowest rungs of the group had a threefold difference in cardiac-disease mortality.[106] In controlling for various factors, noting that everyone had universal, free health care at his or her disposal, the study concluded that psychosocial stress played a prominent role in the outcome. Two decades later a follow-up study was done that confirmed the prior findings, expanding to reveal deeper social determinants of disease by way of social stratification. Again, this phenomenon of psychosocial stress is not an issue of poverty or *absolute deprivation* but one of *perceived relative social status*. Marmot states:

> What we found in Whitehall was that the lower the grade of employment, the higher the risk of heart disease. But not just heart

disease, every major cause of death. And that was a bit shocking. The higher the grade, the better the health. The lower the grade, the higher the mortality rate and the shorter the life expectancy, in this remarkably graded phenomenon . . . The other striking thing . . . is that none of them is poor in the conventional sense. We're used to thinking that poverty is bad for health, and so it is. Poverty is dreadful for health. But even the lowest grades of British civil service are not poor in any absolute sense of the word . . . It was this gradient. It was not just about poverty.

He continues:

So we haven't got the richest people in society, we haven't got the billionaires, and we haven't got the poorest people in society, and we haven't got anybody who's unemployed or has any risk of losing their job. And yet we see this remarkable social gradient. The people at the bottom of the hierarchy had a four times higher risk of death than people at the top. The people in the middle had twice the mortality risk of the people at the top—in people who were not exposed to any of the usual hazards.[107]

The research showed that psychosocial stress seemed to account for about 75 percent of the social gradient in mortality. He continues:

We have strong evidence that there are two important influences on health in explaining the hierarchy in health. The first is autonomy, control [and] empowerment. People who are disempowered, people who don't have autonomy, people who have little control over their lives, are at increased risk of heart disease, increased risk of mental illness . . . The second is . . . being able to take your place in society . . . to benefit from all that society has to offer . . . It's self-esteem; it's the esteem of others. It's saying that I can benefit from the fruits that society has to offer.[108]

The implication is far-reaching: Social inequality is itself problematic. While social status is not necessarily about income, there is no question that income and wealth are signifiers of one's sense of status, belonging, self-respect, and autonomy with regard to society as a whole. *In effect, what we have is a public-health indictment of the very nature of social stratification itself.* Evidence shows, in contrast to propaganda that humans should endure and embrace primitive, stratified power and oppression, that social class and the inferior-superior relationship inherent in it is simply bad for social and personal health. Hence capitalism, which is the embodiment of this market-created hierarchy, is really a poisonous social construct. This study, while performed in Britain, has been replicated across the world, with little variation in the overall outcome. Hierarchy simply makes people sick. This is also made worse by the nature of our commercial, consumer society once again, where advertising's functional role is to make people feel inadequate and subordinate. In the words of neuroscientist and stress-health expert Robert Sapolsky, "So it isn't about being poor, it is about feeling poor."[109]

As touched upon before, the work of Richard Wilkinson of the University of Nottingham has further explored this phenomenon in great detail, examining differences between countries that have different degrees of economic inequality. While we know that poverty is extremely bad for one's health, so is *relative poverty* or relative economic inequality. Research has specifically shown that independent of absolute income, the more income inequality there is in a society, the worse the health and mortality rates are overall. Figure 4b shows aggregated data for a range of developed countries ranked from lowest to highest income inequality and better to worse conditions for the social and health concerns noted on the left side.

While the synergy of the mind-body connection to health has been explored broadly, let's now home in on the more traditional mental health concerns. Though there are often genetic predispositions to issues such as depression, anxiety, personality disorders, suicide, and drug addiction, negative stress and life trauma no doubt have powerful causal connections. A great deal of this stress can be directly correlated to economic problems such as job loss, economic decline, status, and so on. Figure 4b illustrates that from Japan to the US, there is a worsening of mental illness, drug addiction, obesity, and homicides as economic inequality increases. Once again, while there are *absolute deprivation* effects that stress people into unhealthy states and patterns, *relative deprivation* is just as powerful in its own way.

Regarding drug and alcohol addiction, the biopsychosocial nature of this issue has become extremely clear in recent times. While the world still imposes primitive legal punishment for people who self-medicate or are addicted to illegal drugs, recognition of the issue as a problem in public health has been steadily growing.

Dr. Gabor Maté, a Canadian physician who specializes in the treatment and understanding of addiction, said, "The greatest damage done by neglect, trauma or emotional loss is not the immediate pain they inflict but the long-term distortions they induce in the way a developing child will continue to interpret the world and her situation in it."[110] Further, "Not all addictions are rooted in abuse or trauma, but I do believe they can all be traced to painful experience . . . The effects of early stress or adverse experiences directly shape both the psychology and the neurobiology of addiction in the brain."[111]

It has been historically common to conclude that addiction simply emerges from the repeated use of an "addictive" substance or activity,

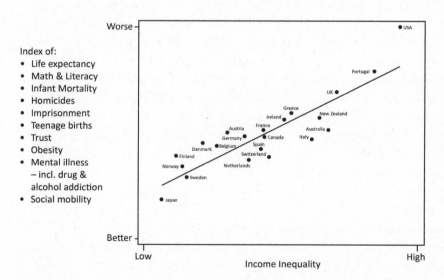

FIGURE 4B. Health and social problems are worse in more unequal countries. *Source:* Wilkinson & Pickett, The Spirit Level. www.equalitytrust.org.uk

coupled with a genetic predisposition. Yet, both conclusions now appear to be secondary when accounting for emotional stress and trauma. These environmental factors take priority. Childhood stress appears particularly defining. One of the largest investigations ever conducted to assess associations between childhood maltreatment and later-life health and well-being is called the "Adverse Childhood Experiences" (ACE) study out of San Diego.[112] Tracking 17,000 participants, it linked severe childhood stress to many adult addictions. It measured a range of stress factors such as having an incarcerated parent, living in a house with domestic violence, losing a parent to death or divorce, and having a mentally ill or addicted parent, along with emotional, physical, and sexual abuse, and neglect.

The study applied a calibrated scoring system to factors, considering their mixture. In other words, something like sexual abuse would be considered one type of ACE, while emotional abuse such as humiliation would be another. These then would be added together to assess the probability of certain addiction outcomes. The study found a vast range of increased propensities for drug use, such that the more ACEs in play, the higher the probability. For example, a male child with four or more ACEs was found to be seven times more likely to be an alcoholic than a person with no ACEs.[113] In a separate study using the same framework, "economic hardship," or an inability to meet financial needs, was also included.[114] Unsurprisingly, "economic hardship" was deemed "the most common adverse childhood experience reported." However, that economic correlation is just one of many. While the study includes economic hardship singularly, which is more often than not linked to low socioeconomic status, the study overlooked how the other ACEs considered, such as child abuse, are also highly correlated to poverty and economic inequality.

As far as mental illness overall is concerned, it has been well established that low socioeconomic status is a risk factor. A report published by the American Psychological Association, examining a database of 34,000 patients with repeat psychiatric hospitalizations, found that unemployment, poverty, and housing unaffordability were correlated with a risk of mental illness. The study states, "One of the most consistently replicated findings in the social sciences has been the negative relationship of socioeconomic status (SES) with mental illness: The lower the SES of an individual is, the higher is his or her risk of mental illness."[115] Similarly, an analysis by M. H. Brenner covering 120 years of data from New York State mental institutions found that instabilities in the national economy are the single most important source of fluctuations in mental-hospital admissions or admission rates.[116]

As far as depression is concerned, a study by researchers at Washington University in St. Louis in 2016 actually found that child poverty can alter "brain connectivity," weakening important connections between regions, leading to future clinical depression. Deanna M. Barch, PhD, chair of Washington University's Department of Psychological & Brain Sciences in Arts & Sciences, stated:

> In this study, we found that the way those structures connect with the rest of the brain changes in ways we would consider to be less helpful in regulating emotion and stress . . . [I]t behooves us to remember that adverse experiences early in life are influencing the development and function of the brain. And if we hope to intervene, we need to do it early so that we can help shift children onto the best possible developmental trajectories.[117]

Likewise, in a 2014 survey published by the US government's Substance Abuse and Mental Health Services Administration, clinical psychologist Bruce E. Levine stated that "suicidality, depression, and mental illness are highly correlated with involvement in the criminal justice system, unemployment, and poverty."[118] Given the fact that the lower classes are more prone to experience the criminal justice system, one cannot dismiss the socioeconomic connection to this attribute on its own, reinforcing the broad influence of economic conditions overall. It appears the justice system's imposed restraint of freedom and loss of control helps lead one to such mental illness.[119] A study in Denmark from 2011 found an increased suicide rate not only for people who had been found guilty and incarcerated, but also for those who simply had general exposure to the process—that is, found innocent and set free.[120] The author concludes, "Thus, exposure to the criminal justice system in itself may contribute to elevating a person's suicide risk, rather than simply reflecting the traits and characteristics of people who come into contact with the system." Again, while one may see vulnerability to the criminal justice system as detached from economic forces, systemic reasoning forces the realization that most all crime in the world is property-driven to one degree or another. In other words, if there were no scarcity pressure, no core survival stress or status-shaming inequality, crime would drop dramatically compared with what we endure today.

As for suicide, this phenomenon is a profound existential tragedy. It is the tenth-leading cause of death in the United States. Approximately 105 Americans commit suicide every day, with an attempt made every thirty-one seconds.[121] Globally, about 800,000 commit suicide annually, with many more attempts. Seventy-five percent occur in low- and middle-income countries, with 30 percent occurring by way of pesticide self-poisoning in recent times.[122] This pesticide self-poisoning has become a powerful pattern in rural regions in the developing world. While part of a larger global pattern of farmer suicides, patterns in the Global South have specific characteristics that link it directly to changes in international trade policy and effectively *neoliberal globalization*. In fact, of all the variations of structural violence we could categorize, the economically induced mass suicides by farmers who have lost their means of survival due to austerity, economic adjustment programs, trade policy, and ultimately the stress of debt, have been staggering in number.

India is now home to one out of every three suicides worldwide. Between 1997 and 2014 more than 280,000 farmers committed suicide in India. This averages out to roughly 16,000 suicides per year.[123] The most common reason found has to do with debt and crop failure. While crop failure is not necessarily a structural outcome, as poor weather is partly to blame, the vast debt farmers have recently endured creates stress that, in combination, pushes them over the edge. It isn't just the predominantly male death toll that is tragic—it's the desperate families left behind. For every farmer committing suicide there is almost always a wife with multiple children left in economic and personal despair.

Indian journalist Palagummi Sainath, who studied the problem for decades, is one of many who argue the phenomenon is directly tied to the arrival of neoliberal "trade liberalization" in the 1990s. He states, "[E]very suicide has a multiplicity of causes . . . but when you have 300,000 . . .

in the same occupation within a compressed period of time, then you want to start looking for . . . the common factors."[124] He concluded, along with many others, that debt is the "central driving factor behind the suicides," noting that agricultural costs and interfering foreign subsidies had increased greatly following the implementation of neoliberal agricultural policies. General debate on the issue is wide, with a well-oiled PR machine that has worked to dismiss any assignment of blame to commercial, corporate, or government policy. It's widely speculated that the Indian government underreports the numbers and shifts contexts to downplay the reality, while large agriculture-related companies such as Monsanto have directly countered and denied any systemic links.[125] The truth is that while the defensive position portrays "trade liberalization" and the forced introduction of Western-patented seeds as having no correlation with the rise and persistence of debt-driven farmer suicide, a detailed analysis proves otherwise.

The spread of neoliberal globalization and Western transnational agribusiness to India began by way of World Bank/IMF "structural adjustment" policies in the late 1990s. A structural adjustment is a contractual condition for obtaining or restructuring a loan from these international institutions. In most cases, changes to national economic policies must be made. Privatization is one such contractual demand, forcing once-nationalized or public services into the hands of private corporations, often with dire consequences. Once again, at the core of neoliberal conception is the theory of self-regulation and total open-market competition. I say theory because that is all it is.

The truth is that "open markets" only give advantage to those with the most economic leverage, coupled with endless amounts of government collusion to ensure that leverage. Such is the inevitable paradox of the "free market," once again. So, to be clear, the neoliberal reality actually has little to do with free trade and everything to do with strategic advantage on the part of vested commercial interests that are far too often directly tied to the international lending and trade institutions. Deregulation, "trade liberalization," and privatization are political tools used to force open a country's economy, making it vulnerable to profit-seeking interests that otherwise wouldn't be able to interfere. Trade liberalization isn't talked about this way at international economic summits, of course, but that is exactly how things have unfolded for numerous developing nations around the world.

In the case of India, the World Bank's structural-adjustment policies required the country to open up its seed and overall agricultural sector to transnational corporations like Monsanto. One area of interest was cotton, for which Monsanto had developed a proprietary genetic type. These seeds, generally called "Bt cotton," cost substantially more than traditional seeds, also requiring supporting chemicals and monoculture regimens to work properly. These seeds also can't be reproduced, owing to genetic modification, forcing farmers to buy the custom products from Monsanto each season. Before the 1990s, seeds were naturally collected upon harvest and used the next year. The increased expense of this new regimen ultimately led to substantial borrowing, under the promise of increased crop yields, diminished pesticide use, and hence more profit.

At the same time, adherence to the new trade policies required the gradual removal or reduction of once-fortifying Indian government agricultural subsidies, leaving the cotton farmers to compete in the market with little support. Simultaneously, the United States and other nations were now free to export cotton to India and sell it much more cheaply than the Indian farmer ever could. The US in the early 2000s was subsidizing its cotton production by about $18 billion a year, thereby making it very cheap and competitive in the consumer market.[126] Given all this, Indian production was at a massive competitive disadvantage. In the words of Vandana Shiva:

> The WTO rules for trade in agriculture are, in essence, rules for dumping. They have allowed wealthy countries to increase agribusiness subsidies while preventing other countries from protecting their farmers from artificially cheap imported produce. Four hundred billion dollars in subsidies combined with the forced removal of import restriction is a ready-made recipe for farmer suicide. Global wheat prices have dropped from $216 a ton in 1995 to $133 a ton in 2001; cotton prices from $98.2 a ton in 1995 to $49.1 a ton in 2001; Soya bean prices from $273 a ton in 1995 to $178 a ton. This reduction is due not to a change

in productivity, but to an increase in subsidies and an increase in market monopolies controlled by a handful of agribusiness corporations.[127]

So, Indian farmers went into debt to buy the new patented products, which reduced their tolerance for crop failure, all while being forced to compete with cheaper, subsidized cotton imports. The structural violence machine accelerated to full speed: Foreign producers earned high profits, Monsanto collected vast seed royalties for its monopoly crop, and Indian cotton farmers spiraled into disarray. A study by Srijit Mishra, a professor at the Mumbai-based Indira Gandhi Institute of Development Research, found that in 2006, 86.5 percent of farmers who took their own lives were in debt and about 40 percent had suffered a crop failure.[128]

A 2014 analysis published in *Globalization and Health*, directly addressing the question of quantitative evidence for the suicides, concluded "that the liberalization of the agricultural sector in the early 1990s led to an agrarian crisis and that consequently farmers with certain socioeconomic characteristics—cash crops cultivators, with marginal landholdings, and debts—are at particular risk of committing suicide."[129] It found that "there is a significant and positive relationship between the percentage of marginal farmers and suicide rates, but only when we control for either or both cash crop production and indebted farmers."[130]

In other words, a small farmer growing cash crops, which include Bt cotton, coupled with being in severe debt, is highly correlated to suicide. The central focus here is psychological stress related to debt. Debt and the mechanisms that have preceded its creation by way of neoliberal globalization and "free trade" is killing people. Before global intervention in the 1990s, such debt levels did not exist, nor did the level of suicides.

DESTABILIZATION

Now to complete this chapter, I will address the second half of the two outcomes at the bottom of Figure 4a. These are *reduced social stability* and *increased behavioral violence*. While these outcomes can include issues such as human dispossession from a regional pollution crisis or refugees produced by war, the main focus here is behavioral violence. Most people who hear the term "violence" simply imagine interpersonal and intergroup conflict. But violence includes self-inflicted acts such as suicide, toxic socioeconomic conditions that cause mental and physical disease, or economic policies that ensure the perpetuation of genocidal outcomes in the Third World.

As touched upon in chapter one, our social nature guides us to great empathic concern for acts of direct violence such as person-to-person murder. Murder gets much more attention than more indirect mortality such as death from heart disease. It is certainly emotionally dramatic to witness a terrorist behead a victim on television, see photos of torture from the Abu Ghraib prison, or to be reminded of the genocidal horrors of World War II. Yet, while these visceral, certainly horrific and heart-breaking events may challenge our humanity and cause deep existential pain, from an objective public-health standpoint, they are statistically lower in priority as far as overall unnecessary human suffering and death are concerned. For example, heart disease, which is correlated to low socioeconomic status, is far more of a threat to general public health than behavioral violence. In this way, structural violence challenges our most common intuitions about what is or isn't inflicted harm.

However, as expressed by Dr. James Gilligan earlier, "[T]he most powerful predictor of the murder rate is the size of the gap in income and wealth between the rich and the poor. And the most powerful predictor of the rate of national or collective violence—war, civil insurrection, and terrorism—is the size of the gap between income and wealth between the rich and poor nations."[131] I reiterate this as it is critical to our conception of interpersonal and group violence. Taking a *structuralist* perspective of behavioral violence is to take a scientific or public-health perspective. No human being suddenly wakes up one day with extremely bigoted or racist views, nor does he or she choose to harm others without reason or by way of some kind of biopsychosocial distortion that pollutes the mind. While it is true that some people are born with strong propensities for sociopathology or psychopathology, statistically these predispositions do not come close to explaining the vast prevalence of behavioral violence across the world today.

As Gilligan points out, while behavioral violence pales in comparison to the deaths caused by structural violence, behavioral violence itself is also an *outcome* of structural violence. The through-line of inequality and deprivation manifests in shame, anger, and psychological distortion. It can occur in something of a novel way during one's life, or it can be an extension of culturally developed bias. There is no doubt cultures of violence have been created around the world, as notably seen with multi-generational terrorism and gang behavior, along with racism and bigotry. This is problematic from a causal perspective since it is easy to forget that causality for violent propensities can run deeper than a single generation.

Loss of opportunity, loss of social inclusion, loss of material support, loss of security and the life or cultural history of people enduring intersecting inequalities and deprivation, all link to personal and social destabilization. How these outcomes tie back to the competitive market structure is certainly more complex than the prior investigation of health disparities resulting from inequality, or loss of economic means. Yet they can be traced. When the smoke clears we find that the main cause of human conflict and the destabilization it creates links back to economically induced desperation, fear, and contempt. Just as we find that research on interpersonal violence links to poverty, low socioeconomic status, lack of education, and exclusion, we see that the same basic attributes apply to group behavior.

At the same time, the logic of the market economy, firmly rooted in competition and exploitation, creates justification for direct acts of state violence through war, along with imperially imposed global trade policies. Neoliberalism is the modern adaptation of state violence, in which Western power uses trade sanctions, embargoes, and austerity to ensure global compliance of nations that are not in line with its economic interests. This tendency is not to be confused with a flaw of "state power," as some in modern libertarian circles propose. Rather, this Mafia-like behavior is tied to the ethic of market competition at the root. "Free trade" agreements and the now global laissez faire obsession systemically create conditions ripe for group violence on many levels.

With that overview stated, this section will explore three dominant areas of group violence: hate crime/racism, terrorism/gang violence, and national war.

A hate crime is generally defined as a crime motivated by bias against a race, religion, disability, ethnic origin, or sexual orientation.[132] Unlike normal crime, which is usually about property or money directly, the perpetrator of a hate crime is motivated only by the desire to make the victim worse off. As for analysis, the first problem with measuring these events is the lack of reporting. Using the United States as an example, a 2013 study released by the Bureau of Justice Statistics found that only one in three hate crimes was generally ever reported to law enforcement.[133] Of those reported cases, for the period of 2007–2011 the average number of hate crimes was about 259,700 a year. It also found that about 92 percent of those crimes were of a violent nature. For the same period, 21 percent were reported as due to religious bias and 54 percent due to racial bias. Similar patterns are found around the world to varying degrees, with ideological and ethnic bias also dominant.

There is no doubt that the cultural factors involved in generating bigotry are complex. However, as with all human development, there are long-term and short-term causal influences. A common short-term influence is the direct impression made by parents and communities during a person's upbringing. It is commonly understood that religious and racial bias often forms during early development, influenced by parents and peers. While weak biological arguments for innate racial bias have floated around for years, a 2013 study in the *Journal of Cognitive Neuroscience* found that the part of the brain that is responsible for racial recognition, the amygdala, does not show a response until the age of fourteen.[134] It also found through neuroimaging scans that the amount of measured activity correlated to the amount of racial diversity experienced in the child's life history. The more racially diverse the peer group, the less strong the amygdala effect indicating racial sensitivity. This basically means the brain is "programmed" by the child's exposure. The authors state, "these findings suggest that neural biases to race are not innate and that race is a social construction, learned over time."[135]

Regarding long-term influence, it can be multigenerational or cultural, with bias spreading as something of a "thought gene," passed down and around over time. This has been touched upon previously with respect to America's white vs. black racism, largely attributed to early abject slavery. Again, the notion of racial bias against those of African origin has been well established as artificially cultivated, advertently and inadvertently, through economic interests simply seeking to save money on labor. Over time, as slavery and then Jim Crow segregation faded, the class battle for survival in the capitalist order kept the poor white and black cultures at odds, in the same way the rise of immigration and loss of jobs in the US has been accompanied by bigotry and xenophobia toward Mexicans and other subcultures migrating from the Global South.

A unique parallel to American racism is India's caste bigotry. In his work *Castes of Mind: Colonialism and the Making of Modern India*, Nicholas Dirks explains how the arrival of the British in India changed the nature of ancient caste relationships, morphing them during the colonial period into hierarchies for political and economic dominance.[136] The British politically incorporated the existing religious caste structure into a method of social organization and control, dividing ranks and structuring elitism. They basically added new meanings, connotations, and implications to the existing caste system to suit their own colonial needs, in a kind of "divide and rule" approach. Once colonial rule ended, the associations created remained in place, perpetuating caste bias and discrimination to this day. While this may seem vague from a socioeconomic perspective, remember that the purpose of the Indian colony was fundamental for economic exploitation. The "drain of wealth," as termed by Dadabhai Naoroji, helped make the British rich through robbing India and exploiting human labor.[137] This links the pursuit of profit and the primary logic of capitalism to such social manipulation and hence the chain reactions still plaguing the country. Today, about 165 million lower-caste people are routinely subject to discrimination, exploitation, and violence as a result.[138]

Now, as far as hate crime in general goes, social science researchers trying to find patterns usually seek out influences that may accelerate or diminish occurrences over time. Periodic economic downturns and poverty have been widely debated as related to the prevalence of hate crime in a given period. However, the problem is that unlike more readily measurable correlations such as the link between suicides and economic recession, hate crime behavior is far more sporadically distributed. Yet that doesn't disprove a socioeconomic correlation. The root of such behavior comes from a sense of threat. Perceived threat is a psychosocial phenomenon with great variance in how it manifests in an individual or culture. For example, as of the time of writing, waves of anti-Muslim hate crimes have been occurring in the US and Europe, noticeably spiking when a terror attack is blamed on Muslims by the media.[139] The perceived threat in this case is directly related to a fear of personal harm. The media presents the image of the minority subculture as a symbol of bombing, violence, and attack. Fearful people absorb the associations, and sometimes lash out vindictively—a neurotic reaction.

The average person with no prior bias does not simply hear about Islamic extremism and terrorism and then suddenly choose to participate in anti-Muslim hate crimes. People have to be groomed in some way to reach such a state of susceptibility. What sociologists have found is that while the issue is complex, xenophobic and minority fears ultimately link to fear of loss; specifically loss of a community's material and social resources. These resources include jobs, health services, welfare, and other assets that are directly or indirectly economic by nature. This is not to say underlying economic factors are a sole cause since there are many different forms of threat perceived, such as the protection of cultural identity. In sociologist Allen E. Liska's classic work *Social Threat and Social Control*, the idea of group threat in the context of *conflict theory* is explored. He highlights the need to expand considerations away from overly simplistic ideas such as mere group power plays. He states:

> Economic interests, ethnic antagonism, and cultural identity are the new terms in the current debate. The new discussion has set aside the simplistic initial formulation of a struggle between dominant and subordinate group interests in favor of an investigation of the implications of minority group's threat, fear of crime, social disorganization, and competition for sociopolitical dominance.[140]

"Fear of crime" is certainly a commonly discussed threat, often talked about in media and political circles with respect to immigration. There has been no shortage of politicians and pundits who blame legal or illegal immigrants for crime and other social problems. Yet, the real problem has nothing to do with minority culture and everything to do with unseen, underlying economic deprivation.

For example, it has been well established that the implementation of NAFTA in the mid-1990s has had highly negative consequences for rural Mexico. Similar to the case of subsidized Western agriculture that has damaged India through globalized "free trade," Mexican farming was deeply inhibited by dramatic price drops of staple exports due to competition with foreign corporations.[141] By 1998 rural poverty stood at 82 percent.[142] This poverty increased the drive for immigration to the North. In the 1990s the Mexican-born population in the US doubled from 4.5 million to 9 million.[143] This consequence in and of itself has been an atrocity, not to mention the profoundly destabilizing acceleration of gang warfare and drug-cartel violence that can also be linked to neoliberal economic adjustments.[144] And Mexico is not alone. According to USAID, "The lack of economic opportunities in Latin America . . . makes the region the number one source of illegal immigration into the United States, with 88 percent of illegal immigrants coming from these countries."[145]

Given this, returning to the subject of "fear of crime," out-group bias common to the United States and other countries where immigrants now effectively seek refuge, proper causality must go to the impoverished condition such people have come from. Since destitution and poverty have been long correlated to general crime, this is far from a surprise.[146] Sadly, the modern cliché, especially in the West, is that immigrants are a source of crime and this fear is perpetuated without an understanding of the deeper root cause.

Historically, this is all very old sociological behavior. Immigrants and minorities have always been used as scapegoats, even as they were being exploited and excluded. People often forget that in the early United States, vast ethnic antagonism was in play, beyond the dominant white vs. black issue. The Irish, Italians, Jews, Poles, and other immigrant groups experienced deeply bigoted, xenophobic reactions as they competed for socioeconomic resources and labor. When the Irish, for example, who had been viewed as "white Negros" in nineteenth-century Britain, came to the US, they were ostracized for their perceived cultural traits.[147] I can even remember my grandmother once bad-mouthing the Irish, revealing she was brought up in a culture of ethnic bias during her generation.

The point here is that while racism and bigotry have numerous cultural roots, the "meeting ground" has generally been socioeconomic competition. As noted by Stanford University historian George M. Fredrickson:

> The Nineteenth century was an age of emancipation, nationalism, and imperialism—all of which contributed to the growth and intensification of ideological racism in Europe and the United States. Although the emancipation of blacks from slavery and Jews from the ghettos received most of its support from religious or secular believers in an essential human equality, the consequence of these reforms was to intensify rather than diminish racism. Race relations became less paternalistic and more competitive. The insecurities of a burgeoning industrial capitalism created a need for scapegoats. The Darwinian emphasis on "the struggle for existence" and concern for "the survival of the fittest" was conducive to the development of a new and more credible scientific racism in an era that increasingly viewed race relations as an arena for conflict rather than as a stable hierarchy.[148]

A 2014 study by Ipsos Mori polled people in Britain who thought immigration should be reduced, asking them why. The top answer was that "Immigrants are taking jobs from British people—causing a job shortage."[149] In fact, the top five answers were based on economic fears, including concerns of "over-crowdedness," "resource drains," and "housing shortages." This factor of economic stress and the fear derived from it casts a shadow over society, with racism, bigotry, and hate crimes seeping out as a kind of negative externality resulting from a social order driven by scarcity and competition for income. While difficult to source at first glance, the economic relationships inherent in these psychological problems are ever apparent. This reality indicts capitalism distinctly since its structural attributes of competition and advantage have normalized inequality and class. Once again, as will be argued in the next chapter, none of this is necessary.

Moving on, this same undercurrent of historical and modern economic pressures and consequences are found at the root of terrorism.

Terrorism has become a defining characteristic of modern times, with growing media hype. From the Middle East to Europe, terrorism in the twenty-first century appears to have become a household awareness, sparsely but consistently peppered across the world each year. However, the popular idea that it is rooted in extreme religious thought alone or fueled by fringe ideologies is mostly a myth. This isn't to say aspects of extreme ideology are not present, but religious, national, and ideological hatreds that foment violence require more than mere words on a page. It requires insult, shame, pain, humiliation, and/or oppression. Terrorism involves an active need for retribution. This is not to absolve the problem of religion and violence, as all major theistic religions have written into their scriptures prescribed acts of revenge and bigotry to some degree or another. The issue is interpretation and motivation. People backed into a corner, feeling abused, will start to see things as a Rorschach blot, justifying ideas and acts that they otherwise would not support. Theistic religion has always been a handy tool for irrational justification of preconceived action.

In the aftermath of a 2015 attack in Paris that killed 130 people, blame quickly went to an Islamic extremist group operating mostly out of Iraq and Syria called Islamic State (IS). IS has emerged as something of an upgraded version of the notorious al-Qaeda, famously linked to the attacks of September 11, 2001. Unlike al-Qaeda, IS has (as of the time of this writing) succeeded in taking over fairly substantial amounts of territory in postwar Iraq and beyond. The suffering and death inflicted in their wake has been complemented by self-produced media documenting and glorifying their mass murders and beheadings. Unlike the crude media produced by prior groups, IS approaches these films with music, sound effects, professional editing, visual effects, and an overall Hollywood gesture. These aesthetic presentations have added to the emotional public outcry to see an end to the group, with now large sums of money being spent on military action and anti-terrorist surveillance in an attempt to collar the problem.

Yet, in the midst of the panic and outrage, little perspective is given as to where IS came from. While the group is deemed a *Salafist jihadist* group, believing in an ultra-orthodox Sunni Muslim interpretation and strict Sharia law, the basis of its views is not original. In fact, the dominant religion and political system of Saudi Arabia is also based on Salafist, Sunni views operating under Sharia law. Saudi Arabia is also a central ally and high-value commercial partner with the United States, while IS distinctly expresses its hatred of everything US and the West. So, if it is purely ideological, why such extremes? Why does the overwhelmingly vast majority of Muslims condemn such violence, disassociating from such groups?

With 1.8 billion Muslims in the world, those who do commit violent acts are very few by regional comparison. A University of Berkeley study found that when it came to the context of crime, "Muslim countries average 2.4 murders per annum per 100,000 people, compared to 7.5 in non-Muslim countries."[150] This was after controlling for authoritarianism and political regime, meaning state oppression was considered not a determinant factor. Yet it is still true that Muslims have been responsible for the majority of terrorist attacks in the world. According to political scientist M. Steven Fish, "Contemporary terrorism is disproportionately Islamist . . . [B]etween 1994 and 2008, the world suffered 204 high-casualty terrorist bombings. Islamists were responsible for 125, or 61 percent of these incidents, which accounted for 70 percent of all deaths."[151] On the surface, this contrast seems strange, compounded by the fact that this rise in Islamic terrorism is fairly new, with few occurrences by comparison decades ago.

The only real explanation is a social one. There is a social problem in play, arguably the result of long periods of interference coming from the Western world. A cursory examination of the Middle East regions most plagued by insurrection, violence, and terror systemically links to dramatic geopolitical and economic events. Again, this perspective is not to excuse acts of murder or violence but to show how such acts are cultivated. Just as an individual with certain natural vulnerabilities can be distorted by life experiences that eventually drive the development of psychological problems, generating destructive behavior, so too can whole subcultures that share a common identity be pushed into aberrant acts.

The story of Iraq is perhaps the clearest example. While its broad history is quite interesting, including the US-backed coup d'état in the 1960s that helped install dictator Saddam Hussein, destabilization of the region really began with the harsh economic sanctions imposed in the 1990s. Economic sanctions are financial and trade restrictions placed on a nation intended to force political or economic change. In effect, such sanctions are a form of coercive economic warfare. After Saddam Hussein invaded Kuwait in 1990, the United Nations, led by the US and the UK, effectively cut off all economic trade with Iraq for the next thirteen years. With the first Gulf War invasion in 1991 devastating Iraq's infrastructure, the toxic and restricted condition of the country fueled mass poverty, starvation, and disease. Just four years after the sanctions started, 576,000 children were reported as systemically killed through poverty.[152] Defended as a means to ensure Iraq couldn't gather resources to build weapons of mass destruction (WMDs), the sanctions by 1999 are argued to have killed up to 1.5 million people.[153] Denis Halliday, who spent 34 years with the UN, resigned in disgust over the issue, referring to the situation as genocide. In 1999, he stated publicly:

> [There are] 4,000 to 5,000 children dying unnecessarily every month due to the impact of sanctions because of the breakdown of water and sanitation, inadequate diet and the bad internal health situation . . . It doesn't impact . . . governance effectively and instead it damages the innocent people of the country . . . It has also produced a new level of crime [and] street children . . . [There] is a town where people used to leave the key in the front door, leave their cars unlocked, where crime was almost unknown. We have, through the sanctions, really disrupted . . . quality of life, the standard of behavior that was common in Iraq before.[154]

Halliday has also spoken of cultural changes, with great foresight of the future. He talked about the growing sense of exclusion, desperation, and consequential rise of more-extreme religious views. He discussed how mosque attendance soared as sanctions continued, with Iraqis seeking solace in religion. This was a change from the more moderate nature of the nation prior. He then prophetically predicted in 1999: "What should be of concern is the possibility at least of more fundamentalist Islamic thinking . . . It is not well understood as a possible spin-off of the sanctions regime. We are pushing people to take extreme positions."[155]

By 2012, some estimates put the cumulative death toll since 1990 at 3.3 million.[156] The 2003 Iraq invasion, justification of which has been categorically proven as a fraud with respect to claims of present WMDs, served to shatter what little integrity Iraq had left.[157] Securing control over Iraqi oil has been corroborated by numerous insiders as the real motivation for war, with associated profits in the hundreds of billions for Western corporations.[158] At the same time, while the party line was that postwar Iraq would be able to "rebuild" with great vigor given its energy-resource wealth, reconstruction has been dismal.[159] Iraqi employment and public health now rank at the bottom among Third World nations.[160] As far as postwar violence is concerned, the UN reported that between January 2014 and October 2015 about 19,000 people were killed in sectarian violence.[161] This also includes more than 3 million people displaced during the same period, adding to what has become a global refugee crisis, amounting to roughly 60 million displaced people due to violent social destabilization as of 2015.[162]

Now, I pose the question: If you were a young child surviving in Iraq during the 1990s sanctions, growing up through both US-led wars, now enduring a profoundly devastated, destabilized, and destitute situation, would you be angry at the forces that caused your society's collapse? Do you think others might be angry as well, willing to twist their frustration and deprivation into violence? Would it not seem fairly reasonable that views of the West would become synonymous with suffering and oppression, slowly molding a culture of anti-American sentiment, passing these values onto children as they grow up?

The truth is, modern Islamist extremism, specifically the rise of IS, has been cultivated by Western geo-economic politics and undeniable US imperialism over the past few decades. The Middle East has been a target, along with Africa and Latin America before that. It is a kind of neo-post-colonialism, if you will, where the long-term side effect of intervention and its resulting suffering has been anger and blowback. Former CIA official and Middle East expert Graham Fuller stated that the US "is one of the key creators" of IS, explaining how its intervention has fostered the violence.[163] From Libya to Syria to Afghanistan to Iraq and other interventions in the twenty-first century, the destabilizing effects are consistent. In fact, before the 2011 US-backed NATO overthrow of Libya's government, many strides were being taken to improve and evolve the society in a more progressive, more democratic way. Libya actually had the highest standard of living in Africa, with a steady trend of public-health improvement.[164] Though far from perfect, it was changing notably. Today, like Iraq, Libya is now fractured, impoverished, and replete with violence—including the presence of IS.[165]

So, terrorism and the rise of violent extremism in the world did not come out of nowhere, nor is it merely a result of religious or ideological fervor. It has been actively bred by a destabilizing process of intervention, economic exploitation, and marginalization. And the more it goes on the worse it seems to become. Noam Chomsky, a famous social theorist and critic, stated, "You can be pretty confident that as conflicts develop, they will become more extremist. The most brutal, harshest groups will take over. That's what happens when violence becomes the means of interaction . . . That's true in neighborhoods; it's true in international affairs . . . That's where [IS] comes from. If [Western allies] manage to destroy [IS], they will have something more extreme on their hands."[166]

This brings us to gang violence (terrorism's cousin). The same underlying precondition of social destabilization extends to this epidemic, as recognized in inner cities and through drug cartels. While cultures of outlaws have indeed been created over time, even taking on a life and "style" of their own, the origins of gangs inevitably root back to socioeconomic insecurity.

For example, the Italian Mafia actually originated as a means of local protection against outside forces in Sicily in the nineteenth century. The term "mafioso," or Mafia member, initially had no criminal connotations and was used to refer to a person who was suspicious of authority. It then evolved into private armies, or "mafie," morphing into the criminal organizations famous today.[167] Likewise, the Los Angeles–rooted Crips and Bloods, two notorious street gangs that have been in a feud for decades, started in South Central Los Angeles in the late 1960s. At that time, given high unemployment and concentrated urban poverty, local crime and police brutality flourished. The Crips were started by two high school students who felt the need for protection to defend against the destabilized circumstances in their neighborhood. They based their idea on the

Black Panthers Movement. Crip stands for "Community Resources for Independent People."[168] Yet, over time, they corrupted, and themselves became a threat as street war evolved. As with the Mafia, illegal trade for money, such as drug dealing, became common. In this chain reaction, the Bloods emerged then to protect themselves from the Crips, sparking the ongoing war still happening today.

All across the world we see variations on the same theme, often centered on prohibitive economies, incorporating great violent force. These gangs are universally born from a lack of economic opportunity, fear, and overall deprivation. A detailed four-year study measuring the relationship between socioeconomic factors and gang violence in Los Angeles unsurprisingly concluded, "At the community level, gang-related homicide in Los Angeles is most closely associated with lower income and unemployment."[169] It is also interesting to note that, in a time of great pressure to reduce gun violence in the United States, half of all violent crime in America actually originates from the 33,000 existing gangs, according to the FBI as of 2011.[170] Yet, with all the political debate over gun control, no one is talking about poverty control. Guns are not killing people in the gangland world—the precondition of poverty, lack of opportunity, and inequality is. Guns are just hastening the process.

The same causal roots apply to the infamous drug cartels and street gangs of Mexico and Colombia. In Colombia there are between 4 million and 5 million internally displaced people.[171] Many of these people have been forcibly removed from their land to make way for commercial industry by way of neoliberal globalization. In a detailed work by Jasmin Hristov titled *Blood & Capital: The Paramilitarization of Colombia*, the connection between corporate-backed neoliberalism and state violence is firmly established. In the 1990s, sweeping pro-US economic policies were put in place, largely in response to prior international debt pressures. Hristov states, "[The] main cause that led to the official adoption of neoliberal policies by the developing countries in Latin America and elsewhere was the pressure to service their external debts in the late 1970s. In order to receive loans from the World Bank (WB) or the International Monetary Fund (IMF), nations had to agree to a program of structural adjustment that included drastically reducing public spending in health, education, and welfare."[172] These structural adjustments also included "trade liberalization," the trademark of neoliberalism, opening borders to foreign interests.

Long story short, Colombia opened its doors to transnational corporations, kicked millions of people off of commercially useful land, and began "economic development." Only this development produced profit only for a small Colombian and Western elite; any objection from the public was met with violent oppression by paramilitary forces, largely sanctioned by the government.[173] As with much of Latin America over the past century, highly dictatorial regimes with horrendous human rights violations have been backed by US interests to ensure neoliberal adherence and transnational corporate profit. Overthrows and assassinations have never been out of the question.

The now declassified information about the 1954 coup d'état against democratically elected Guatemalan President Jacobo Árbenz is a classic example.[174] After Árbenz was elected, creating reforms to help the public by returning land dominated by the United Fruit Company of America, United Fruit lobbied the US government to intervene. The CIA then overthrew Árbenz and installed a violent military dictator, Carlos Castillo Armas. Armas was the first of a long line of US-backed dictators who favored Western neoliberalism at the expense of the public's well-being.[175]

Colombia was yet another nation in this process of coerced market expansion ravaging the general population through neoliberalism's structural violence. While Colombia has historically been a turbulent and politically corrupt place, the country's embrace of "free market" policies dramatically worsened conditions. It increased the already high level of economic stress, giving rise to powerful gangs and militias that today move mountains of illicit drugs around the world. Colombia's drug cartels and related street gangs have become world-famous for their horror and dominance. Despite billions of dollars in military aid given to the government to fight the cartels and insurgencies, little progress has been made. In fact, many have speculated that the aid sent to Colombia, while partly used to fight the cartels, is also being used to support paramilitary operations that further oppress the general public and those opposed to the government trade policies that are impoverishing them.[176]

As far as Mexico is concerned, its modern destabilization and gang violence is yet another thematic variation. The 1994 NAFTA implementation set in motion a deteriorating economic condition for the general public, specifically affecting the agricultural sector. In summary, structural adjustments placed on loans to Mexico by the IMF restricted its ability to subsidize agriculture production.[177] Given the "free trade" reality of NAFTA, this effectively meant Mexico could not compete with other producers that actually were subsidizing their agricultural production, such as the US and Canada. This inability to compete ruined millions of Mexican farmers, specifically corn producers. Losses in Mexico's agricultural sectors are estimated at over a billion dollars annually since the start of NAFTA.[178]

As noted prior, this led to an exodus from farm regions to inner cities and eventually outside the country to find work. While jobs were created in some cities, touted by some as a mark of NAFTA's success, the surplus of labor was enormous. Wages were also extremely low, while some factories started to move overseas, compounding local poverty and unemployment.[179] For many, the question then was whether to leave Mexico to find work, as millions have, or to work in black-market economies such as the drug trade. NAFTA unintentionally made moving drugs across the border to the US much easier. As summarized in a detailed study, *A Narco History*:

> [US] agribusiness pushed thousands of Mexican farmers out of their own markets. The price of corn dropped by around 50 percent after the NAFTA agreement, and the number of farmers living in poverty rose by a third. In the six years following the introduction of NAFTA, two million farmers abandoned their land ... The army of the urban unemployed gave the cartels a deep pool from which to recruit foot soldiers, and the miserably paid (and eminently corruptible) police and military provided the muscle with which to protect their interests. The spread of everyday crime—aided by the rapid declension and corruption of local police forces—demoralized civil society, and provided a climate within which grander forms of criminality would flourish. The adoption of free trade and the deeper

integration of the Mexican economy with that of the United States dramatically increased cross-border traffic, making it far easier to insert narcotics into the stream of northward-bound commodities.[180]

The result has been horrific gang violence and bloodshed. Some 85,000 people are estimated to have died from drug-gang violence since 2006, with cartels dominating many cities.[181] In effect, we see the chain reaction of structural violence unfold through the gateway of poverty, scarcity, and lost opportunity, exacerbated by neoliberal economics once again. To make matters worse, the degree of degradation is so severe, the social distortion so deep, that commonsense economic alleviations to reduce poverty will likely now have very little effect. This is the problem once cultures of corruption have been created.

As a secondary issue related to this subsection, as it pertains to the broad context of terrorism and gang violence, the modern era has also seen a marked increase in seemingly random mass shootings in public settings. As the media tends to slap labels on such events as being acts of "domestic terrorism" and so on, the nuanced nature of this specific phenomenon goes largely unaddressed in sociological terms. From the Columbine High School massacre in 1999 to the Virginia Tech mass shooting in 2007 to the Pulse nightclub massacre in Florida in 2016, the frequency of such explosive rage has been steadily increasing. While the obvious mixture of mental illness and a need for revenge are apparent in all cases, along with the unique prevalence of most mass shootings of this nature occurring the United States (noncoincidentally the global center of extreme socioeconomic inequality), each case study of this seemingly random violence shares a common thread. That thread is a psychological need by those perpetrating such acts to feel like they are winning and in control and that people are paying attention to them. In virtually all such cases, the perpetrator(s) seek to express their power and contempt, often making videos explaining their acts in advance, writing detailed manifestos online, calling media and police to make sure everyone knows who they are, and so on. The underlying sense of such perpetrators is generally of having endured great shame, hurt, humiliation, and helplessness, even if they cloak those sensitive feelings in outward rage and hate. More often than not, the violent act is a precursor to their suicide, connecting the interest to die with the need to hurt others and perhaps become famous. While taking a structuralist view of this complex phenomenon is difficult, Italian theorist Franco Berardi has attempted to find some order in the chaos. In his work, *Heroes: Mass Murder and Suicide*, he provides valuable speculation correlating what it means to live in our competitive, neoliberal society—a society that structurally produces winners and losers, along with shame and humiliation for those who see themselves as the latter.[182]

He states:

> [S]uicide has increased particularly rapidly in the last 45 years— by 60 percent according to the World Health Organization. It is epidemic . . . And what else has happened in last 40 years? Neoliberal transformation . . . We are seeing an all-time high in the need to compete economically, and a general low in sensibility and human relations . . . The frequency of psychopathology is [also] on the rise.
>
> What is the core of neoliberal ideology? Firstly, that you are alone, that you are an individual competing with everybody else. Secondly, that the real distinction among human beings is between winners and losers . . . There's no more stable class identity, no more stable political identity—the real divide is between neoliberalism's winners and losers. And if you are a young person who has grown up in this capitalist environment, and you understand that actually you can never be a winner, what will you do?
>
> In some cases, you decide that you are going to be a winner for a second, for an hour, for a moment. Because you feel like a winner when you kill all the people around you and then kill yourself. And this is not just my theory; it's not me saying all these horrible things. It's Eric Harris and Dylan Klebold, the two young men who committed mass murder and killed themselves at Columbine High in 1999. They wrote in their diaries, which are available to read for anyone: "You gave me all this shit, telling me I am a loser, but I will be a winner for a minute." And so

you see, it's not so much the neoliberal ideology [that motivates mass murderers]; it's much more the particular psychological effects of this neoliberal ideology.[183]

"FREEDOM AND DEMOCRACY"

Now we finally come to the largest of all conflict types—*national war* itself. While terrorism and gang behavior are largely rooted in socio-economic destabilization, often metastasizing cancerous subcultures of violence, bigotry, and hate over generations, national war is more of an advanced stage of brute economic competition. The fundamental difference is that national war has become fully institutionalized, with a general public sanction of systematic, industrial-scale violence. Historians peg the origins of standing armies in protection of statehood as emerging some 6,000 years ago, developing ever more deadly weapons through the Bronze and Iron Ages, arriving at the advanced modern condition of today's massively destructive nuclear and nano-tech weapons.

As touched upon in chapter two, the rationale for armies links back to the post-Neolithic period. Early settlements had different geographical advantages, such as being near a fresh water source or having more fertile land. This led cultures lacking such advantages to invade those that had them. Hence, regional armies served to both protect and conquer. During the vast stretch of time within the Malthusian Trap period, state warfare and literally thousands of national wars have shifted territorial boarders on the world map like a kaleidoscope. Within this disorder empires periodically emerge, formed on the basis of military dominance and expansionism. Imperialism, by way of territorial dominance and control over the political and economic life of a region, has become the central role of military might in the world today.

As a kid, I was taught in school that war was mostly a last resort when two or more nations simply couldn't get along. I was also taught that the United States is the "Good Samaritan" empire and it takes it upon itself to rid the world of ruthless dictators, seeking to help the poor and oppressed. If only this were really true. Rather, empires are like socio-geographic diseases, born of the dominant social psychology of the root socioeconomic orientation of the social system. Empires, like corporate monopoly, are inevitable when economic competition flourishes unabated. But government can break up a corporate monopoly, if it chooses to. Empires spread their dominance like malignant tumors over the planet and the only means to combat them is by defensive war, as we saw in the two world wars, or by a grand shift in economic policy, undermining the sociological tendency that grows from the market structure to begin with.

Now, as mentioned previously, all wars are indeed class wars when root motivations are observed. Virtually all can be linked to the acquisition of resources and economically related factors. The United States, a country that proclaims its mission to assist "global peace," happens also to be the largest exporter of arms, to the tune of billions of dollars.[184] With an annual global military expenditure at almost $1.8 trillion as of 2014, it is clear the general business of killing people and destroying corners of civilization is huge.[185] Of course, this business is also about power and control—but power and control don't exist without economic dominance first.

Since the official fall of Soviet communism and the USSR, Western pro-market forces have pushed neoliberalism as hard as possible not only to increase transnational market share and assist capital accumulation, but also to "mark" the world in the same way a dog marks a tree. Any country that isn't hip to the demanded "freedom and democracy" of markets is often met with some nasty pushback. It generally starts with economic sanctions and ends with military invasions. Perhaps one of the most direct forms of structural violence, national war—the decision to enter a region for purely economic reasons, routinely killing thousands of civilians along the way—reveals just how primitive our geopolitical condition really is.

Maj. Gen. Smedley D. Butler, often regarded as the most famous decorated US army officer of the early twentieth century, wrote a book after World War I aptly called *War Is a Racket*. Upon retirement in the 1930s, he gave speeches around the country to spread his message—a message that sheds light upon the hidden internal dialogue underlying US military history. In 1935, Butler boldly stated:

I spent 33 years and four months in active military service and during that period I spent most of my time as a high class muscle man for Big Business, for Wall Street and the bankers. In short, I was a racketeer, a gangster for capitalism. I helped make Mexico and especially Tampico safe for American oil interests in 1914. I helped make Haiti and Cuba a decent place for the National City Bank boys to collect revenues in. I helped in the raping of half a dozen Central American republics for the benefit of Wall Street. I helped purify Nicaragua for the International Banking House of Brown Brothers in 1902–1912. I brought light to the Dominican Republic for the American sugar interests in 1916. I helped make Honduras right for the American fruit companies in 1903. In China in 1927 I helped see to it that Standard Oil went on its way unmolested. Looking back on it, I might have given Al Capone a few hints. The best he could do was to operate his racket in three districts. I operated on three continents.[186]

As a final note, the terms "freedom and democracy" actually have a double meaning today. We often hear these words when government is defending its decision to invade or sanction some country. In my lifetime, I cannot think of a Western-driven war that didn't at some point have politicians talking about bringing "freedom and democracy" to its target. In fact, most economic sanctions and embargoes being imposed in the world today by the United Nations also include "lack of democracy" or "violations of human rights" as a reason. While there is some truth to this gesture in certain cases, a deeper examination reveals a unique sublety to the language.

In 1962, economist Milton Friedman wrote a classic text called *Capitalism and Freedom*. Arguing for the association of democracy and liberty with markets, he stated, "Underlying most arguments against the free market is a lack of belief in freedom itself."[187] This declaration embraces the seed of the neoliberal, "free market" ethic. This ethic sits at the root of dominant sociopolitical theory. It effectively links antidemocratic processes and oppression to anything that isn't "free market." This is not to defend any existing system of state control that may or may not be totalitarian. This is simply to show how the philosophy of free markets has usurped the most foundational social ideal of what true freedom and democracy could be, limiting perception.

Today, the co-opted term "freedom" has nothing to do with one's right to well-being, justice, opportunity, expression, or ability to choose how one is to focus his or her life in the pursuit of happiness. Rather, freedom now refers only to the freedom of trade—the freedom of the movement of money and deregulation of business. It is about economic freedom, but not economic freedom in the sense of sovereign nations' being able to choose how they wish to govern, with democratic sanction of their populace. Rather it is about the freedom of the most dominant and powerful businesses to enter, abuse, pillage, and exploit as they see fit. It is *their* economic freedom, not anyone else's. In the words of Noam Chomsky:

> Neoliberalism operates not only as an economic system but as a political and cultural system as well . . . [B]ecause profit-making is [considered] the essence of democracy, any government that pursues anti-market policies is being antidemocratic, no matter how much informed popular support they might enjoy . . . [E]quipped with this particular understanding of democracy, neoliberals like [Milton] Friedman had no qualms about the military overthrow of Chile's democratically elected Allende government in 1979, because Allende was interfering with business control of Chilean society.

He then adds, regarding the nature of political democracy in neoliberal cultures, "That is neoliberal democracy in a nutshell: trivial debate over minor issues by parties that basically pursue the same pro-business policies regardless of formal differences and campaign debate. Democracy is permissible as long as the control of business is off-limits to popular deliberation or change; that is as long as it *isn't* democracy."[188]

It is time the world began to understand and see beyond the mythology of "free markets," realizing that no matter how idealized theoretical assumptions may be, the structural bigotry and systemic oppression will forever harm the lower-class majority. Please note that I do not see the rise of modern capitalism and neoliberalism as some evil that could have been prevented. Rather, we are dealing with a natural progression of social evolution and at a certain point in time market capitalism was indeed the best method we had. Yet, as can occur with any socially perpetuated phenomenon, we are now stuck in a feedback loop that perversely restricts our ability to take the next evolutionary step as an intelligent species. It is in this stage, a stage philosopher John McMurtry calls "the cancer stage of capitalism," that a great deal of energy is now needed to deliberately shift the course of civilization. What defines this course and how it may come about will be explored in the next and final chapter.

....

Chapter Five

DESIGNING OUT: WHERE
WE GO FROM HERE

*We must rapidly begin the shift from a thing-oriented society
to a person-oriented society. When machines and computers,
profit motives and property rights are considered more important than people, the giant triplets of racism, extreme materialism and militarism are incapable of being conquered.[1]*

—DR. MARTIN LUTHER KING JR.

THE PREVIOUS FOUR CHAPTERS have covered a range of diverse issues,
linked by a train of thought. This train of thought carves out a model
by which we can better understand society, resolve major problems, and
set a course for more productive social progress. As stated, the dominant
view here is *structuralist*, defined in this context as respecting the influence of larger-order system dynamics and realizing the disproportionate
power of these influences over our lives. Given this perspective, general
patterns of violence, mortality, disease, crime, oppression, and other
seemingly separate outcomes are found to share common roots, linked to
our social system. Just as a clean water supply is foundational to a city to
prevent poor health and other social problems, an appropriately designed
social system is the starting point of healthy social psychology, peaceful
cohabitation, positive public health, and an all-around quality of life.

Putting aside the market's perpetuation of socioeconomic inequality and inhumane patterns of hierarchical dominance, we can see that
the general loss of improved technical efficiency and overall productive

inferiority is a serious problem. Apologists for capitalism often declare that it is superior to all known systems in terms of productivity. But this is a shallow conclusion since there hasn't been any kind of real departure from market-based organization in thousands of years. System variations such as historical communism, socialism, and fascism have varied more politically and ideologically than economically. The shared mechanisms of competition, cost efficiency, exploitation, trade, and overall monetary practice show little real variance across modern history, regardless of nuances or theoretical ideals.

The main problem with the capitalism-works-best defense is that it ignores modern economic potentials that far exceed what the market is capable of. Since technological progress is at the root of increasing standards of living, along with consequential alleviations of social tension, the question becomes: What specific economic approaches can optimize technological progress? For example, today the world produces 17 percent more calories per person than it did thirty years ago, despite an increase in population of 70 percent. We can produce enough food to provide everyone with at least 2,720 kilocalories (kcal) per day. This is more than enough to maintain good health for most.[2] Yet a substantial portion of the world is still malnourished, dying of starvation. This simple fact shows that there are flaws in the economic pipeline that are producing distribution inefficiencies and exceptional waste.[3]

When the current state of productive capacity and efficiency is examined overall, we discover underutilized and potential methods that are far superior to what is being applied. As will be described, society currently uses only a fraction of known technical means that can increase efficiency greatly. This lack of application is caused by general ignorance of such potentials and by core problems inherent to the market's mechanistic structure, as well as the stagnating tendency of business to fight change. As discussed in chapter four, business does not favor optimized technical efficiency. It favors market efficiency, which is basically the opposite. Companies also seek self-preservation to remain profitable in the short-term, naturally pushing back interfering change. Capitalism's competitive incentive, promoted as the virtuous force behind world progress, has now become the greatest detriment to social advancement. If we cannot update and redesign our society to embrace its modern technical capacity to increase economic efficiency, including equitable distribution, the major problems we see today will find little resolution, including the growth of xenophobia and in-group/out-group bigotry.

The goals of this final chapter are to highlight how human-perpetuated scarcity and inequality are now the central drivers of human disorder; how current negative trends are on pace to severely destabilize society in ways never before possible; and finally, to explore potential solutions that can overcome these problems, improving public health and social stability. However, before those aspects are addressed, let's quickly summarize the prior chapters for clarity.

Chapter one introduced the systems-based, structuralist perspective that underscores this entire book. As expressed, this kind of thinking goes against our most basic perceptual intuition. It is also at odds with the way society is currently oriented; after all, that orientation has been largely built upon the same faulty intuition that fails to see society and culture in a systemic or interconnected way. It took the advancement of physical and social science for us to start recognizing facts our intuition previously failed to reveal. Just as weather balloons and satellite imagery have confirmed that hurricanes emerge from atmospheric collisions of differential weather systems, statistical analysis and longitudinal studies have revealed the origins of outcomes related to public health and human behavior. This chapter featured a case study focused on systemic racism and the evolution of America's bigoted criminal justice system. When historical events are considered in combination with modern oppressed conditions, we can begin to understand how institutional and interpersonal racism have been created and perpetuated as a systemic consequence related to socioeconomic phenomena.

In other words, drivers of racism, xenophobia, and similar forms of human bigotry very often link to economic circumstances on one level or another, as argued. Yet, there are naturally exceptions, for certain issues are indeed more cultural in origin. Gender bigotry and LGBT discrimination are examples. These two important issues have not been focused on in this work as their roots are less driven by socioeconomic dynamics. In the case of LGBT bigotry, there appear to be normative cultural identity problems that inspire fear of people with non-normative lifestyle practices. Yet there is still an economically linked tendency to exacerbate such "out-group" fear and condemnation when economic stress arises.[4] Gender discrimination is also cultural, deeply rooted in civilization's long, mostly patriarchal history. However, economic motivations accentuate this problem as well. While one may argue that the modern wage gap between men and women is a consequence of cultural disrespect of women, we can't forget that underpayment is a basic feature of labor exploitation, hence driven by economic motivations rather than just sexist ones.[5]

The link between economic deprivation and female vulnerability to abuse should also be highlighted. Prostitution, sexual violence, and the trafficking of women is still epidemic in the world today. This outcome of our social system's manifest inequality, commodification, and basis in exploitation arguably reinforces male-perpetuated sexism, chauvinism, and the general abuse of women. There is no argument regarding the link between economic deprivation and female sexual exploitation. From the bikini model plastered on a billboard, to the far less culturally respected stripper who undresses on stage, to those actresses who engage in pornography, to prostitutes walking the streets late at night, we cannot understand these patterns of behavior without accounting for the need for income. If there is any remaining gravitation of society to remain patriarchal, perpetuating female exploitation and subservience to males, the existing condition of socioeconomic inequality and deprivation reinforces that gravitation. From the standpoint of the lowest, most immoral sexist mentality, keeping women poor and financially desperate is a strategic means to ensure the future exploitation and abuse of them on various levels. Over generational time, this pattern furthers a culture of violence against woman in general, creating distortions in both male and female perceptions.

That being said, it is important to reiterate the fact that historical events can snowball, generating cultural patterns, values, and customs that take on a life of their own long after their apparent point of origin. The reason systemic black oppression and race antagonism continues to this day in America is partly that the engine that created it and pushed it forward is still in place. As an analogy, imagine a train that symbolizes American racism, built in the period of abject slavery and set in motion down a track. The fuel that keeps that train moving forward is socioeconomic inequality. The train may have traveled far away from its origins, but the mechanisms that keep it going remain. This is just as true for American social relations as it is for other countries with similar histories.

Chapter two focused on both the history of our social system and the legitimizing myths that perpetuate it. Like white blood cells seeking and destroying foreign invaders, the social system reacts to impositions that conflict with its normative functions. However, the reactionary cells in this case are beliefs, people, and institutions that form a kind of *cultural hegemony*. Deep identity associations have also been generated, helping to create an Orwellian cognitive dissonance or doublethink. These associative mechanisms are reinforced by humanity's long history of social dominance, wherein the custom of competition and human abuse has become codified as not only a natural phenomenon but also a virtuous one. The dominant ethic today isn't about coexistence and mutual concern. It is about "winning" and disproportionate "success." This ethic is driven by the post-Neolithic evolution of what we now innocuously call business.

Commercial enterprise, the center of human affairs today, has built-in, self-preserving mechanisms that repress any urge to alter its expression. One mechanism is the mere conception of success in the market game, which is rewarded by not only material wealth and social status but also societal power. Those statistically rare few who do rise through the ranks of privilege and economic class are naturally the least likely to find motivation for social change. It is in their most basic self-interest to keep things the same given how well they have been rewarded. Also, since the wealthy own society's major organs of communication—television networks, newspapers, production companies, and other influential media—they intentionally or unintentionally filter out social perspectives that contradict those they favor. This is only natural, based upon operant conditioning principles. All this assists an already expansive social mythology associating only positive outcomes with the market economy, since the general population has been groomed to covet the success of the wealthy. Such ambition is mostly wasted, of course, since the model structurally limits high levels of wealth and power to a very small few, effectively ensuring class war.

Chapter three further expanded on this class-war reality, homing in on the structurally generated inevitability of poverty, oppression, and deprivation. The system is certainly rigged; however, it is rigged in ways that are less about direct conspiracy or malicious intent and more about the procedural dynamics of the model itself. From the dawn of agriculture, our economic structure evolved with a *root socioeconomic orientation* based upon competition, exploitation, and scarcity. The social system that results is foundationally elitist and oppressive, ensuring those with the most wealth and power will maintain the most wealth and power. When we realize that elitism and oppression are structural, we reduce the age-old confusion that pins the world's woes on a lack of morality and ethics. While morality and ethics are important for orienting cultural values, they can't compete with the prevailing social psychology and mechanistic (primary) logic that manifests from the economic requirements of survival. Unless the moral conclusion is literally to change this dominating structure, morality has little effect in the long run. Moreover, though it may seem an overgeneralization, class war lies beneath most forms of oppression, discrimination, and bigotry. Whether historically rooted or birthed in modern times, the battle for economic resources and human labor exploitation sit at the root of our divided world and continue to do so *unnecessarily*, as will be discussed.

Chapter three also described some aspects of the market system's maturation over the last century. These are worth consolidating here because, just as an apple rots till only the core is left, the essence of the market system is rapidly surfacing, and with great discord. This core consists of massive, flawed incentives and problematic economic contradictions that were not apparent in the market's earlier stages. Six of these in total have been expressed in Figure 5a. With the exception of technological unemployment, which will be discussed later in this chapter, the other five have already been touched upon. For the sake of clarity, I will reiterate these as they are important to understand as a group trend.

From top to bottom, first is the rise of what we now call capitalism itself, specifically how the presence of social dominance has become obscured by "free trade." All major historical economic systems since the Neolithic Revolution have been market-based in the sense that the

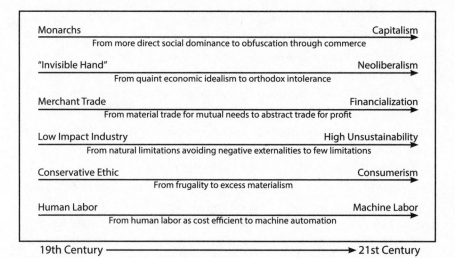

FIGURE 5A. Conceptual trend depiction of six notable issues that have evolved since the Industrial Revolution. Each of these developments are natural to the market ecomony, consequential as social and technological conditions have changed.

root socioeconomic orientation of competition, exploitation, and scarcity has been dominant. The molding of modern-day capitalism over time was inevitable as more complex labor roles and technology unfolded. In this, the once-obvious social inequities and undemocratic power imbalance of early societies slowly became cloaked by the idealism of the "free market." Unlike in earlier eras, which featured intolerant government monarchs, abject slavery, and other more primitive forms of dictatorial power and direct oppression, this new structure provided the needed illusion of democratic participation, rights, and freedom by structurally submerging social dominance within the mass competitive act of "free trade." The beauty of this means of social dominance is that it facilitates the pretense that totalitarianism doesn't exist. Kings and regimes no longer wield total control over the lives of their subjects. Rather, power and wealth remain concentrated by way of a process of competitive advantage in the market—a process that is provably undemocratic and structurally rigged to favor a small, undefined, transient minority in the same basic manner (yet obscured) by which a monarch exerted control.

In effect, the ethic of trade and markets has become synonymous with democracy and freedom. Any talk today of government directly assisting a population in an organized, streamlined capacity—efficiently using resources in a way only larger-order design and organization can achieve—is derailed derisively as "socialist" interference with "market freedom." This process of maturation of capitalism has sanctified or normalized the idea that some should be very rich and powerful and most should be very poor and impotent. This ethos is preserved by the mythology that any other way can only be "anti-freedom."

The second form of maturation worth reiterating, as noted in Figure 5a, is the rise and spread of *neoliberalism*, specifically through *globalization*. In effect, this is the expression of the market economy's fully realized belief structure. The once-passive, quaint, and generally ignored "invisible hand" comment by Adam Smith has grown into full-blown orthodox religious extremism. Neoliberal globalization includes not only the ethic that "free trade" and business power should prevail over democratic institutions and state policy, it also embraces capitalism's tendency toward constant hegemonic expansion.

Capital accumulation, which is a fancy term for the business interest in reinvesting profit in new capital assets that will in turn further increase profits, rests at the heart of globalization. Like cancer, businesses always seek to expand and multiply. Transnational corporations forge extensive international trade contracts such as the North American Free Trade Agreement (NAFTA) or the more recent Trans-Pacific Partnership (TPP) not with an interest in respecting public choice or improving global health, but to further their trade interests and exploit labor for corporate profit. Such agreements increase government and public-policy subservience to corporate interests on the international level. This process is transforming and conforming the world to one governed only by business logic and competitive gaming.

I will add that as is characteristic of most religious extremism, intolerance of nonbelievers is acute. Any contrary economic belief system on the planet today has been effectively condemned as sacrilegious, the behavior of socioeconomic savages. Countries that attempt to praise a different economic god are quickly struck down in the holy name of "freedom" and "democracy." Of course, the only real freedom apparent is the freedom of moneyed interests to do as they please, seeking constant capital accumulation across the world, leaving no stone unturned. Neoliberal globalization is the evolving process of homogenizing the world into one economic belief system.

The third form of maturation to reiterate is the rise of financialization. In earlier times, the practice of labor specialization and trade was minimalistic in that people mostly sought to satisfy their most basic needs. For example, a man milks a cow and sells that milk to buy some bread. The man who sold the bread then uses that money to buy a needed tool, etc. If we lived during the Malthusian Trap, this behavior would be indispensable given how arduous and slow production was. During the time of Adam Smith, trade was a powerful and useful tool and represented a mutual pursuit through networked specialized labor. The agrarian and handicraft-oriented time period of capitalism's formal inception clearly justified the act of exchange.

Yet under the surface of this behavior is still the abstract framework of buying and selling for gain, no matter what is bought and sold. This once-cloaked feature led to the practice of wealth speculation and ultimately to today's vastly profitable and increasingly powerful financial sector. While speculation in some form goes back hundreds of years, what we find now is truly an extreme. Perhaps the best term to use is "decoupled." The purpose of trade in its most notable handicraft-oriented conception is now decoupled from any true, tangible utility. Today, people buy and sell and employ for no other reason than the pursuit of income, with no true concern over *what* is being bought and sold.

The buying and selling of mere digits on a screen, the economically irrational appreciation and depreciation of physical assets, and the trade of functionally meaningless certificates of ownership have grown to supplement the original productive utility of the market economy. Wall Street and the nonproductive financial sector are indicative of just how detached from reality the idea and purpose of trade has become. The original purpose of market interaction has been lost in our technologically advanced society, distorted into abstract, economically meaningless perversions that do little more than further ensure socioeconomic inequality, social dominance, and environmental destruction.

The fourth form of maturation worth reiterating is the inherently unsustainable nature of the market's need for economic growth and turnover, a topic covered in chapter four. While true economic logic recognizes earthly scarcity as a condition to be respected and avoided by efficient and sustainable management, market logic sees scarcity as yet another mechanism for exploitation, while paradoxically pushing for as much production and consumption as possible. Without this growth and consumerism the system cannot work, since labor demand comes from consumer demand. This cyclical consumption is demanded by the market. Once again, this feature went unexpressed in earlier times since the technical means to reach such high levels of productivity simply didn't exist. It has only been within the post-Malthusian period that this productivity is now possible.

This maturation from low-impact industry to high unsustainability has necessarily occurred in tandem with the fifth form, consumerism. As noted, the rise of consumer culture and conspicuous consumption is best thought of as a transfer of the structural demands of the market system to the social psychology of the masses. This evolution has not only worked to assist needed cyclical consumption, but also has further distorted psychology by turning once-arbitrary wants into emotionally demanded needs. This leads culture into general emotional confusion, as it copes with trying to decide what is important to social existence and what is not. It is this distorted aspect of social maturation by way of market influence that now correlates reduced happiness to increased material gain, once one's basic survival needs have been met.[6]

As for the sixth and final form of maturation, technological unemployment, this will be explored later in this chapter. However, to introduce the issue, the rapid rise of mechanization around the Industrial Revolution has been the main reason for the vast increases in productive efficiency. While the rise of this phenomenon has been responsible for increased ease and the development of more-complex industries, it has also shifted labor roles such that machine automation is proven to be more effective and less expensive. Due to the market economy's structural interest in cost efficiency, the gravitation toward machine labor has been natural. Yet this trend clashes with the system's need for human employment: serious problems occur when the automation of jobs moves faster than society's ability to create new jobs. If people do not have income from labor, they cannot spend money back into the economy, keeping it going. Of all the issues of maturation, this is perhaps the clearest contradiction of system processes, something that was hard to predict long ago. Even the very idea of arbitrarily "creating new jobs" simply for the sake of having jobs reveals a unique and neurotic social distortion.

I will now conclude this introductory summation by reiterating what is perhaps the most important systemic concept that links human suffering to market economics—structural violence. As detailed in chapter four, structural violence is the mother of all negative economic externalities. It can be viewed in a macro and micro context. Whether dealing with mental-physiological disease or behavioral distortions directly linked to poverty, the psychosocial stress that reduces well-being and life span as one moves down the socioeconomic ladder, or the broad international trade dynamics that continue to isolate, deprive, and kill millions annually in the Global South alone, socioeconomic inequality can rightfully be deemed the most destructive manmade force on the planet. This inequality, combined with deeper systemic problems resulting from what is an outdated and unsustainable economic foundation that now threatens species survival itself, inspires the charge for change.

SCARCITY

If there is any single idea that gets to the heart of the negative social effects addressed in this book, it is scarcity. While simple in conception, scarcity is difficult to quantify in reality since its presence and effects can be relative. We may understand in principle that we have a finite amount of physical resources on the planet, but exactly how and why those resources are processed, allocated, and used is really what decides the state of earthly scarcity. The degree and effects of resource and means scarcity are hence defined by a nuanced interaction, not a static state.

Despite this rather obvious fact, the market economy is explicit and unnuanced in its perception of scarcity. All the market assumes is that scarcity is universal and hence all engagement should be equal in that understanding. From there, the aforementioned *root socioeconomic orientation* is built, pushing the framework of competition and exploitation. In addition, the prevailing contradiction has evolved in which infinite growth is sought to ensure cyclical consumption. Professor of Science and Civilization at Oxford University Steve Rayner refers to these interlocked mechanisms as "narratives." He states:

> "Scarcity" is a key term in contemporary human development discourse. It is deeply embedded in two competing narratives. In one of these, the "limits-to-growth" narrative of a finite world in which a recklessly expanding human population is rapidly depleting resources on which it depends, the idea of scarcity represents the explicit boundary conditions of discourse and policy. In the other narrative, scarcity serves a more technical role in defining neoclassical economics as the "science of resource allocation," which places markets at the centre of ever-expanding economic growth. In both cases, the idea of scarcity is seldom interrogated. To do so is intellectually dangerous. It is to question the underlined worldviews upon which each of these narratives, and the policies that flow from, depend.[7]

These two narratives combine to justify the existence of inequitable resource allocation and hence the foundation of socioeconomic inequality. Malthusian in origin, the overall view also implies that premature human death and disproportionate suffering is not only to be expected but required. From this perspective, the state of the modern world begins to make more sense; the Malthusian worldview, already implicit in the structure of the market economy, has no doubt deeply permeated culture. In this worldview, nature takes the blame for poverty, inequality, and the host of related problems, not manmade mechanisms of social organization.

This "appeal to nature" defense also applies to human beings, who have been conveniently deemed hedonistic, insatiable, and irrational. Old philosophical theories of human freedom and liberty further compound this issue, justifying inequitable allocation of resources since any attempt to repress the source of inequality is viewed as "anti-choice." We often see this in conservative political circles, which frequently spout such "anti-socialist" rhetoric. The result is an economic system that is interpreted as an extension of nature, with any attempt to alter the system seen as a violation of immutable natural laws and human dignity itself. In effect, scarcity has become politicized and used to justify the way of the world. In the words of sociologist Lyla Menta: "For too long has scarcity been used by powerful actors in compelling ways as a political strategy either to maintain the status quo, prevent redistributing limited resources or to legitimize certain solutions and interventions. This has contributed to reproducing inequalities and hindering social justice. This process must now be rolled back."[8]

Scarcity, while indeed an empirical fact of life, again expresses itself according to our intelligent use of resources and means. Proper strategic management ideally mitigates scarcity to such a degree that we barely see its negative effects. In the past, scarcity was an obvious and heavy burden since advanced means of production were limited. Today, our advanced technological civilization has the capacity to tame scarcity to a profound extent through intelligent design and efficient organization. The disappointing truth is that the most prominent form of scarcity in the twenty-first century is that which is created artificially through market behavior.

In fact, I would argue that what we have today isn't really an economic system at all. It is an *anti*-economic system. Its focus on trade and profit translates into the system preference for general privation and conflict. It is grossly unfair in its allocation of resources, and by inherent design concentrates wealth among a few, dividing the rest of humanity into subclasses of varying relative insecurity. One cannot define a system as being "economic" when its structural characteristics support the opposite of thrift (i.e., growth), the opposite of problem solving (i.e., profit from servicing problems, not solving them), and the opposite of equitable allocation across the population.

As this chapter will explore, there is no technical reason for any human being to be without a generally high standard of living in modern terms. This is a bold statement, requiring great defense since our society has become so alienated from what a high standard of living means in terms of human happiness, sustainability, and coexistence. By high standard, I do not mean the excesses of the modern upper 1 percent.

That extremity is not a condition of sound mind and intelligence but a neurotic, disrespectable condition of immaturity and irresponsibility. Just as no human being should be poor, starving, and living on the streets, no human being should have such material excess that it pollutes the whole of society by way of social alienation. As expressed, modern social science makes it clear that given our social nature as a species, we tend to adjust our self-perception based upon how we perceive others. People who flaunt extreme status and wealth are, in effect, harming the sense of integrity of others, instigating conflict and insecurity. Wealth signaling and class stratification itself is really a social pollutant, not an inspiration for progress, as is often argued.

When I refer to a high standard of living, I am including the ability to engage in society without exclusion or alienation, have all basic material needs met, and have access to high-order luxuries that can only be determined by the culture itself. What one culture sees as a need, another may see as a luxury or want. This relativity proves the arbitrary nature of material excess, showing that such luxuries are social tools, sought for social purposes. As such, it is time the drive for material excess be seen for what it is—a sociologically driven mental illness.

At the same time, our misconception of scarcity and sense of lack is so deeply ingrained that the mere suggestion that modern means and available resources can currently elevate the whole of humanity to a relatively high standard of living is quickly dismissed as utopian. This reaction is natural; we've been brainwashed with the exact opposite message across all mainstream economic and political discourse. For example, for centuries now talk of the Earth's "carrying capacity" has been in the background of global affairs.[9] Simplistically, we assume the rate of resource consumption that supports a given number of people will always be the same; if the human population doubles, the resources required to support them doubles too, as a 1:1 correlation. However, this isn't accurate. While the rapid rise of global population over the past two centuries is attributed to increased productive means, extracting and processing more and more resources, there has also been a parallel rise in efficiency of use. This means our increased scientific understandings have reduced the amount of resources needed over time to satisfy the needs of the same proportionate number of people.

In other words, we have learned to do *more with less*. The Malthusian Trap ended with what has been termed the *Great Divergence* around the Industrial Revolution in the early nineteenth century. This Great Divergence started an exponential advance in productive capacity and efficiency. *Ephemeralization*, a term coined by R. Buckminster Fuller, embraces this "more with less" phenomenon, while other theorists, such as Jeremy Rifkin, refer to it as approaching *zero marginal cost*.[10] Approaching zero marginal cost means that once systems are set up to produce goods, each consecutive good gets cheaper and cheaper, approaching zero cost or zero value in terms of production. For example, imagine a good-producing machine that costs $1,000 to build. The very first good that machine outputs effectively costs $1,000, if we leave aside any additional resources required. The second good produced would then cost $500 to create, since the output value of the machine is now divided into two goods. Now, imagine that machine has produced 100,000 goods with no costly need to service the machine. The value of that last good produced is now one cent. This is the nature of approaching "zero marginal cost." Digital media is the best example of this, for music, film, and other forms can be reproduced and distributed at virtually no cost across the Internet, nearly an infinite number of times.

R. Buckminster Fuller's assessment of ephemeralization was more general in that the whole of economic production could be viewed as a move toward ever-increasing efficiency, based upon advancement in design. An example is the first computer. The ENIAC computer of the 1940s contained 17,468 vacuum tubes, along with 70,000 resistors, 10,000 capacitors, 1,500 relays, 6,000 manual switches, and 5 million soldered joints. It covered 1,800 square feet of floor space, weighed 30 tons, and consumed 160 kilowatts of electrical power.[11] It also cost about $6 million in modern value. Today, a nearly zero-cost, cheap, pocket-size cellphone chip computes substantially faster than ENIAC and uses vastly less resources and energy.

This is the most important economic development of human civilization. It debunks the longstanding mantra that "there simply isn't enough to go around," and in so doing it discredits the core rationale of market competition—scarcity. As will be discussed, there is plenty to go around if certain economic adjustments are made, and if we reverse the market-spawned value system disorder that increasingly perverts modern culture. The only ostensibly real reason that exists today for poverty and inequity is the idea that "not everyone can have a fifty-room mansion or a private jet." It is this "infinite wants" view of reality that supports the market's arbitrary emphasis on scarcity, through which we justify starving almost a billion people so .01 percent of the population can rationalize neurotic material excess.

It is not enough to imagine a world that has streamlined its economic system to maximize the reduction of scarcity and the reduction of socioeconomic inequality. We must also imagine a state of social maturity that recognizes the true natural limits to human existence. This maturity includes understanding the immutable need to coexist with our habitat, along with realizing the socially destabilizing public-health problems that ultimately arise due to the practice of economic competition, exploitation, and resulting inequality. While values against these practices and outcomes can be realized on a personal level with a heartfelt interest to see change, real sociological transformation will not occur until the most dominant influence on our social psychology—our economic mode—is replaced. If what it is replaced by favors behavior that condones sustainable, collaborative, and socially just outcomes, then a cultural shift is possible. Otherwise, it is all talk. Until the social system is designed to support these new humane values and practices, there is no chance of any serious human rights expansion in the future. This is not to say that educational activism isn't critically important, as that is the path to influencing and inspiring this revolution. However, we cannot be naïve enough to think the problem exists in the moral aptitude of individuals when, as described in chapter two, there is really no such thing as an individual expressing free will without inhibitions.

Likewise, since our social nature often distorts our perception as we tend to conform to normative society, thereby preventing painful social exclusion or feelings of inferiority, we gravitate toward the irrational. Material inequality, for example, creates a psychological perception of scarcity that can be almost as real and stressful as absolute scarcity, even though the goods in question are not core to survival. In the words of anthropologist Mary Douglas: "A person wants goods for fulfilling personal commitments. Commodities do not satisfy desire; they are only tools or instruments for satisfying it . . . [R]estricting consumption of goods restricts participation in the extended social conversation for which they are used."[12] This again explains why in some societies what are deemed basic needs are often luxuries elsewhere, revealing the arbitrary nature of socially contrived "needs."

So, scarcity is just as much of a physical problem as it is a spiritual one. I use the term *spiritual* in its most technical sense, being "of or relating to." Spirituality, despite the endless poetic rhetoric associated with it, relates to feelings of connection with something outside the self. This can be our connection to one another, to the planet, to the universe, or to anything and everything. From our narrow, individualistic perspectives, locked into localized perceptions, we limit our sense of connection at our peril (that is, peril to ourselves as individuals, to our greater society, and to the planet as a whole). A systems-based worldview raises the question of who and what we are and how we fit. Truly embracing this understanding, accepting its limitations and new possibilities, may be the very realization that has confounded our deepest sense of identity and purpose as a species. It is my personal view that our spiritual fulfillment rests in coming to terms with organizational and behavioral approaches that establish a truly sustainable and socially just society. At the core of this quest is an understanding of what scarcity truly means and how to overcome it on all relevant levels, ending socioeconomic inequality. From the structuralist perspective, this *poverty of the spirit* can only be resolved by building a new social precondition that fosters proper awareness, respect, and responsibility.

NEGATIVE TRENDS

Now, before such a proposal is made, we must explore the severity of our current situation. Figure 5b is a conceptual chart showing seven negative trends that, assuming a "business-as-usual" scenario, suggest a perfect storm of social destabilization by around 2050. Each of these issues will be discussed in order, from top to bottom.

However, I would like to point out that there has been no shortage of doomsayers in modern history predicting vast crises due to human incompetence.[13] Over time, dire predictions seem to fade, making everyone wonder what happened. It isn't that most in the scientific community who have warned of such trends have been delusional; it is that our technical ingenuity continues to surpass expectations. For example, for many decades we've been warned of "peak oil," a theory predicting the irreversible decline of Earth's oil reserves. Proponents of this theory simply analyzed the known state of reserves at the time, noting negative supply trends. With growing global energy demand, it's easy to understand the concern. Yet, the focus was on the nature of extraction at the time, something we can call *conventional* extraction or production. Conventional oil production is drawing raw crude from large reservoirs under the Earth's surface. In this context, the peak-oil proponents were correct; the US peaked in the 1970s as far as conventional extraction goes, with an additional thirty-seven countries deemed past their peak today.[14]

What no one expected was the technology-enabled rise of *nonconventional* extraction, including shale, tar sands, and hydraulic fracturing or "fracking," referring mostly to natural gas. These practices are now driving down hydrocarbon prices, making the peak-oil debate mostly moot. This pattern is an aspect of ephemeralization or increased efficiency. Unfortunately, the application of technology is just as important as its power, for the alleviation of hydrocarbon pressures has only stifled what is a deeply needed shift to renewable energy sources. The rapid rise of pollution-induced climate change, along with other related environmental issues, has made this innovation in nonconventional extraction a terrible advent in the long run. While people sigh in relief at the lower cost of gas, the long-term ecological damage will no doubt harm the generations ahead. The Center for Biological Diversity put it clearly in 2013:

> The development of "oil shale" and "tar sands" has been shown to be environmentally destructive, and water and energy intensive. Extracting oil from U.S. public lands through oil shale or tar sands would deal a disastrous blow to any hope of reducing atmospheric CO_2 levels to below 350 parts per million—the level we need to reach soon to stabilize Earth's climate. Besides helping push us toward global warming catastrophe, oil shale and

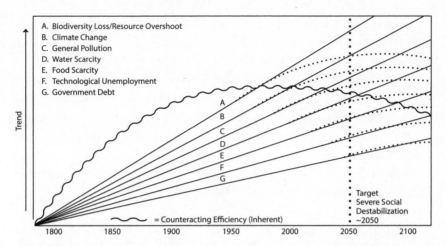

FIGURE 5B. Conceptual trend depiction of the top seven factors that may lead to severe social unrest. Based on independent studies conducted for each issue, targeting ~2050 for peak problems. This figure begins at 1800 BCE, around the first Industrial Revolution, where most of the issues take root. The "counteracting efficiency" factor marks the possibility that current trends may slow due to increased efficiency in some form. This is noted as "inherent" since it is assumed conduct will still be "business as usual."

tar sands development destroys species habitat, wastes enormous volumes of water, pollutes air and water, and degrades and defiles vast swaths of land.[15]

Today, we have passed 400 parts per million and climbing, with ever-increasing biodiversity loss.[16]

Regarding Figure 5b, we begin with *biodiversity loss* and *resource overshoot.* At the cost of $24 million, a four-year study sponsored by the United Nations utilizing more than 1,300 scientists from 95 countries found that 60 percent of the world's forests, grasslands, farmlands, rivers, lakes, and other known ecosystem attributes are being depleted and disturbed in an unsustainable manner.[17] In the words of Jonathan Lash of the World Resources Institute: "This report is essentially an audit of nature's economy, and the audit shows we've driven most of the accounts into the red."[18] Corroboration of these conclusions is extensive, showing things getting worse as time goes on.

Today, species are now going extinct 1,000 times faster than the rate recorded during the previous 65 million years.[19] The "sixth great extinction" is upon us. There have been five large extinction events in the past, from the Ordovician-Silurian, some 400 million years ago, to the Cretaceous-Paleogene, some 60 million years ago.[20] However, unlike prior events, it appears this one is entirely manmade.[21] A 2011 study found that though we've put millions of square kilometers of land and ocean under legal protection, it has done little to slow the trends of ecological decline.[22] The same study also analyzes resource overshoot in tandem with biodiversity loss, stating:

> [The] "excess" use of the Earth's resources or "overshoot" is possible because resources can be harvested faster than they can be replaced . . . the cumulative overshoot from the mid-1980s to 2002 resulted in an "ecological debt" that would require 2.5 planet Earths to pay. In a business-as-usual scenario, our demands on planet Earth could mount to the productivity of 27 planets by 2050.[23]

In effect, all life-support systems are in decline, with nothing currently sustainable about major industrial practices. As the population inches toward 9–10 billion by 2050, any positive outlook on future ecological integrity is arguably delusional.[24] In the words of Professor Sir John Lawton, former chief executive of the UK's Natural Environment Research Council: "There will undoubtedly be gainsayers, as there are with the IPCC [Intergovernmental Panel on Climate Change]; but I put them in the same box as the flat-Earthers and the people who believe smoking doesn't cause cancer."[25] Given that the entire foundation of human civilization depends on biodiversity, including the regenerative resources needed for day-to-day survival, the general political silence on the issue is quite unsettling. From fish and marine species halved in number since the 1970s to 6 million hectares of primary forest lost or damaged each year since 1990, there are no positive trends occurring on the whole.[26] Only in a world based upon capital accumulation and environmental exploitation could the denial seen today become so opaque.

As for *climate change* (trend B in Figure 5b above), the cognitive dissonance is also profound. Even though the overwhelming majority of scientists agrees on its effects and manmade sources, and even though the research goes back many decades now, conservative political and economic forces continue to pretend it is unimportant or a mere fantasy. In a 2015 work titled *Climate Change, Capitalism, and Corporations*, authors Wright and Nyberg explore the powerful corporate resistance to any meaningful adjustment to market economics, exposing the myth of "green" capitalism.[27] They report that profit-seeking businesses simply work around policy shifts designed to help the environment, while spending a great deal of money on lobbying and counteractivist influence to ensure the security of their bottom line. They write:

> Our economies are now reliant upon ever more ingenious ways of exploiting the Earth's fossil fuel reserves and consuming the very life-support systems we rely on for our survival. This is evident in the rush by some of the world's largest companies to embrace deep-water and Arctic oil drilling, tar-sands processing, new mega-coalmines, and the "fracking" of shale and coal-seam gas. These examples highlight both the inventive genius of corporate capitalism, and the blindness of industry and government to the ecological catastrophe they are fashioning.[28]

The authors make a clear case that the current capitalist orientation will only drive humanity into an ever-deepening hole, despite the green rhetoric and impressive, high-profile international meetings. No significant change is happening in real terms, because the social psychology generated by the market—the root orientation of the system that guides narrow, self-interested behavior—is larger than personal discipline. Consequently, predictions forecasting the state of affairs by 2050 are bleak, with a 2013 paper in *Nature* projecting a complete climate transformation for the worse. This transformation will affect the low-income tropics first, destabilizing core ecosystems.[29]

A 20-year study by Yale sociologist Justin Farrell found that "[C]orporations have used their wealth to amplify contrarian views [of climate change] and create an impression of greater scientific uncertainty than actually exists . . . The contrarian efforts have been so effective for the fact that they have made it difficult for ordinary Americans to even know who to trust."[30] A leaked draft report from the United Nations published by the *New York Times* stated "that governments of the world were still spending far more money to subsidize fossil fuels than to accelerate the shift to cleaner energy, thus encouraging continued investment in projects like coal-burning power plants that pose a long-term climate risk."[31]

The report also warned that if the 500 ppm threshold of CO_2 is passed, as is predicted if trends stay the same, future generations will need to find ways to "suck greenhouse gases out of the atmosphere and store them underground to preserve the livability of the planet."[32] The *Times* also published that it was the opinion of the report that "[w]hile emissions appear to have fallen in recent years in some of the wealthiest countries, that is somewhat of an illusion . . . The growth of international trade means many of the goods consumed in wealthy countries are now made abroad—so that those countries have, in effect, outsourced their greenhouse gas emissions to countries like China."[33]

Since the start of industrial society, there has been a 40 percent increase in greenhouse gases, reaching levels higher than anything recorded in the past 800,000 years. The effects on the cryosphere (the frozen-water part of our planet) have provided empirical evidence of the damage. As the ocean warms and ice formations shrink, sea levels rise in synergy with many other factors that set the stage for a litany of negative future effects.[34]

Moving on to *general pollution* (trend C in Figure 5b), we see that in concert with greenhouse-gas emissions, air, land, and water integrity are all experiencing negative trends. A 2016 study linked household and outdoor air pollution to an astounding 5.5 million premature deaths each year, based upon 2013 data.[35] Half of those deaths are occurring in China and India, two countries that are employing the mid- to late-twentieth-century Euro-American model of economic expansion through dirty industrialization means. A 2015 study, tracking current trends, concluded: "Model projections based on a business-as-usual emission scenario indicate that the contribution of outdoor air pollution to premature mortality could double by 2050."[36]

Land degradation is equally dire. According to the World Wildlife Organization, half of the topsoil on Earth has been lost in the last 150 years.[37] Topsoil is the uppermost layer of soil that possesses the greatest concentration of organic matter and microorganisms, where plants obtain the majority of their nutrients and thrive. Today, it is disappearing at an alarming rate, primarily due to conventional agricultural practices such as monoculture. According to the National Academy of Sciences, topsoil is being eroded ten times faster than it can be replaced.[38] This erosion often sends toxic farm chemicals and pollutants into streams and sensitive water supplies, hurting ecology and potable reservoirs.

Some have considered soil destruction as rivaling global warming as an environmental threat, with 1 percent lost every year.[39] Given that it takes about 1,000 years to generate three centimeters (a bit over an inch) of topsoil, it has been predicted that by 2050, only 25 percent of the productivity experienced in the 1960s will be possible, posing extreme challenges for a population two times larger.[40] As expressed by trend E, unless topsoil destruction is rapidly stopped, or there is a mass incorporation of different agricultural methods such as soilless agriculture, serious food-scarcity problems are on the horizon. A 2013 study published in the journal *Plos ONE* found that even with current yields, ignoring looming problems, a near doubling of global crop production is going to be needed to meet demand by 2050.[41]

This problem will be compounded by water pollution and increased freshwater scarcity (trend D). Water pollution from farming and industrial activity has been extensive, as evidenced by "dead zones" in lakes, excess nitrates in water tables, and growing mercury pollution in the ocean and fish stock sourced to coal plants.[42] While the rise of the now multibillion-dollar bottled-water industry has been good for GDP, the environmental destruction underlying it is devastating, expressing yet another example of the distorted incentive of the market structure. According to the United Nations, about 1.8 billion people will live in areas plagued by water scarcity by 2025, with two-thirds of the world's population living in water-stressed regions.[43] The *OECD Environmental Outlook to 2050* reported that fresh-water demand will rise by 55 percent by 2050, corroborating the UN water-stress statistic; using the OECD demand estimate of 55 percent, we can expect that 3.9 billion people will be living in water-stressed regions by 2050.[44]

Professor Janos Bogardi of the Global Water System Project (GWSP) has stated that severe water shortages will affect more than half the world's future population by 2050, sparking mass migrations of people likely followed by destabilizing political tensions.[45] A 2013 GWSP study concluded that:

> In the short span of one or two generations, the majority of the nine billion people on Earth will be living under the handicap of severe pressure on fresh water, an absolutely essential natural resource for which there is no substitute . . . This handicap will be self-inflicted and is, we believe, entirely avoidable . . . Mismanagement, overuse and climate change pose long-term threats to human well-being, and evaluating and responding to those threats constitutes a major challenge to water researchers and managers alike.[46]

Overall, from a broad environmental perspective, as warned by a 2016 study by the UN Environment Programme (UNEP) involving 1,200 scientists, hundreds of scientific institutions, and 160 governments, radical and rapid change is needed to stop the looming global catastrophe.[47]

Beyond these environmental concerns, the final two issues, *technological unemployment* and *government debt* (trends F and G in Figure 5b), if left unaddressed, will further increase social stress. With "47 percent of . . . jobs at high risk of being taken by computers within the next two decades" and all the financial incentives to do so by business, there is no stopping this trend without major policy adjustments.[48] This trend also shows an exacerbation of inequality as the fruits of automated productivity continue to go into the pockets of the upper class (as will be explored in more detail in this chapter). As physicist Stephen Hawking stated in 2015:

> If machines produce everything we need, the outcome will depend on how things are distributed. Everyone can enjoy a life of luxurious leisure if the machine-produced wealth is shared, or most people can end up miserably poor if the machine-owners

successfully lobby against wealth redistribution. So far, the trend seems to be toward the second option, with technology driving ever-increasing inequality.[49]

As for government debt, it has been estimated that by 2060 60 percent of all the countries in the world will be bankrupt, while the US alone will have a debt of 415 percent of GDP by 2050.[50] On a certain level, debt is a customary fiction and can be erased by the flick of a pen. Yet the very integrity of the capitalist system is based on the idea that the math of financial interaction, hence competitive self-regulation, will work out in the end. That is the façade that must be upheld, while behind the scenes large powers never play by the rules. The truth is, dominant nations can extend their debts to near infinity, moving goal posts as they go along.

The US's having a federal debt of $19 trillion or $190 trillion is actually only as relevant as its position in the global power hierarchy. The US will never default as long as it remains a global empire, and all major nations buying US bonds know this deep down. The US can just make it up by way of its central bank, the Federal Reserve, which extends to a financial system with great global power, also ensuring the power of the US dollar. If debts are in dollars, the US simply makes more. Although people often argue that the US is in debt to a private banking cartel (its central bank) and that is a problem in itself, it is really irrelevant in the broad view. The whole thing is mostly a sleight-of-hand arrangement that lets the US government borrow endlessly while the banking system gets special political treatment. No one in the US government and its central bank cartel really cares about US government debt because money is made out of thin air. They only care about public regulation and public perception, not government spending or government debt. In the words of former Federal Reserve Chairman Alan Greenspan: "The United States can pay any debt it has because we can always print money to do that. So there is zero probability of default."[51]

However, that is not the case with smaller nations, which are highly susceptible to international debts. Small nations face serious repercussions imposed by way of sanctions, structural adjustments, and austerity if they cannot meet debt requirements. These repercussions reduce the welfare of their citizens, decreasing standards of living and increasing the probability of destabilization. They are forms of oppression, in truth: punishment for simply being poor. Again, it is market discipline for the poor and socialist protections for the rich. The true "free market" is really the freedom of those with the most money and hence control.

So, in this midst of all this, with mass global bankruptcy pending for most nations and a general pressure to reduce spending, the odds of seeing the kind of economic reforms required to stop the vast environmental crises looming are very low. The pressure is also against any large-scale social-welfare compensation for the population to ease economic stress, along with any hope to finance the mass shifts needed to revise the global energy infrastructure. In short, we are entering into a situation that, if we are to respect capitalism's financial dynamics, will require enormous amounts of money to make the sustainable changes required. With a world in debt to itself at many times its GDP, it is very hard to feel optimistic about such changes actually occurring. Capitalism and markets simply cannot be respected if we expect to move forward with integrity.

As a final note on Figure 5b, which targets 2050 as a perfect storm of negative trends, the wiggly line is the hopeful wild card. It is termed the "counteracting efficiency" trend, suggesting a possible tapering off of these trends to a limited degree as unexpected forms of ingenuity prevail. In the same spirit of the decline of "peak oil," the figure expresses hope that these negative trends will slow so as to allow more time for large-order change. Ephemeralization, which is really the only positive economic feature of modern times, guides this trend. This wiggly line is labeled "counteracting efficiency" that is "inherent" to point out that some alleviation of negative trends will likely be natural to a "business-as-usual" scenario. Be that as it may, unless a deliberate and highly specific effort to counter these trends occurs, far beyond this *inherent counteracting efficiency*, the social destabilization on the horizon is going to be spectacular.

RECONSTRUCTION

In stark contrast to the aforementioned trends, the possibility of returning to ecological balance is still very much within our reach. While a point of no return is certainly possible, if we remove the "business-as-usual" scenario from the equation and take a fresh look at our potentials, from the ground up, the light at the end of the tunnel is profoundly bright. So bright, in fact, that we are not only able to end socioeconomic inequality, and dramatically increase public health and social justice, but we can also move society toward a truly *sustainable abundance*. When I say abundance I am not referring to some infinite amount of everything. I am referring to a society focused on maximizing its efficiency to reduce scarcity and economic inequality as much as technically possible, while ensuring *homeostasis* with the planet. This goal may sound utopian but it is entirely practical and simple in conception. As noted throughout this book, scarcity has been ingrained in our social system and harnessed as a political tool. Humanity's sense of possibility has been severely limited in consequence, and we have unfortunately cultivated a highly competitive, dehumanized, and warlike culture as a result.

In this section, attributes of an idealized economic model will be inferred to describe a system focused on maximizing technical efficiency to circumvent any pressures of resource scarcity and lack of sustainability. While what will be discussed is, indeed, literal in principle and general application, I encourage the reader to first view this as a thought exercise in order to try to avoid subjective bias. This thought exercise is simply about reasoning what an ideal economic system would be if logically constructed from the ground up, based upon modern understandings. The goal is maximum efficiency to meet all human needs in a sustainable way. This basic reasoning, as implied throughout this book, regards structurally linking public health to social organization. It is a scientific fact that if I do not consume water, I will eventually die as a result. By extension, the means by which water is accessed, utilized, and preserved for future use becomes just as much of a technical, nonsubjective issue of organization as the need to drink it.

This is how, from a structuralist view, we can argue that those dying from dehydration, water-transmitted disease, and starvation in the world perish due not to the actual lack of food or water, but to societal inefficiencies that allow (or create) such deprivation. The mechanics that enable these inefficiencies exist in the territory of the objective, not the subjective, since we can quantify the cause-and-effect relationships that link food or water scarcity to broader influences and eventually larger-order system dynamics. Suddenly, we see that the nearly 1 billion people on Earth who lack safe drinking water are in that condition because of the structural nature of the global economy, not due to some natural, immutable imposition of our habitat.[52]

So, this exercise (or train of thought) is about constructing an economic system technically and objectively, in the same way one builds an airplane to fly. The only decision to be made is that of purpose. An airplane is built with the purpose of safely and efficiently moving cargo from one location to another. This new economic model is built with the purpose of providing for all the people in the world in the most efficient and sustainable way possible. What has been argued in this text is that either this new approach is adopted or humanity is on a fast track to increased destabilization. In other words, as odd as this may sound, it is less about the moral issue of what is "right" or "wrong" in terms of social fairness and more about what works and what doesn't. If the goal is ongoing human survival as a species with the least amount of violence, premature mortality, habitat destruction, and other ultimately public-health issues, what we have now is simply unworkable.

Five attributes that form the foundation of this new economic model are conceptualized in Figure 5c. They include (a) Automation, (b) Access, (c) Open Source, (d) Localization, and (e) Networked Digital Feedback (also generally referred to in popular literature as "the *Internet of Things*" or *IoT*). Each of these represents a more efficient mechanism to achieve higher productivity and the least amount of waste and environmental impact feasible. The logic is no different in principle from the practical decision to reject using a manual screwdriver in favor of an electric one, increasing productive efficiency. Yet they contradict the structural logic of the market system as they are based upon technical efficiency, not market efficiency—two very different approaches to economic behavior, once again. Interestingly enough, these five ideas are actually not obscure, randomly idealized, or pulled out of thin air. People who pay attention to current social and technological trends are aware of them, yet have not thought about their broader implications. Signposts pointing us in new directions surround us, in fact, and the following thought exercise will extend their implications, showing how they complement one another in optimizing economic efficiency.

In effect, what underscores these new attributes is a dramatic change of our current *root socioeconomic orientation*. Unlike with the market, which is structurally based on scarcity, trade, competition, and exploitation, this new model focuses on strategic and sustainable abundance, collaboration, and balance. In a single word, it is about *design*. I wish to express that I am not using these terms poetically. I am not gesturing, saying: "Hey, let's all just collaborate, be sustainable, and seek abundance." Wishful thinking has proven to be of little help without a structural foundation to support goals, which is why all the poems, stories, and songs about peace, love, and human solidarity have remained an idealistic backdrop in the midst of constant human conflict, deprivation, and abuse. Also, the degree to which any or all of these changes are made is proportional to the benefits achieved. In other words, even if only partial transitions were made toward the ideal goals expressed, it would

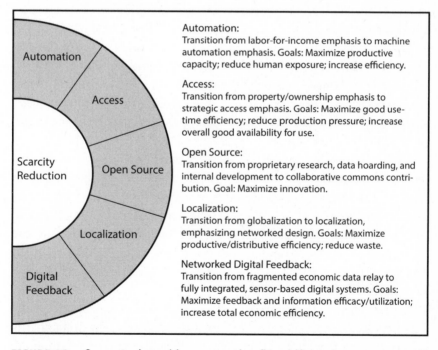

FIGURE 5C. Conceptual graphic representing five shifts to increase economic efficiency and reduce the scarcity pressure. These adjustments will decrease socioeconomic inequality and the consequential spectrum of disorder and oppression.

still improve things. However, the more one examines the implications of these changes, the more it will become clear how they work against the current economic system's incentives and structure. This means the ideal of a step-by-step transition (and improvement) is improbable. Rather, it will likely take large and dramatic leaps to move from one state to another, revealing the need for serious activism to get things done.

The first attribute in Figure 5c is the deliberate application of (a) labor automation. This means the conscious reduction of human labor-for-income roles, replacing jobs by machine automation wherever possible. As radical as this may seem to some, it is common sense given current trends. I will note three.

First, in contradiction to the market's framework, human employment is now inverse to productivity in the sectors where automation has been applied.[53] This means human labor is becoming obsolete and human employment is actually economically inefficient when the automation option is available. It doesn't make sense, in the same way that farming a field with eighteenth-century equipment is inappropriate today.

Second, machine automation has greatly helped facilitate the vast increase in productive efficiency and resulting standard-of-living increases experienced by much of the globe. As such, it becomes a matter of social responsibility and prudence to maximize this potential. Rather than enduring the relatively slow process of cost-efficiency-induced automation, where companies automate *only* when it is cheaper than human labor, the intent should be full automation overall, favoring technological unemployment. This is contrary to the market system, which structurally disfavors automation in the interest of preserving human jobs. Structural adjustments would need to be made to incentivize automation liberally, not fight it. This approach makes obsolete the overall labor-for-income framework. The effect would be a rapid increase in production efficiency through the "zero marginal cost" phenomenon, furthering the creation of a goods surplus.

Third, even with the nondeliberate rise of technological unemployment due to the pursuit of cost efficiency alone, the socially destabilizing effects emerging must be countered. At the time of writing, pressure is being put on the industrialized labor force as technological unemployment inches ahead. The growth of information technology, applied robotics, and artificial intelligence are projected to move faster than society is able to create new jobs to replace the ones being automated.[54] Because the costs to produce these machines are increasingly inverse to their productivity, they will also continue to become cheaper than human labor in most sectors over time. Statisticians tracking this rapid rise find no reason to assume any sector will be off-limits from automation in the future.[55]

Economist John Maynard Keynes, writing in 1931, is perhaps the most famous for foreshadowing this issue, stating:

> We are being afflicted with a new disease of which some readers may not yet have heard the name, but of which they will hear a great deal in the years to come—namely, *technological unemployment*. This means unemployment due to our discovery of means of economizing the use of labour outrunning the pace at which we can find new uses for labour. But this is only a temporary phase of maladjustment.[56]

Classical economist David Ricardo, writing before Keynes, in 1821, also recognized the pattern, and, like Keynes, wrongly dismissed the issue as a mere "temporary phase of maladjustment," not a true system contradiction. Ricardo stated:

> I have been of the opinion that . . . an application of machinery to any branch of production as should have the effect of saving labour was a general good . . . [but] that the substitution of machinery for human labor is often very injurious to the interests of the class of laborer . . . I have been supposing, that improved machinery is suddenly discovered, and extensively used; but the truth is, that these discoveries are gradual, and rather operate in determining the employment of the capital which is saved and accumulated, than in diverting capital from its actual employment.[57]

Naturally, machine technology of the nineteenth century would appear limited in effect, functioning more as a means of complementing human labor than replacing it. It wasn't sophisticated and it developed very slowly. Today, this is no longer the case. Professor of computer science Moshe Vardi, speaking at the annual meeting of the American Association for the Advancement of Science, said: "We are approaching a time when machines will be able to outperform humans at almost any task."[58] Using the United States as a basis, a 2013 analysis released by the Oxford Martin Programme on the Impacts of Future Technology found that 47 percent of jobs will be susceptible to computerization in a few decades.[59] This speculation is far from unfounded. In May 2016 the Adidas company announced it was moving much of its shoe production to Germany. However, rather than bringing new jobs to the region, as would commonly be assumed, the company described its new "Speed-factory" process that will rely on near full robotic automation.[60] More revealing, in 2016 US minimum-wage protests successfully forced a move to raise the hourly rate in some states. This was considered a victory for the working class. In response, the Wendy's fast-food restaurant corporation announced it was going to simply counter the move by deliberately moving to automation, reducing the workforce to avoid paying the wage increase.[61] This pattern of bypassing increased lower-class wages and labor union demands through automation is just starting and will only increase as the primary market logic to reduce costs will naturally force increased unemployment as technology becomes cheaper.

Aside from the need to adjust the economic system to allow for this new productive reality, compensating the loss of jobs, this trend also poses unique existential challenges. The idea of a paid occupation has become so ingrained in our social identity and sense of purpose that loss of opportunity can cause emotional harm, such as with the correlation between suicide and employment noted earlier.[62] At the same time, a limited view of human nature bleakly asks, "What would people do?" if they had no coerced labor role. This is like asking a curious child what will consume his time if it is not imposed upon. A future not based upon labor-for-income shouldn't be confused with a future of no creativity, progress, or incentive. While a pattern of laziness exists, often derisively associated with the working class, this can be linked to job dissatisfaction and a loss of purpose, not a blanket lack of interest in exerting any effort. As put by psychologist Barry Schwartz:

We want work that is challenging and engaging, that enables us to exercise some discretion and control over what we do, and that provides us opportunities to learn and grow. We want to work with colleagues we respect and with supervisors who respect us. Most of all, we want work that is meaningful—that makes a difference to other people and thus ennobles us in at least some small way.[63]

There is also an age-old notion that people should only "get what they work for." We all understand the ethic of work as a virtue and also the necessity for property as a means to protect one's work. However, we forget that work is part of a social process and that process provides countless things to us that are achieved without our need to assist in development. While a person may need to work a job to get money to purchase a computer, the value of that computer does not truly represent the countless years of scientific advancement and the countless minds it took to manifest it. In other words, for the "you get what you work for" ethic to be real, each human would need to reject the social reality and evolution of eco-scientific development and, upon birth, begin to create the entire world's industrial network from scratch. This is a ridiculous proposal, of course, but just as scarcity is viewed with no nuance through the eyes of market economics, so too is the idea of work as the only justifiable means to earn the "right to life."

As philosophers have argued, work, in its truest state, is the creative act of inquiry, invention, and development. The drive to solve problems is inherent in us; our minds are simply wired that way. People have no problem working hard on what they enjoy. Unfortunately, the exploitative drudgery of our historical existence, coupled with an economic system that requires work for income, has distorted this inherent drive through arduous and monotonous labor. "Jobs" are not vocations. Jobs are structural prerequisites for survival in an economic system based upon labor-for-income. At the same time, some (rightly) see the "earn a living" reality as a mechanism of social control. London School of Economics anthropologist David Graeber, in his amusing essay, "On the Phenomenon of Bullshit Jobs," says: "It's as if someone were out there making up pointless jobs just for the sake of keeping us all working . . .

The ruling class has figured out that a happy and productive population with free time on their hands is a mortal danger."[64]

The science of human motivation has found that while drudgery is burdensome, creative tasks, a sense of inclusion, and feelings of contribution are stimulating and sought after.[65] Adam Smith was famous for cynically stating: "It is the interest of every man to live as much at his ease as he can . . . it is certainly his interest, at least as interest is vulgarly understood, either to neglect [work] altogether . . . or to perform it in as careless and slovenly a manner [as possible]."[66] This view may have held at the time Smith wrote, as noted, at the edge of the Malthusian Trap, but today our understanding is different. Once monotonous drudgery is removed, and independent, meaningful work is instilled, the floodgates of creativity, enthusiasm, and productivity open.

In the words of Stanford University Professor of Psychology Carol S. Dweck: "Effort is one of the things that gives meaning to life. Effort means you care about something, that something is important to you and you are willing to work for it. It would be an impoverished existence if you were not willing to value things and commit yourself to working toward them."[67] This helps explain the exceptional amount of work people do for no monetary reward in the world, simply seeking purpose and meaning. For instance, a 1992 Gallup Poll found that more than 50 percent of American adults volunteered time for social causes at an average of 4.2 hours a week, for a total of 20.5 billion hours a year.[68] This was calculated to equate to about $176 billion in value.[69] Even in times of recession, average people continue to give and help at high rates.[70]

Aside from how this structural shift to labor automation will dramatically help create a more equitable standard of living for all due to increased efficiency, it will free humanity from dictatorial, dehumanizing, monotonous labor roles. This freedom opens the door to a new world of incentives, shifting motivation into creative, collaborative, and exploratory fields. As a natural course, the first areas that automation becomes applicable in are generally the most monotonous since they are the easiest to mechanize. This means the path of adjusting society to an automated economy first removes the type of work people do not wish to do, refocusing on areas with greater fulfillment.

Furthermore, highly specific to the theme of this book, this adjustment has many implications for improving interpersonal affairs and the
alleviation of social dominance. For thousands of years, labor has been
the main focus of human exploitation and abuse. The rise of automation breaks the need for human commodification and dehumanization,
assuming we adjust accordingly to remove labor-for-income as a universal economic requirement. In the words of Jeremy Rifkin:

> A half century from now, our grandchildren are likely to look
> back at the era of mass employment in the market with the same
> sense of utter disbelief as we look upon slavery and serfdom in
> former times. The very idea that a human being's worth was
> measured almost exclusively by his or her productive output
> of goods and services and material wealth will seem primitive,
> even barbaric, and be regarded as a terrible loss of human value
> to our progeny living in a highly automated world.[71]

How the system adapts to such a shift is a complex discussion, but many
theorists today have returned to the idea of Martin Luther King's universal, guaranteed minimum income (or Universal Basic Income). The
idea is to simply compensate for unemployment and poverty with money
given directly by the state to the public.[72] This is a logical step, along
with the parallel idea of shortening the workday, as has already been
experimented with in some Nordic countries.[73]

The second attribute noted in Figure 5c is (b) access over property,
by which I mean tilting the balance toward access and away from ownership. Ownership and property are foundational to the market economy.
This idea goes back to the philosophical work of John Locke.[74] However,
things have changed since the time of Locke, and our high-technology
society is now being hindered by the tradition of ownership, proving it
wasteful and impractical. From the standpoint of technical efficiency,
the general idea of everyone owning one of everything is irrational for a
species sharing a finite planet. The fact is, very few goods are constantly
utilized over time, with some goods, such as cars, dormant the majority of the time. This ethic of individual ownership has also been a large

contributor to resource overshoot, environmental destruction, pollution, and waste. It promulgates a materialist conception of reality that further fuels detrimental cyclical consumption.

Sharing and the *communal commons* have also existed to a fair degree, from libraries to rental systems to public transit. Interestingly, due to pressures of eco-concern and an increased democratization of commerce, we have seen a mild increase in more advanced sharing systems, from street-bike depots in cities, to car-sharing networks, to home sharing.[75] While the term "sharing" is actually not entirely accurate since it is really consumer-driven renting overall, the phenomenon has still been dubbed "the rise of the sharing economy" or *collaborative consumption*. The term *access* will be used here, as the root of the trend is about people gravitating away from ownership, relying on access to sharing networks as needed.

Yet, like the rise of automation, entry into this territory has been slow and tenuous. That is because the core of the market system fights it. Access instead of ownership interferes with cyclical consumption and growth. Generally, there is no economic benefit in a market economy when fewer goods are produced to meet the demands of more people. Today, the sharing economy isn't really an *access economy* but a fad based around consumer recycling of current ownership. A true access-based approach to distribution means good use is spread across the population, just as a thousand people over a generation may check out a single book from a library. Let's consider the example of automobile transport. If fifty people need to drive a car, the market benefits from all fifty of them each buying a car. However, if fifty people were to share ten cars, the economy would suffer a theoretical contraction of 80 percent.

It has been reported that the average American only uses his or her car about 5 percent of the time.[76] In 2015, there were 257.9 million consumer vehicles in the United States.[77] Abstractly, given the 5 percent use-time, only 13.8 million cars would be needed to meet demand if they were shared and not owned. The real number would be much higher given the logistics of such a sharing arrangement, but it certainly wouldn't come close to 257.9 million. This would mean a deep reduction of traffic and parking congestion since the vast majority of cars wouldn't be needed. Likewise, the pollution reduction would also be substantial, especially given that hydrocarbon power is unfortunately still the norm.

As with automation, driverless-car technology has advanced markedly in the past few years, as well. It has been estimated that this development, in combination with collaborative-consumption car networks, is on pace (conservatively) to eliminate 10 million jobs.[78] If this approach were to be combined with a more deliberate access focus, magnified to incentivize the removal of private, single-use car ownership whenever possible, the access abundance and positive ecological effects would be staggering by comparison to today. This is just one example, as the idea of incentivizing access over property can be applied to a wide range of goods genres, from tools to recreation equipment to apartments.

Access is really at the heart of economic necessity, while ownership is a creation of the market system's need to store value and protect property from theft in a world based on the assumption of universal scarcity. Most property crime is generally driven by want and a lack of access. The creation of an "access abundance," seeking to give everyone equal opportunity to use, means property crime would drop as abundance is achieved. This ideal may seem fanciful given the crude world we endure today, but it is logically sound. People do not steal things they can gain access to.

This is not to argue an abstraction where property no longer exists and no material rights of any kind are enforced. The efficiency logic here is simply to shift the focus from property to access, supporting access rights more than property rights. The result would be the cultivation of a kind of shared *commons* that would be not only more sustainable and less wasteful, but also able to extend goods and services to those who once were not able to afford them. As a proxy for the creation of abundance, consider the car example again. In theory, with only 13.8 million cars needed, the other 262.1 million would be an abundant surplus. If you extend this reasoning to other categories of goods, suddenly our state of scarcity begins to look much different.

The third attribute is the full incorporation of (c) *open-source* contribution, making all industrial and scientific information freely available. This could be deemed the cultivation of a *collaborative commons*.[79] The market economy treats ideas as property to be owned and sold, and uses the term "intellectual property," about which a host of laws exist. The market incentivizes the proprietary hoarding of information and closed internal development rather than open, collaborative development. This makes sense in such an economy as today's, since information and development lead to new products sold for profit, assisting market survival. Sharing information is rarely in the best interest of any company, as it makes it vulnerable to others' using the information more strategically, possibly undercutting its market share and business success. The same goes for intellectual development of most kinds, since "time is money" in this world. A scientist who has spent years researching and writing a detailed book on a subject usually needs to copyright, sell, and protect that work since he or she needs income to compensate for the time spent. It is just what the system demands.

For years, this kind of competitive arrangement has been interpreted as the driver of innovation in the commercial arena. While this may have been true to a certain degree, today it has become clear that technical innovation is actually occurring more quickly and efficiently through open-source collaborative contribution than through proprietary, closed development. While there is plenty of empirical evidence to support this truth, basic common sense also prevails. If we understand that technological progress is an inherently social process, with parties constantly building upon and improving existing ideas over time, then logic recognizes that more minds thinking about a given problem or proposal will always be better than a few, if organized properly.

The development of the Linux operating system is a classic example. Started in 1991 by students as an experiment, the global, mass-contribution project was completed in just three years, with little monetary involvement.[80] In 2000, NASA started the "Clickworkers" project that allowed online volunteers, with no prerequisite knowledge, to engage in visual analysis generally reserved for professional scientists or graduate students. More than 85,000 people voluntarily visited the site in six months and made almost 2 million entries. An analysis of the markings found that "the automatically-computed consensus of large numbers of Clickworkers is virtually indistinguishable from the inputs of a geologist with years of experience in identifying Mars craters."[81]

In 2009, famous mathematician Tim Gowers decided to start the Polymath Project. This is today an ongoing, networked collaborative project to solve complex math problems. Since inception, it has solved numerous problems through public interaction.[82] Wikipedia, a user-driven online encyclopedia, is another example of overflowing public interest in collaborative contribution. While structurally limited in its bureaucracy and famous for its often opinionated undertone, it has still been found to have an error rate that isn't much higher than the proprietary *Encyclopedia Britannica Online*.[83]

The scope of open-source development and collaborative mass decision making and contribution has been expanding rapidly since the dawn of the Internet. As Thomas Goetz reports in *Wired* magazine:

> Open source has spread to other disciplines, from the hard sciences to the liberal arts. Biologists have embraced open source methods in genomics and informatics, building massive databases to genetically sequence E. coli, yeast, and other workhorses of lab research . . . There is open source publishing . . . books open to any use, modification, or redistribution, with readers' improvements considered for succeeding editions . . . Distributed Proofreading, [which] deploys legions of copy editors to make sure the Gutenberg texts are correct. There are open source projects in law and religion. There's even an open source cookbook.[84]

The open-source movement is a testament to the power of the group mind and the wisdom of crowds, and also shows that people feel an incentive to contribute to ideas even when no money or material reward is involved. While in its infancy, as numerous pro-open-source organizations now plead with industry to open their intellectual vaults, the emerging reality is that the efficacy of proprietary development is losing steam as an optimized means of innovation. Yet, due to market pressures, there has naturally been a limited range of open-source engagement overall. While we see great poetry in the spirit of open source, such as Elon Musk's famous release of his Tesla automobile patents, poetry is not enough.[85] The power of open source ultimately depends on how effective the communicative medium being used is. In the digital, online realm, this harnessing of group analysis and creativity is becoming increasingly more effective.

The ideal next stage of this trend is to apply the method to major industrial design projects. Through *CAD (computer-aided design)* and *CAE (computer-aided engineering)* projects, linked online, it is now possible for economic creation to be engaged by anyone who has the skills and interest to contribute.[86] There is no reason that the same structure and shared goals that created Linux cannot be applied to the creation of a smartphone, a boat, or an entire industrial transit system. Such capacity forms the basis of what could be *participatory economics*, creating efficiency not only in design but also in public demand. Today, demand is assessed, created, and manipulated by advertising, market research, and guesswork. In essence, product developers are testing the waters of what people may or may not seek. The intent is not to help but to sell. A system of open-source *participatory economics* reverses the process, using a democratic means to decide what should or should not be produced. Other positives would be the elimination of wasteful, duplicate proprietary components that otherwise perform the same function, and movement toward *universal standardization* across as many categories of goods as possible, also reducing waste.[87]

On the whole, while all forms of open source should be encouraged to whatever degree possible today, the full potential of the revolution simply cannot develop within a market economy. The market economy, which monetizes information and thereby places a premium on information control, deeply limits the efficiency potential of truly collaborative, strategic, and holistic development.

The fourth attribute is (d) *localization*. In stark contrast to globalization, localization is about regaining efficiency and reducing waste by locally producing as much as possible, streamlining the supply chain. Extraction, production, distribution, and recycling should be subject to design itself, organized in the closest proximity to the population group in need. This may seem like common sense, but mostly because of the competitive pursuit of lower labor costs, commodities and goods are moved all over the world unnecessarily. This pattern has become increasingly wasteful in light of new production means that are highly versatile and effective, such as advanced 3D fabrication (additive manufacturing) or soilless indoor agriculture.[88] Modern productive potentials are changing rapidly, further supporting the interest to end globalization in its current form, focusing on regional production through advanced means. In effect, the rise of ephemeralization expands local capacity to degrees never known before, as we are able to produce much more with increasingly simplified production means and less resources.

Historically, there has been ongoing debate over how a society's "means of production" is to be organized and controlled. This argument has often been considered the defining difference between socialist societies and capitalist societies. *Means of production* refers to the nonhuman capital goods used to create products, such as factories, machines, and so forth. In this polarized view, capitalism is said to have "private ownership of the means of production" while socialism or communism is said to have "public ownership of the means of production."[89] Yet, there is a deep culture lag here. It is becoming increasingly difficult to classify modern trends since capital goods (the means of production) are now turning into consumer goods. An advanced 3D printer, for example, is really a mini "means of production" that may be privately owned by the person using it, and yet it may very well have been created through socialist arrangements. In the reverse case, a capitalist system may output a 3D printer, but it may then be used communally in a town to assist the production of local interests in a socialist way. In other words, the lines are blurred as ephemeralization makes production means smaller, more portable, and more powerful.

Likewise, with the advent of automation, we now see labor power, once deemed a core, human-performed economic factor of production, collapsing into the context of capital goods. In effect, labor power, capital goods, and consumer goods are now blending together. Taking this trend to its logical conclusion, it isn't difficult to envision advanced fabrication systems capable of producing, through mostly automated means, virtually everything material a region needs, locally. This would be a dramatic shift from current practices. The only imports perhaps required would be raw materials the machines used to produce the goods. This notion may seem utopian but it isn't. It is simply where ephemeralization is headed: doing more with less. The point here is that society should refocus its intention in this way to maximize this efficiency, bypassing the highly wasteful practice of globalization, in which we unnecessarily import goods from thousands of miles away to "save money," while using exploited labor in distant lands for the same reason. If intelligently developed and applied, localization by way of modern means would increase efficiency greatly in comparison with current methods. To put this idea into perspective with respect to global food production, according to the Institution of Mechanical Engineers:

> [W]e produce [globally] about four billion metric tonnes of food per annum. Yet due to poor practices in harvesting, storage and transportation, as well as market and consumer wastage, it is estimated that 30–50% (or 1.2–2 billion tonnes) of all food produced never reaches a human stomach. Furthermore, this figure does not reflect the fact that large amounts of land, energy, fertilizers and water have also been lost in the production of foodstuffs which simply end up as waste.[90]

This example of a problem could be resolved today by the application of strategic localization to food production through advanced, soilless agricultural systems. Localized "vertical farming" systems, for example, would be effective if liberally employed.[91] Yet, once again, market dynamics complicate this shift. One problem is that attempts at larger-order industrial design across the Earth's surface to efficiently link the supply chain are restricted by random land ownership. It is almost impossible in the current economy to design an optimized regional production network in the same way one would design an airplane to function as a single system. It is as though one person owned the wings, another the fuselage, a third the electronics, etc., and all had to be in agreement to make the system work. The chaotic web of landowner relationships confounds sensible macro-industrial design.

However, as production means become smaller and less resource-intense, and, if (or when) society incentivizes such streamlining, regional production networks *can* be designed and hence optimized. This shift would require a democratic, community process of organizing the landscape to be most efficient, as opposed to the current market system in which land is randomly acquired and sold—again, as though the airplane's wings were sold while in flight to an owner who wanted to use them for some other purpose. Overall, it is very difficult to embrace the power of efficient, holistic design in a market economy, specifically on this macro level. Current mechanisms that attempt to accomplish this, such as zoning, eminent domain, or massive capital investment, are cumbersome in the extreme and therefore limit the potential. I bring up this lack of integrated design not only to point out this property-related disorder, but to again highlight how ephemeralization will assist localization, embracing smaller and increasingly more simplistic industrial mechanisms. Assuming a transition over time to this localization approach, strategic macro-industrial design will become easier to harness, increasing total efficiency.

I would also like to mention that there is an underlying human liberation to be achieved by localization and community self-containment, in contrast to the current hierarchical, power-concentrated capitalist reality. In his writings, Mahatma Gandhi made clear his opposition to emerging capitalist industrialization on the grounds of a loss of control and misguided incentive. When asked in conversation about his view on the rise of industrial mass production, he stated, in 1931:

> I would categorically state my conviction that the mania for mass production is responsible for the world crises. If there is production and distribution both in the respective areas where things are required, it is automatically regulated, and there is less chance for fraud, none for speculation. Because while it is true that you will be producing things in innumerable areas, the power will come from one selected centre. That, in the end, I think, would be found to be disastrous. It would place such a limitless power in one human agency that I dread to think of it. The consequence, for instance, of such a control of power would be that I would be dependent on that power for light, water, even air, and so on. That, I think, would be terrible.[92]

Aside from our context of modern efficiency, this objection has certainly been validated by reoccurring problems of centralized economic power. Gandhi saw the use of localization, even at that early time, as possibly as efficient as centralized industrial activity, while much better at safeguarding liberty and social justice. He stressed the importance of parallel systems of mutual power, like "oceanic circles" overlapping in synergy, avoiding centralized pyramid structures common to industrial capitalism.[93] "Every village has to be self-sustained and capable of managing its affairs even to the extent of defending itself against the whole world," he wrote.[94] However, it has really only been in the modern day that Gandhi's localized, "oceanic circles" economic ideal can be facilitated through new high technology. The advanced means of production that was once only accessible to large, proprietary entities is now coming into the realm of consumer use. Ephemeralization continues to move this transition forward. The goal here is a kind of decentralization that, to the highest degree possible, makes communities economically self-contained. This does not mean a global consciousness is not present, of course, as maintaining a holistic synergy between population centers to ensure overall global sustainability is very important. But the focus to organize a region's needs in a localized way is the first step to a vast improvement in efficiency and community integrity.

This brings us now to the fifth and final attribute to address, (e) networked digital feedback. This has been popularly embraced by what is often called the "Internet of Things" (IoT).[95] While the IoT has no exact definition, it is about networking technology and sensors to optimize information flows. Using the Internet and instruments to measure, track, and feed back information, this process, in the ideal, can unify numerous disparate elements and systems, greatly advancing awareness and efficiency potentials. Some ambitious ideas are "smart cities" where various components of the urban infrastructure become networked for rapid response, from personal health sensors that link to hospitals, to lights that dim when no one is detected in order to save energy.[96] The imagination can run wild with possibilities. If properly incorporated, this ability could allow for a powerful integration, unifying and simplifying the once extremely complex technical processes of society.

In an economic context, the IoT approach could relay and connect data regarding how best to manage resources, production processes, distribution, consumption, recycling, waste disposal behavior, consumer demand, and so on. It may seem abstract, but such a process of networked economic feedback would work on the same principle as modern systems of inventory and distribution found in major commercial warehouses.

Many companies today use a range of sensors and sophisticated tracking means to understand rates of demands, exactly what they have, where it is or where it may be moving, and when it is gone. It is ultimately an issue of detail and scalability to extend this kind of awareness to all sectors of the economy, macro and micro.

Today, the market economy is mostly driven by feedback from consumer purchases and little more. Through people's preferences expressed by way of buying and selling, business alters its productions and designs to accommodate them. As termed in older economic circles, this feedback comes from the "price mechanism." Austrian school economist Ludwig von Mises, in his work *Economic Calculation in the Socialist Commonwealth*, famously argued that without the use of price and exchange, it would be impossible for efficient information to be communicated within the economy. Money changing hands was the bridge to all transactions, feeding back critical supply and demand information.[97] At the time of his writing, in 1920, it is safe to say he was mostly correct in this view, even though there was no shortage of rebuttals. However, today there is no doubt his view is outdated. Not only is price no longer needed to gain critical economic feedback, but the information price communicates is long delayed and incomplete in terms of economic measures required to dramatically increase efficiency. Mechanisms related to the IoT make it possible to efficiently monitor shifting consumer preference, demand, supply, and labor value, virtually in real time. Moreover, IoT can also be used to observe other technical processes price cannot, such as shifts in production protocols, allocation, recycling means, and so on. A true system of economic feedback and management is about understanding the total interaction of economic components on all levels, in a unified way, not just supply and demand or what people are buying and selling. It is now possible to track trillions of economic interactions related to the supply chain and consumer behavior by way of sensors and digital relay, far surpassing what we are doing today.

Needless to say, we are far away from this kind of holistic approach to economic management despite its vast potential. But not because it isn't technically feasible. The ideological tension common in conservative circles, which view fragmentation and competition as a means of "liberty," quickly pollutes the power of this kind of systems-based thinking. The protectionist needs of the market also thwart such collaboration, since even something as basic as releasing inventory data of a natural-resource stock is often kept secret by commercial powers. Overall, poor economic information is generally available since the competitive ethic fosters fear. Hence, this holistic means of improved efficiency, like the other four attributes noted, finds little traction today as far as truly harnessing positive potentials is concerned.

Now, with all five attributes introduced, I suspect some readers may be alienated or bewildered by these counter-market ideas. In all my public engagements, I find that while people are generally open to criticism of our social system, the moment the conversation turns to solutions, the discomfort level rises substantially. While the five proposals may seem radical, they are merely extrapolated from existing trends, oriented by the structuralist train of thought presented throughout this work. Though I understand the cynicism and the repeatedly expressed mantra, "that can never happen!," this also isn't about absolutes. As noted, the five attributes are actually happening right now, proving their importance and superiority to current methods—but only to a very limited and largely unnoticed degree. I can't stress enough the need for an expanded sense of creativity and inquiry in this regard. Naturally, any relevant proposal for true social change is going to feel awkward given how acclimated people are to normality, as we know it. Despite this discomfort, unless people wish to keep things the same—that is, to preserve the social disorder, violence, disease, injustice, and overall spectrum of oppression present today—then this train of thought can't be ignored. *The New Human Rights Movement* must march forward, working to forge these socioeconomic adjustments as best we can, by whatever means we can. How far we as a society move down such a path is proportional to the degree of improvement experienced.

Taking this economic logic to the ultimate extreme, the most advanced adjustment—one that ensures the highest reduction of scarcity and hence lowest amount of induced socioeconomic oppression—is one that focuses solely on design, holistic development, and direct economic participation by the general population. In other words, an economic system that actually has no market at all. While perhaps perceived as highly radical, the whole of sociological, public-health science, along with the most advanced principles of economic management and habitat sustainability, support this conclusion. This is simply the direction society must now move if any true alleviation of socioeconomic inequality and ecological destruction is to occur.

Indeed, the shift from fragmented economic processes driven by monetary incentives to economic processes directly focused on producing the highest state of abundance possible in harmony with our habitat is a dramatic detour from how most of us are taught economics. As discussed throughout this book, there is an underlying structure to capitalism that results in the social and environmental outcomes we see today. *True* economics is a technical design process, without subjective ideology, in the same way the creation of an airplane or any technical tool is. There is no right-wing, liberal, Christian, populist, socialist, or Islamic methodology to the design of a car. The same can be said of how the whole of economic activity is organized, as it is a system or machine like any other, set to perform a given task. Our task again is to optimize economic behavior to further human well-being while remaining ecologically sustainable. Once this goal is understood, bypassing the cultural dogma of our market-based existence, rational thought will naturally arrive at the same set of technical conclusions.

In Appendix B, a highly simplified theoretical model for economic calculation has been reproduced for consideration. This has been included for those who may wish to further explore a more technical, systems-based approach to economic management. This model was introduced in a 2014 work I helped coauthor on behalf of a 501(c)3 nonprofit organization called The Zeitgeist Movement. While abridged and general, the proposed model in Appendix B is considered a good overview in the right direction, accounting for economic factors that today go unaccounted for. The functional expression arrived at is:

$$f_p(E_{design}, E_p, E_{dist}, E_r) \to \max$$

While the above symbolic-logic representation may appear intimidating to some, it is simply a way of organizing complex, connected sets of information in a shorthand way to help clarity. To generalize the expression, from left to right in the parenthesis, we have our four core economic processes that we wish to optimize in terms of efficiency. The letter E symbolizes efficiency while the connected subscripts (design, p, dist, and r) represent how the processes (or rules) of product design, production, distribution, and recycling logically occur. This process is embraced by the total production function (f_p) on the far left, with the arrow pointing to "max" on the far right symbolizing the maximization of economic efficiency. Again, please review Appendix B for a more extensive and accurate explanation.

In addition, Appendix A has been included to provide a raw exploration of *post-scarcity* potentials, examining certain trends and extrapolating theoretical possibilities. This is provided to show what is possible, albeit in theory, if the kind of efficient approach just mentioned were put in place. The scarcity-driven, socioeconomic imbalances seen today are politically justified through public ignorance of modern potentials. What we are doing today vs. what we could be doing, with outstanding improvements, is important to understand. Many in technology communities today do talk about positive future possibilities, with the implication being "We are just not there yet." The truth is that currently existing methods, not trending potentials, can already solve the food, water, energy, pollution, and basic material stress problems common today, if scaled out properly in a systems-based approach. Appendix A sources this empirical research in detail, with noted calculations, but I will summarize the conclusions here.

With respect to food availability, it has already been established that the world produces more than enough food in its current capacity. However, if we were extrapolating what would be possible if advanced agricultural methods were applied, specifically the use of *vertical farm* and soilless systems, we find an astounding increased potential toward abundance. Extrapolated from work done at Columbia University, only 0.006 percent of the current amount of land used today for agriculture would be needed to meet global needs with a vegetarian diet. These systems would also account for a major reduction in water use, since traditional agriculture is extremely water-intensive and wasteful.[98] If we extrapolate the theoretical potential of this method and all agricultural land on Earth was modified to only use vertical farming methods, the output would be enough to feed 34.4 trillion people. Again, this is purely

theoretical, ignoring many other factors. However, since it would only
need to feed 9–10 billion by 2050, only 0.03 percent of that theoretical
potential is needed. This makes moot any seemingly practical objections
to this extrapolation.[99]

With respect to fresh or potable water, while current trends show
water stress growing in the world, our technical potentials for problem
resolution are great. Through proper organization and the use of modern
purification and desalination processes, it is possible to resolve all water
stress in the world. Given the average use per person of 1,385 cubic meters
a year and a population of 7.2 billion, we arrive at a total annual use of
9.972 trillion cubic meters. According to ultraviolet water-purification
statistics produced by a facility in New York, only 3,324 facilities would
theoretically be needed to purify all the water currently used, requiring
only 12,309 acres of land. As for desalination, the process is more intense.
Using a reverse-osmosis seawater plant out of Victoria, Australia, as a
basis, it would take 60,000 plants to process all potable water usage. This
is, again, an extreme extrapolation to make a point. We would never need
to desalinate that much water in reality.[100]

With respect to renewable, sustainable, nonhydrocarbon energy,
the potential of geothermal, solar, wind, and hydropower means show
powerful combined potential. Geothermal has been estimated as having
a possible 2,000 zettajoules (ZJ) of constant power that is harvestable,
assuming minor technological improvements. The total energy consumption of all the countries on the planet is currently only about half
a zettajoule (0.55 ZJ) a year. Wind farms show similar potential, even
with general intermittency problems. Based upon the output of the Alta
Wind Energy Center in California, 13,231 9,000-acre wind farms would
be needed to meet total global energy use; 0.3 percent of Earth's land
surface. Once again, this is not to suggest such a thing is ideal given what
land is feasible for wind farms, along with other required factors. This is
simply to give a general perspective of possibility. Solar fields also show
similar potential. Using the Ivanpah Solar Electric Generating System in
California as a basis, it would take 141,767 fields or 496,184,500 acres to
theoretically meet total current global demand; 1.43 percent of total land
surface on Earth. And as for hydropower, combining existing statistics
for wave, tidal, ocean current, ocean thermal, and osmotic, we arrive at

130,320 TWh/yr or 0.46 ZJ a year. This is roughly 83 percent of current global use.[101]

Put together, along with critically important mixed-use and reuse approaches, only a fraction of current potentials existing today are needed to end hydrocarbon dependence, assisting a dramatically increasing surplus. Again, please see Appendix A for more details.

MOVING FORWARD

In late 2011, I was asked to give a speech in downtown Los Angeles at the encampment of the regional chapter of Occupy Wall Street. Originating in New York City, this organic uprising against inequality, the financial system, and ultimately the whole of capitalism, had sparked to life quite suddenly some months before. Today, its echoes are felt not only in America but globally, as the terms "Occupy" and "We are the 99%" have become symbols against inequality and social injustice. Having already been to New York earlier that year to speak, I was honored to now participate in the parallel L.A. culmination.

Upon arriving at city hall, I was informed that a large protest march would be making its way to an outdoor stage in the middle of an adjacent street. As I conversed with various organizers, the distant sound of mass chanting grew from afar. The sprawling tent city surrounding the city hall campus grew more and more active with excitement. Eventually, the march flooded in, saturating the area and revealing a spectrum of demographics across the thousands of participants. From the stage, the congregation could be seen going back into the horizon along the street, blurred by the signature glare of Los Angeles smog. The energy was overwhelming.

Nervously awaiting my cue to speak, I realized I was following John Densmore, the former drummer of the famous rock group The Doors. His presence added to the already retro feel of the scene, reminiscent of the 1960s counterculture. Listening to Densmore's rhetoric, I felt like I had been sucked into a documentary on Vietnam-era civil rights and antiwar protests. Yet, this time it wasn't a singular issue such as voting rights or seeking to end a specific hegemonic war. This time it was about the dysfunction of the whole social system, most notably the undemocratic power of business and the emergence of vast economic inequality.

What I witnessed looking out from the stage that day was the gradual fortification of our social immune system. The public is increasingly coming to terms with the structural flaws of our economic system. Occupy Wall Street, no matter how crude or unfocused its critics may declare it, has been a preliminary step in what I think will eventually be the greatest social transition of human culture since the Neolithic Revolution. The eon-long battle to overcome injustice, group dominance, and oppression has expanded in awareness to realize a deeper context. Activist concerns that have been historically detached, from the environment to war to social rights, are slowly being recognized as sharing a common root. That root, as explored in this text, is an economic mode with a distorted incentive structure and a mechanistic framework that conflicts with the basic laws of human and ecological nature.

Unlike prior moves against capitalism, specifically the rise of Marxism and the failed Soviet experiment, modern social and physical science has clarified nuances of the problem, helping us better understand what is specifically wrong and why. In the context of public health and socio-environmental sustainability, a move away from market-based economics is no longer an ideological or moral proposal. It is a foundational requirement for progressing society in a positive, increasingly humane way, thwarting powerful negative externalities that mount as the clock ticks down. This is compounded by the now-overwhelming potential of our advanced capacity to provide for all human beings on Earth, also allowing for true harmonic balance with our regenerative habitat.

Tired arguments based upon false dualities such as "individualist" or "collectivist" or "capitalist" or "socialist" can be put to rest. Our increased awareness of how the world works as a unified, systemic synergy shatters such ideological polarity. As Martin Luther King put it in his final work, *Where Do We Go From Here?*: "Communism forgets that life is individual. Capitalism forgets that life is social, and the kingdom of brotherhood is found neither in the thesis of communism nor the antithesis of capitalism but in a higher synthesis. It is found in a higher synthesis that combines the truths of both."[102]

Traditional cultural beliefs and values, no matter how rich and meaningful, do not compete with the laws of human sustainability and public health. The dynamics of what comprises a healthy society transcend our customary loyalties. Instead of arguing about the way we think the world should be, based upon our values, we should first argue about what is working and what isn't, based upon observable facts. Again, while many have viewed civil or human rights as a moral debate, I would argue that the real issue isn't just moral but really one of social stability.

We cannot sustain ourselves in the long run without resolving socioeconomic inequality and the undercurrent of environment incompatibility. Either destruction through environmental forces will create mass social instability or the more desperate victims of unequal economic conditions will ensure deprivation-sparked backlash. The creation of the atomic bomb and the rise of terrorism are two diverse examples of how insecurity, competition, and fear lead to broad dangers. As more-advanced weapons emerge that can cause extreme destruction through smaller and more powerful mechanisms (that is, as ephemeralization affects weapons development), the alienated populace will increase its capacity for destruction, with the effects becoming increasingly catastrophic. Security can no longer be about laws, locks, surveillance, and punitive threat. True global security will come from removing socioeconomic inequality and the oppression/deprivation that defines it. It is also worth considering how the threat of global disease epidemics, something the twenty-first century seems to flirt with more and more each year, will arise from the tropics of the Global South given the vast poverty and overall loss of public health. This puts the whole world at risk, not just the region. Reducing global poverty and improving public health is no longer an isolated concern. It is an international one given the widespread travel common today.

Furthermore, our social immune system must be careful to avoid false solutions. One such myth is the idea that the market will arrive at a global, "zero marginal cost," post-scarcity condition in environmental harmony with further equality all by itself. This view has become popular in technologist circles today; people believe that only minor economic adjustments are needed to allow the fruits of post-scarcity and resulting equality to thrive. Many books have been written in the past decade by generally well-to-do, tech-centric entrepreneurs who isolate the "more with less" trend, falsely arguing that it proves the efficacy of the market economy in the long term. I use the term "techno-capitalist apologists" to refer to those who view the market as a facilitator of, rather than a hindrance to, material and social progress. The mantra is that since the increased rise in efficiency is being accompanied by lower costs, society must therefore be on pace to equalization as a whole as goods become more affordable. They mistakenly believe the market is creating the power of increased efficiency when the real cause is our increasing capacity to intelligently *design*. The market is merely an incentive-and-distribution system, and a poor one at that. (Recall that in chapter four, I discussed that business values only market efficiency, not technical efficiency.)

While there are no doubt parts of the world, specifically the industrialized nations, that have seen a rise in standard of living at lower costs, we will never reach the level of truly optimized potentials if the market remains in its basic form. It matters little what the intentions of "green" or "social" entrepreneurs are. The entire goal of seeking a reduction of socioeconomic inequality, ecological sustainability, and post-scarcity is simply incompatible with the market's *root socioeconomic orientation*. Yet, this myth that we need only tweak the market to birth an abundant, equitable society continues to prevail. For example, many techno-capitalist apologists boast that the affordability of cellphones has brought service and options to millions in Africa who previously lacked any form of telephone. As great as this is, the anecdote misses the deeper problem: more Africans have cellphones than running water.[103] Hence, these are not prioritized developments. The fruits of ephemeralization, without comprehensive design inspired by specific intentions to resolve problems, will never be inclusive enough to be effective. Though some improvements will occur, they will be chaotic, while the overall system consequence will continue to generate destructive inequality and structural violence.

Humanity cannot afford to pander to the superstition of market self-regulation and Adam Smith's invisible hand, pretending everything will be fine in the end because we see fragmented evidence of approaching "zero marginal cost" in some sectors. While the positive intentions of the techno-capitalist apologists should be respected, their delusion should not. The grace period of market-driven development is ending.

The chickens—climate change, technological unemployment, biodiversity loss, and resource overshoot—are coming home to roost in the form of multiple negative externalities that have no "in-system" resolution. Without a unified *design* approach to the economy—one that undoes the current system's structural intentions—only minor progress will occur.

Remember, the market economy's first priority is not to help the world but to increase cost efficiency and profits. Therefore profit, not social benefit, is what drives its efforts. If it happens to be that this process of competition improves more lives, great. But that is not a priority when it comes to market logic. A company that sells a good for $5 that costs $3 to make, finding that it can reduce that production cost to $2, does not lower its original selling price if it can avoid doing so. The whole point is to increase profits, not equalize them based on production savings. This creates self-limiting thresholds toward "zero marginal cost." No company is going to make itself obsolete by reducing its costs to near zero, selling at near zero value. That is the antithesis of a model based, once again, on the benefits of scarcity.

Now, how these changes are to be made is no doubt the ultimate question. While it is easy to theorize such ideal changes and their merit, transitioning to them smoothly involves many considerations. Generally, assuming the sanction of society to make such an adaptation, moving from here to there can be done by replacing attributes of the current economy with ones that increasingly orient away from the market's basis in scarcity, competition, and exploitation. Returning to Figure 5c, going from top to bottom, we can consider some possibilities. However, I wish to point out that what follows regarding ideas of how to transition to each of the five shifts in Figure 5c is presented to inspire further thought by the reader. It is not the scope of this text to expand this line of thinking into extensive specifics, owing to the inherent complexity. Also, I wish to remind the reader that what follows assumes the overall sanction of society, meaning the majority would seek these changes, with little political or establishment resistance. Needless to say, as will be stated at the end of this brief exploration, the truth is that things will never be so easy.

The move from *human labor to automation* could be made by the use of a Universal Basic Income (UBI) and the strategic shortening of the workday, as touched upon prior. It is a matter of replacing lost income from increased automation through compensating adjustments. The source of the Universal Basic Income is open to debate but, as per Thomas Piketty's observations, a large tax on the wealth of the super-rich would be an obvious start. This step would also directly assist the reduction of economic inequality, which, in and of itself, is a dire imperative in order to improve public health and stabilize society. Any debate about the importance of the ownership class's role as "job creators" and hence the need for upper-class tax breaks and the like can finally be rejected permanently on the grounds that the focus of society is no longer on creating jobs but on *removing* them in favor of more efficient means. Likewise, with the shift to labor automation and efforts to maximize zero marginal cost, the value of goods will drop in general, causing positive deflation of prices directly. This means less income will be needed in general to purchase the same amount of goods.

It's also important to express that when people criticize UBI by asking where the money will come from to begin with, they forget that *wealth is not money*. In fact, wealth is not even a store of value, nor is wealth an outcome of acquisition or investment. We are taught these crude interpretations of wealth because capitalism is based around individual success, not social or technical success, while value is associated with property. True wealth, in the purest economic sense, can only describe a kind of strategic leverage over nature—an economic strategy for personal and group prosperity that can only be measured in terms of *efficiency trends*, not stores of value or property. For example, years ago, a simple electric calculator cost $1,000. Today, you can get one for a dollar or less. The real value or wealth inherent in any calculator (or any good) is the efficiency trend achieved over time, doing "more with less." In this sense, what allows for UBI is the ever-increasing economic efficiency we are seeing (as driven by technology), not the arbitrary level of money, incomes, or goods in circulation. The same logic applies to the shortening of the work week or the reduction of daily work hours. It isn't about money as related to labor—it is about efficiency achieved, and the more efficiency, the less need for money or labor.

The move from *property to access* could be assisted by further incentivizing a rental or so-called "sharing economy," where it becomes more cost-effective to rent than own. At the same time, the liability of ownership should be moved from the user/consumer to the producer as much as possible. This shift incentivizes the creation of more optimized, durable goods that don't suffer from planned obsolescence or other common production weaknesses currently occurring due to the need for cyclical consumption. While today we see a passive attempt at durable production through product warranties, this is not enough. Further shifting most all liability to the producing company in an access or rental society will ensure more-efficient and sustainable products, with less waste. The overall benefit will reduce the production footprint greatly through access while increasing goods integrity through producer-based liability. Fewer goods will be produced, but they will be used by more people through rental systems, with those goods becoming more efficient, pliant, and long-lasting since the company no longer has an incentive to produce low-quality or soon-to-be obsolete goods (planned obsolescence).

The move from *intellectual property to open source* could be assisted by a program of royalty or single-reward incentives for those contributing. For example, if Apple Inc. decided to open-source all of its software and hardware designs, utilizing a democratized platform that people could engage to assist development, monetary reward for those with the most measurably helpful contributions could be effective. Yet it should again be pointed out that such an idea really moves against the grain of how capitalism works in terms of intellectual property. Because the public interaction or collaboration would be out in the open for all to see and learn from, such a move would quickly erode the vast profit potential currently occurring. To void Apple's patents means to remove a major aspect of their profitability by extension, meaning it would invariably hurt the company in traditional economic terms. However, that is also the point, expressing the role of such a transition away from market economics. This intermediate step involving royalty shares or rewards for public contributions is still feasible to inch us forward, keeping one foot on each side of the paradigm. It is complex to think about, but what safeguards the current market mode is the fact that a major company such as Apple still owns the specific means of production, ensuring final sale value goes to the company overall. So, the general contributing public wouldn't be able to simply "steal" and produce an Apple product on its own since it doesn't (yet) have access to such complex production facilities.

Overall, to maximize open-source potential the ethos would have to shift away from profit as the first focus of incentive, to where any and all companies exist to further the well-being of the society as a whole. One step in this direction could be to mandate corporate sharing of all information within its sector first. For example, imagine all the cell-phone companies being required by law to share their designs with each other, forming a genre-wide cooperative of sorts. This doesn't remove the company and its basic material operations, income structure, or specific decisions, but it reduces the wasteful effects of competition by enabling collaboration across the genre or sector. This would accelerate the design progress since, in the context of modern open-source approaches, more minds looking at a problem are always better than fewer minds. Likewise, if properly networked, it would be far more environmentally sustainable since the competitive ethic encourages companies to seek *differential advantage* and this means they constantly seek to "one-up" their competitors in the eyes of consumers, reproducing and duplicating with mild variation what is already occurring in their market genre. This can be as minor as a new add-on feature or some idea another company already came up with. With open source, this repetitive, duplicate waste would diminish, rapidly accelerating design efficiency.

The move from *globalization to localization* could unfold naturally if automation and the power of ephemeralization are allowed to flourish without restriction. Global product distribution wouldn't make financial sense after a while since costs would be reduced enough to incentivize localization over globalization. Unfortunately, this trend is currently unrealized with no real incentive to pursue it. In terms of *market efficiency* it is still too cheap and profitable to exploit poverty in distant lands, wastefully moving resources around the globe. For example, it has been estimated that the average American foodstuff now travels an absurd 1,500 miles before being consumed.[104]

To deter such behavior, disciplinary action could be used. The state (assuming it could be disengaged enough from its elitist business loyalties) could directly incentivize local production, fining companies that engage in unneeded globalization for profit on the grounds of environmental waste. It could also reward companies through tax breaks and the like to focus on localized production as well. While this is certainly a big challenge given the "anti-free market" nature of such a move, I suspect such impositions are going to be forced in the future regardless, given the need to counter climate change and the clear relationship it has to globalization. Moreover, if time allows for it, assuming the "inherent counteracting efficiency" noted in Figure 5b is strong enough, it may actually become natural and logical for localization to occur as we approach "zero marginal cost" within the market system. The reduced size and needs of the means of production simply won't be complex enough to warrant Third World labor and resource exploitation anymore, making it more profitable to localize. However, that is a personal hope and not an expectation given the reality of circumstances today.

Overall, localization in the context in this text would synergistically incorporate all the attributes noted in Figure 5c. The establishment of a highly efficient and advanced industrial network would be needed. The general transition would be to "socialize" or generally make free (without direct purchase) goods from as many industries as possible. Logically, the least complex production needs would be socialized before the more complex, likely starting with food production, moving to energy production, and then to basic goods production. As a process, in addition to shorter work hours and Universal Basic Income to compensate for reduced purchasing power, less-complex products would be made free before the more-complex, in the same kind of step-by-step logic. Those sectors most approaching "zero marginal cost" through automation could then be subsidized for the final margin, allowing fully free access to the public. Food and energy would again be the easiest to provide, assuming the advanced economic methods denoted earlier in this chapter were applied.

As for the final attribute, the move from *fragmented economic feedback to networked, digital feedback* through sensors and measures related to the IoT, this involves scaling out current systems already in use to incorporate the widest range possible. Within a market economy, this is difficult given the inherently nonintegrated nature of things on the technical level. It would perhaps be easiest to start with sector-wide networking and data sharing. Sector-accessible databases could be created that dynamically show all related activity, including environmental impact, raw resource use, recycling efficacy, processing rates, waste output, etc. One important mandate would be the use of an intelligent calculation system to ensure steady-state equilibrium and design optimization. As in the crude conception in Appendix B, if each sector utilized such an integrated system, the regulatory nature of this calculation would thwart many unsustainable practices. Monitoring this activity, fines or sanctions could then be placed on companies that violate basic protocols. Ideally, this integration would extend to the entire global economy so a total-Earth system/habitat perspective could be understood.

To reiterate, taken to its logical extreme, the end goal of achieving a truly sustainable, post-scarcity economy would logically be one that has no trade or money at all, but rather focuses on design and management processes that have become democratized and made participatory. And again, despite the controversy of such a proposal or conclusion, that is exactly what the train of thought presented here suggests in terms of optimized public health, habitat sustainability, and ultimately reduced social oppression. This level of organization through design has only really become possible in the past few decades. It may seem like a fantasy goal, given what we have been conditioned to believe about society, economics, and human nature, but from a systems-based scientific perspective, what is proposed here is simply what a *real* economy is, by definition.

Now, a great deal more could be said as far as technical steps go. The goal is, again, a transitional move focused on not only *designing out* socioeconomic inequality and unsustainable practices, but also furthering the move toward post-scarcity. In this, there are many possible avenues and degrees of incorporation, most of which are fairly straightforward. But, as stated, this isn't the real problem at hand. The real problem is that such moves will never happen without a massive amount of activist pressure put on the business-run establishment. It is very easy to rationally theorize a transitional process once the general approval of the community and government is achieved, supporting the overall change. Unfortunately, such approval is far from being achieved at this time given the vast ignorance of the public and the coercive, nondemocratic power of the world's business-run governments.

Before this complex problem is addressed, I wish to summarize how *The New Human Rights Movement* has four basic levels of realization:

1. The structuralist realization that the most detrimental social patterns existing today are sourced to a flawed economic orientation.
2. These resulting detrimental social patterns include socioeconomic inequality as the core public-health threat. Socioeconomic inequality is the precondition for a spectrum of other problems, also linking to unsustainable negative externalities produced by the market.
3. Adjusting away from this flawed economic orientation and seeking to reduce socioeconomic inequality and generate environmental sustainability means shifting focus to maximize economic efficiency through strategic, systems-based, technical design. This will reduce scarcity, reduce inequality, and reduce the environmental footprint. It will also better harness ephemeralization, moving us ever closer to a "post-scarcity" abundance.
4. Accomplishing this transition will require both creative initiative and activist initiative. The creative initiative has to do with developing the efficiency-enhancing systems that will compose the new economic mode. The activist initiative has to do with strategic pressure and demands placed upon the existing power structure, coercing change from the bottom up.

It is realization four that is the real problem. Different conditions in different regional cultures and socioeconomic extremes require different actions. However, a major growing advantage is the pressure that technological unemployment is slowly creating. This, combined with the pressure of growing environmental crises such as climate change, is forcing new considerations regarding what the future should look like, slowly eroding confidence in the current economic establishment. These and other factors consequential of capitalism's increased incompatibility with nature and progress itself open the door to new levels of influence.

Broadly, I refer to the "Four Ds" when thinking about activism: Demand, Design, Detach, and Deter.

Demand:
Political influence, whether through grassroots protest or institutional lobbying via NGOs, will naturally be important. This is the arena of democracy that most think of, though often they

misunderstand its limitations. Public appeals to directly reduce socioeconomic inequality and stop environmental degradation are always going to go against the grain within a market system, which will resist every step.

Regardless, we should constantly demand things such as Universal Basic Income; maximum wage and wealth caps per person, government subsidies to incentivize cooperative businesses rather than hierarchical ones, universal standardization of goods components by industry sector to reduce waste, and other socializing and income/wealth equalizing means. Basic public-health services, as common to Nordic countries, should also be pushed to ease social stress while larger strides are made. These are not solutions in and of themselves, but they will help.

Design:
At the root of a socially just, post-scarcity, and sustainable economic mode is design. It is design not only in the sense of tangible means, but also in the sense of philosophy. One great efficiency flaw in market economics is that it is void of any larger-order design. As with any system, the more relevant factors directly incorporated, the more streamlined the total system is. A simple analogy is a transit system. If you were tasked to design a transit system for a city from scratch, it would logically form in a far different and more efficient way than if you had to build around already existing infrastructure that's in the way.

So, designing new systems, both macro and micro—from individual goods to integrated goods genres and sectors—is an important step. This requires think tanks and engineers employing the most advanced efficiency principles in a holistic way. Appendix B is a starting point for a calculation system that needs development. Other projects could include localization approaches seeking to get a town, city, or community "off the grid" and self-sustaining.

Detach:
Some degree of rejection of the current system must occur in order to increase the pressure to change the whole structure. One method

is to work to reduce economic involvement in money and trade as much as possible. The use of collectives, shared library systems, time banks, mutual credit systems, and other mechanisms can help not only reduce economic growth but also help those currently suffering. This is a difficult line to walk, however, as the systemic chain reaction of a loss of economic growth is also a loss of work and purchasing power for some.

Yet, this kind of negative pressure can further incentivize politically driven reforms as per the "Demand" section. If more people become unemployed, more will see the need for Universal Basic Income, and so on. This may seem controversial but in the broad view it is simply speeding up what is now a natural process. Also, increasing community involvement through sharing systems and the like will help set the stage for localization. Any method that uses integrated design and sharing systems to reduce trade is going to be productive.

Deter:
As mentioned, Johan Gultang coined the term *cultural violence* as an extension of structural violence. This is embedded in the value-system disorder common to modern culture. It is part of our *poverty of the spirit* as also mentioned. While the social psychology emanating from the social system will continue to pollute culture as long as capitalism exists, those of us who identify with a new value system, as described in this text, need to utilize our shared social nature to influence what others believe. Specifically, a polite level of disrespect and shame should be put upon those promoting high wealth, consumerism, and materialism. No longer should any respect or praise be placed on those engaging in conspicuous consumption or wealth signaling. Those driving Ferraris down the street or sporting overly expensive designer handbags should be made to feel embarrassed for their wasteful and insulting decadence.

It needs to be communicated that such values only symbolize the structural violence of the world, not the individual's own ostensible success or status. Extreme luxury goods today really signify dehumanization and a lack of empathy. It is this pattern of materialism and the false idea of "infinite wants" that helps pollute attempts to create a sustainable and equitable society. To such minds, "there isn't enough to go around" seems real because they choose to see elitism and rarity as a virtue. The new measures of success must be based upon finding balance with nature and one another, not gaming, exploitation, and advantage seeking. Only sustainable values can create a sustainable culture.

As I think again of gazing out upon Occupy Wall Street that California day, it is clear to me that very little faith can be put in the established political and business leaders of our time. The change I speak of will not originate from existing authority but rather from the raw masses. As noted, those who reach high levels of power and opulence in the world are usually conditioned to favor the mechanisms of their reward. As such, it is up to the average majority to realize this change can only come from the ground up. This means courage and confidence must manifest in areas that may be unfamiliar to some. I am convinced that while there is a technical learning curve to some of what has been described in this book, it is not out of the reach of the average person.

People may think that if they have no background in economics, sociology, political science, or engineering, they have no right to engage in such subjects. Our overly specialized and fragmented society has created gaps between disciplines, discouraging exploration. I'm here to tell you that nothing is off-limits in this world when it comes to learning, understanding, and contribution. However, a new level of creativity and vulnerability is critical. No one told two bicycle mechanics called the Wright Brothers that it was impossible to design a manmade flying machine, which was the scientific consensus at the time. But that is exactly what they did when they built the first airplane. Yet, I have no doubt many reading this work will hastily dismiss its proposals as impossible, not understanding how such changes can be implemented in real life. I also have no doubt that these final proposals will spark great discomfort and even fear, given the numerous unanswered questions and considerations they raise.

The purpose of this book has been to explain the roots of social distress in the twenty-first century and the train of thought that will resolve it, if a well-informed and diligent activist movement succeeds in implementation. It was not the intention of this book to cover all possible scenarios or to pretend they even could be covered. The new human rights movement at hand will necessarily be an outcome of our collective efforts, following this train of thought. It is my hope that the ingenuity of humanity can coalesce in building upon this reasoning, turning theory into reality. It is really up to you to decide which side of history you will be on. And to those who do outright reject these observations and proposals for whatever reason conjured, I offer a provocative prediction: The kind of change proposed in this book is going to happen one way or another. The only question is how much suffering has to occur before it does. Returning to the prophetic words of Bayard Rustin:

> We are all one. And if we don't know it, we will find out the hard way.[105]

POST-SCARCITY POTENTIALS[1]

I N THIS SECTION, basic statistics and trends will be presented to show the potential for a global "post-scarcity" social system.[2] While scarcity in absolute terms will always be with humanity to one degree or another in this closed system of earthly resources, scarcity on the level of *human needs* and *basic material success* is no longer a viable defense of the market system's allocation methods.[3] Below is a list of current life-support potentials available to the global population that have gone unharnessed due to inhibiting factors inherent in the market economy. Each point will be addressed in its own subsection.

1. Food Production: Current production methods already produce more than enough food to feed all human beings on Earth. Furthermore, current trends toward more optimized technology and agricultural methods also show a capacity to further increase production efficiency and nutrition quality to a state of active abundance, using minimal human labor and increasingly less energy, water, and land.

2. Clean Water: Desalination and decontamination processes currently exist to such a vast degree of application that no human beings, even with our current levels of pollution, should ever need to be without clean water, regardless of where they are on Earth.

3. Energy: Between geothermal, wind, solar, and hydropower, coupled with system-based processes that can recapture expelled energy and reuse it directly, there is an absolute energy abundance that can serve the current world's population many times over.

FOOD PRODUCTION

According to the United Nations Food and Agriculture Organization, one out of every eight people on Earth (nearly 1 billion people) suffers from chronic malnutrition. Almost all of these people live in developing countries, representing 15 percent of the population of these countries.[4] First World waste patterns can create price increases for the global food supply due to increased demand resulting from those very waste patterns. In other words, the First World adds to the world hunger epidemic because its consumers waste food, resulting in increased demand, which ultimately pushes price values past what is affordable for many.

While there is certainly an educational imperative for the consuming world to consider the relevance of its waste patterns, both in terms of real food waste and waste's effect on global prices, the most effective and practical means to overcome this global deficiency is to update the system of food production itself with more modern methods. This updating of production methods can also be coupled with deliberate localization to reduce the waste caused by inefficiencies in the current global food-supply chain. The combination of improved methods and localization would reduce waste, demand, inefficiency, and price problems in general, and it would dramatically increase productivity, product quality, and output overall.[5]

While the active use of arable land and land-based agriculture should continue (ideally, of course, with more-sustainable practices than we are using today),[6] a great deal of pressure can be alleviated now with advanced soilless methods, which require less water, less fertilizer, fewer (or no) pesticides, less land, and less labor. These facilities can now be built in city environments or even off coastlines, at sea.[7]

It appears the most promising of all such arrangements is what is known today as "vertical farming."[8] Vertical farming has been put to test in a number of regions, with extremely promising results regarding efficiency. Extrapolating these statistics, coupled with parallel trend advancement (increases in efficiency) of the associated mechanisms of this process, reveals that the future of abundant food production will use fewer resources per unit of output (compared to the current land-based tradition), cause less waste, reduce the ecological impact of food production, increase food quality, and the like; it will also use less of the surface of the planet and enable types of food once restricted to certain climates or regions to be grown virtually anywhere in enclosed vertical systems.

While approaches vary, common methods include rotating crop systems in transparent enclosures to use natural light, coupled with hydroponic,[9] aeroponic,[10] and/or aquaponic[11] water and nutrient servicing systems. Artificial-light systems are also being used along with other means to distribute natural light, such as parabolic mirror systems that can move light without electricity.[12] Many "waste to energy" approaches to these structures are increasingly common, along with advanced power systems based on regenerative processes.[13] Between various approaches, the capacity is dramatically increased since food can, in many cases, be grown almost twenty-four hours a day, seven days a week.

Common objections to this type of farming have mostly been concerns over its energy footprint, criticizing the use of artificial light in some arrangements as too power-intensive. However, the use of renewable energy systems, such as photovoltaics, coupled with regional placement most conducive to renewable methods, such as near wave, tidal, or geothermal sources, are plausible solutions for sustainable, nonhydrocarbon-based powering.

However, it is best to think about this in a comparative context. In the US, up to 20 percent of the country's fossil-fuel consumption goes into the food chain, according to the UN's Food and Agricultural Organization (FAO), which points out that fossil-fuel use by the food systems in the developed world "often rivals that of automobiles."[14]

In Singapore, a vertical farm system, custom built in a transparent enclosure, uses a closed loop, automated hydraulic system to rotate the crop in circles between sunlight and an organic nutrient treatment, costing only about $3 *a month* in electricity for each enclosure.[15] This system is also reported as *ten times* more productive per square foot than conventional farming, using much less water, labor, and fertilizer, as noted above. There is also little transport cost as all produce is distributed locally, saving more resources and energy.

Overall, there is a spectrum of applications. In many cases, preexisting structures not originally built for vertical farming are being utilized.[16]

In Chicago, the world's largest certified organic vertical farm is in operation. While producing mostly greens for the local Chicago market, this 90,000-square-foot facility uses an aquaponic system, with waste from tilapia fish providing nutrients for the plants.[17] The farm reportedly saves 90 percent of its water, compared with conventional farming techniques, and produces no agricultural runoff. Additionally, all of its waste, such as plant roots, stems, and even biodegradable packaging, is recycled in collaboration, making it nearly a zero-waste facility.[18]

Current statistics vary with respect to the efficiency, often due to monetary-based limitations and inherent profitability concerns. In line with the market system, promising technology finds development only if it proves competitive. Given how new these ideas are, we cannot expect to see many examples, nor can we expect to see an optimization of such methods to a high degree for measurement without "market acceptance."

However, we can extrapolate the realized potential of existing systems, scaling the application out as if it were incorporated in every major city, in its most relatively efficient form. The following list confirms the superiority of this approach as compared to current, traditional land-based models. Not only is it a more sustainable practice, it is also a more productive practice. In contrast with existing methods, it can provide the entire world's population with vegetable-based nutrition many times over.[19]

Versatile

Unlike traditional farming, vertical farms can be constructed anywhere, even on water, using upward layers to multiply output capacity (i.e., a 10-story farm will produce one-tenth of a 100-story farm). This space utilization is limited mostly to architectural possibility. Likewise, the plants grown can be "on demand" in many ways; the farms can grow virtually any crop, since regional soil, climate, and similar restrictions have been lifted.

Reduced resource use

Vertical farming uses substantially less water and pesticide, and is more conducive to nonhydrocarbon-based nutrient/fertilizer methods. Its energy use can vary by application, but in its most efficient setting it uses dramatically less energy both to power the farm itself and with respect to the greatly diminished need for hydrocarbon fertilizer and oil-fueled transport, which is a heavy burden in the current, farm-based process.

More sustainable/less ecological damage

The current tradition of farming has been recognized as one of the most ecologically destructive processes of modern society. In the words of environmental writer Renee Cho:

> As of 2008, 37.7 percent of global land and 45 percent of U.S. land was used for agriculture. The encroachment of humans into wild land has resulted in the spread of infectious disease, the loss of biodiversity and the disruption of ecosystems. Over-cultivation and poor soil management has led to the degradation of global agricultural lands. The millions of tons of toxic pesticides used each year contaminate surface waters and ground-water, and endanger wildlife. Agriculture is responsible for 15 percent of global greenhouse gas emissions, and accounts for one-fifth of U.S. fossil fuel use, mainly to run farm equipment, transport food and produce fertilizer. As excess fertilizer washes into rivers, streams and oceans, it can cause eutrophication: algae blooms proliferate; when they die, they are consumed by microbes, which use up all the oxygen in the water; the result is a dead zone that kills all aquatic life. As of 2008, there were 405 dead zones around the world . . . more than two-thirds of the world's fresh water is used for agriculture.[20]

Post-scarcity capacity

Students at Columbia University working on vertical farm systems determined that in order to feed 50,000 people, a thirty-story building the size of a "New York City" block would be needed.[21] A New York City block is about 6.4 acres.[22] If we extrapolate this into the context of the city of Los Angeles, with a population of about 3.9 million[23] and a total acreage of about 318,912,[24] it would take roughly seventy-eight such thirty-story structures to feed the local residents, for a total of 499 acres. This amounts to about 0.1 percent of the total land area of Los Angeles to feed the population.[25]

The Earth, consisting of about 29 percent land, has roughly 36,794,240,000 acres and a human population of 7.2 billion as of late 2013.[26] If we extrapolate the same basis of a thirty-story vertical farm covering 6.4 acres to feed 50,000 people, we end up needing 144,000 vertical farms, in theory, to feed the world.[27] This amounts to 921,600 acres.[28] Given that roughly 38 percent of all the Earth's land is currently being used for traditional agriculture (13,981,811,200 acres),[29] we find that we need only 0.006 percent of the Earth's existing farmland to meet production requirements.[30]

Now, these extrapolations are clearly theoretical and obviously many other factors need to be taken into account with respect to placement of such farm systems and critical specifics. Also, within the 38 percent land-use statistic, much of that land is for livestock cultivation, not just crop production. However, the raw statistics are quite incredible with respect to possible efficiency and capacity. In fact, if we were to build these same vertical farms on the land currently used for crop production—about 4,408,320,000 acres—the food output would be enough to feed 34.4 trillion people.[31]

Given that we will need to feed only 9 to 10 billion by 2050, we only need to harness about 0.03 percent of this theoretical capacity, which, it could be argued, likely makes rather moot any seemingly practical objections common to the aforementioned extrapolation. As a final note, vegetable protein from vertical crops offer a solution for the pollution and waste related to animal farming. From a sustainability standpoint, ignoring the common moral objections and arguably inhumane practices commonly associated with industrialized livestock cultivation, the production of meat and animal-based products is an environmentally unfriendly act as practiced today.

According to the International Livestock Research Institute (ILRI), livestock systems occupy about 45 percent of the Earth's land.[32] According to the FAO, the livestock sector produces more greenhouse-gas emissions than modern gas-consuming transport.[33] Given that 90 percent of all the large fish once thriving in the ocean are gone due to overfishing, as well,[34] new solutions are needed.

One such solution is aquaculture, which is the direct farming of fish, crustaceans, and the like. This direct approach, if sustainably driven, can provide farm-raised, protein-rich fish for human consumption, replacing the demand for land-based meat. Another approach is the production of "in vitro meat." In vitro meat may be produced as strips of muscle fiber, which grow through the fusion of precursor cells, either embryonic stem cells or specialized satellite cells found in muscle tissue. This type of meat is usually cultured in a bioreactor.

While still experimental, in 2013 the world's first lab-grown burger was cooked and eaten in London.[35] Benefits include the reduction of livestock-sourced disease, which is very common, along with eliminating certain negative health characteristics of traditional meat, such as fatty acids.

CLEAN WATER

Given that the human body can survive without fresh water for only a few days,[36] making this most basic resource abundantly available to all is critical. Likewise, it is the backbone of many industrial production methods, including agriculture. Fresh water is naturally occurring water on the Earth's surface in ice sheets, ice caps, glaciers, icebergs, bogs, ponds, lakes, rivers, and streams, and underground as groundwater in aquifers and underground streams. Of all the water on Earth, 97 percent of it is saline and not directly consumable.

According to the World Health Organization: "About 2.6 billion people—half the developing world—lack even a simple 'improved' latrine and 1.1 billion people have no access to any type of improved source of drinking water. As a direct consequence:

- 1.6 million people die every year from diarrheal diseases (including cholera) attributable to lack of access to safe drinking water and basic sanitation and 90 percent of these are children under 5, mostly in developing countries.
- 160 million people are infected with schistosomiasis; causing tens of thousands of deaths annually; 500 million people are at risk of

trachoma from which 146 million are threatened by blindness and 6 million are visually impaired.

- Intestinal helminths (ascariasis, trichuriasis and hookworm infection) are plaguing the developing world due to inadequate drinking water, sanitation and hygiene with 133 million suffering from high intensity intestinal helminthes infections; there are around 1.5 million cases of clinical hepatitis A every year."[37]

According to the United Nations, by 2025, an estimated 1.8 billion people will live in areas plagued by water scarcity, with two-thirds of the world's population living in water-stressed regions.[38] As with most all of the world's current resource problems, it is an issue of both poor management and a lack of industrial application. From the standpoint of management, the amount of water wasted in the world due to pollution, overuse, and inefficient infrastructure is enormous. About 95 percent of all water that enters most people's homes goes back down the drain in one shot.[39]

A systems-based solution to optimize water use is to design kitchens and bathrooms so that they recapture water for different purposes. For example, the water running through a sink or shower can be made available for a toilet. Various companies have slowly put such ideas into practice recently, but overall most infrastructures do not include plans for such reuse. The same is true of large commercial buildings, which can create reuse networks throughout the whole structure, capture rainwater for other purposes, and otherwise use water more efficiently.

Water pollution is another problem. It affects both developed and developing nations on many levels. The American Environmental Protection Agency (EPA) estimates that 850 billion gallons of untreated discharges (waste) flow into water bodies annually, contributing to more than 7 million illnesses each year.[40] The Third World Centre for Water Management estimates that only about 10 to 12 percent of wastewater in Latin America is treated properly. Mexico City, for example, "exports" its untreated wastewater to local farmers.

Though the farmers value this wastewater because the water increases crop yields, the wastewater is heavily contaminated with pathogens and toxic chemicals, representing a serious health risk for both farmers and consumers of the agricultural products grown in this area. In India, major cities discharge untreated wastewater into the bodies of water that serve as their drinking water. Delhi, for example, discharges wastewater directly into the Yamuna River—the source of drinking water for some 57 million people.[41]

Solutions to this problem must in part address the issue of this enormous inefficiency, which itself has most likely been driven by the expense of instituting proper waste-management systems. By coupling good waste management with an industrial-design imperative that systems should include reuse, we can better preserve and utilize our existing resources.

That aside, the broadest solution to compensate for these emerging water problems is through (a) purification and (b) desalination systems, both on the macro-industrial and micro-industrial scale. This approach can alleviate current water problems affecting more than 2 billion people and also transcend the current condition into one of relative abundance.

(a) Purification

Advancements in water purification have been accelerating rapidly with many technological variations of approach. Perhaps one of the most efficient today is what is called "ultraviolet (UV) disinfection." This process is highly scalable, low energy, and works quickly.

Engineer Ashok Gadgil has invented a portable UV system that can disinfect water at the rate of one ton per hour, or fifteen liters per minute. It uses only sixty watts of electrical power, which is comparable to the power used by one ordinary table lamp. This is enough to meet the drinking-water needs of a community of 2,000 people."[42] Gadgil developed this device for rural, poor areas; it can run off solar panels, weighs only fifteen pounds, and has no toxic discharge.

Of course, there is no silver bullet. While UV disinfection works very well for bacteria and viruses, it is less effective with other types of pollution such as suspended solids, turbidity, color, or soluble organic matter.[43] In large-scale applications, UV is often combined with more standard treatments, such as chlorine, as is the case with the world's largest UV drinking-water disinfection plant, in New York, which can treat 2.2 billion US gallons (8,300,000 cubic meters) per day.[44] That is 3,029,500,000 cubic meters a year.

The average person in the United States uses 2,842 cubic meters a year.[45] This includes fresh water used for industrial purposes, not just for direct (i.e., drinking) consumption. The global average is 1,385 cubic meters per year.[46] China, India, and the United States are currently the largest freshwater users in the world and the majority of that water is used in production, mainly agriculture.[47] In fact, about 70 percent of all fresh water is used for agriculture globally.[48]

For the sake of pure statistical argument, ignoring the highly needed changes in strategic water use, reuse systems, and conservation possibilities through more advanced and efficient industrial applications, let us assess the simple question of what it would require to disinfect all the fresh water currently being used in the world on average by the population, in all contexts. Given the global average of 1,385 cubic meters and a population of 7.2 billion, we arrive at a total annual use of 9.972 trillion cubic meters.

Using the New York UV plant's output capacity of roughly 3 billion cubic meters a year as a base per installation of such a plant, we find that 3,324 plants would be needed globally.[49] The New York plant is about 3.7 acres (160k sq. ft.).[50] This means, in theory, that about 12,300 acres are needed to facilitate a purification process of all the fresh water currently used globally by the population. Of course, needless to say, there many other "footprint" factors that come into play, such as power needs, coupled with the critical importance of location.

However, let's put this into a larger, more thoughtful comparison. The United States military alone, with its roughly 845,441 military buildings and bases, occupies about *30 million acres* globally.[51] Only 0.04 percent of that land would be needed to disinfect the total freshwater use of the entire world, if it were even needed at that scale, which it is not.

(b) Desalination

The realistic possibility of mass, global purification of polluted fresh water aside, likely the most powerful means to assure usable, potable water is to convert directly from a saline source, namely the ocean. With a planet composed mostly of salt water, this technique, if done properly, would assure global water abundance alone.

The most common method of desalination used today is *reverse osmosis*, a process that removes water molecules from salt water, leaving salt ions in a brine waste byproduct. According to the International Desalination Association; "Currently, reverse osmosis (RO) . . . accounts for nearly 60 percent of installed capacity, followed by the thermal processes multi-stage flash (MSF) at 26 percent and multi-effect distillation (MED) at 8.2 percent."[52] As of 2011, there were roughly 16,000 desalination plants worldwide. The total global capacity of all plants online (e.g., in operation) was 66.5 million cubic meters per day, or approximately 17.6 billion US gallons per day.[53]

As with everything technological, many advancing methods currently considered experimental suggest a powerful increase in efficiency as the trends unfold. One such method called "capacitive desalination" (CD), also known as capacitive deionization (CDI), has been shown to operate with greater energy efficiency, lower pressures, and no membrane components, all without the production of a waste discharge like conventional practices. It can also be easily scaled-up simply by an increase in the number of flow electrodes in the system.[54]

If we examine the existing methods, coupled with emerging methods, we see a general trend of increasing efficiency in both power conservation and performance.[55] That briefly noted, the focus of this extrapolation toward a "post-scarcity" utilization of desalination will consider only current, proven, in-use methods, namely the reverse-osmosis system.

The Wonthaggi Desalination Plant is an advanced reverse-osmosis seawater desalination plant on the Bass Coast near Wonthaggi, in southern Victoria, Australia. It was completed in December 2012. It can produce, conservatively speaking, about 410,000 cubic meters of desalinated water per day (150 million cubic meters a year),[56] while occupying about 20 hectares (about fifty acres of land).[57] Since, as noted, the total annual water use of the world today is about 9 trillion, 972 billion cubic meters, this means that it would take 60,000 plants[58] to process all potable water usage. Once again, this extreme extrapolation is to make a relative point, since we do not need to desalinate that much water in reality.

However, assuming that we did need to desalinate seawater constantly to match current global use, 3 million acres of land would be needed in total. Earth has about 217,490[59] miles of coastline, which means, loosely using the Wonthaggi model of roughly twenty hectares (fifty acres) with 100 meters per hectare (or 328 feet), assuming the construction was 4 hectares deep and 5 hectares long, parallel to the coastline, the plant would take up 1,640 feet along the coast. This means, assuming 60,000 plants of the same dimension, it would take up 98,400,000 feet or 18,636 miles of coastline (8.5 percent of the world's coastline).

Of course, that is a great deal of coastline and naturally many other factors come into play in the choice of an appropriate location for such a plant. Again, it is not the purpose of this extrapolation to suggest these statistics are of any other use than to gauge a broad sense of what such capacity means, in light of the water scarcity/stress issues occurring today. Yet, the fact is, it is clearly *within the range* of such application to meet the needs of people suffering from water scarcity via desalination alone, coupled with an infrastructure and distribution system to move water inland.

As a final example, let's reduce this abstract extrapolation even more and apply it to a real-life circumstance. On the continent of Africa, for example, which has about 1 billion people as of 2013, roughly 345 million people lack sufficient access to running water.[60] If we apply the noted global average consumption rate of 1,385 cubic meters a year, seeking to provide each of those 345 million people that amount, we would need 477,825,000,000 cubic meters produced annually.

Using the Wonthaggi annual capacity of 150 million cubic meters produced as the base figure, Africa would need 3,185 fifty-acre plants along its coastline to meet such demand, taking up about 5,223,400 feet or 989 miles. Given Africa has about 26,000 km (16,000 miles) of coastline, this would take up about 6 percent of Africa's coastline.

However, if we divided this number in half, and used UV purification systems for one section and desalination for the other, the desalination process would need about 3 percent, or 494 miles of coastline for desalination facilities, and only about 296 acres of land for purification facilities, which is a minuscule faction of Africa's total landmass of about 7 billion acres. This approach is highly workable and obviously, in this case and in all other cases, we would strategically maximize purification processes since they are more efficient, while using desalination for the remaining demand.

Such crude statistics reveal that between UV and traditional decontamination, coupled with traditional desalination processes, as they currently exist (and ignoring the rapid advancements occurring in both fields,[61] which will likely have an exponentially advanced level of efficiency in the coming decades), the idea of enduring water scarcity on planet Earth is absurd. Both of these isolated extrapolations have assumed only one or the other was applied, in only large-scale form, assuming there are no other existing sources of potable water.

In reality, we have the technical capacity to bring potable water availability to absolute global abundance. This can be done by respecting existing freshwater availability through the use of intelligent use/reuse water network schemes to further preserve the existing capacity. At the same time, both large- and small-scale desalination *and* decontamination processes can be applied as specific regions require. Moreover, we can power these plants using rapidly advancing renewable energy processes.

ENERGY

Renewable energy sources are sources that are continually replenished. Such sources include water, wind, solar, and geothermal. In contrast, fuels such as coal, oil, and natural gas are nonrenewable, as they are based on Earth stores that show no near-term regeneration.

As of the early twenty-first century, the recognition of clean, renewable energy possibilities has been substantial.[62] The spectrum of application, scalability, and degree of efficiency, coupled with advancing methods for energy storage and transfer, have arguably made our current, mostly hydrocarbon-based energy methods appear outdated, especially given the ongoing negative consequences of their use. Nuclear energy, while effective and considered a "renewable" form by some, works at very high risk given the unstable materials involved and the large-scale accidents on record that have brought the safety of this form of production into question.[63]

In the world today, the five most commonly used renewable sources are hydropower (via dams), solar, wind, geothermal, and biofuels. Renewable energy sources currently represent about 15 percent of global energy use, with hydropower accounting for 97 percent of this figure.[64]

More than 1.2 billion people lack access to electricity worldwide.[65] Additionally, nonrenewable energy sources are plagued by ongoing pollution and periodic crises. Hence, the purpose of this subsection is to show how the dangerous realities associated with fossil fuels and nuclear energy are no longer needed, even as we ramp up to serve those who lack sufficient electricity. We can now power the world many times over with clean, renewable, relatively low-impact methods, largely localized to the needs of a single structure, city, or industrial application.

However, it is important to point out upfront that there is no single solution at this time. Different areas of the Earth have different propensities for renewable energy, so application must be developed as a system or network of a combination of mediums. That noted, and narrowing down the most relevant of these abundance-producing possibilities, it is perhaps best to think of renewable energy extraction/harnessing and use in two categories: (a) large-scale/base-load and (b) small-scale/total mixed-use systems.

(a) Large-scale/base-load

Large-scale generation, such as for "base-load" needs required to power a city or industrial center, includes four main mediums: (a1) geothermal plants, (a2) wind farms, (a3) solar fields, and (a4) water (ocean/hydropower).

(A1) GEOTHERMAL

Geothermal power[66] is energy harnessed essentially from the natural heat of the Earth's molten core. Plants are usually placed where heat centers are closer to the surface of the Earth.[67] A 2006 MIT report on geothermal energy, promoting an advanced extraction system called EGS, found that 13,000 zettajoules of power are currently available in the Earth, with the possibility that 2,000 additional zettajoules could be harvested through improved technology.[68]

The total energy consumption of all the countries on the planet is about half a zettajoule (0.55) a year,[69] which means thousands of years of planetary power could be harnessed via geothermal sources alone. The MIT report also estimated that there was enough energy in hard rocks 10 kilometers below the US to supply all the world's current needs for 30,000 years.

Even with an expected 56 percent increase in consumption by 2040, geothermal capacity is enormous if properly tapped.[70] Likewise, the extraction of heat needing to take place from within the Earth appears quite minor in comparison to its store, making the source virtually limitless in proportion to actual human consumption.[71] Also, since the energy is produced constantly, there are no intermittency problems; this type of energy can be produced constantly without the need for storage.

The environmental impact of geothermal is relatively low. Iceland has been using it almost exclusively for some time and its plants produce extremely low emissions (and zero carbon) compared with hydrocarbon-based methods.[72] This problem has been acknowledged as human induced[73] and improvement in the engineering process is offered as the solution, along with a clear understanding of the nature of the location for drilling.

In terms of location, it is theoretically possible to place geothermal-energy extraction plants anywhere, if the capacity to drill deeply enough is available, coupled with other advancements in technology.[74] However, today most plants need to exist near the junction of tectonic plates.[75] A geothermal map of emitted heat on the surface of the Earth, made by satellite, can show such ideal spots.[76] These maps show possibilities near most coastlines around the world,[77] and while most studies are ambiguous with respect to the number of available locations, the recognized potential is enormous.

The US Department of Energy has noted that geothermal energy also uses much less land than other energy sources, including fossil fuel and currently dominant renewables. Over thirty years, the period of time commonly used to compare the lifecycle impacts from different power sources, a geothermal facility uses 404 square meters of land per gigawatt hour, while a coal facility uses 3,632 square meters per gigawatt hour.[78] If we do a basic comparison of geothermal with coal using this ratio of square meters to gigawatt hour, we find that we could fit about *nine* geothermal plants in the space of one coal plant.[79]

Likewise, it is important to note that new, more efficient methods of tapping geothermal are imminent with respect to possible output potential. In 2013 it was announced that a 1,000-megawatt power station was to begin construction in Ethiopia.[80] A megawatt is a unit of power, and power capacity is expressed differently from energy capacity, which is expressed, in this context of megawatts, as megawatt hours (MWh). To put it another way, energy is the amount of work done, whereas power is the rate of doing work. So, for example, a generator with one MW capacity that consistently operates at that capacity for one hour will produce 1 MW-hour (MWh) of electricity.

This means if a 1,000 MW geothermal power station operated at full capacity for twenty-four hours a day, seven days a week (365 days), it would produce 8,760,000 MWh/yr.[81] The world's current annual usage in MWh is about 153 billion,[82] which means it would take, in abstract, 17,465 geothermal plants to match global use.[83]

According to the World Coal Association, there are over 2,300 coal power plants in operation worldwide.[84] Using the aforementioned plant size/capacity comparison of about nine geothermal plants fitting into one coal plant, the space of 1,940[85] (or 84 percent of the total in existence) coal plants would be needed, in theory, to contain the 17,465 geothermal plants. Also, given that coal today accounts for only 41 percent of the world's current energy production,[86] this theoretical extrapolation also shows that geothermal energy could supply 100 percent of our global energy requirements while occupying only 84 percent of the space required by our current coal plants (which produce only 41 percent of our energy). All this without the pollution from coal, one of the most polluting energy sources in the world and arguably the largest contributor to the human-made increase of CO_2 in the atmosphere.

(A2) WIND FARMS

US Department of Energy studies have concluded that wind harvesting in the Great Plains states of Texas, Kansas, and North Dakota could provide enough electricity to power the entire USA.[87] More impressively, a 2005 Stanford University study published in the *Journal of*

Geophysical Research found that if only 20 percent of the wind potential on the planet were harnessed, it would cover the entire world's energy needs.[88]

In corroboration, two more recent studies by unrelated organizations published in 2012 calculated that with existing wind-turbine technology the Earth could produce hundreds of trillions of watts of power. This is much more than what the world currently consumes.[89] Wind power is perhaps one of the most simple and low-impact forms of renewable energy and its scalability is limited to location only.

The 9,000-acre Alta Wind Energy Center California has an active capacity of 1,320 MW of power. Using that plant as a basis, a theoretical annual output of 11,563,200 MWh is possible.[90] This means 13,231 nine-thousand-acre wind farms would be needed to meet the current output figure of 153 billion MWh. It also means 119,079,000 acres of wind-sufficient land would be required.[91] This amounts to 0.3 percent of the Earth's surface that would be needed to power the world, in abstract.[92] Once again, this is not to suggest such as an ideal situation given what land is feasible for wind farms, along with other important factors. This is simply to give a general perspective of possibility.

However, one unique reality of wind-power generation is the potential of offshore harnessing. Compared to land-based wind power, offshore wind power has, on average, a much larger yield, as wind speeds tend to be higher. This reality also alleviates land-based pressures given land scarcity and regional restrictions.

According to the *Assessment of Offshore Wind Energy Resources for the United States*, 4,150 gigawatts (4,150,000 MW) of potential wind-turbine capacity from offshore wind resources are available in the United States.[93] Assuming this power capacity were consistent for a year, we end up with an energy conversion of 36.354 billion MWh/yr. Given that the United States, in 2010, used 25,776 25.78 billion MWh, we find that offshore wind harvesting *alone* would exceed national use by about 10.6 billion MWhs, or 41 percent.

Extrapolating this US capacity to the rest of the world's coastlines, and taking into account the aforementioned land-based statistic that showed we could power the world many times over onshore as well,[94] the possibilities of wind-based energy abundance are exceptional.

(A3) SOLAR FIELDS

The upper atmosphere receives about $1.5 \times 1,021$ watt-hours of solar radiation annually. This vast amount of energy is more than 23,000 times that used by the human population of the planet.[95] If humanity could capture one-tenth of 1 percent of the solar energy striking the Earth, we would have access to six times more energy than we consume in all forms today, with almost no greenhouse-gas emissions. The ability to harness this power depends on the technology and how high the percentage of radiation absorption is.

Conventional photovoltaics, currently the most common form, used mostly for smaller applications, use silicon as the semiconductor and exist in something like a flat cell or sheet. Concentrated photovoltaics (CPV) are generally more efficient than nonconcentrated on average; however, they tend to require more direct exposure to focus the light properly.

Concentrated solar power (CPS) is a large-scale approach that uses mirrors or lenses to concentrate a large area of sunlight, or solar thermal energy, onto a small area. Electrical power is produced when the concentrated light is converted to heat, which drives a heat engine (such as a steam turbine) connected to an electrical power generator or the like. Unlike photovoltaics, which convert directly to electricity, this technology converts to heat. Recently, large-scale storage methods have also been used to prolong access at night.

A variation of CSP is STE, or *solar thermal energy*. The Ivanpah Solar Electric Generating System in California is a 3,500-acre field[96] with a stated annual generation of 1,079,232 MWh.[97] Ivanpah does not use any form of storage, but it serves about 140,000 homes in the region. Using Ivanpah as a basis, it would take 141,767 fields or 496,184,500 acres to theoretically meet current global energy use based on output. This is 1.43 percent of total land on Earth.[98]

Once again, this is not to suggest such a thing is practical, nor is it to ignore the radiation-yield differences found in different areas of the Earth. However, deserts, which tend to be highly conducive for solar fields while often less conducive to life support for people, are roughly a third of all the land mass in the world, or about 12 billion acres. Compared with the roughly 500 million acres theoretically needed to "power the world" as per our extrapolation, only 4.1 percent of the world's desert land would be needed.[99]

Likewise, other projects similar to the Ivanpah field have been incorporating storage systems. The Solana 280 MW solar power plant in Arizona combines parabolic-trough mirror technology with molten-salt thermal storage and is able to continue outputting up to six hours after the sky goes dark.[100]

In general, photovoltaic, solar thermal, storage methods, and other existing and emerging technologies continue to rapidly develop, suggesting that many installations seen as highly efficient today will be grossly inefficient in a decade or two. As will be addressed further with respect to smaller-scale renewable energy solutions, future efficiencies are likely to occur through the use of solar power localized into the construction of buildings and domiciles. The issue is making the technology compact and efficient enough for local use.

However, solar-field power stations, just like geothermal and wind, have an enormous global potential in and of themselves. There is little doubt that given proper resources and attention, these fields alone could theoretically establish an infrastructure and efficiency level to power the world.

(A4) WATER/HYDRO ENERGY

Water-based renewable energy extraction could generally be said to have two broad sources: the ocean and river-type water flows, which use the gravitational force of falling or flowing water, usually in an inland watercourse. The latter is generally referred to in practice as *hydroelectric* and, as noted before, it is currently a fairly large part of the existing renewable energy infrastructure.[101]

On the other hand, the vast potential of the ocean has yet to be harnessed within a fraction of its capacity. It is not far-fetched to suggest that ocean water power could power the world alone.[102] This could be done through the intelligent harvesting of the various mechanical movements of ocean water as well as through exploiting the differences in heat, known as *ocean thermal energy conversion* (OTEC). Given the existing, fairly large-scale use of hydroelectric power (dams) already, this section will instead focus on the ocean potentials.

The most pronounced sea-based potentials at this time appear to be wave, tidal, ocean current, ocean thermal, and osmotic power. Waves are primarily caused by winds; tides are primarily caused by the gravitational pull of the moon; ocean currents are primarily caused by the rotation of the Earth; ocean thermal energy results from solar heat absorbed by the surface of the ocean; and osmotic power is when fresh water and salt water meet, exploiting the difference in salt concentration.

Wave—It has been found that wave power's *usable* global potential is about 3 TW[103] or about 26,280 TWh/yr assuming constant harnessing. This is almost 20 percent of current global use. This amount of power has been ascertained essentially by analysis of deep-water regions off continent coastlines. (The theoretical power estimate has been estimated at 3.7 TW, with the final net estimate reduced by about 20 percent to compensate for various inefficiencies related to a given region, such as ice coverage.) Energy output is basically determined by wave height, wave speed, wavelength, and water density.

Wave farms, or the construction of wave-harnessing plants off a coastline, have seen limited large-scale application at this time, with only about six countries sparsely applying the technology. Locations with the most potential include the western seaboard of Europe, the northern coast of the UK, and the Pacific coastlines of North and South America, Southern Africa, Australia, and New Zealand.

Tidal—Tidal power has two subforms: range and stream. Tidal *range* is essentially the "rise and fall" of areas of the ocean. Tidal *streams* are currents created by periodic horizontal movement of the tides, often magnified by the shape of the seabed.

Different locations of Earth have large differences in range.[104] In the United Kingdom, an area with high levels of tidal activity, dozens of sites are currently noted as available, with a forecast that 34 percent of all the UK's energy could come from tidal power alone.[105] Globally, older studies have put tidal capacity at 1,800TWh/yr.[106] More recent studies have put the theoretical capacity (both range and stream) at 3TW, assuming only a portion would be extractable.[107]

Tidal power, while very predictable, is also subject to daily periods of intermittency based around tidal shifts. Assuming only 1.5 TW could be harnessed in a year through advanced technology, this means about 7 percent of the world's power could come from tidal power.

Ocean Current—Similar to tidal streams, ocean currents have shown great potential. These currents flow consistently in the open ocean and various technologies have been emerging to harness this largely untapped medium.

As with all renewables, the capacity to harness such potential is directly related to the efficiency of the technology employed. The European Ocean Energy Association estimates the current potential at 400 THW/yr.[108] However, there is good reason to assume this figure is outdated. Prior applications of turbine/mill technologies to capture such water flows have needed an average current of five or six knots to operate efficiently, while most of the Earth's currents are slower than three knots.[109] However, recent developments have revealed the possibility to harness energy from water flows of less than two knots.[110] Given this potential, it has been suggested that ocean current alone could power the entire world.[111]

Osmotic—Osmotic power or salinity gradient power is the energy available from the difference in the salt concentration between seawater and river water. The Norwegian Center for Renewable Energy (SFFE) estimates the global potential to be about 1,370 TWh/yr,[112] with others putting it at around 1,700 TWh/yr[113]—the equivalent of half of Europe's entire energy demand.[114]

While still largely in its baby shoes, osmotic power harnessing through advancing technology is promising. Power plants can, in principle, be built any place where fresh water meets sea water. They can generate power 24/7, regardless of weather conditions.

Ocean Thermal—The final ocean-based means for energy harnessing worth noting is ocean thermal energy conversion (OTEC). Exploiting the differences in heat existing on the surface of the ocean and below, technology can use warmer surface water to heat a fluid, such as liquid ammonia, converting it into vapor, which expands to drive a turbine. That, in turn, produces electricity. The fluid is then cooled using cold water from the ocean depths, returning it into a liquid state so the process can start all over again.

Of all ocean-based energy sources, OTEC appears to have the most potential. It has been estimated that 88,000 TWh/yr could be generated without affecting the ocean's thermal structure.[115] While this figure may not express total usable capacity, it implies that well over half of all current global energy consumption could be met with OTEC alone. As of 2013, most of the existing OTEC plants are experimental or on very small scale. However, a few major industrial capacity projects have been set in motion, including a 10 MW plant off the coast of China[116] and a 100 MW facility near Hawaii.[117] One 100 MW offshore plant can theoretically power Hawaii's entire Big Island alone,[118] 186,000 people according to a 2011 census.

Total Oceanic Power—Consistent with the prior categorical estimations set forward for solar, wind, and geothermal power, it is worthwhile to consider the total combined (largely conservative) potential of each noted oceanic medium. This is a crude extrapolation since there are many complex variables, including the fact that some applications are still semi-experimental and difficult to assess. Nevertheless, this general figure still conveys the broadest perspective of the potential of ocean renewables. Here is a list of the noted global potentials:

Wave: 27,280 TWh/yr
Tidal: 13,140 Twh/yr (1.5 TW × 8,760 hr)
Ocean Current: 400 Twh/yr (old estimate with old tech)
Osmotic: ~1,500 TwH/yr (average of noted statistics)
Ocean Thermal: 88,000 Twh/yr

All of this added together brings us to 130,320 TWh/yr or 0.46 zettajoules a year. This is roughly 83 percent of current global use (0.55 ZJ). It is important to note that such numbers are derived, in part, from traditional technologies, with no adjustment made for more recent improvements. If we bring traditional hydroelectric (watercourse based) power back into the equation, which according to the IEA has a potential of 16,400 TWh/yr,[119] this brings the figure up to 146,720 TWh/yr or 96 percent of current global use.

(b) Small-Scale & Total Mixed-Use Systems

The prior section described the vast potential of large-scale, base-load renewable energy harnessing. Wind, solar, water/hydro, and geothermal power have all shown that they are capable, individually, of meeting or vastly exceeding the current 0.55 zettajoule annual global energy consumption at this time.

The true question is how to intelligently apply these methods. Given regional limitations and other issues such as intermittency, any design should incorporate a workable combination of sources. Such a systems approach is the real solution, harmonizing an optimized fraction of each of those renewables to achieve global, total-use abundance.

For example, imagine a series of manmade floating islands off select coastlines, harnessing wind, solar, thermal difference, wave, tidal, and ocean current power—all at the same time and in the same general area. Such "energy islands" would then pipe their harvest back to land for human use. Various combinations could also be applied to land-based systems, as well, such as constructing wind/solar combinations to take advantage of the fact that wind is often more present at night, while solar is present during the day.

Likewise, we can combine various methods to harness energy on a more local level. Smaller-scale renewable methods that are conducive to single structures or small areas find the same systems logic regarding combination. These localized systems could also, if need be, connect back into the larger, base-load systems as well, creating a mixed-medium integrated network.

A common example today is the use of single-structure solar panels, such as for home use. While the efficiency of these panels is still improving and the market imposes return-on-investment challenges, most people utilizing these solar power systems are only able to complement their home's electricity use rather than gain 100 percent utilization. (For example, most systems are applied to power the home during the day, while pulling power from the regional base-load grid at night.) *Maximizing localized possibilities first, before resorting to larger-scale energy use, is the key to practical energy abundance, efficiency, and sustainability.*

To understand the relevance of this concept more thoroughly, let's expand the example of the household solar array to its theoretical potential. In 2011, the average annual electricity consumption for a US residential utility (household) customer was 11,280 kWh.[120] Given 114,800,000 households in 2010,[121] this means 1,295 TWh/yr was used. Total electrical energy consumption for the US in 2012 was 3,886.4 TWh. This means 33 percent of all electric consumption occurred in people's homes, with the majority of that energy coming from fossil-fuel power stations.

If all households in the United States were able to power themselves for electricity using solar panels alone—a localized energy production capacity that is simply wasted at this time—the base-load stress reduction would be dramatic. Contrary to popular belief, as of 2016 this is a real possibility given the state of solar-cell efficiency and storage technology.[122] The problem is that the current energy industry is not prepared for such efficiency and consumer solar systems currently available suffer from high expense as a result of limited mass production, competition, and a lack of social initiative to advancement.

It is worth stating here that the financial system and its price-oriented mechanisms are barriers to ubiquitous and optimized household-solar development. (This is also true for every other developing technology after a certain point of proven efficacy.) While defenders of capitalism argue that the process of investment-to-market of an in-demand good generally reduces the cost of that good over time, making it more available to those who could not afford it before, these defenders conveniently forget that the entire process is a contrivance.

If price and profit were removed from the system, we could focus on the technology and its merit both at the current time and with regard to its longer-term efficiency trends (future improvements). This design focus would enable us to employ proper resource allocation strategies and research to hasten the introduction of promising technology. Given the incredible capacity of home-solar arrays to alleviate base-load energy stress and thereby reduce fossil-fuel emissions and pollution, it is very unfortunate that this technology is subject to the whims of the market.[123]

If we survey the commercial expense of a typical solar array as of 2013, an average home using 11,280 kWh a month would require about thirty panels, with a solar-cell efficiency of about 9 to 15 percent and a nighttime battery system. This would cost well over $20,000.[124] Such an expense is unaffordable for the vast majority of the world, even though the basic materials used in traditional PV systems are simple and abundant and manufacturing is increasingly efficient.

Likewise, it is equally disappointing that modern home construction has made little to no use of other basic, localized renewable methods that can further facilitate the real-world capacity to bring all households (not only in the United States but also in the world) to a place of energy independence.

Noting solar power, other nearly universal applications also apply. Small wind-harvesting systems[125] and geothermal heating and cooling technology[126] can be combined with architectural design that makes better use of natural light and conserves heating and cooling. Many other design adjustments could make apartments and houses self-sufficient and more ecologically sustainable. Coupling this with use-reuse designs for water preservation, along with other approaches to optimize energy/resource efficiency, it is clear that our current methods are enormously wasteful when compared with the possibilities.

City infrastructure exhibits the same failure almost everywhere with respect to such applied systems. For example, an enormous amount of energy is used in transportation. While the electric vehicle has proven viable for full global use despite lobbying efforts and other market limitations that keep its application well behind the gasoline-powered norm, many system-based methods also go unharnessed.

Apart from a general necessity to reorganize urban environments to be more conducive to convenient mass-transit networks, removing the need for numerous autonomous vehicles, simply re-harnessing the powered movements of all transport mediums could dramatically alleviate energy pressures.

A technology called "piezoelectric,"[127] which is able to convert pressure and mechanical energy into electricity, is an excellent example of an energy-reuse method with great potential. Existing applications have included power generation by people walking on piezo-engineered floors[128] and sidewalks,[129] streets that can generate power as automobiles cross over them,[130] and rail systems that can also capture energy from passing train cars through pressure.[131] Aerospace engineer Haim Abramovich has stated that a stretch of road less than a mile long, four lanes wide, and trafficked by about 1,000 vehicles per hour can create about 0.4 megawatts of power, enough to power 600 homes.[132]

Other theoretical applications extend to pretty much anything that engages pressure or action, including minor vibrations. For example, there are projects working to harness seemingly small-scale energy production, such as charging a cellphone with the extra movement caused by texting or moving it,[133] applications to harvest energy from airflow from airplanes,[134] and even an electric car that uses piezo tech, in part, to charge itself as it travels.[135]

If we think about the enormous mechanical energy wasted by vehicle transport and high-traffic walking centers such as downtown streets, the potential of that regenerated energy is quite substantial. It is this type of *systems thinking* that we need in order to maintain sustainability while actively pursuing global energy abundance.

In conclusion, the key to a sustainable energy abundance comes down to an integrated systems approach combining base-load and more localized mixed-use/reuse systems. Each region and situation would necessarily be customized according to the kind of renewable sources available. As described, base-load means including geothermal energy, wind farms, solar fields, and water (ocean/hydropower). Each of these sources has potential that far exceeds current global needs, but also circumstantial limitations. While critics of renewables routinely cite the native limitations, such as the intermittency of wind farms or solar energy, the key rests in the combination of these means, along with intelligent localized sources, such as domiciles with heat pumps, small wind turbines, and so on. In many cases, any energy harnessed in excess of local needs can be loaded into a base-load grid for a region, turning each mixed-use domicile into a publicly accessible energy source.

Industrial designers of the future should focus on this type of fully integrated and circular approach. As a general design rule, the greater the integration, the more productive, efficient, and protected the outcome. This approach builds in multiple levels of redundancy and thereby ensures that any regional-source power outages are limited or uneventful due to the interconnected supplemental sources.

Appendix B

··

ECONOMIC CALCULATION AND
BROAD SYSTEM CONCEPTION[1]

T HE FOLLOWING outlines a model for optimized economic efficiency
to maximize productivity and increase goods surplus (abundance)
while minimizing any environmental footprint. This model is a theoretical arrangement to reach the goals of reducing scarcity across a
population while achieving equitable distribution, thereby decreasing or removing socioeconomic inequality and the associated public-
health harms described in this book. The degree of incorporation of
such principles and systems-based approaches is directly proportional
to the degree of positive advancement achieved. What follows is not
intended as complete or thorough. It is a general framework emphasizing a systems-based, nonmarket/nonmonetary approach to economic
calculation and management.

An economic model can be thought of as representing component
processes by a set of variables or functions, describing the logical relationships between them. Traditional or market-based economic models
rely on contrived features such as price trends, utilitarian purchase patterns, inflation, labor cycles, currency fluctuations, and so forth. These
are considered contrived since they relate to the market mode only and
are irrelevant to the foundation of pure economics. By pure economics,
I mean technical methods to optimize the economic process, satisfying
in a conservative and sustainable way the needs of a population.

Rarely, if ever, do modern economists focus on technical processes
that underscore innovation, production, distribution, or regeneration;
nor do they factor in actual relationships that directly improve public or
ecological health. Rather, the market system functions as a proxy means,

based only on the act of exchange and exchange preferences. As a result, market economics is "life-blind"; it is decoupled from the actual science of life support and sustainability.

True economic efficiency must first and foremost be thought of not in market-oriented terms but in terms of industrial or technical efficiency, in a systems approach. This considers interrelated input processes such as design proposals and demand assessment, along with what could be called *sustainability* and *efficiency* protocols. Before the rise of increased economic activity in the post-Malthusian period, sustainability and efficiency were mere afterthoughts in general economic behavior, since impact and technical knowledge was so minor compared to today.

Such protocols are, in effect, the basic rules of economic activity that pursue optimized economic efficiency and sustainability. The model here is scalable, meaning the principles and protocols can be applied to small communities or to the entire world. Naturally, given the reality of our habitat as unified and synergic, the highest level of efficiency would arise from a global approach.

STRUCTURE AND PROCESSES

Figure 1 shows a linear schematic of the proposed model, moving from design to production to distribution to recycling. Figure 2 shows the same from a mathematical point of view, as a minimization or maximization of functions. Because we are talking about efficiency, we can consider the problem as a maximization of the production function f_p.

Figure 3 on page 332 is a table of the symbols and descriptions that will be used in the explanations. Again, it is important to note the generalized nature of this. The purpose of this analysis is to give an overview of optimized economic calculation on the core, technical level, highlighting the most relevant, overarching needs or attributes. A more detailed and complete algorithmic calculation, taking into account all related subprocesses in real-life terms, along with democratic interaction (participatory economics), would require a great deal more expansion. It is not the scope of this appendix to extend that far. However, I will state

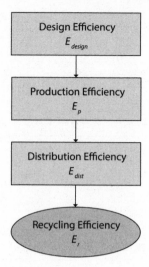

FIGURE 1.   Block-scheme of system process

$$f_P(E_{\text{design}}, E_p, E_{\text{dist}}, E_r) \to \max$$

FIGURE 2.   System process as expression

that this process would unfold in real terms by way of a software plat-form that has these measures, rules, and data streams built in, engaged by the user or organization as a critical interaction to ensure the most optimized outcomes possible at that given point in time.

DESIGN EFFICIENCY

Efficiency standards are standards by which a given design must conform to ensure optimal integrity. This can also be thought of as a *filtering* process. Proposed designs are filtered through a series of sustainability and efficiency protocols to optimize performance. This is the first stage of intelligent product creation.

Symbol	Description
E_{design}	Design efficiency
E_p	Production efficiency
E_{dist}	Distribution efficiency
E_r	Recycling efficiency
f_p	Production function
E_{design}^i	Design efficiency standards
t_d	Durability
A_{design}	Adaptivity
c_r	Recycling conduciveness
$g_c^1, g_c^2, \ldots g_c^i, \ldots g_c^{Nc}$	Genre components
Nc	Minimum number of genre components
H_L	Human labor
A_L	Automated labor
f_{design}	Design efficiency function
D_s	Demand splitting value
$\tilde{A}$	Flexible automation process
$\bar{A}$	Fixed automation process
C_i	Consumer with index i
D_i	Distributor with index i
d_p	Distance to the production facilities
d_{dist}	Distance to the distribution facilities
P_{reg}	Regenerative protocol

FIGURE 3.   Logic Symbols and Description

$$E_{\text{design}} = f_{\text{design}}(t_d, A_{\text{design}}, c_r, Nc, H_L)$$

FIGURE 4.   Expression for the "optimized design efficiency" function

These include the following:

a. Strategically Maximized Durability
b. Strategically Maximized Adaptability
c. Strategic Standardization of Genre Components
d. Strategically Integrated Recycling Conduciveness
e. Strategic Conduciveness for Labor Automation

As expressed in Figure 4, design efficiency E_{design} is a critical step affecting the overall efficiency of the manufacturing and distribution process. This design efficiency depends on several key factors, which can be called *current efficiency standards* E_{design}^i. Here the index i corresponds to some particular standard. Each standard will be generally explored as follows, expanding in certain cases with respect to the logic associated.

a. "Strategically Maximized Durability" means to make the good as strong and lasting as relevant. The materials utilized, comparatively assuming possible substitutions due to levels of scarcity or other factors, would be dynamically calculated, likely automatically by the design system, to be most conducive to an optimized durability standard.

   This *durability* $t_d(d_1, d_2, \ldots, d_i)$ maximization can be considered a local optimization issue. It can be analyzed by introducing the factor d_i, which affects it where $d_1^o, d_2^o, \ldots, d_i^o$ are some optimal values of the factors.

$$t_d(d_1, d_2, \ldots, d_i) \to \max, \, t_d = t_{\max}(d_1^o, d_2^o, \ldots, d_i^o)$$

b. "Strategically Maximized Adaptability" A_{design} means designing for the highest state of flexibility for replacing component parts. In the event a component part of a certain good becomes defective or out of date, the design facilitates easy replacement to maximize full product life span, always working to avoid replacing the good as a whole.

c. "Strategic Standardization of Genre Components"

$$g_c^1, g_c^2, \ldots g_c^i, \ldots g_c^{Nc}$$

means all new designs either conform to or replace existing components, which are either already in existence or outdated due to a lack of comparative efficiency. This logic should apply not only to a given product, but also to the entire good genre, however possible.

$$Nc \rightarrow \min$$

The aim is to minimize the total number of genre components Nc. In other words, the standardization of the process will make it possible to lower the number Nc to a possible minimum.

d. "Recycling Conduciveness" c_r means every design must conform to the current state of regenerative possibility. The breakdown of any good must be anticipated in the initial design and allowed for in the most optimized way.

e. "Strategic Conduciveness for Labor Automation" means that the current state of optimized, automated production is also taken into account in an effort to refine the design to be most conducive to production with the least amount of complexity, human labor, or monitoring. Again, we seek to simplify the way materials and production means are used so that the maximum number of goods can be produced with the least variation of materials and production equipment.

This is denoted by human labor H_L and automated labor A_L. The aim is to minimize the human interaction with the production process.

This can be written as:

$$H_L / (H_L + A_L) \rightarrow \min$$

Using this equation, we could also write a simpler condition:

$$H_L(l_1, \ldots, l_i) / A_L(l_1, \ldots, l_i) \rightarrow \min$$

l_i are factors that influence human and automatic labor.

So, returning to Figure 4, this "Optimized Design Efficiency" function can be described as f_{design}, where t_d is durability, A_{design} is adaptability, c_r is recycling conduciveness, Nc is the minimum number of genre components, and H_L is human labor.

PRODUCTION EFFICIENCY

Dynamic feedback and monitoring of production factors are critical to integrity, especially in a world where extensive resource overshoot now occurs. Maintaining equilibrium with the Earth's regenerative processes while also working strategically to maximize the use of the most abundant materials, strategically minimizing any emerging scarcity, is critical to efficient production. The scope of this accounting is vast; hence only three issues will be discussed here. The first two deal with (a) "scarcity" and the degree of (b) "labor complexity."

a. "Scarcity value" could be assigned a numerical value, from 1 to 100. One would denote the most severe scarcity with respect to the current rate of use, and 100 would denote the least severe; 50 would be the steady-state dividing line. The scarcity value of any given resource would exist at some value along this line, dynamically updated by whatever feedback systems are tracking such inventory. Figure 5 expresses this visually.

    For example, if the use of lumber passes below the steady-state level of 50, which would mean consumption is currently surpassing the Earth's natural regeneration rate, this event would encourage a countermove of some kind, such as "material substitution" or finding a replacement for lumber in any future productions.

    In a market system the price mechanism is used to decide which material is more cost-efficient, assuming a given price will have already accounted for relevant technical information. This accounting is only weakly accurate. This new approach accounts for a direct given technical quality by a comparative quantification, rather than

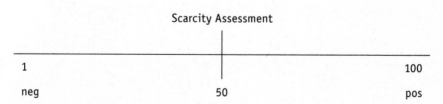

FIGURE 5.   Scarcity rank visual aid

using price to assess value. In the case of scarcity concerns, it is best to organize genres or groups of similar-use materials and then quantify, to the highest degree possible, their related properties and degrees of efficiency for any given purpose. Then, a general numerical value spectrum is applied to those relationships. This isn't done at all today.

For example, there is a spectrum of metals with different efficiencies for electrical conductivity. These efficiencies can be physically quantified and then compared by value. So, if copper, a conductive metal, goes below the 50 value of equilibrium regarding its scarcity, calculations are triggered by the management program to compare the state of other conducive materials, their *scarcity level* and their *efficiency level*, preparing for substitution. This is only one example of many. This type of reasoning would get extremely complicated depending on the material and purpose posed, which is why computer calculation is required. This type of direct value calculation, based around purpose, conduciveness, and sustainability, dramatically eclipses the price mechanism when it comes to true resource awareness and intelligent resource consideration.

b. "Labor complexity" is about estimating the difficulty of a given production, drawing a numerical value based upon the degree of complexity. In the context of an automation-focused industry, complexity can be quantified by defining and comparing the number of "process stages." Any given good production can be foreshadowed as to how many stages of production processing it will take. It can then be compared to other good productions, ideally in the same good genre. In other words, the units of measurement are these stages.

For example, a chair that can be molded from polymers in one process and in three minutes will have a lower labor-complexity value than a chair that requires automated assembly across a more tedious process using mixed materials. Generally, the intent in this kind of pursuit of efficiency is to avoid increased complexity when possible.

c. The final issue to note is how different degrees of complexity are organized through the network. We can think of this as a classification system based on difficulty. As stated in chapter five, the focus in this new economic model is generally on automating labor and production, rather than on monetary remuneration and employment, which tend to interfere with efficiency when prioritized. Means of production in this way would likely evolve as automated factories, small and large, that are increasingly able to produce more with fewer material inputs and fewer machine configurations (that is, "more with less").

The number of production facilities would be strategically distributed topographically based on population statistics and concentrations. This is a "proximity strategy." Parameters can change according to the nature of the facilities and how much machine variation in production (fixed automation vs. flexible automation) is required at a given time.[2] For the purpose of exemplification, two facility types will be distinguished: one for high demand or mass production (generally less complex) and one for low demand or short-run, custom goods (generally more complex). Figure 6 expresses this based on these parameters.

A simple class determination is made that splits D_s, the destination facilities, based on the nature of production requirements. The "high demand" target assumes fixed automation $\bar{A}(a_i)$, meaning unvaried production methods ideal for high demand/mass production. The "low demand" target uses flexible automation, $\bar{A}(t, D_c(t), a_i)$, which can do a variety of things but usually in shorter runs.

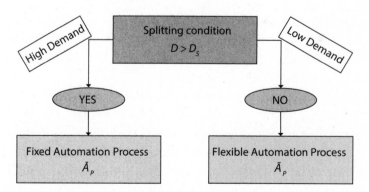

FIGURE 6.   Dividing by low and high; class-determination process

t is time,
$D_c(t)$ is the current demand value
a_i are additional factors

Again, this scheme assumes only two types of facilities are needed. There could be many more facility types based upon production factors, generating more splitting conditions. This is just an example. However, if the design rules are respected, there shouldn't be too much variation over time as the intent is always to reduce complexity. Given current trends, it is not difficult to envision a single-factor design that could produce 25 percent or more of all known good variation.

Figure 6, stated in linear form, starts with product designs filtered by a [Demand Class Determination] process. The [Demand Class Determination] process filters based on the standards set for [Low Demand] or [High Demand]. All [Low Consumer Demand] product designs are to be manufactured by the [Flexible Automation] process. All [High Consumer Demand] product designs are to be manufactured by the [Fixed Automation] process. Also, both the manufacturing of [Low Consumer Demand] and [High Consumer Demand] product designs will be regionally allocated as per the [Proximity Strategy] d_p of the manufacturing facilities.

DISTRIBUTION EFFICIENCY

Distribution, given modern means, could either occur directly from the production facility, usually in the case of an on-demand, one-off type production, or be sent into a distribution system based upon access, not ownership, as denoted in chapter five.

Generally, some goods will be conducive to low-demand, custom production and some will not. Food is the easiest example of a mass-production necessity, while a personally tailored piece of furniture would come directly from the manufacturing facility once created. It is worth reiterating that regardless of whether the good is classified to go to an access-based distribution system for rotational use or directly to a consumer, it is still an "access system" in principle. At any time, the user of the custom or mass-produced good can return the item for reprocessing or restocking. (This nonmarket approach removes the incentive for resale as the accessed good was not bought to begin with.)

As per Figure 7, upon product creation, the process moves to the [Optimized Distribution Efficiency] stage. In short, all products are allocated based on their prior [Demand Class Determination]. [Low Consumer Demand] products follow the [Direct Distribution] process. [High Consumer Demand] productions follow the [Mass Distribution] process. Both the [Low Consumer Demand] and [High Consumer Demand] product will be regionally allocated as per the [Proximity Strategy], as before.

In the case of [Low Consumer Demand]

$$D_c < D_s$$

the distribution scheme is direct (Figure 8a). In this case the product goes directly to the consumer without the help of network intermediaries.

In the case of [High Consumer Demand]

$$D_c > D_s$$

the distribution scheme is mass (Figure 8b). In this case the product goes to intermediary facilities, such as "libraries" D_i, to engage the potential consumers C_i.

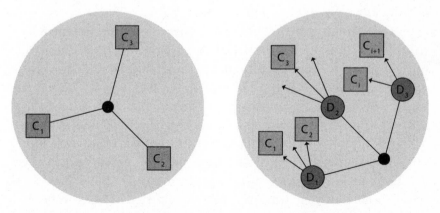

FIGURE 7.   Illustration of the distribution schemes A (left)—Direct Distribution—low-demand case; B (right)—Mass Distribution—high-demand case

Similar to the production efficiency considerations, in the case of "Distribution Efficiency" E_{dist}, for the low and high demand, the distribution process will be optimized in terms of the distance d_{dist} to the existing facilities. In this case the facilities are strategically localized based on the level of demand in the given region. [Proximity Strategy d_p.]

RECYCLING EFFICIENCY

After distribution, the product goes through its life cycle. Once its life cycle ends, the product becomes "void" and moves to the fourth process noted in Figure 1, the [Optimized Recycling Efficiency] process. In short, all voided products will follow a [Regenerative Protocol] P_{reg}. This protocol embraces the standards employed at that time to ensure the optimized reuse or reincorporation of any given good or component. Naturally, the subprocesses of this are extensive and subject to a great deal more technical specificity.

Recycling facilities would likely exist as part of the production facility, allowing access to returned parts for updating and reprocessing. As noted in the design protocol, all goods have been pre-optimized for "conducive recycling." The goal here is a zero-waste economic system. Whether it is a phone, a couch, a computer, a jacket, or a book, everything goes back to a recycling facility, likely the point of origin, which will directly reprocess any item as best it can.

In conclusion, it should be restated that the outline presented here is necessarily limited and oversimplified to inspire further exploration of such a truly technical process of economic calculation. This kind of approach was not possible years ago, without the powerful calculation, sensory, and feedback capabilities of modern computers and technology. Once this kind of algorithmic process can be created and interacted within the course of industrial production, the logic of sustainable and efficient design and production becomes a natural-order regulatory factor. In other words, these rules, imposed in recognition effectively of nature itself, transcend what has been a long period of highly subjective and ultimately irresponsible economic decision making and industrial practice. Without connecting human industrial activity to the natural regenerative process of our habitat, and without a newfound respect for the possibilities and limits inherent, our economic activity will continue to be life-blind and dangerous. In turn, not only must we adapt our industry to conform to the reality of this "natural law," we must also adapt our culture and its beliefs.

Glossary

....

Aberrant Behavior
Also defined as deviant behavior, moving away from normality. The text refers to it mostly in the context of antisocial behavior or "criminal"/ socially offensive behavior. (See pages 9 and 222.)

Absolute Deprivation
The condition in which one's most basic physical needs are not being met, such as a lack of food and water. (See pages 182, 190–191, 204–205, and 206–207.)

Absolute Poverty
As a broad social distinction, this is the condition of basic human needs not being met, generally including food, safe drinking water, sanitation facilities, health, shelter, education, and information. (See page 157.)

Access Economy
An economy focused on people's gaining access to goods and services rather than through ownership or property. (See page 272.)

Appropriative Conflict
Conflict caused by one party seeking the material property of another, usually driven by scarcity or inequality. (See pages 42 and 47–48.)

Automaticity
Generally refers to habits of behavior usually based on repetition. In the context of this text, it is about culturally conditioned reactions and reasoning that have become habituated, in combination with existing biological/ psychological propensities. (See page 95.)

Automation
The application of machines to labor, usually replacing human jobs. (See pages 246, 264–273, 277, 290–291, 293, 294, 334, and 336–337.)

Biological Determinism
While never absolute, this generally refers to genetic expressions that can influence one's physical state or behavior. (See pages 40 and 94–95.)

Biopsychosocial
The synergy of biological, psychological, and social forces, shaping a person at the individual level. (See pages 2–5, 8, 25, 87, 95–56, 100–101, 207, and 214.)

Boom and Bust Cycle

Economic cycle of contraction and expansion. This text emphasizes the destructive nature of the phenomenon since it serves to enhance class division given a redistribution of wealth from bottom to top. This text also points out the artificial nature of the phenomenon as it is correlated to credit expansion and increased liquidity in the money supply more than any true economic factor. Characteristic of market economies only, it has no true relationship to pure economic unfolding. (See pages 133 and 178.)

CAD/CAE (Computer-Aided Design/Engineering)

Programming advancement in which people can design physical objects in virtual environments and test them as though they were physical. This is mentioned in the text regarding the possibility of open-source design for industrial goods and participatory economics. (See page 276.)

Capitalism

Generally defined as "an economic and political system in which a country's trade and industry are controlled by private owners for profit, rather than by the state"; a deeper understanding of this social system reveals a synergy between state power and private power. This synergy, as expressed in this book, shows how state power is actually composed of private power, blurring any lines between the state institution and the market institution. (See pages xviii, 57, 62, 63, 84, 86, 111, 139–140, 146–147, 151, 154, 173, 191–192, 238–239, 242–247, 277, and 283.)

Capitalist Ownership

Also termed the "ownership class," this highlights the traditional labor-role separation between workers and owners in capitalism. Underscoring this relationship is socioeconomic inequality. While often classified as a Marxist concept, the phrase is merely the observation of power imbalance and how there are hierarchy-enhancing aspects of market economics, along with incentivized state policy in favor of power and wealth consolidation for the upper class overall. (See pages 150 and 192.)

Class

Distinction denoting the economic stratification of society based on income and wealth. Can also be extended socioeconomically in terms of social status and access enabled/disabled by differential income and wealth levels. (See pages xviii, 23–28, 100–105, 111–114, 146–156, 158, 180, 193–194, 198–199, and 206.)

Classism

Like the meaning of the term "racism," classism is an equivalent conception of bigotry, whether direct or systemic, creating social antagonism through socioeconomic inequality. (See pages 39–40, 113, 131, and 176.)

Class War

In Marxist terms, class war is considered an economic and political power struggle between capitalist owners and workers. More broadly, as argued in this book, class war is a structural inevitability of the market system's incentive psychology and competitive procedural dynamics, creating a constant state of imposed economic and political deficiency upon the lower classes while the upper classes are naturally supported by the structure, in contrast. This outcome occurs without personal intent to oppress or elevate. (See pages 58, 134, 146–156, 232, and 241.)

Climate of Opinion

Observation put forward by Carl Becker regarding how dominant cultural influences bias recorded history and social loyalties, polluting objectivity. (See pages 146 and 150.)

Cognitive Bias

A systematic pattern of deviation from rationality in judgment, whereby inferences may be drawn in an illogical fashion. This idea is emphasized as the tendency reduces the integrity of our free will, highlighting our vulnerability to social and cultural conditions, unknowingly. (See pages 91–92.)

Cognitive Dissonance

The state of having inconsistent thoughts, beliefs, or attitudes. The text specifically argues that the incentive structure of market economics interferes with one's sense of ethics, often forming contradictory psychological confusion and detrimental rationalizations. (See pages xxi, 164, 241, and 257.)

Collaborative Commons

Notably used by author Jeremy Rifkin, this refers to interdisciplinary collaborative systems where information and resources can be shared through both online and offline means. It is contrary to proprietary or closed development, as common to the market economy. (See pages 265 and 273.)

Collaborative Consumption

Refers to sharing systems for goods, such as rental services, often originating from consumers themselves and not formal commercial industry. (See pages 272–273.)

Communal Commons

Refers to specific shared community services, such as a public library. (See page 272.)

Communism

In Marxist theory, communism is a social system based upon the common ownership of the means of production, the absence of social classes, and the end of state power. It is generally considered the final stage of a socialist evolution. As touched upon in this book, the confusion between communist theory and communist history is widespread, with the assumption that the principles of communism, which were largely poetic and existed as a moral philosophy rather than a tangible social approach, are responsible for the true historical outcomes of its apparent implementation. Rather, what has been called communism throughout history was mostly dictatorship and oligarchy, with little public influence in the unfolding of those societies or economies. Moreover, as this book also argues, from the standpoint of social oppression or social control, both capitalism and historical communism operate in the same basic elitist capacity to ensure social control, albeit using different approaches. (See pages xviii, 34, 62, 105–106, 147, 232, 238, 277, and 287.)

Competitive Self-Regulation

The idea that the market economy is capable of various forms of self-correction by way of mutual parties engauging in competition. As per this text, this idea is argued as false and dangerous. *Also see* Market Self-Regulation. (See pages 117, 121–123, 190–192, 211, and 261.)

Conflicting Moral Dilemmas

In morality theory, these are rationalization problems that occur when a person is forced to decide between two or more nonpreferred moral choices. The existence of this common situation supports the argument for a more coherent epistemological approach to moral decision making, rather than a static or dogmatic one (i.e., moral objectivism). (See pages 76 and 83.)

Conflict Theory

Also called social-conflict theory, this is the view that social dynamics, especially class conflict, are related to competition over economic and social resources. Social change is viewed as an outcome of opposing forces, specifically conflict between the upper and lower classes. This view is in contrast to Functionalism. (See pages 29, 41, 42, 50, 215, and 218.)

Conspicuous Consumption

Coined by Thorstein Veblen, this refers to the expenditure on or consumption of luxuries in an attempt to enhance one's prestige. It is deemed as a consequence of consumer culture and power hierarchy, based upon materialism and wealth being tied to a social perception of success. (See pages 24, 173, 246, and 298.)

Consumerism

Generally a derogatory term referencing the preoccupation of society with the acquisition of consumer goods. However, it was also an economic theory of preferred behavior that started in the early twentieth century, seeing the act of purchasing goods as a socially progressive act. (See pages xviii, 25, 171–177, 192–193, and 243.)

Continuum Fallacy

When two or more different states or distinctions are assumed, while those distinctions actually exist along a fluid continuum that cannot be distinctly differentiated. This term is applied specifically to principles that are falsely delineated and made morally relativistic. (See page 77.)

Convict Leasing

Post–Civil War practice in America that started during the Reconstruction Period, consisting of arresting former slaves/African Americans and using the legal system to return them to forced labor. (See pages 125–128.)

Corporate Welfare

Behavior on the part of the state and legal system that favors upper-class, business interests over the general public. An example are the "too big to fail" corporate bailouts. (See page 151.)

Cultural Hegemony

Coined by Antonio Gramsci, this is the idea of societal domination by cultural influence of the thoughts, behavior, and expectations of general society, such that people are conditioned to appreciate and support the worldview of the ruling class. So influenced, people tend to support the mechanisms and institutions that may actually oppress them. (See pages 57 and 241.)

Cultural Relativism

Notably used by anthropologist Franz Boas, it is the principle that an individual person's beliefs and activities can be understood in terms of that individual's external culture. (See pages 75–76.)

Cultural Violence

Introduced by Johan Galtung as an extension of structural violence, this idea focuses on aspects of culture that normalize both direct and structural violence and their mechanisms, sanctifying it as natural. (See pages 188–189 and 298.)

Culture of Conflict

This phrase expresses the creation of competitive, dominating, and often violent behavioral patterns that have been reinforced over generations. The original reasoning or justification for such aggressive behavior has been lost, replaced by the cultural custom of aggression itself. As argued in this text, those groups or societies who do develop a culture of conflict are far more difficult to change over time than an individual who has succumbed to violent tendencies due to more immediate deprived or oppressive circumstances. (See page 43.)

Cyclical Consumption

Denoting the market economy's need for constant turnover through buying and selling in order to increase or maintain economic stability. This term is used to highlight the foundationally unsustainable nature of the system as it disfavors conservation or thrift. (See pages 165, 173, 176, 190–191, 193, 246, 248, 272, and 292.)

Debt Slavery

As one of the oldest mechanisms of slavery, debt slavery or debt bondage uses financial liability to coerce behavior. As argued in this text, the existence of debt slavery is still a global phenomenon, running a spectrum from abject debt-bondage conditions afflicting up to 46 million people, to the more common "wage slave" condition of billions, bound by consumer credit. (See pages 123–128.)

Differential (or Competitive) Advantage

Whereas competitive advantage is about the broad scope of competing for personal or group gain, differential advantage is an economic term regarding how a competitor separates himself from other competitors in public perception. As noted in this text, this competitive intent partly composes the *root socioeconomic orientation* of market economics and is proven destructive in the long term since it overrides more productive and stabilizing collaborative possibilities. (See pages 64, 192, and 293.)

Displaced Aggression

A social phenomenon that can be seen in both nonhuman and human primate species, where shame or offense experienced by one inspires motivation to exert control, power, or dominance over others that were previously uninvolved. Domestic abuse is a common example, in which stress experienced outside a family triggers abuse within a family. The idea highlights the importance of reducing socioeconomic stress overall. (See page 27.)

Doublethink

Coined by George Orwell, this is the acceptance of contrary opinions or beliefs at the same time, generally as a result of political indoctrination. (See pages 33 and 241.)

Empathy Gap

While a few definitions exist, the term is used in this text to describe a relativism in interpretation in the context of what triggers increased or decreased empathic responses. An example is how different cultures react to negative events occurring in different places. A bombing killing people in a distant city may have little emotional impact on a distant culture, while a closer bombing, harming a similar demographic, may have a large impact. (See page 104.)

Ephemeralization

A term coined by R. Buckminster Fuller, it is the ability and trend of technological advancement to do "more with less." It is complemented by other ideas denoting increased efficiency, such as Moore's Law, or approaching zero marginal cost. (See pages 251, 254, 262, 277–280, 289, 293, and 296.)

Epistemological Coherentism

Philosophical view that verifiable truth is an issue of how well it is supported by, or coherent with, other held beliefs. (See pages 81–82.)

Ethical Poverty Line

Devised by Peter Edward of Newcastle University, this calculation challenges established poverty-line figures put forward by the UN, WHO, World Bank, and other international institutions. It states that in order to achieve normal human life expectancy of just over seventy years, people need roughly 2.7 to 3.9 times the traditional poverty line put forward by such institutions (as of 2014). (See page 163.)

Exceptionalism

Used in both a legal and military context, exceptionalism has to do with the expressed elitism of state or business power not to abide by national/international laws or regulations. This text argues that the market system is premised on exceptionalism for an elite by its very design, inherent in its competitive structure. (See pages 39, 100, and 150–151.)

Externality

A consequence of economic activity that is generally experienced by unrelated third parties and can be positive or negative. The text focuses on negative externalities, highlighting the incapacity of the market economy to solve the problems it is creating. (See pages xix, 118–122, and 220.)

Feudalism

A decentralized social system based on mutual obligations and services going up and down a set social hierarchy, resting essentially on an agricultural foundation. It occurred from roughly the ninth to the sixteenth centuries. (See pages xviii and 62.)

Financial Capitalism

In contrast to merchant capitalism, this term expresses the modern evolution of markets and trade such that the selling of physical goods and services for profit becomes replaced by the selling of intangible assets such as stocks, bonds, and futures. *Also see* Financialization. (See page 142.)

Financialization

A pattern of accumulation in which profit making occurs increasingly through financial channels rather than through physical trade and commodity production. This text contextualizes the rise of financialization as a maturation process of market economics, moving from the tangible to the intangible. (See pages 138, 142–146, 166–167, 243, and 245.)

Foundationalism

In contrast to epistemological coherentism, this is the view that all knowledge ultimately rests on a foundation of noninferential understandings. (See pages 80–83.)

Free-Market Theory

An idealized form of a market economy in which buyers and sellers transact freely on the basis of mutual agreement and price, without state intervention in the form of taxes, subsidies, or other regulations. As argued at length in this book, this ideal is a destructive myth, as it is technically impossible to have a pure free market since regulation—and hence a means to stifle or coerce market competitors—can be created, bought, and sold, as well. *Also see* Paradox of Free Trade. (See pages 59–60 and 67.)

Free Will

The power of acting without the constraint of necessity, influence, or fate; the ability to act at one's own discretion. (See pages 8–9, 85–96, 178–179, and 252.)

Fundamental Attribution Error

The error of judgment made when people experience another's behavior a certain way, without knowing about other factors involved that would change their interpretation. (See page 89.)

Game Theory

Discussed in the context of utilitarianism, game theory embodies the strategic approach inherent in market competition. While it is common to see descriptions of market theory and behavior in terms of mutual benefit, human service, voluntary trade, and other aspects that sound as though market incentives gravitate toward social or human concern, the truth is that market logic is based upon a gaming strategy for income first and foremost, existing as the most dominant ethos of economic engagement. (See page 90.)

General Equilibrium Theory

General theory that seeks to explain the functioning of the market economy in terms of dynamics related mostly to supply, demand, and price interaction. The focus of the theory (and those who utilize it) is usually to prove markets have a natural propensity to find balance and stability through uninhibited free-market dynamics. (See pages xviii and 60.)

Geographical Determinism

Notably attributed to author Jared Diamond, this is about how characteristics of a particular culture have been historically shaped by geographic conditions. (See pages 46–47, 58, and 96.)

Gift Economy

An economic acquisition mechanism in which goods are given without an explicit agreement for immediate exchange. The context expressed in this book relates to the nature of early hunter-gather societies, which are documented as generally being based not upon exchange or reciprocation but rather on mutual altruistic giving. (See page 45.)

Globalization

A process of interaction and integration among the people, companies, and governments of different nations, driven by international trade and investment. (See pages 138, 144, 153–154, 210–211, 244–245, 265, 276–278, and 293–294.)

Golem Effect

In social psychology, this is the phenomenon in which lower expectations placed upon individuals lead to poorer performance by those individuals. (See page 101.)

Great Divergence

This refers to the end of the Malthusian Trap period, generally around the first Industrial Revolution in the late eighteenth century. This is when a marked rise in economic efficiency and productivity due to advancements in technology followed many prior centuries of near-static economic development, low incomes, and low population growth. (See page 251.)

Green Capitalism

General view that with incentive adjustments and policy shifts, capitalism can evolve out of its unsustainable and destructive environmental tendencies. In the view of this text, this idea is untenable on the whole. (See pages 171 and 257.)

Hedonic Treadmill

The tendency of a person to remain at a relatively stable level of happiness despite a change in fortune or the achievement of major goals. Accordingly, as a person makes more money, expectations and desires rise in tandem, which results in no permanent gain in happiness. This tendency can also relate to dissatisfaction, in that people seeking further material gain cannot increase happiness. In the context of this text, vanity, materialism, and consumerism are considered negative generators of this tendency, with more gain having less and less relevance. (See page 25.)

Heuristic

In psychology, this is about mental shortcuts that allow people to solve problems and make judgments quickly. However, their decisions are not necessarily thorough or accurate. (See pages 9 and 76.)

Hierarchy-Attenuating

In reference to social dominance theory, this has to do with structural or cultural influences that reduce the power of hierarchy and dominance. (See page 40.)

Hierarchy-Enhancing

In reference to social dominance theory, this has to do with structural or cultural influences that increase the power of hierarchy and dominance. (See pages 40 and 55.)

Homeostasis

The property of a system in which variables are regulated so that internal conditions remain stable and relatively constant. In this text, maintaining ecological sustainability in concert with economic behavior means homeostasis is achieved. (See pages 263 and 288.)

In-Group Bias

In conflict-and-identity theory, this is the propensity to favor one's identified group for inclusion (in-group) while generally disfavoring or being apathetic to those outside it (out-group). As argued in this book, while there appears to be a strong, natural propensity for humans to form groups due to associations and shared intents, the competitive and scarcity-based foundation of capitalism ensures this tendency will gravitate toward economic and political discrimination, dehumanization, and elitism. (See pages 93, 113, and 192.)

Inherent Counteracting Efficiency

This custom phrase from chapter five denotes the natural progress of increased efficiency, notably occurring since the start of the Industrial Revolution. It is an efficiency growth inherent in current established economic norms; this text argues that it is far from optimized to surpass the growing problems or negative externalities that also naturally emerge from capitalism. While counterintuitive, this phrase expresses how there will predictably be a mild slowing of many negative future trends as time moves forward, creating a false sense of security, while the force and momentum of the emerging negative externalities themselves in the twenty-first century will arguably outpace this inherent counteracting efficiency, making it undependable in a "business as usual" scenario. In other words, while things will improve due to the natural growth of efficiency in capitalism, there is little evidence to show that without a large, grand shift of our social system, this problem-solving capacity inherent in market economics will alleviate the accelerating negative public-health and environmental trends at hand. (See pages 255, 262, and 294.)

Institutional Racism

A form of racism expressed in the practice of social and political institutions, as distinct from racism expressed by individuals or informal social groups. Popularized by civil rights activist Stokely Carmichael, this concept and reality expresses a systemic process of bigotry and oppression, generally independent of an individual's personal bias. (See pages 16–23, 28, 112, and 239.)

Invisible Hand

As coined by Adam Smith, this is a metaphor to describe unintended social benefits resulting from self-interested, individual actions with a nonsocial intent. (See pages 60–61, 73, 86, 90, 106, 117, 243–244, and 289.)

IoT (Internet of Things)

Generalized term referencing the networking of physical objects, devices, vehicles, buildings, and other items embedded with electronics, software, and sensors. This networking through the Internet enables vast data exchange and feedback. This text views this advent as a means to assist more-advanced forms of economic calculation. (See pages 264, 280, and 294.)

Legitimizing Myths

Attitudes, values, beliefs, stereotypes, and ideologies that provide moral and intellectual justification for the social practices that distribute social value within the social system. (See pages 32 and 62.)

Localization

This is the interest in reversing globalization and seeking to employ as much production and distribution as possible locally in a given region. Localization is emphasized in the modern day since the democratization of the means of production through advanced technology and ephemeralization is a growing reality, coupled with the known waste and inefficiency of globalization. (See pages 264–265, 276–280, 293–298, and 330.)

Localized Perception

Truncated perception due to an overreliance on intuition, traditional ideas, and immediately perceived assumptions. It is in contrast to systems perception, which extends causality via systems theory in order to better explain the phenomenon. An example is the old idea or rhetoric that the sun "rises," when physically the Earth is moving to create the false perception of the sun's motion. (See pages 8–9, 21, 112, 186, and 253.)

Malthusian Trap

Named after the nineteenth-century political economist Thomas Malthus, this denotes the idea that population can or will outgrow its means to feed itself, as described by Malthus's population theories. Use in this text refers to how we can historically see population growth and die-offs occurring cyclically due to a lack of economic efficiency. This is generally considered to have started with the Neolithic Revolution and ended with the Industrial Revolution around the late eighteenth century. This is referred to as the *Malthusian Trap period*. (See pages 48–49, 124–125, 231, 245, 251, and 270.)

Market Economy (Free Market)

An economy that ideally operates by voluntary exchange and is not planned or controlled by a central authority; an economy run by supply and demand through self-regulation. As per the implications of this text, there are only mixed economies that fall under the market umbrella, utilizing varying degrees of state coercion. A theorized free market is argued as impossible. *Also see* Paradox of Free Trade. (See pages xviii–xix, 53, 59, 62, 63–65, 75, 106, 114, 118, 123, 143, 161, 165, 177, 186, 189, 201–202, 215, 241–248, 271–281, 289–294, and 329.)

Market Efficiency

As used in this text, this is the form of efficiency that assists the market system to maintain optimized functionality in and of itself. This is in contrast to technical efficiency, which is about actual resources, earthly sustainability, and what could be considered true economic factors in real life. (See pages 127, 172–173, and 293.)

Marketization

While generally defined as "the exposure of an industry or service to market forces," the context employed in this text has to do with dehumanization and the commodification of human affairs itself. (See page 176.)

Market Self-Regulation

The principle that free markets will regulate themselves through supply, demand, and inherent corrective dynamics, removing the need for state intervention or regulation. As argued in this book, this idea is mostly a myth or superstition, with very little evidence to support such assumed integrity beyond very basic price-and-trade relationships. (See pages 60, 63–65, 117, and 123.)

Mechanization

The use of machines to replace human labor or to aid human labor. (See pages 124 and 246–247.)

Mercantilism

An economic theory and practice dominant in modernized parts of Europe from the sixteenth to the eighteenth century that promoted governmental regulation of a nation's economy for the purpose of augmenting state power at the expense of rival national powers. This book contextualizes mercantilism as a stage of an ongoing economic evolution linking back to the Neolithic Revolution as the general starting point. (See pages xviii, 49, and 62.)

Merchant Capitalism

A distinction made that differentiates the pattern of manufacturing and trading tangible, physical goods from the historically recent and accelerating rise of the buying and selling of intangible financial assets. *Also see* Financial Capitalism. (See pages 140, 142–143, and 191.)

Moral Objectivism

The view that moral truths exist independently of opinion or subjective analysis. There are several versions of moral objectivism with varying levels of strength. From an epistemological perspective, it can be viewed as a derivative of foundationalism. (See pages 75, 76–77, 80, and 82–83.)

Moral Relativism

The view that moral or ethical propositions do not reflect objective and/or universal moral truths, but instead make claims relative to social, cultural, historical, or personal circumstances. From an epistemological perspective this can be viewed as related to coherentism. (See pages 75, 76, and 82–83.)

Negative Externality

See Externality.

Neoliberal Globalization

The ostensible philosophy of unregulated trade applied to international commerce. As argued in this book, this combination has served as an advanced form of colonization and exploitation of weak regions by larger commercial and governmental powers. *Also see* Neoliberalism. (See pages 210–213, 226, and 244–245.)

Neoliberalism

An approach to economics and social study in which control of economic factors is shifted from the public sector to the private sector. This text views neoliberalism as birthed from the free-market superstition triggered by

Adam Smith. At the same time, the practiced reality of neoliberal application is in fact contrary to pure free-market principles, assuming a true free market is even possible. (See pages 144, 153–155, 192–194, 215, 226–227, 230–234, and 243–244.)

Neolithic Revolution

Starting roughly 10,000 years ago, this was the social shift from nomadic hunting and gathering to agriculture and permanent settlements, the establishment of social classes, and the eventual rise of civilization as we know it. As argued in this text, this shift instilled the root socioeconomic orientation of market economics. (See pages 44–52, 53, 58, 96, 138, 192, 242–243, and 287.)

Open Source

A development model that promotes universal access to a product's design or blueprint, along with universal redistribution of that design or blueprint, including subsequent improvements to it by anyone. (See pages 265, 273–276, and 292–293.)

Oppression Equilibrium

With respect to social dominance or conflict theory, this has to do with limits to social oppression in order to prevent destabilizing insurrection and backlash. (See pages 72–73.)

Paradox of Free Trade

The observation that to decide what is and is not for sale in the market is entirely subjective, leading to a systemic contradiction. In a pure free market, one has the right to freely compete as one sees fit, assuming competitive self-regulation and voluntary trade. This also includes the ability to inhibit the freedom of others by coercive spending, such as paying off a politician. Therefore, the free market promotes the incentive to actually eliminate the free market, preferring cartel, monopoly, cronyism, and so on. (See page 68.)

Participatory Economics

A form of decentralized economic planning usually involving the common ownership of the means of production, with a democratization of access and influence. (See pages 276 and 330.)

Planned Obsolescence

In industrial design, this is the policy of designing a product with an artificially limited useful life, so it will become obsolete after a certain period of time. (See pages 173 and 292.)

Post-Scarcity

While idealistically termed, post-scarcity is an intention rather than a static state. It is the pursuit of abundance in society by way of increased efficiency, seeking to eliminate aspects of economic behavior that benefit from the existence of scarcity. Since the foundation of market economics is based upon an unnuanced assumption of scarcity, a move toward post-scarcity means a move away from what justifies the existence of capitalism. (See pages 284–285, 288–297, and 329–341.)

Poverty of the Spirit

As famously used by Dr. Martin Luther King Jr., this form of poverty references a lack of empathy and lost sense of social priority in society. (See pages 158–160, 176, 188–189, 197, 253, 275, and 298.)

Precondition

Generally defined as a condition that must be fulfilled before other things can happen or be done. This text specifically uses the term to highlight the systemic nature of cause and effect as related to social or public-health outcomes. (See pages xviii, xx, 6–9, 12–16, 22–28, 41, 46, 50, 54, 78 87–89, 100, 107, 152, 178–180, 186, 190, 203, 225, and 253.)

Primary Considerations

As used in this text, primary considerations have to do with the root incentive logic of markets. This means reducing costs and maximizing income. This is in contrast to "secondary conditions" that attempt to fulfill the classical utilitarian view that actions should always promote a greater good. Also termed "primary logic." (See pages 115–118.)

Psychosocial Stress

A form of stress that links one's social environment to his or her psychological health. Examples include threats to our social status, social esteem, respect, or acceptance within a group; threats to our self-worth; or threats that we feel we have no control over. It has been found that this form of stress has very direct physiological consequences, as well. (See pages 158, 180, 190–193, 204–208, and 247.)

Public Health

Generally defined as "the health of the population as a whole, especially as monitored, regulated, and promoted by the state," public health is argued in this book as embracing not only physical problems occurring across a population, but also behavioral actions and psychology. (See pages xvii, 7, 13, 25, 56, 62, 84, 95, 101, 111–120, and 157–235.)

Purchasing Demographic

This term expresses how companies strategically produce goods to target certain income or wealth levels. As argued in this book, this is a wasteful and unnecessary practice since it results in inferior goods quality to match lower-class consumers' purchasing power. (See pages 201–202.)

Rational Choice Theory

A framework for understanding and often formally modeling social and economic behavior, largely derived from utilitarianism. It assumes that people always make prudent, logical decisions in their highest self-interest. As argued in this text, what is deemed rational through market logic is very often irrational when it comes to the real world. (See pages 115–123.)

Relative Deprivation

The experience of being deprived of something to which one believes oneself entitled, or something that is causing social exclusion; emotional discontent people feel when they compare their positions to others and realize that they have less of what they believe themselves to be entitled to. (See pages 190–191 and 207.)

Relative Poverty

As a broad distinction and dependent on social context, relative poverty is usually a measure of income inequality. However, it also relates to wealth and the overall loss of material and social resources at one's disposal. In contrast to absolute poverty, relative poverty is based on economic comparison rather than a specifically tangible loss of health requirements. (See pages 63, 158, 199, and 206.)

Reverse Dominance Hierarchy

Popularized by anthropologist Christopher Boehm, this is the observation that hunter-gatherer tribes maintained nonhierarchical social structures by deliberately stopping anyone who attempted to rise up and be dominant. (See pages 50–51.)

Root Socioeconomic Orientation

As used frequently in this text, this is the guiding orientation underlying market economics and capitalism. This has to do with justifying competition, self-interest, hierarchy, inequality, oppression, and other factors born from the assumption of universal and unnuanced earthly scarcity. (See pages 53–54, 62–63, 84, 85–87, 96, 116, 138, 159, 232, 242–243, 247–248, 265, and 289.)

Secondary Considerations

In contrast to primary considerations, these are considerations that tend to be prioritized only after the basic competitive pursuit of profit and income has occurred. These may include social concern, ecological respect, charity, and habitat sustainability. The argument posed is that empathic considerations of social concern are more of an afterthought when it comes to the competitive gaming logic inherent in market economics. The result of this focus on primary considerations systematically thwarts true problem resolution, detrimentally forcing a short-term focus. (See pages 115–116 and 117–118.)

Self-Maximization

As per game theory in the context of market incentives, this is the basic interest of all economic players in maximizing their potential immediate gain however possible. The result is primitive, impulsive, and shortsighted behavior, often creating short-term gain at the expense of long-term negative repercussions. (See pages 90, 196, and 200.)

Self-Preservation

Similar to self-maximization, this is the specific need to preserve one's income sources, even if doing so goes against the natural unfolding of economic progress or development. A common example is a business that has invested in a certain kind of income-producing infrastructure, willfully working to slow any further advancement of the specific service or product since that could destabilize existing market share. The term also applies to the use of government as a means of strategic advantage by business powers, stopping more advanced competitors by regulatory force, again preserving the existing, established norms. (See pages 170, 192, and 238.)

Social Dominance Orientation (SDO)

Related to social dominance theory, this is the implied evolutionary trait built into human psychology that is alleged to generate a tendency toward favoring domination of others and other nonegalitarian effects. (See pages 40–41, 43–44, and 50–52.)

Social Dominance Theory (SDT)

Established by psychologists Jim Sidanius and Felicia Pratto, this theory purports to explain the origin and consequences of social hierarchy and resulting oppression, seeing it as immutable in the human condition. (See pages 39–43, 50–52, 72, 85, 90, and 158.)

Social Identity Theory

The theory that people derive their sense of identity and self-esteem largely from group-based social inclusion. (See page 92.)

Socialism

Generally, a political and economic theory of social organization advocating that the means of production, distribution, and exchange should be owned or regulated by the community as a whole. In modern use, the term often expresses the use of state power to supply social services, bypassing the market system in whole or in part. As related to this book, while the end proposals can be deemed socialistic by association, the focus has been to argue that beyond the ideal of a system without a dominant power/economic class, the real issue is the need for synergetic design to increase efficiency and reduce socially destabilizing socioeconomic inequality. From this perspective, the original conception of socialism becomes obsolete as this larger train of thought transcends the original moral premise of the idealized "socialist" community interaction. (See pages xviii, 60, 147–151, 238, and 277.)

Sociobiology

The scientific study of the biological aspects of social behavior in animals and humans. (See page 81.)

Socioeconomic

Relating to or concerned with the interaction of social and economic factors, specifically regarding how economic pressures result in larger-order social consequences in terms of both personal and public health. (See pages xviii–xx, 9, 12–16, 20–21, 25–28, 49, 52–54, 73, 84–86, 96, 98, 103–104, 111, 119, 179–180, 226, 282–284, 288–289, and 295–297.)

Socioeconomic Inequality

A condition in which physical and social resources are unevenly distributed across a population, with the source of this uneven distribution rooted in economic activity. (See pages xix, xvii–xix, 15, 20–22, 24, 86, 152, 179–180, 191–193, 199, 240, 245–253, and 288–297.)

Strategic Access

In contrast to property and product investment, strategic access is about strategizing ways to do "more with less" in terms of distribution, allowing people access to goods in rotation rather than singular ownership. (See page 265.)

Structural Bigotry

Building upon the idea of Stokely Carmichael's institutional racism, structural bigotry recognizes mechanisms in the social structure itself that create and reinforce social oppression indirectly. These mechanisms, as described in this text, are almost exclusively linked to the economy on some level. (See pages 16–17, 97–126, 156, and 160.)

Structuralism

Methodology where elements of human culture are to be understood in terms of their relationship to larger, overarching systems or structures. (See page xvii.)

Structural Violence

Preventable violence, death, and suffering resulting from human-generated institutions, specifically socioeconomic inequality. (See pages 28, 108, 118, 180–215, 227–229, 232, 247, 289, and 298.)

Sustainable Abundance

In contrast to the utopian ideal of infinite material abundance, the concept of a sustainable abundance qualifies and associates two complementary intents. The first (sustainable) is the need for habitat respect by the human species, using advanced measures and practices to ensure homeostatic coexistence with nature, avoiding resource overshoot, pollution, and so forth. The second (abundance) connects as an economic focus, maximizing efficiency through harnessing the "zero margin cost" or "ephemeralization" phenomenon. In capitalism, the orientation is around scarcity, with incentives built around its preservation and exploitation. In a post-scarcity or abundance-focused society, the goal is to remove such incentives, creating more efficient and system-based design methods to overcome any and all basic human material deficiencies. As argued, there is no technical reason today for any human being to starve, be without water, or exist in poverty as we know it. (See pages 263, 265, and 329.)

Systemic Racism

Developed by sociologist Joe Feagin, the idea of systemic racism is composed of intersecting, overlapping, and codependent racist institutions, policies, practices, ideas, and behaviors. The racist outcomes manifest are not necessarily intentional but rather a product of systemic chain reactions. (See pages 12 and 16–23.)

Systemic Servicing

As discussed in the context of negative externalities, this term relates to the extended chain reactions that occur when certain problems arise through economic practice. Each of these chain reactions tends to require servicing (costs) that can appear as separate or disconnected. A polluted water supply leading to an individual's cancer and treatment is an example, since the servicing costs to fix such consequences are spread out, ranging from cleaning up the pollution to the medical costs of the individual with cancer, etc. (See page 119.)

Systems Perception

In contrast to localized perception, this is the general analytical perspective that seeks to find and focus on intersecting processes and chain reactions rather than reductionism or the isolation of phenomena. (See page 8.)

Systems Theory

Made popular by biologist Ludwig von Bertalanffy, this is a nonreductionist approach to understanding complex phenomena, focusing attention on larger-order relationships and intersections rather than smaller or detached parts. In the context of this text, systems theory can be applied not only to mechanistic systems such as industrial economic methods, but also to understanding public-health science, preconditions, and so forth. (See pages xvii, 3–10, 16, and 117.)

Technical Efficiency

In contrast to market efficiency, technical efficiency refers to pure economic creation/production/distribution methods that are optimized in the most direct way, without any monetary or business influence. (See page 172.)

Technological Unemployment

The loss of jobs caused by the introduction of labor-saving machines or more-efficient processes. *Also see* Automation. (See pages 255, 260, and 266.)

Thought Syntax

In linguistics, syntax is the set of rules, principles, and processes that govern the structure of sentences in a given language. In this custom usage, a thought syntax has to do with mental associations that, through repetitive customs, belief systems, and operant conditioning, create orientations and resolutions of thought irrespective of the objective information perceived. This discrepancy ultimately creates a mental schema that is biased, unconsciously so. (See page 54.)

Universal Standardization

In manufacturing and design, this ideal has to do with strategically working to reduce the amount of variance occurring across goods genres, making more items more compatible. A simple example is the common wall-outlet plug design to draw electricity. While there is some variance in the world, it is relatively small so as to help people interchange needed powered devices with ease across regions. This simple idea is counter to differential and planned-obsolescence strategies common to market competition, wherein keeping components proprietary, changing, and unrelated throughout a sector or product genre is seen as a means to inspire more purchases or brand loyalty. (See pages 276 and 297.)

Utilitarianism

As made famous by John Stuart Mill, this is the view that the correct moral choice in any given situation is the one that produces the greatest utility in terms of generating happiness and reducing suffering. (See pages 90, 91, and 115.)

Voluntarism

While generally defined as the principle of relying on voluntary action, in market economics this term is often used to idealize free choice in market behavior. As argued in this text, this is fallacious idealism due to the immutable existence of structural coercion throughout capitalism. (See page 91.)

Wage Slavery

A pejorative term, this expresses the market-system-generated pressure on people to feel coerced into unpreferred labor roles for the sake of maintaining basic survival levels of income. As argued in this book, a continuum between abject slavery and historical debt bondage links to the phenomenon of wage labor since the coercive pressure to gain income for survival is just as present, albeit less severe than earlier forms of slavery. The main difference rests in how the coercive pressure manifests, forcing people into vulnerable positions unnecessarily. In the modern period, slavery is argued as hidden by an ostensible range of employment choices, yet driven by pressures such as consumer debt that constantly oppress the lower classes through imposed scarcity. In traditional thinking, coercion is seen as an interpersonal or institutional force, such as a person holding a gun to another and forcing action. Wage slavery is rather a consequence of systemic economic forces and survival pressures that exist only due to the structure of capitalism, not the natural order itself. *Also see* Structural Bigotry. (See pages 149–150.)

Zero Marginal Cost

Approaching zero marginal cost means that once technical systems are set up to produce goods, each consecutive good gets cheaper and cheaper, approaching zero cost or zero value in terms of production. (See pages 251, 266, 288–291, and 294.)

Endnotes

Acknowledgments

1. Carl Sagan, *Cosmos* (Ballantine Books, 1980), 279.

Introduction

1. Larry Dane Brimner, *We Are One: The Story of Bayard Rustin* (Calkins Creek, 2007), 46.
2. Kate Pickett and Richard Wilkinson, *The Spirit Level* (Bloomsbury Press, 2011).
3. Frederick Douglass, *Slavery and the Civil War: Selections from His Writings* (Dover Publications, 2003), 42.

Chapter 1

1. Jim Wallis, "Martin Luther King, Jr. Was a Social Justice Christian," *Huffpost Religion blog*, 2011, accessed February 3, 2016, http://www.huffingtonpost .com/jim-wallis/martin-luther-king-jr-was_b_695964.html.
2. "White flight" is a twentieth-century term that originated in the United States. It applied to the migration of people of various European ancestries from racially mixed urban regions to more racially homogeneous suburban or exurban regions.
3. Ludwig von Bertalanffy, *General System Theory: Foundations, Development, Applications* (George Braziller, 1968), 30–53.
4. Richard M. Frankel, Timothy E. Quill, and Susan H. McDaniel, *The Biopsychosocial Approach* (University of Rochester Press, 2003).
5. Niklas Luhmann, *Introduction to Systems Theory*, 1st ed. (Polity, 2012, republication).
6. Bruce Hood, *The Self-Illusion: How the Social Brain Creates Identity* (Oxford University Press, 2013).
7. Robert Sapolsky, *Why Zebras Don't Get Ulcers* (Owl Books, 2004), 103.
8. L. Eugene Arnold, *Childhood Stress* (John Wiley & Sons, 1990).
9. Michael Newton, *Savage Girls and Wild Boys* (Thomas Dunne Books/St. Martin's Press, 2003).

10. Such research has been explored by public health and addiction expert Dr. Gabor Maté. He states, "The human infant and toddler is a highly vulnerable creature, and emotional stresses of all kinds in the rearing environment can create long-lasting wounds in the psyche that a person will later try to soothe or numb with addictive behavior. In addition to things that do happen that shouldn't happen, like abuse, there are things that (developmentally speaking) ought to happen that don't. For instance, any sustained sense of emotional disconnection with the parenting figure—which can often happen when the parent is excessively stressed or preoccupied over a period of time—has the capacity to have this sort of impact, especially if the child is constitutionally very sensitive. In a stressed society like ours, with fewer and fewer supportive resources for parents, this is more and more common."

    Gabor Maté, "Addiction—Dr. Gabor Maté," 2016, http://drgabormate.com/topic/addiction/.

    Also see: Gabor Maté, *In the Realm of Hungry Ghosts* (North Atlantic Books, 2012).

11. P. E. Mullen et al., "The Long-Term Impact of the Physical, Emotional, and Sexual Abuse of Children: A Community Study," *Child Abuse & Neglect* 20, no. 1 (1996): 7–21, doi:10.1016/0145-2134(95)00112-3.

12. Evan L. Ardiel and Catharine H. Rankin, "The Importance of Touch in Development," *Paediatrics & Child Health* 15, no. 3 (2010): 153–156, http://www.ncbi.nlm.nih.gov/pmc/articles/PMC2865952/.

13. Tiffany M. Field et al., "Tactile/Kinesthetic Stimulation Effects on Preterm Neonates," *Pediatrics* 77, no. 5 (1986): 654–658.

14. Science Daily, "Unemployment Linked with Child Maltreatment," 2010, http://www.sciencedaily.com/releases/2010/10/101003081452.htm.

15. Ming Jen Lin, "Does Unemployment Increase Crime? Evidence from US Data, 1974–2000," *Journal of Human Resources* 43, no. 2 (2007), 413–436.

16. Carlos Nordt et al., "Modelling Suicide and Unemployment: A Longitudinal Analysis Covering 63 Countries, 2000–11," *The Lancet Psychiatry* 2, no. 3 (2015): 239–245, doi:10.1016/s2215-0366(14)00118-7.

17. Madeleine Côté, "How Categorical Thinking Creates a Biased View of the World," Dawson College, 2013, http://inspire.dawsoncollege.qc.ca/2013/11/13/how-categorical-thinking-creates-a-biased-view-of-the-world/.

18. Gerd Gigerenzer, *Reckoning with Risk: Learning to Live with Uncertainty* (Penguin Books, 2003).

19. Anuj K. Shah and Daniel M. Oppenheimer, "Heuristics Made Easy: An Effort-Reduction Framework," *Psychological Bulletin* 134, no. 2 (2008): 207–222, doi:10.1037/0033-2909.134.2.207.

20. Kenneth A. Dodge and Gregory S. Pettit, "A Biopsychosocial Model of the Development of Chronic Conduct Problems in Adolescence," *Developmental Psychology* 39, no. 2 (2003): 349–371, doi:10.1037//0012-1649.39.2.349.

21. Pew Charitable Trusts, *One in 100: Behind Bars in America 2008*, Public Safety Performance Project, 2008, http://www.pewtrusts.org/~/media/legacy/uploadedfiles/pcs_assets/2008/one20in20100pdf.pdf.

    And

    Annie E. Casey Foundation, "Youth Incarceration in the United States," accessed February 13, 2016, http://www.aecf.org/m/resourcedoc/aecf-YouthIncarcerationInfographic-2013.pdf.

22. NAACP, "Criminal Justice Fact Sheet," accessed February 13, 2016, http://www.naacp.org/pages/criminal-justice-fact-sheet#.

    And

    "And Justice for Some: Differential Treatment of Youth of Color in the Justice System," National Council on Crime and Delinquency, 2007, http://www.nccdglobal.org/sites/default/files/publication_pdf/justice-for-some.pdf.

    And

    Annie E. Casey Foundation, "Youth Incarceration in the United States."

23. Michelle Alexander, *The New Jim Crow: Mass Incarceration in the Age of Colorblindness* (The New Press, 2012), 118.

24. Anna Aizer and Joseph J. Doyle Jr., "Juvenile Incarceration, Human Capital and Future Crime: Evidence from Randomly-Assigned Judges," 2013, http://www.mit.edu/~jjdoyle/aizer_doyle_judges_06242013.pdf.

    And

    Pew Charitable Trusts, "Re-Examining Juvenile Incarceration," 2015, http://www.pewtrusts.org/en/research-and-analysis/issue-briefs/2015/04/reexamining-juvenile-incarceration.

25. Alexander, *The New Jim Crow*.

26. James E. Mazur, *Learning and Behavior*, 6th ed. (Psychology Press, 2012).

27. Bertrand Russell, *Proposed Roads to Freedom: Socialism, Anarchism and Syndicalism* (Henry Holt and Co., 1919), 125.

28. Richard Orange, "Sweden Closes Four Prisons as Number of Inmates Plummets," *The Guardian*, 2013, accessed February 3, 2016, http://www.theguardian.com/world/2013/nov/11/sweden-closes-prisons-number-inmates-plummets.

    Regarding low recidivism of Sweden and Scandinavians countries:

    Doran Larson, "Why Scandinavian Prisons Are Superior," *The Atlantic*, 2013, accessed February 3, 2016, http://www.theatlantic.com/international/archive/2013/09/why-scandinavian-prisons-are-superior/279949/.

29. Prisonpolicy.org, "Global Comparisons—Prison Index | Prison Policy Initiative," 2016, http://www.prisonpolicy.org/prisonindex/globalincarceration.html.

30. Far from uncommon in modern social theory, social preconditions have a clear effect on human behavior as a kind of modulating force. A notable and long-standing sociological example has been the "economic deprivation

argument," also known as the "opportunity-cost argument." An overwhelming number of studies have corroborated a spectrum of effects surrounding poverty, scarcity, and deprivation, including crime in general.

Haiyun Zhao, Zhilan Feng, and Carlos Castillo-Chavez, "The Dynamics of Poverty and Crime," 2015, https://mtbi.asu.edu/research/archive/paper/dynamics-poverty-and-crime.

31. EJI, "United States Considered Most Punitive Country in the World," 2010, http://www.eji.org/node/423.

32. Annie E. Casey Foundation, 2013, "Youth Incarceration in the United States."

33. Regarding adult incarceration, the National Institute of Justice has compiled extensive data, sourcing Bureau of Justice statistics that found up to 76.6 percent of 404,638 prisoners tracked were rearrested in five years.

National Institute of Justice, 2014, "Recidivism," accessed January 3, 2016, http://www.nij.gov/topics/corrections/recidivism/pages/welcome.aspx.

Regarding juvenile incarceration, the Annie E. Casey Foundation produced a detailed study, "No Place for Kids: The Case for Reducing Juvenile Incarceration." This report sources recidivism statistics, while also concluding, "Many studies find that incarceration actually increases recidivism among youth with lower-risk profiles and less-serious offending histories."

Annie E. Casey Foundation, 2011, "No Place for Kids: The Case for Reducing Juvenile Incarceration," http://www.aecf.org/m/resourcedoc/aecf-NoPlaceForKidsFullReport-2011.pdf.

Regarding the US's recidivism, increasing by comparison to other nations' incarceration practices, these studies vary in absolute numbers due to different systems of measurement in different countries. However, the Pell Center for International Relations and Public Policy produced a report, "Incarceration and Recidivism: Lessons from Abroad," by Carolyn Deady, concluding this was the case, on the basis of available evidence.

Carolyn Deady, "Incarceration and Recidivism: Lessons from Abroad," Pell Center for International Relations and Public Policy (Rhode Island, 2014), http://www.salve.edu/sites/default/files/filesfield/documents/Incarceration_and_Recidivism.pdf.

34. James Gilligan, "A New Approach to Violence Treatment: An Interview with Dr. James Gilligan," *PSYCHALIVE*, 2009, http://www.psychalive.org/a-new-approach-to-violence-treatment-an-interview-with-dr-james-gilligan/.

35. FBI, "Persons Arrested," accessed February 13, 2016, https://www.fbi.gov/about-us/cjis/ucr/crime-in-the-u.s/2011/crime-in-the-u.s.-2011/persons-arrested/persons-arrested.

36. Map of world, "Countries with Highest Reported Crime Rates—World Top Ten," 2013, http://www.mapsofworld.com/world-top-ten/countries-with-highest-reported-crime-rates.html.

37. As of 2014, more than 50 percent of inmates currently in federal prison are there for drug offenses, according to the Federal Bureau of Prisons.

    Federal Bureau of Prisons, "BOP Statistics: Inmate Offenses," accessed February 13, 2016, http://www.bop.gov/about/statistics/statistics_inmate _offenses.jsp.

38. Jeremy Travis, Bruce Western, and Steve Redburn, *The Growth of Incarceration in the United States* (National Academies Press, 2014).

39. Christopher J. Lyons and Becky Pettit, "Compounded Disadvantage: Race, Incarceration, and Wage Growth," *Social Problems* 58, no. 2 (2011): 257–280, doi:10.1525/sp.2011.58.2.257.

40. *Falling Further Behind: Combating Racial Discrimination in America*, ebook, 1st ed. (Washington: The Leadership Conference Education Fund, 2014), 6, http://www.civilrightsdocs.info/pdf/reports/CERD_Report.pdf.

41. Stokely Carmichael and Charles V. Hamilton, *Black Power: The Politics of Liberation in America* (Vintage Books, 1976), 4.

42. Ibid., 22.

43. Peter H. Wood, *Strange New Land: Africans in Colonial America*, 1st ed. (Oxford University Press, 2003), 25.

44. Louis Menand, "Morton, Agassiz, and the Origins of Scientific Racism in the United States," *The Journal of Blacks in Higher Education* 34 (Winter, 2001–2002): 110–113, doi:10.2307/3134139.

45. Ellis Cashmore and James Jennings, eds. *Racism: Essential Readings* (Sage Publications, 2011), 113.

46. William J. Wilson, *The Declining Significance of Race: Blacks and Changing American Institutions*, 3rd ed. (Chicago: The University of Chicago Press, 2012), 28.

47. Carter A Wilson, *Racism* (Sage Publications, 1996), 50–51.

48. Ibid., 51–52.

49. Edmund S. Morgan, *American Slavery, American Freedom* (Norton, 1975), 331.

50. *New York Times*, "Haldeman Diary Shows Nixon Was Wary of Blacks and Jews," 1994, http://www.nytimes.com/1994/05/18/us/haldeman-diary -shows-nixon-was-wary-of-blacks-and-jews.html.

51. Todd R. Clear, *Imprisoning Communities* (Oxford University Press, 2007).

52. Jeanette Covington, *Crime and Racial Constructions: Cultural Misinformation about African Americans in Media and Academia* (Lexington Books, 2010), 58–60.

53. American Friends Service Committee, "The Unfinished Business of the Poor People's Campaign," accessed February 13, 2016, http://www.afsc.org/ resource/unfinished-business-poor-peoples-campaign.

54. Martin Luther King Jr., *Where Do We Go From Here? Chaos or Community,*

Convention of the Southern Christian Leadership Conference (Beacon Press, 1968).

55. Ibid.

56. Marshall Frady, *Martin Luther King, Jr: A Life* (Penguin, 2005), 192.

57. Jesse Bricker, Rodney Ramcharan, and Jake Krimmel, "Signaling Status: The Impact of Relative Income on Household Consumption and Financial Decisions," *SSRN Electronic Journal*, n.d., doi:10.2139/ssrn.2435503.

58. Niro Sivanathan and Nathan Pettit, "Protecting the Self Through Consumption: Status Goods as Affirmational Commodities," *Journal of Experimental Social Psychology* 46, no. 3 (2010): 564–570.

59. Emily Chertoff, "The Racial Divide on . . . Sneakers," *The Atlantic*, 2012, http://www.theatlantic.com/national/archive/2012/08/the-racial-divide-on-sneakers/261256/.

60. Kipling D. Williams, Joseph P. Forgas, and William Von Hippel, *The Social Outcast: Ostracism, Social Exclusion, Rejection, and Bullying*, 1st ed. (Psychology Press, 2005).

61. Studies of social exclusion and the generation of antisocial or neurotic behaviors have been corroborated in many contexts, including primitive studies with nonhuman primates. A classic study of social isolation was the controversial Harlow monkey study, in which baby monkeys were left alone for up to one year from birth or repetitively separated from their peers and isolated in a chamber. These procedures quickly produced monkeys that were severely psychologically disturbed; they were used as models of human depression.

    Harry F. Harlow and Stephen J. Suomi, "Production of Depressive Behaviors in Young Monkeys," *Journal of Autism and Developmental Disorders* 1, no. 3 (1971): 246–255, doi:10.1007/bf01557346.

62. A. Malika Auvray, Erik Myin, and Charles Spence, "The Sensory-Discriminative and Affective-Motivational Aspects of Pain," *Neuroscience & Biobehavioral Reviews* 34, no. 2 (2010): 214–223, doi:10.1016/j.neubiorev.2008.07.008.

    M.-P. Paladino et al., "Synchronous Multisensory Stimulation Blurs Self-Other Boundaries," *Psychological Science* 21, no. 9 (2010): 1202–1207. doi:10.1177/0956797610379234.

    Frank H. Wilhelm et al., "Social Anxiety and Response to Touch: Incongruence between Self-Evaluative and Physiological Reactions," *Biological Psychology* 58, no. 3 (2001): 181–202, doi:10.1016/s0301-0511(01)00113-2.

63. The predictable negative outcomes related to social exclusion, feeling disrespected, and social stratification are abundant. With respect to the examples present, select studies are provided respectively.

    Michael Bond, "How Extreme Isolation Warps the Mind," BBC.com, 2014, http://www.bbc.com/future/story/20140514-how-extreme-isolation-warps-minds.

Kipling D. Williams, "Ostracism," *Annual Review of Psychology* 58, no. 1 (2007): 425–452, doi:10.1146/annurev.psych.58.110405.085641.

Paul Gilbert and Jeremy Miles, "Sensitivity to Social Put-Down: Its Relationship to Perceptions of Social Rank, Shame, Social Anxiety, Depression, Anger and Self-Other Blame," *Personal and Individual Differences* 29, no. 4 (2000): 757–774.

Mark Stemmler, Thomas Bliesener, and Andreas Beelmann, *Antisocial Behavior and Crime* (Hogrefe Publishing, 2012).

Stephen J. Bunker et al., "'Stress' and Coronary Heart Disease: Psychosocial Risk Factors," *US National Library of Medicine, National Institutes of Health* 178, no. 6 (2003): 272–276.

Michael Marmot, "Epidemiology of Socioeconomic Status and Health: Are Determinants within Countries the Same as between Countries?," ncbi.nlm.nih.gov, 1999, http://www.ncbi.nlm.nih.gov/pubmed/10681885.

64. David G. Myers, *The American Paradox: Spiritual Hunger in an Age of Plenty* (Yale University Press, 2001).

65. David G. Myers, "The Funds, Friends, and Faith of Happy People," *American Psychologist* 55, no. 1 (2000): 56–67.

66. Roy F. Baumeister and Brad Bushman, *Social Psychology and Human Nature, Brief Version* (Wadsworth Publishing), 2013, 192.

67. Avner Offer, *The Challenge of Affluence: Self-Control and Well-Being in the United States and Britain Since 1950* (Oxford University Press, 2007), 327.

68. Ibid., 152.

69. James Gilligan, "Shame, Guilt, and Violence Social Research," *New School Press*, Winter 70, no. 4 (2003): 1148–1180.

70. Chris Poulson, "The Root of Violence, the Standing Conference on Organizational Symbolism," *Institutions and Violence*, 2011.

71. Richard Wilkinson, "Why Is Violence More Common Where Inequality Is Greater?," *Annals of the New York Academy of Sciences* 1036, no. 1 (2004): 1–12, doi:10.1196/annals.1330.001.

72. James Gilligan, "Violence in Public Health and Preventive Medicine," *The Lancet* 355, no. 9217 (2000): 1802–1804, doi:10.1016/s0140-6736(00)02307-2.

Also see: Susan Evans, "Beyond Gender: Class, Poverty and Domestic Violence," *Australian Social Work* 58 (1) (2005): 36–43, doi:10.1111/j.0312-407x.2005.00182.x.

R. C. Kramer, "Poverty, Inequality, and Youth Violence," *The Annals of the American Academy of Political and Social Science* 567 (1) (2000): 123–139. doi:10.1177/0002716200567001009.

73. Robert Sapolsky, *Why Zebras Don't Get Ulcers*, 3rd ed. (Henry Holt, 2004) 255–263.

74. Katherine S. Van Wormer and Albert R. Roberts, *Death by Domestic Violence* (Westport, CT: Praeger, 2009).

Also see: David M. Buss and Todd K. Shackelford, "Human Aggression in Evolutionary Psychological Perspective," *Clinical Psychology Review* 17, no. 6 (1997): 605–619, doi:10.1016/s0272-7358(97)00037-8.

75. Ibid., 102–103.

76. James Gilligan, *Violence: Reflections on a National Epidemic* (Random House, 1997), 236.

77. Robert Smyth and Patrick McGrain, "The Nature of Riots: Socioeconomic and Political Conditions Inherent in Collective Action," accessed February 4, 2016, http://www.desales.edu/_fileserver/salesian/PDF/HonorsProgram Smyth2006.pdf.

78. "The Siege of L.A.," *Newsweek*, 5/10/1992, http://www.newsweek.com/siege-la-199112.

79. Gandhi has been quoted often in history and original sources are often lost. Third-party sourcing is all that exists in many cases, even though the usage and credit is ubiquitous.

Metta Center, "Structural Violence—Metta Center," 2010, http://metta center.org/definitions/gloss-concepts/structural-violence/.

80. Ibid., 4.

81. Johan Galtung, "Violence, Peace, and Peace Research," *Journal of Peace Research* 6, no. 3 (1969): 167–191.

82. Thomas Weber, *Gandhi as Disciple and Mentor* (Cambridge University Press, 2004), 210.

Chapter 2

1. John McMurtry, *The Cancer Stage of Capitalism* (Pluto Press, 1999), 7.

2. Kevin Schilbrack, ed., *Thinking Through Myths: Philosophical Perspectives* (Routledge Press, 2002), 174–189.

3. Shanto Iyengar and William J. McGuire, eds., *Explorations in Political Psychology* (Duke University Press, 1993), 208.

4. Stephen Ingle, *The Social and Political Thought of George Orwell: A Reassessment* (Routledge, 2006), 83.

5. John Luskin, *Lippmann, Liberty, and the Press* (University of Alabama Press, 1972), 229.

6. George Orwell, *The Orwell Reader: Fiction, Essays, and Reportage* (Houghton Mifflin Harcourt, 1961), 363.

7. George Carlin publicly stated this phrase in a live address to the National Press Club, May 13, 1999.

8. M. J. Heale, *McCarthy's Americans: Red Scare Politics in State and Nation, 1935–1965* (The University of Georgia Press, 1998).

9. Alexander Kouzmin, Matthew T. Witt, and Andrew Kakabadse, eds., *State*

Crimes Against Democracy: Political Forensics in Public Affairs (Palgrave Macmillan, 2012), 1945.

10. Carl Schmitt, *The Concept of the Political* (Rutgers University Press, 1927).

11. Srikant Sarangi and Stefan Slembrouck, *Language, Bureaucracy and Social Control* (Routledge, 2014).

12. Democracy Now!, "U.S. Ally Saudi Arabia Prepares To Behead, Crucify Pro-Democracy Protester Ali Mohammed Al-Nimr," 2015, http://www .democracynow.org/2015/10/22/us_ally_saudi_arabia_prepares_to.

13. Hamid Dabashi, *The Arab Spring: The End of Postcolonialism* (Zed Books, 2012).

14. Edward L. Bernays and Mark Crispin Miller, *Propaganda* (Ig Publishing, 1928).

15. Stuart Ewen, *PR!: A Social History of Spin* (Basic Books, 2008), 446.

16. Bernays and Miller, 37.

17. James W. Loewen, *Lies My Teacher Told Me about Christopher Columbus: What Your History Books Got Wrong* (New Press, 2014).
    And
    Tamra Orr, *A History of Voting Rights* (Mitchell Lane Publishers, Inc., 2012), 9.

18. Wilson Lloyd Bevan, *The World's Leading Conquerors: Alexander the Great, Caesar, Charles the Great, the Ottoman Sultans, the Spanish Conquistadors, Napoleon* (H. Holt and Company, 1913), 311–312.

19. John Neville Figgis, *The Theory of the Divine Right of Kings* (University Press, 1896).

20. It is true that there are two or more sides to a war and one or more sides may indeed be seeking to simply protect itself from aggressive interests. However, this fact doesn't change the reason for the initiation of war itself, which starts from interests involving dominance, conquest, resources, colonialism, or imperialism.

21. Ziauddin Sardar, *American Dream, Global Nightmare* (Icon Books, 2009), 258.

22. Roy Harvey Pearce, *Savagism and Civilization: A Study of the Indian and the American Mind* (University of California Press, 1988), 63.

23. Angeliki E. Laiou and Roy P. Mottahedeh, *The Crusades from the Perspective of Byzantium and the Muslim World* (Dumbarton Oaks, 2001), 10–18.

24. "Fighting Radicalism, Not 'Terrorism': Root Causes of an International Actor Redefined," *SAIS Review* no. 2 (2009): 75–86.

25. General Assembly, *Contemporary Forms of Racism, Racial Discrimination, Xenophobia and Related Intolerance*, Elimination of Racism, Racial Discrimination, Xenophobia and Related Intolerance: Comprehensive Implementation of and Follow-Up to the Durban Declaration and Programme of Action

(United Nations, 2013), http://idsn.org/wp-content/uploads/user_folder/pdf/ New_files/UN/SP/SR_racism_-_report_Sep_2013.pdf.

26. Jose D. Fermin, *1904 World's Fair: The Filipino Experience* (University of the Philippines Press, 2004).

27. Theodore Roosevelt, *A Compilation of the Messages and Speeches of Theodore Roosevelt, 1901–1905*, vol. 1 (Bureau of National Literature and Art, 1906), 29.

28. Chris Woods, "Drone Strikes in Pakistan," The Bureau of Investigative Journalism, 2011, https://www.thebureauinvestigates.com/2011/08/11/more -than-160-children-killed-in-us-strikes/.

29. Dana Hughes, "US Drone Hits in Pakistan Called Illegal," ABC News, 2013, http://abcnews.go.com/blogs/politics/2013/03/us-drone-strikes-in-pakistan -are-illegal-says-un-terrorism-official/.

30. Jim Sidanius and Felicia Pratto, *Social Dominance: An Intergroup Theory of Social Hierarchy and Oppression* (Cambridge University Press, 2001).

31. Felicia Pratto et al., "Social Dominance Orientation: A Personality Variable Predicting Social and Political Attitudes," *Journal of Personality and Social Psychology* 67, no. 4 (1994): 741–763, doi:10.1037/0022-3514.67.4.741.

32. Jim Sidanius et al., "Social Dominance Theory: Its Agenda and Method," *Social Dominance and Intergroup Relations* 25, no. 6 (2004): 845–880.

33. Paul M. Sniderman and Philip E. Tetlock, *Prejudice, Politics, and the American Dilemma* (Stanford University Press, 1993), 173.

34. Paul A. M. Van Lange, Arie W. Kruglanski, and E. Tory Higgins, *Handbook of Theories of Social Psychology*, vol. 2 (Sage Publications, 2011), 419.

35. Daniel J. Christie, *The Encyclopedia of Peace Psychology*, vol. 1 (John Wiley & Sons, 2011), 1015.

36. As far as the denial of any biological determinism is concerned, they state, "In short, we should regard human action as the result of an enormously complex interaction between an array of *weakly determinative factors*, including genotype, specific environmental conditions at multiple levels of organization (e.g., inter-cellular, interpersonal, intergroup, etc.), and pure chance" (Sidanius et al., "Social Dominance Theory,": 845–880).

    Yet, this ambiguous distinction is contradicted by other declarations of the theorists, such as, "SD theory views group conflict as having less to do with 'structural' features of the economy or culture than as being primarily driven by a ubiquitous human drive towards domination and group-based hierarchical social organization." (Sniderman and Tetlock, 181.) The phrase *ubiquitous human drive* can only be construed as implying biological determinism via evolutionary psychology.

37. Sniderman and Tetlock, 181.

38. Felicia Pratto et al., "Social Dominance Orientation: A Personality Variable Predicting Social and Political Attitudes," *Journal of Personality and Social Psychology* 67, no. 4 (1994): 741–763, doi:10.1037/0022-3514.67.4.741.

39. Sidanius and Pratto, 33–34.

40. Ibid, 33.

41. Jim Sidanius et al., "Social Dominance Theory: Its Agenda and Method," *Social Dominance and Intergroup Relations* 25, no. 6 (2004): 845–880.

42. Thomas F. Homer-Dixon, *Environment, Scarcity, and Violence* (Princeton University Press, 1999).

43. For a modern example and analysis: Chris Arsenault, "Risk of Water Wars Rises with Scarcity," Aljazeera.com, 2012, http://www.aljazeera.com/indepth/features/2011/06/2011622193147231653.html.

44. A. R. Krosch and D. M. Amodio, "Economic Scarcity Alters the Perception of Race," *Proceedings of the National Academy of Sciences* 111, no. 25 (2014): 9079–9084, doi:10.1073/pnas.1404448111.

    Also see: UKEssays, "Need for Peaceful Co-Existence and Resolution," 2011, http://www.ukessays.com/dissertation/examples/politics/need-for-peaceful-co-existence-and-resolution.php.

45. Robert B. Textor, *A Cross-Cultural Summary* (HRAF Press, 1967).

46. James DeMeo, *Saharasia: The 4000 BCE Origins of Child Abuse, Sex-Repression, Warfare and Social Violence, in the Deserts of the Old World* (Natural Energy Works, 2011).

47. Kay Prüfer et al., "The Bonobo Genome Compared with the Chimpanzee and Human Genomes," *Nature* 486, no. 6 (2012): 527–531, doi:10.1038/nature11128.

48. Frans de Waal, Frans B. M. de Waal, and Frans Lanting, *Bonobo: The Forgotten Ape* (University of California Press, 1998).

49. Ann Gibbons, "Bonobos Join Chimps as Closest Human Relatives | Science | AAAS," Sciencemag.org, 2012, http://www.sciencemag.org/news/2012/06/bonobos-join-chimps-closest-human-relatives.

50. Thomas F. Homer-Dixon, *Environment, Scarcity, and Violence* (Princeton University Press, 1999).

51. Herschel I. Grossman and Juan Mendoza, "Scarcity and Appropriative Competition," 2002, http://citeseerx.ist.psu.edu/viewdoc/download?doi=10.1.1.445.4113&rep=rep1&type=pdf.

52. E. J. Peltenburg and Alexander Wasse, *Neolithic Revolution: New Perspectives on Southwest Asia in Light of Recent Discoveries on Cyprus* (Oxbow Books, 2004).

53. Stephen Boyden is notable for describing four ecological phases of human existence. (1) The hunter-gatherer phase, by far the longest of the four phases, lasting for hundreds of thousands of years. (2) The early farming phase, which began in some parts of the world 11,000 to 12,000 years ago. (3) The early urban phase, which began in southwestern Asia around 6,000 to 9,000 years ago. (4) The high-energy phase, which began in Western Europe and North America 150 to 200 years ago.

Stephen Boyden, "The Fundamental Questions Program and Its Conceptual Basis," 1990, https://hec-forum.anu.edu.au/2015/Fundamentals/Boyden-1990-Fundamentals_1.pdf.

54. Kerry Sheridan, "Warfare Was Uncommon Among Hunter-Gatherers: Study," Phys.org, 2013, http://phys.org/news/2013-07-warfare-uncommon-hunter-gatherers.html.

55. John Gowdy, *Limited Wants, Unlimited Means: A Reader on Hunter-Gatherer Economics and the Environment* (Island Press, 1998), 115.

56. Marshall Sahlins, *Stone Age Economics* (Routledge, 2013).

57. Carolyn C. Pertsova, *Ecological Economics Research Trends* (Nova Publishers, 2007), 178.

58. Richard Heinberg, *The End of Growth: Adapting to Our New Economic Reality* (New Society Publishers, 2011), 29.

59. Tim Ingold, *The Perception of the Environment: Essays on Livelihood, Dwelling and Skill* (Psychology Press, 2000), 70.

60. Jared M. Diamond, *Guns, Germs, and Steel: The Fates of Human Societies* (W. W. Norton & Company, 1997).

61. An example was the battle of Cajamarca in 1532, where about 170 Spaniards faced an army of 80,000 Inca soldiers. In the first ten minutes, there were 7,000 Incas dead, with all Spaniards alive. This was because they could advance with swords and crude guns while the Incas had wooden clubs. This battle is reflective of the different stages of development.
Stefan Lovgren, "'Guns, Germs and Steel': Jared Diamond on Geography as Power," News.Nationalgeographic.com, 2005, http://news.national geographic.com/news/2005/07/0706_050706_diamond_2.html.

62. Gregory Clark, *A Farewell to Alms: A Brief Economic History of the World* (Princeton University Press, 2008), part 1.

63. Thomas Robert Malthus, *An Essay on the Principle of Population* (Dent, 1973).

64. Ibid., book IV, chap. V.

65. Clark, 1.

66. Kathy S. Stolley, *The Basics of Sociology* (Greenwood Publishing Group, 2005), 140.

67. Robert Sapolsky, *Why Zebras Don't Get Ulcers* (W. H. Freeman, 1998), 383.

68. Peter Gray, "How Hunter-Gatherers Maintained Their Egalitarian Ways," *Psychology Today*, 2011, https://www.psychologytoday.com/blog/freedom-learn/201105/how-hunter-gatherers-maintained-their-egalitarian-ways.

69. Christopher Boehm et al., "Egalitarian Behavior and Reverse Dominance Hierarchy [and Comments and Reply]," *Current Anthropology* 34, no. 3 (1993): 227–254.

70. Peter Gray, "How Hunter-Gatherers Maintained Their Egalitarian Ways," *Psychology Today*, 2011, https://www.psychologytoday.com/blog/freedom

-learn/201105/how-hunter-gatherers-maintained-their-egalitarian
-ways.

71. John C. Turner and Katherine J. Reynolds, "Why Social Dominance Theory Has Been Falsified," *School of Psychology, The Australian National University* 42, no. 2 (2003).

72. Thomas Hobbes, *Leviathan* (Cosimo, Inc., 2009).

73. Clark, 112.

74. N. Mankiw, *Principles of Microeconomics* (Cengage Learning, 2014), 4–5.

75. Robert Sapolsky, "Are the Desert People Winning?," *Discover Magazine*, 2005, http://discovermagazine.com/2005/aug/desert-people.

76. D. C. Park and C.-M. Huang, "Culture Wires the Brain: A Cognitive Neuroscience Perspective," *Perspectives on Psychological Science* 5, no. 4 (2010): 391–400, doi:10.1177/1745691610374591.

77. Robert W. Sussman and C. Robert Cloninger, *Origins of Altruism and Cooperation* (Springer Science & Business Media, 2011).

78. Keith Francis, *Charles Darwin and The Origin of Species* (Greenwood Publishing Group, 2007), 53.

79. Margaret Mead, *Cooperation and Competition Among Primitive Peoples* (Transaction Publishers, 2002).

80. Gordon Ervin Moss, *The Dawning Age of Cooperation: The End of Civilization as We Know It—and Just in Time* (Algora Publishing, 2011), 20.

81. Sussman and Cloninger, chap. 7.

82. Douglas P. Fry, *War, Peace, and Human Nature: The Convergence of Evolutionary and Cultural Views* (Oxford University Press, 2013), 551.

83. Pauline V. Rosenau, "Competition as a Public Health Problem," 2002, accessed February 4, 2016, https://apha.confex.com/apha/responses/130am/362.doc.

84. Kurt Edward Kemper, *College Football and American Culture in the Cold War Era* (University of Illinois Press, 2009), 37.

85. NPR.org, "Pentagon Paid Sports Teams Millions for 'Paid Patriotism' Events," 2015, http://www.npr.org/sections/thetwo-way/2015/11/05/45483 4662/pentagon-paid-sports-teams-millions-for-paid-patriotism-events.

86. Sam Pizzigati, "The 'Self-Made' Myth: Our Hallucinating Rich," Inequality. org, 2012, accessed February 4, 2016, http://inequality.org/selfmade-myth -hallucinating-rich/.

87. Walter L. Adamson, *Hegemony and Revolution: A Study of Antonio Gramsci's Political and Cultural Theory* (University of California Press, 1983).

88. Amanda Doherty, "Violence in Sports: A Comparison of Gladiatorial Games in Ancient Rome to the Sports of America," *Open SIUC* 8 (2001), http:// opensiuc.lib.siu.edu/cgi/viewcontent.cgi?article=1011&context=uhp_theses.

89. Joshua Holland, "Raising the Minimum Wage Is the 'Free Market' Thing to Do," Billmoyers.com, 2014, accessed February 4, 2016, http://billmoyers

.com/2014/01/14/raising-the-minimum-wage-is-the-%E2%80%9Cfree
-market%E2%80%9D-thing-to-do/.

90. Adam Smith, *An Inquiry into the Nature and Causes of the Wealth of Nations*, 1776 (Doig and Stirling, 1817), par. IV.2.9.

91. Bernard Hodgson, *The Invisible Hand and the Common Good* (Springer Science & Business Media, 2013).

92. Jonathan Schlefer, *The Assumptions Economists Make* (Harvard University Press, 2012), 9.

93. Vlasta Kunova and Martin Dolinsky, *Current Issues of Science and Research in the Global World: Proceedings of the International Conference on Current Issues of Science and Research in the Global World, Vienna, Austria; 27–28 May 2014* (CRC Press, 2014), 26.

94. Schlefer, 9.

95. Pam Bennett, "The Forum for Family and Consumer Issues (FFCI)," *4H & Family/Consumer Sciences*, 2012, https://ncsu.edu/ffci/publications/2012/v17-n1-2012-spring/index-v17-n1-may-2012.php.

    And

    Reeves, M. McKee and D. Stuckler, "Economic Suicides in the Great Recession in Europe and North America," *British Journal of Psychiatry* 205, no. 3 (2014): 246–247, doi:10.1192/bjp.bp.114.144766.

    And

    Rawstory.com, "Global Financial Crisis Linked to 500,000 Cancer Deaths in New Study," 2016, accessed June 4, 2016, http://www.rawstory.com/2016/05/global-financial-crisis-linked-to-500000-cancer-deaths-in-new-study/.

96. Stéphane Courtois and Mark Kramer, *The Black Book of Communism: Crimes, Terror, Repression* (Harvard University Press, 1999), 76.

97. Oxfam.org, "Annual Income of Richest 100 People Enough to End Global Poverty Four Times Over," 2013, accessed February 4, 2016, https://www.oxfam.org/en/pressroom/pressreleases/2013-01-19/annual-income-richest-100-people-enough-end-global-poverty-four.

98. Julie Mertus and Jeffrey W. Helsing, *Human Rights and Conflict: Exploring the Links Between Rights, Law, and Peacebuilding* (US Institute of Peace Press, 2006), 72.

99. Gandhi has been quoted often in history and original sources are often lost. Third-party sourcing is all that exists in many cases, even though the usage and credit is ubiquitous.

    Metta Center, "Structural Violence—Metta Center," 2010, http://mettacenter.org/definitions/gloss-concepts/structural-violence/.

100. Marlene Podritske, *Objectively Speaking: Ayn Rand Interviewed* (Lexington Books, 2009), 39.

101. Thorstein Veblen, *The Theory of Business Enterprise* (Kessinger Publishing, 2006), 269.

102. Carly Cody, "Majority in Congress Are Millionaires," NPR.org, 2014, accessed February 4, 2016, http://www.npr.org/sections/itsallpolitics/2014/01/10/261398205/majority-in-congress-are-millionaires.

103. Lee Fang, "Where Have All the Lobbyists Gone?," *The Nation*, 2014, accessed February 4, 2016, http://www.thenation.com/article/shadow-lobbying-complex/.

104. Thomas Edsall, "The Trouble with That Revolving Door," *Campaign Stops*, 2011, accessed February 4, 2016, http://campaignstops.blogs.nytimes.com/2011/12/18/the-trouble-with-that-revolving-door/?_r=0.

105. Martin Gilens and Benjamin I. Page, "Testing Theories of American Politics: Elites, Interest Groups, and Average Citizens," *Perspectives on Politics* 12, no. 03 (2014): 564–581, doi:10.1017/s1537592714001595.

106. United States Constitutional Convention, *The Records of the Federal Convention of 1787*, vol. 1 (Yale University Press, 1911), 431.

107. John Cunningham Wood, *Thorstein Veblen: Critical Assessments* (Psychology Press, 1993), 236.

108. Sniderman and Tetlock, 178.

109. Thorstein Veblen, *Absentee Ownership and Business Enterprise in Recent Times* (Augustus M. Kelley, 1964), 220–221.

110. Derek Robbins, *Cultural Relativism and International Politics* (Sage Publications, 2014).

111. Louis P. Pojman and Peter Tramel, *Moral Philosophy: A Reader* (Hackett Publishing, 2009).

112. Michael Ruse, "Evolutionary Ethics: A Phoenix Arisen," *Zygon* 21, no. 1 (1986): 95–112, doi:10.1111/j.1467-9744.1986.tb00736.x.

113. Elizabeth Palermo, "Religion Doesn't Make People More Moral, Study Finds," Livescience.com, 2014, http://www.livescience.com/47799-morality-religion-political-beliefs.html.

114. *Internet Encyclopedia of Philosophy*, "Foundationalism," accessed February 4, 2016, http://www.iep.utm.edu/found-ep/.

115. Jack S. Crumley II, *An Introduction to Epistemology*, 2nd ed. (Broadview Press, 2009), 108.

116. Terence Irwin, *Aristotle's First Principles* (Clarendon Press, 1989).

117. René Descartes, Donald A. Cress, *Discourse on Method*, 3rd ed. (Hackett Publishing, 1998).

118. Edward O. Wilson, *Sociobiology: The New Synthesis* (Harvard University Press, 2000).

119. Matteo Rizzato, Davide Donelli, and Giacomo Rizzolatti, *I Am Your Mirror: Mirror Neurons and Empathy* (Edizioni Amrita SL, 2014).

120. George Kohlrieser, Susan Goldsworthy, and Duncan Coombe, *Care to Dare: Unleashing Astonishing Potential Through Secure Base Leadership* (John Wiley & Sons, 2012).

121. Paul K. Moser, *The Oxford Handbook of Epistemology* (Oxford University Press USA, 2005).

122. Catherine Z. Elgin, "Non-Foundationalist Epistemology: Holism, Coherence, and Tenability," *Contemporary Debates in Epistemology*, 2005, doi:10.5860/choice.43-0232.

123. Kay Codell Carter and Barbara R. Carter, *Childbed Fever: A Scientific Biography of Ignaz Semmelweis* (ABC-CLIO, 1994), 64–68.

124. Peter Tse, *The Neural Basis of Free Will: Criterial Causation* (MIT Press, 2013).

125. Wilkie A. Wilson and Cynthia M. Kuhn, "How Addiction Hijacks Our Reward System," *Cerebrum: The Dana Forum on Brain Science* 7, no. 2 (2005): 53–66, https://science.madison.k12.wi.us/files/science/How_Addiction_Hijacks_Our_Reward_System.pdf.

126. Gabor Maté, M.D., *In the Realm of Hungry Ghosts: Close Encounters with Addiction* (North Atlantic Books, 2011).

127. M. H. Teicher, C. M. Anderson, and A. Polcari, "Childhood Maltreatment Is Associated with Reduced Volume in the Hippocampal Subfields CA3, Dentate Gyrus, and Subiculum," *Proceedings of the National Academy of Sciences* 109, no. 9 (2012): E563-E572, doi:10.1073/pnas.1115396109.

128. Christopher D. Webster and Margaret A. Jackson, *Impulsivity: Theory, Assessment, and Treatment* (Guilford Press, 1997), 122.

129. David G. Myers, *Exploring Psychology, 8th ed., In Modules* (Macmillan, 2010), 545.

130. This is not to ignore the consideration of "insanity" in the justice system, but to show how rare and extreme that view of involuntary control is. Generally, the courts view everyone as a free agent, making choices on his or her own, with no inhibiting factors.

131. John Stuart Mill, *Utilitarianism* (Dover Publications, 2007).

132. E. K. Hunt and Mark Lautzenheiser, *History of Economic Thought: A Critical Perspective* (Routledge, 2015).

133. J.P. Caverni, J.M. Fabre, and M. Gonzalez, *Cognitive Biases* (Elsevier, 1990), 333–336.

134. Emanuele Bardone, *Seeking Chances: From Biased Rationality to Distributed Cognition* (Springer Science & Business Media, 2011), 44–46.

135. David F. Barone, James E. Maddux, and C. R. Snyder, *Social Cognitive Psychology: History and Current Domains* (Springer Science & Business Media, 2012), 35–37.

136. Andrew J. Fuligni, *Contesting Stereotypes and Creating Identities: Social Categories, Social Identities, and Educational Participation* (Russell Sage Foundation, 2007), 66, 78.

137. Charles Mackay, *Extraordinary Popular Delusions* (Templeton Foundation Press, 2015), preface.

138. V. A. Klucharev, P. Zubarev, and A. N. Shestakova, "Neurobiological Mechanisms of Social Influence," *Experimental Psychology (Russia)* 7, no. 4 (2015): 20–36, http://psyjournals.ru/en/exp/2014/n4/73771.shtml.

139. R. Custers and H. Aarts, "The Unconscious Will: How the Pursuit of Goals Operates Outside of Conscious Awareness," *Science* 329, no. 5987 (2010): 47–50, doi:10.1126/science.1188595.

140. Eben Harrell, "Think You're Operating on Free Will? Think Again," Time .com, 2010, http://content.time.com/time/health/article/0,8599,2000994,00 .html.

141. D. Rigoni et al., "Inducing Disbelief in Free Will Alters Brain Correlates of Preconscious Motor Preparation: The Brain Minds Whether We Believe in Free Will or Not," *Psychological Science* 22, no. 5 (2011): 613–618, doi:10.1177/0956797611405680.

142. John A. Bargh and Tanya L. Chartrand, "The Unbearable Automaticity of Being," *American Psychologist* 54, no. 7 (1999): 462–479, doi:10.1037//0003 -066x.54.7.462.

Chapter 3

1. Kimberley A. Bobo, *Wage Theft in America* (New Press, 2009), 204.

2. Nicholas Rayfield, "National Student Loan Debt Reaches a Bonkers $1.2 Trillion," *USA Today College*, 2015, http://college.usatoday.com/2015/04/08/ national-student-loan-debt-reaches-a-bonkers-1-2-trillion/.

   And

   Shelly Banjo, "American Student Loan Debt Has Surpassed the GDP of Australia, New Zealand, and Ireland Combined," *Quartz*, 2015, http:// qz.com/346342/american-student-loan-debt-has-surpassed-the-gdp-of- australia-new-zealand-and-ireland-combined/.

3. Drew DeSilver, "U.S. Students Improving—Slowly—in Math and Science, but Still Lagging Internationally," Pew Research Center, 2015, http://www .pewresearch.org/fact-tank/2015/02/02/u-s-students-improving-slowly-in -math-and-science-but-still-lagging-internationally/.

4. Brad Plumer, "America's Staggering Defense Budget, in Charts," *Washington Post*, 2013, https://www.washingtonpost.com/news/wonk/wp/2013/01/07/ everything-chuck-hagel-needs-to-know-about-the-defense-budget-in -charts/.

   And

   Cbpp.org, "Policy Basics: Where Do Our Federal Tax Dollars Go?," 2015, http://www.cbpp.org/research/policy-basics-where-do-our-federal-tax -dollars-go?fa=view&id=1258.

5. Coalitionforthehomeless.org, "Basic Facts about Homelessness: New York City," accessed February 8, 2016, http://www.coalitionforthehomeless.org/basic-facts-about-homelessness-new-york-city/.

6. Buzzflash, "Disney's Sad Sweatshop History," 2006, http://www.truth-out.org/buzzflash/commentary/disneys-sad-sweatshop-history/429-disneys-sad-sweatshop-history.

7. F. Scott Fitzgerald, *The Short Stories of F. Scott Fitzgerald*, Matthew J. Bruccoli, ed., n.d., 318.

8. Richard Wilkinson and Kate Pickett, "Belief Systems and Durable Inequalities, Policy Research Working Paper," *Chart from the Spirit Level*, 2009, 113–114.

9. Peter David Blanck, *Interpersonal Expectations* (Cambridge University Press, 1993), 155–156.

10. Drake Morgan et al., "Social Dominance in Monkeys: Dopamine D2 Receptors and Cocaine Self-Administration," *Nature Neuroscience* 5, no. 2 (2002): 169–174, doi:10.1038/nn798.

11. A. Randrup, I. Munkvad, and R. Pog, "Mania, Depression, and Brain Dopamine," *Current Developments in Psychopharmacology* 2, W. Essman and L. Valzelli L, eds., (1975): 206–248.

12. Pamela Paul, "The Rich Lack Empathy, Study Says," *New York Times*, 2010, http://www.nytimes.com/2011/01/02/fashion/02studied.html.

    And

    M. W. Kraus, S. Cote, and D. Keltner, "Social Class, Contextualism, and Empathic Accuracy," *Psychological Science* 21, no. 11 (2010): 1716–1723, doi:10.1177/0956797610387613.

13. "Having Less, Giving More: The Influence of Social Class on Prosocial Behavior," *Personality and Social Psychology, 2010* 99, no. 5 (2012): 771–784, http://www.rotman.utoronto.ca/phd/file/Piffetal.pdf.

14. Robert Frank, "The Rich Are Less Charitable than the Middle Class: Study," CNBC, 2012, http://www.cnbc.com/id/48725147.

    And

    Frank Greve, "America's Poor Are Its Most Generous Givers," McClatchy DC, 2009, http://www.mcclatchydc.com/2009/05/19/68456/americas-poor-are-its-%20most-generous.html.

15. Ken Stern, "Why the Rich Don't Give to Charity," *The Atlantic*, 2013, http://www.theatlantic.com/magazine/archive/2013/04/why-the-rich-dont-give/309254/.

16. P. K. Piff et al., "Higher Social Class Predicts Increased Unethical Behavior," *Proceedings of the National Academy of Sciences* 109, no. 11 (2012): 4086–4091, doi:10.1073/pnas.1118373109.

17. Q. Ashton Acton, ed., *Issues in Behavioral Psychology* (Scholarly Editions, 2013), 803–805.

18. Daniel Goleman, "Rich People Just Care Less," Opinionator blog, 2013, http://opinionator.blogs.nytimes.com/2013/10/05/rich-people-just-care-less/?_r=0.

19. Katia Savchuk, "Wealthy Americans Are Giving Less of Their Incomes to Charity, While Poor Are Donating More," *Forbes*, 2014, http://www.forbes.com/sites/katiasavchuk/2014/10/06/wealthy-americans-are-giving-less-of-their-incomes-to-charity-while-poor-are-donating-more/.

20. John Tozzi, "Income Inequality Makes Rich People Stingier," *Bloomberg*, 2015, http://www.bloomberg.com/news/articles/2015-11-23/income-inequality-makes-rich-people-stingier.

21. Paul Piff, "Does Money Make You Mean?," Ted.com, 2013, https://www.ted.com/talks/paul_piff_does_money_make_you_mean?language=en#t-287828.

22. Lisa Miller, "The Money-Empathy Gap," *New York News & Politics*, 2012, http://nymag.com/news/features/money-brain-2012-7/.

23. Ken Stern, "Why the Rich Don't Give to Charity," *The Atlantic*, 2013, http://www.theatlantic.com/magazine/archive/2013/04/why-the-rich-dont-give/309254/.

24. Wfp.org, "Hunger Statistics—Fighting Hunger Worldwide," UN World Food Programme, accessed February 8, 2016, https://www.wfp.org/hunger/stats.

25. Jeffrey Dorfman, "Income Redistribution's Logical Conclusion Is Communism," *Forbes*, 2014, http://www.forbes.com/sites/jeffreydorfman/2014/01/16/income-redistributions-logical-conclusion-is-communism/.

26. Oxfam International, "Richest 1% Will Own More than All the Rest by 2016," 2015, https://www.oxfam.org/en/pressroom/pressreleases/2015-01-19/richest-1-will-own-more-all-rest-2016.

27. Bill Gates, "Why Inequality Matters," Gatesnotes, 2014, http://www.gatesnotes.com/Books/Why-Inequality-Matters-Capital-in-21st-Century-Review.

28. Advisor of the People's Health Movement Dr. David McCoy states, regarding the power of the Gates Foundation: "Through its funding it also operates through an interconnected network of organizations and individuals across academia and the NGO and business sectors. This allows it to leverage influence through a kind of 'group-think' in international health." In 2008 the WHO's head of malaria research, Aarata Kochi, accused a Gates Foundation "cartel" of suppressing diversity of scientific opinion, claiming the organization was "accountable to no-one other than itself."

    Andrew Bowman, "The Flip Side to Bill Gates' Charity Billions," *New Internationalist Magazine*, 2012, http://newint.org/features/2012/04/01/bill-gates-charitable-giving-ethics/#sthash.MP3jXKN8.dpuf.

29. Jennifer Yang, "Bill Gates, the World's Chequebook Doctor," *Toronto Star*, 2015, http://www.thestar.com/news/world/2015/04/06/bill-gates-the-worlds-chequebook-doctor.html.

30. Donald G. McNeil Jr., "Gates Foundation's Influence Criticized," *New York Times*, 2008, http://www.nytimes.com/2008/02/16/science/16malaria.html?_r=0.

31. Slavoj Žižek, *Violence* (Picador, 2008), 22.

32. Jackie Wattles, "10 More Billionaires Join Buffett-Gates Giving Pledge," CNN Money, 2015, http://money.cnn.com/2015/06/02/news/companies/giving-pledge-billionaires-buffett-gates/.

33. Meena Hartenstein, "Bill Gates and Warren Buffett Ask Oprah, Bloomberg, Other Billionaires to Give Big Money to Charity," *Daily News*, 2010, http://www.nydailynews.com/news/money/bill-gates-warren-buffett-oprah-bloomberg-billionaires-give-big-money-charity-article-1.184375.

34. Josh Bivens, "Inequality, Exhibit A: Walmart and the Wealth of American Families," Economic Policy Institute, 2012, http://www.epi.org/blog/inequality-exhibit-wal-mart-wealth-american/.

35. "The Phony Philanthropy of the Walmart Heirs," accessed February 9, 2016, http://walmart1percent.org/files/2014/06/PhonyPhilanthropy.pdf.

36. Chye-Ching Huang and Brandon Debot, "Ten Facts You Should Know about the Federal Estate Tax," Center on Budget and Policy Priorities, 2015, http://www.cbpp.org/research/ten-facts-you-should-know-about-the-federal-estate-tax.

37. Brendan Coffey, "Pledge Aside, Dead Billionaires Don't Have to Give Away Half Their Fortune," Bloomberg Business, 2015, http://www.bloomberg.com/news/articles/2015-06-04/as-billionaires-bask-in-glow-of-pledge-giving-half-is-optional.

38. Jon M. Bakija and William G. Gale, "Effects of Estate Tax Reform on Charitable Giving," Tax Policy Center, 2003, http://www.taxpolicycenter.org/publications/url.cfm?ID=310810.

39. Aviva Aron-Dine, "Estate Tax Repeal—or Slashing the Estate Tax Rate—Would Substantially Reduce Charitable Giving," Center on Budget and Policy Priorities, 2006, http://www.cbpp.org/research/estate-tax-repeal-or-slashing-the-estate-tax-rate-would-substantially-reduce-charitable?fa=view&id=465.
    And
    Jon M. Bakija and William G. Gale, "Effects of Estate Tax Reform on Charitable Giving," Tax Policy Center, 2003, http://www.urban.org/sites/default/files/alfresco/publication-pdfs/310810-Effects-of-Estate-Tax-Reform-on-Charitable-Giving.PDF.

40. Spiegel Oonline, "Negative Reaction to Charity Campaign: German Millionaires Criticize Gates' 'Giving Pledge,'" 2010, http://www.spiegel.de/international/germany/negative-reaction-to-charity-campaign-german-millionaires-criticize-gates-giving-pledge-a-710972.html.

41. Stephanie Storm, "Pledge to Give Away Fortunes Stirs Debate," *New York*

Times, 2010, http://www.nytimes.com/2010/11/11/giving/11PLEDGE
.html?pagewanted=all.

42. Noam Chomsky and Barry Pateman, *Chomsky on Anarchism* (AK Press, 2005), 364.

43. As an aside, US tax policy is quite biased, as has been explored by many researchers.

    See: Bonnie Kavoussi, "Poor People Paying Double the Tax Rate of the Rich," *Huffington Post*, 2012, http://www.huffingtonpost.com/2012/09/21/poor-americans-state-local-taxes_n_1903993.html.

44. Kingencyclopedia.stanford.edu, "Address at the Conclusion of the Selma to Montgomery March," accessed February 8, 2016, http://kingencyclopedia
.stanford.edu/encyclopedia/documentsentry/doc_address_at_the
_conclusion_of_selma_march/.

45. *Investopedia*, "Rational Choice Theory," accessed February 8, 2016, http://www.investopedia.com/terms/r/rational-choice-theory.asp.

46. Leemon McHenry and Mellad Khoshnood, "Blood Money: Bayer's Inventory of HIV-Contaminated Blood Products and Third World Hemophiliacs," *Accountability in Research* 21, no. 6 (2014): 389–400, doi:10.1080/08989621
.2014.882780.

47. As will be discussed in chapter five, "planned obsolescence" is a known practice, which is the deliberate withholding of efficiency for the sake of future purchases and updates. Apple Inc. has been known for this practice.

    Jamie Campbell, "Apple Watch Is Beset by 'Planned Obsolescence,'" *The Independent*, 2015, http://www.independent.co.uk/life-style/gadgets
-and-tech/company-breaks-open-apple-watch-to-discover-what-it-says-is
-planned-obsolescence-10203822.html.

48. Charles M. Kelly, *Class War in America: How Economic and Political Conservatives Are Exploiting Low and Middle Income Americans* (Fithian Press, 2000), 178.

49. Ian Talley, "IMF Estimates Trillions in Hidden Fossil-Fuel Costs," *Wall Street Journal*, 2015, http://www.wsj.com/articles/imf-estimates-trillions-in-hidden-fossil-fuel-costs-1431958586.

50. Reuters, "IMF Says Energy Subsidized by $5.3 Trillion Worldwide," accessed February 8, 2016, http://www.reuters.com/article/imf-energy
-idUSL1N0Y61S220150518.

51. Overseas Development Institute, "Time to Change the Game: Fossil Fuel Subsidies and Climate," accessed February 8, 2016, http://www.odi.org/subsidies-change-the-game.

52. *Natural Capital at Risk: The Top 100 Externalities of Business*, Trucost, TEEB for Business Coalition, April 2013.

53. Ed Dolan, "Why Fuel Subsidies Are Bad for Everyone," Oilprice.com, 2013,

http://oilprice.com/Energy/Gas-Prices/Why-Fuel-Subsidies-are-Bad-for
-Everyone.html.

54. Ibid.

55. World Bank, "Climate Change Complicates Efforts to End Poverty," 2015,
    http://www.worldbank.org/en/news/feature/2015/02/06/climate-change
    -complicates-efforts-end-poverty.

56. United Nations Development Programme, "Climate Change Threatens
    Unprecedented Human Development Reversals," United Nations, November
    27, 2007.

57. Andrea Thompson, "Pollution May Cause 40 Percent of Global Deaths,"
    Livescience, 2007, http://www.livescience.com/1853-pollution-40-percent
    -global-deaths.html.

58. David Graeber, *Debt: The First 5,000 Years,* 3rd ed. (Melville House, 2014).

59. Ibid., 10.

60. Abject slavery is still occurring in places like Mauritania. John D. Sut-
    ter, "Slavery's Last Stronghold," CNN, accessed February 8, 2016, http://
    www.cnn.com/interactive/2012/03/world/mauritania.slaverys.last.strong
    hold/.

61. The Abolition Project, "Why Was Slavery Finally Abolished in the British
    Empire?," accessed February 8, 2016, http://abolition.e2bn.org/slavery_111
    .html.

62. Edward E. Baptist, *The Half Has Never Been Told* (Basic Books, 2014), 313.

63. *Encyclopedia Britannica,* "John Elliott Cairnes, British Economist," 2014,
    http://www.britannica.com/biography/John-Elliott-Cairnes.

64. Edward E. Baptist, *The Half Has Never Been Told* (Basic Books, 2014), 386–387.

65. Ibid., 130.

66. Douglas A. Blackmon, *Slavery by Another Name* (Doubleday, 2008), 53.

67. Eric Arnesen, *Encyclopedia of U.S. Labor and Working-Class History,* 1 (CRC
    Press, 2007), 318.

68. Blackmon, 351.

69. In the Public Interest, "Criminal: How Lockup Quotas and 'Low-Crime
    Taxes' Guarantee Profits for Private Prison Corporations," 2013, http://www
    .inthepublicinterest.org/criminal-how-lockup-quotas-and-low-crime-taxes
    -guarantee-profits-for-private-prison-corporations/.

70. Ian Urbina, "Despite Red Flags about Judges, a Kickback Scheme Flourished,"
    New York Times, 2009, http://www.nytimes.com/2009/03/28/us/28judges
    .html?_r=2.

71. Beth Buczynski, "Shocking Facts about America's For-Profit Prison Indus-
    try," Truthout, 2014, http://www.truth-out.org/news/item/21694-shocking-
    facts-about-americas-for-profit-prison-industry.

72. Joe McGauley, "13 Everyday Items You Never Knew Were Made by

Prisoners," Thrillist, 2015, https://www.thrillist.com/gear/products-made-by -prisoners-clothing-furniture-electronics.

73. Antonio Costa, "UN and Partners Launch Initiative to End 'Modern Slavery' of Human Trafficking," UN News Center, accessed February 8, 2016, http:// www.un.org/apps/news/story.asp?NewsID=22009#.VmB2l99Y6ko.

74. Annie Kelly, "46 Million People Living as Slaves, Latest Global Index Reveals," *The Guardian*, 2016, http://www.theguardian.com/global-devel- opment/2016/jun/01/46-million-people-living-as-slaves-latest-global-index -reveals-russell-crowe.

75. Kevin Bales, *Disposable People* (University of California Press, 1999), 9.

76. Ibid., 11.

77. Ibid., 11., 16–17.

78. Federal Reserve Bank of Chicago, *Modern Money Mechanics*, 9781105038310: Amazon.com: Books, 2011.

79. Richard Dobbs et al., "Debt and (Not Much) Deleveraging," McKinsey Global Institute, 2015, http://www.mckinsey.com/insights/economic_studies /debt_and_not_much_deleveraging.

80. Jeff Desjardins, "All of the World's Money and Markets in One Visualization," Money Project, 2015, http://money.visualcapitalist.com/all-of-the-worlds -money-and-markets-in-one-visualization/.

81. Federal Reserve Bank of New York, *New York Fed Report Finds Advances in Auto Loans, Mortgage Originations*, 2015, https://www.newyorkfed.org/ newsevents/news/research/2015/rp151119.

82. *Trading Economics*, "United States Money Supply M2 | 1959–2016 | Data | Chart | Calendar," accessed February 9, 2016, http://www.tradingeconomics .com/united-states/money-supply-m2.

83. Quentin Fottrell, "Most Americans Have Less than $1,000 in Savings," *Market Watch*, 2015, http://www.marketwatch.com/story/most-americans -have-less-than-1000-in-savings-2015-10-06.

84. Dimitri Papadimitriou, "The Coming 'Tsunami of Debt' and Financial Crisis in America," *The Guardian*, 2014, http://www.theguardian.com/money/2014/ jun/15/us-economy-bubble-debt-financial-crisis-corporations.

85. *Investopedia*, "Inflation Definition," accessed February 9, 2016, http://www .investopedia.com/terms/i/inflation.asp#axzz2JypjmRJs.

86. Reem Heakal, "What Is the Quantity Theory of Money?," *Investopedia*, 2005, http://www.investopedia.com/articles/05/010705.asp#axzz2JypjmRJs.

87. Michael J. Kosares, "The Nightmare German Inflation," USA Gold, 1970, http://www.usagold.com/germannightmare.html.

88. To clarify, inflation is countered by the increase in economic assets. If an economy produces more and more money with a parallel increase in the production of new goods, the effect is balanced out, in principle.

This, of course, is highly nonlinear and hasn't occurred in reality, in the long term.

89. US Inflation Calculator, "Consumer Price Index Data from 1913 to 2016," accessed February 9, 2016, http://www.usinflationcalculator.com/inflation/consumer-price-index-and-annual-percent-changes-from-1913-to-2008/.

90. *Business Insider*, "22 Statistics that Prove the Middle Class Is Being Systematically Wiped Out of Existence in America," accessed February 9, 2016, http://www.businessinsider.com/22-statistics-that-prove-the-middle-class-is-being-systematically-wiped-out-of-existence-in-america-2010-7#83-percent-of-all-us-stocks-are-in-the-hands-of-1-percent-of-the-people-1.

91. Blake Ellis, "Savings Accounts with the Highest Yields," CNN Money, 2013, http://money.cnn.com/2013/10/01/pf/savings-account-yields/.

92. Michael Grimm and Isabel Gunter, "Inflation Inequality and the Measurement of Pro-Poor Growth," *Document De Travail*, 2005.

93. Michael Grimm, "Food Price Inflation and Children's Schooling," *SSRN Electronic Journal*, 2008, doi:10.2139/ssrn.1428836.

94. Hongyi Li and Heng-Fu Zou, "Inflation, Growth, and Income Distribution: A Cross-Country Study," *Annals of Economics and Finance* 3 (2002).

95. Gwendolyn Audrey Foster, *Class-Passing* (Southern Illinois University Press, 2005), 61.

96. Atif Mian and Amir Sufi, *House of Debt: How They (and You) Caused the Great Recession, and How We Can Prevent It from Happening Again*, 9780226081946, Amazon, 2014, http://www.amazon.com/House-Debt-Recession-Prevent-Happening/dp/022608194X.

97. Michael Corkery, "Foreclosure to Home Free, as 5-Year Clock Expires," *New York Times*, 2015, http://www.nytimes.com/2015/03/30/business/foreclosure-to-home-free-as-5-year-clock-expires.html.

98. Mint Press News Desk, "Empty Homes Outnumber the Homeless 6 to 1, So Why Not Give Them Homes?," *Mintpress News*, 2015, http://www.mintpress-news.com/empty-homes-outnumber-the-homeless-6-to-1-so-why-not-give-them-homes/207194/.

99. Federica Cocco, "There Are 10 Empty Homes for Every Homeless Family in England," *Mirror*, 2015, http://www.mirror.co.uk/news/ampp3d/housing-crisis-10-empty-homes-5008151.

100. Claire McKenna and Irene Tung, "Occupational Wage Declines Since the Great Recession: Low-Wage Occupations See Largest Real Wage Declines," National Employment Law Project, 2015, http://www.nelp.org/publication/occupational-wage-declines-since-the-great-recession/.

101. Ibid.

102. Bonnie Kavoussi, "Recession Killed 170,000 Small Businesses between 2008 and 2010: Report," *Huffington Post*, 2012, http://www.huffingtonpost

.com/2012/07/25/us-lost-more-than-170000-small-businesses-2008-2010
_n_1702358.html.

103. Emmanuel Saez, "Striking It Richer: The Evolution of Top Incomes in the United States," UC Berkeley, 2013.

104. Peter Werber, "CHARTS: How the Rich Won the Great Recession," *The Week*, 2013, http://theweek.com/articles/460179/charts-how-rich-won-great-recession.

105. Sovereign Man, "Despite 'Ending' QE, Fed Balance Sheet STILL within 0.3% of Its All-Time High," *Valuewalk*, 2015, http://www.valuewalk.com/2015/07/fed-balance-sheet/.

106. Imad A. Moosa, *Quantitative Easing as a Highway to Hyperinflation* (World Scientific Pub. Co., 2014), 269.

107. Robert Frank, "Does Quantitative Easing Mainly Help the Rich?," CNBC, 2012, http://www.cnbc.com/id/49031991.

108. Andrew Huszar, "Andrew Huszar: Confessions of a Quantitative Easer," *Wall Street Journal*, 2013, http://www.wsj.com/news/articles/SB100014240527023 0376380457918368075147388 4.

109. Tim Ingold, *The Perception of the Environment* (Routledge, 2000), 170.

110. Public Citizen, "The Trans-Pacific Partnership: Empowering Corporations to Attack Nations," accessed February 9, 2016, http://www.citizen.org/tppinvestment.

111. *Encyclopedia Britannica*, "Surplus Value | Economics," accessed February 9, 2016, http://www.britannica.com/topic/surplus-value.

112. Mike Dash, *Tulipomania: The Story of the World's Most Coveted Flower & the Extraordinary Passions It Aroused* (Crown: Archetype, 2010).

113. Richard Frost, "China's Stock Market Value Tops $10 Trillion for First Time," *Bloomberg Business*, 2015, http://www.bloomberg.com/news/articles/2015-06-14/china-s-stock-market-value-exceeds-10-trillion-for-first-time.

    And

    Wallace Witkowski, "Global Stock Market Cap Has Doubled Since QE's Start," *Marketwatch*, 2015, http://www.marketwatch.com/story/global-stock-market-cap-has-doubled-since-qes-start-2015-02-12.

114. Sam Ro, "Here's What the $294 Trillion Market of Global Financial Assets Looks Like," *Business Insider*, 2015, http://www.businessinsider.com/global-financial-assets-2015-2.

115. J. Cooper, "OTC Derivatives Market Notional Tops $700 Trillion. But Gross Credit Exposure—the Number to Watch—Drops to $3 Trillion," *Securities Finance Monitor*, 2014, http://www.secfinmonitor.com/otc-derivatives-market-notional-tops-700-trillion-but-gross-credit-exposure-the-number-to-watch-drops-to-3-trillion/.

116. Statista, "Global GDP 2010–2020 | Statistic," accessed February 9, 2016, http://
www.statista.com/statistics/268750/global-gross-domestic-product-gdp/.
And
Megan Davies and Walden Siew, "45 Percent of World's Wealth Destroyed:
Blackstone CEO," Reuters, 2009, http://www.reuters.com/article/us
-blackstone-idUSTRE52966Z20090311.

117. Gerald A. Epstein, *Financialization and the World Economy* (Edward Elgar,
2005), 3.

118. Jordan Weissmann, "How Wall Street Devoured Corporate America," *The
Atlantic*, 2013, http://www.theatlantic.com/business/archive/2013/03/how
-wall-street-devoured-corporate-america/273732/.

119. Michael Konczal, "Frenzied Financialization," *Washington Monthly*, 2014,
http://www.washingtonmonthly.com/magazine/novemberdecember_2014/
features/frenzied_financialization052714.php?page=all#.

120. Benjamin Landy, "Graph: How the Financial Sector Consumed America's Economic Growth," *Century Foundation*, 2013, http://www.tcf.org/
blog/detail/graph-how-the-financial-sector-consumed-americas-economic
-growth.

121. Jordan Weissmann, "How Wall Street Devoured Corporate America," *The
Atlantic*, 2013, http://www.theatlantic.com/business/archive/2013/03/how
-wall-street-devoured-corporate-america/273732/.

122. Ibid.

123. Lawrance Mishel, "Causes of Wage Stagnation," Economic Policy Institute,
2015, http://www.epi.org/publication/causes-of-wage-stagnation/.

124. Stephen G. Cecchetti and Enisse Kharroubi, "Why Does Financial Sector
Growth Crowd Out Real Economic Growth?," Bank for International Settlements, 2015, http://www.bis.org/publ/work490.htm.

125. Epstein, 6.

126. Baptist, 246–248.

127. Ellen E. Schultz and Theo Francis, "Companies Profit on Workers' Deaths
through 'Dead Peasants' Insurance," *Wall Street Journal*, 2002, http://www
.wsj.com/articles/SB1019165548622630040.

128. Kharunya Paramaguru, "Betting on Hunger: Is Financial Speculation to
Blame for High Food Prices?," *Time*, 2012, http://science.time.com/2012/12/
17/betting-on-hunger-is-financial-speculation-to-blame-for-high-food
-prices/.

129. A. S. Eisenstadt and Charlotte Watkins Smith, "Carl Becker: On History &
the Climate of Opinion," *Political Science Quarterly* 72, no. 2 (1957): 295,
doi:10.2307/2145783.

130. Elizabeth A. Fones-Wolf, *Selling Free Enterprise* (University of Illinois Press,
1994).

131. Scott Martelle, *Blood Passion* (Rutgers University Press, 2007).
132. Hagley Museum and Library, "Research: The National Association of Manufacturers and Visual Propaganda," accessed February 9, 2016, http://www.hagley.org/librarynews/research-national-association-manufacturers-and-visual-propaganda.
133. Fones-Wolf, 51–53.
134. I wish to comment on a common reaction to this. People often say things like, "Well, I have to eat, so that is coercion like any other." Does that mean I am a slave to nature? This is inapplicable as a counterargument since eating is not something any of us can circumvent if we expect to live. However, the way society has organized economic activity is very much in our control and the existence of structural coercion in capitalism is not an immutable phenomenon. It is simply an extension of the slavery/exploitation mindset going back thousands of years.
135. Eugene Robinson, "MLK'S Prophetic Call for Economic Justice," *Washington Post*, 2015, https://www.washingtonpost.com/opinions/eugene-robinson-mlks-call-for-economic-justice/2015/01/15/3599cb70-9cfe-11e4-96cc-e858eba91ced_story.html.
136. Ken Jacobs, "Americans Are Spending $153 Billion a Year to Subsidize McDonald's and Wal-Mart's Low Wage Workers," *Washington Post*, 2015, https://www.washingtonpost.com/posteverything/wp/2015/04/15/we-are-spending-153-billion-a-year-to-subsidize-mcdonalds-and-walmarts-low-wage-workers/.
137. *Macleans*, "Global CEO-to-Worker Pay Ratios," 2014, http://www.macleans.ca/economy/money-economy/global-ceo-to-worker-pay-ratios/.
138. Derek Abma, "Top Canadian CEOs Make Average Worker's Salary in Three Hours of First Working Day of Year," *Financial Post*, 2012, http://business.financialpost.com/executive/top-canadian-ceos-make-average-workers-salary-in-three-hours.
139. United Nations Conference on Trade and Development, *World Investment Report: Reforming International Investment Governance*, 2015.
140. Luke Harding, "What Are the Panama Papers? A Guide to History's Biggest Data Leak," *The Guardian*, 2016, http://www.theguardian.com/news/2016/apr/03/what-you-need-to-know-about-the-panama-papers.
141. Lucy Clarke-Billings, "Panama Papers: Top Ten Tax Havens—Where the Money Is Hidden," *Newsweek*, 2016, http://www.newsweek.com/panama-papers-top-ten-tax-havens-where-money-hidden-444512.
142. Glenn Greenwald, *With Liberty and Justice for Some: How the Law Is Used to Destroy Equality and Protect the Powerful* (Metropolitan Books/Henry Holt and Co., 2011), Chap. 3.
143. Kasper Viita and Kati Pohjanpalo, "Piketty Warns Scandinavia of Growing

Income Inequality Risk," *Bloomberg Business*, 2014, http://www.bloomberg
.com/news/articles/2014-06-12/piketty-warns-scandinavia-of-growing
-threat-of-income-inequality.

144. Kentaro Toyama, "Income Inequality around the World Is a Failure of
Capitalism," *The Atlantic*, 2011, http://www.theatlantic.com/business/
archive/2011/05/income-inequality-around-the-world-is-a-failure-of
-capitalism/238837/.

145. Niall Ferguson, *Colossus*, Google Books, 2004, https://books.google.com/
books?id=Uy23kBDD7WcC&hl=en.

146. Geoff Moore, *Fairness in International Trade* (Springer, 2010), 54.

Chapter 4

1. James Gilligan, stated during an interview in the film, "Zeitgeist: Moving
Forward" (Gentle Machine Productions LLC, 2011).

2. World Health Organization, "Children: Reducing Mortality," 2016, http://
www.who.int/mediacentre/factsheets/fs178/en/.

3. Epidemiology is the study of the patterns, causes, and effects of health and
disease conditions in defined populations. It is the cornerstone of public
health, and shapes policy decisions and evidence-based practice by identifying risk factors for disease and targets for preventive health care.

4. Nobelprize.org, "Martin Luther King Jr. Nobel Lecture: The Quest for Peace
and Justice," 2015, http://www.nobelprize.org/nobel_prizes/peace/laureates/
1964/king-lecture.html.

5. Geological Survey, "Geology's Role in Ohio's Solid Waste Management,"
2005, http://geosurvey.ohiodnr.gov/environmental-geology/solid-waste
-disposal.

6. James Ohwofasa Akpeninor, *Modern Concepts of Security* (AuthorHouse,
2013), 215.

7. Dr. Kenneth Omeje, *Extractive Economies and Conflicts in the Global South*
(Ashgate, 2008).

8. Ilan Kapoor, "Capitalism, Culture, Agency: Dependency Versus Postcolonial
Theory," *Third World Quarterly* 23, no. 4 (2002): 647–664, doi:10.1080/0143
659022000005319.

9. Vandana Shiva, "New Emperors, Old Clothes," *Ecologist*, 2005, http://www.
theecologist.org/blogs_and_comments/commentators/other_comments/
268520/new_emperors_old_clothes.html.

10. G. N. Kitching, *Development and Underdevelopment in Historical Perspective*
(Methuen, 1982), 195.

11. Matilda Dalquist, "Does Economic Growth Reduce Poverty?," (Soderton
University, 2013), 2, 31.

12. United Nations Development Programme, *UNDP and Poverty Reduction in*

Africa, accessed February 9 2016, http://www.africa.undp.org/content/dam/rba/docs/Outreach%20Material/Poverty%20Fast%20Facts%202013.pdf.

13. Jason Hickel, "Could You Live on $1.90 a Day? That's the International Poverty Line," *The Guardian*, 2015, http://www.theguardian.com/global-development-professionals-network/2015/nov/01/global-poverty-is-worse-than-you-think-could-you-live-on-190-a-day.

14. Abraham H. Maslow, *The Psychology of Science* (Harper & Row, 1966), 15.

15. *Forbes*, "Cap-and-Trade Is Fraught with Fraud," 2015, http://www.forbes.com/sites/judeclemente/2015/10/01/cap-and-trade-green-climate-fund-are-fraught-with-fraud/.

16. Martin Livermore, "Cap and Trade Doesn't Work," *Wall Street Journal*, 2009, http://www.wsj.com/articles/SB124587942001349765.

17. Duncan Clark, "Has the Kyoto Protocol Made Any Difference to Carbon Emissions?," *The Guardian*, 2012, http://www.theguardian.com/environment/blog/2012/nov/26/kyoto-protocol-carbon-emissions.

18. Mengpin Ge, Johannes Friedrich, and Thomas Damassa, "6 Graphs Explain the World's Top 10 Emitters," *World Resources Institute*, 2014, http://www.wri.org/blog/2014/11/6-graphs-explain-world%E2%80%99s-top-10-emitters.

19. *The Guardian*, "Canada Pulls Out of Kyoto Protocol," 2011, http://www.theguardian.com/environment/2011/dec/13/canada-pulls-out-kyoto-protocol.

20. Tom Switzer, "The Future of Australian Coal," *Wall Street Journal*, 2016, http://www.wsj.com/articles/the-future-of-australian-coal-1452012514.

21. "Global Biodiversity Outlook 3," *Convention on Biological Diversity*, 2010, 17, https://www.cbd.int/doc/publications/gbo/gbo3-final-en.pdf.

22. Ibid., 9–10.

23. Robert J. Brulle, "Institutionalizing Delay: Foundation Funding and the Creation of U.S. Climate Change Counter-Movement Organizations," *Climatic Change* 122, no. 4 (2013): 681–694, doi:10.1007/s10584-013-1018-7.

24. Ibid., 12.

25. Christine Lagorio, "The Most Polluted Places on Earth," CBS Evening News, 2007, http://www.cbsnews.com/news/the-most-polluted-places-on-earth/.

26. Walden Bello, "Can Capitalism Survive Climate Change?," *Global Policy Forum*, 2008, https://www.globalpolicy.org/component/content/article/212/45366.html.

27. Lee-Anne Broadhead, *International Environmental Politics* (L. Rienner, 2002), 95.

28. Thorstein Veblen, *The Engineers and the Price System* (Batoche, 2001).

29. The practice of "planned obsolescence" is worth noting. This is the deliberate withholding of efficiency in design. See:

    TZM Lecture Team, *The Zeitgeist Movement Defined: Realizing a New Train of Thought* (CreateSpace, 2014), 99–101.

And

Giles Slade, *Made to Break: Technology and Obsolescence in America* (First Harvard University Press, 2007).

30. Max Weber, "Asceticism and the Spirit of Capitalism," *The Protestant Ethic and the Spirit of Capitalism*, 1905, accessed February 9, 2016, https://www.marxists.org/reference/archive/weber/protestant-ethic/ch05.htm.

31. Norbert Haring and Niall Douglas, *Economists and the Powerful* (Anthem, 2012), 21.

32. Charles F. Kettering, "Keep the Consumer Dissatisfied," *Nation's Business* 17, no. 1 (1929): 30–31, 79.

33. Gary Holthaus, *Learning Native Wisdom: What Traditional Cultures Teach Us about Subsistence, Sustainability, and Spirituality (Culture of the Land)*, 2013, 9780813141084, http://www.amazon.com/Learning-Native-Wisdom-Sustainability-Spirituality/dp/0813141087.

34. Lizabeth Cohen, "A Consumers' Republic: The Politics of Mass Consumption in Postwar America," *Journal of Consumer Research* 31, no. 1 (2004), 2, doi:10.1086/383439.

35. Ibid., 3.

36. R. A. Easterlin et al., "The Happiness-Income Paradox Revisited," *Proceedings of the National Academy of Sciences* 107, no. 52 (2010): 22463–22468, doi:10.1073/pnas.1015962107.

37. Michael J. Sandel, *What Money Can't Buy: The Moral Limits of Markets* (Farrar, Straus, and Giroux, 2012).

38. Michael Sandel, "The Moral Limits of Markets: Live Interview with Michael Sandel," *Big Think*, 2012, http://bigthink.com/videos/the-moral-limits-of-markets-live-interview-with-michael-sandel.

39. Michael J. Sandel, *What Money Can't Buy: The Moral Limits of Markets* (Farrar, Straus, and Giroux, 2012), 6.

40. Merriam-Webster.com, "Definition of Public Health," 2016, http://www.merriam-webster.com/dictionary/public%20health.

41. "Diarrhea: Common Illness, Global Killer," U.S. Department of Health and Human Services, accessed February 9, 2016, http://www.cdc.gov/healthywater/pdf/global/programs/Globaldiarrhea508c.pdf.

42. Aaron Reeves, Martin McKee, and David Stuckler, "Economic Suicides in the Great Recession in Europe and North America," *British Journal of Psychiatry* 208, no. 2 (2014), doi:10.1192/bjp.bp.114.144766.

43. University of Oxford, "Recession 'Linked with' over 10,000 Suicides across Europe and North America," 2014, http://www.ox.ac.uk/news/2014-06-12-recession-%E2%80%98linked-with%E2%80%99-over-10000-suicides-across-europe-and-north-america.

44. Carlos Nordt et al., "Modelling Suicide and Unemployment: A Longitudinal

Analysis Covering 63 Countries, 2000–11," *The Lancet Psychiatry* 2, no. 3 (2015): 239–245, doi:10.1016/s2215-0366(14)00118-7.

45. James Gilligan, "Violence in Public Health and Preventive Medicine," *The Lancet* 355, no. 9217 (2000): 1802–1804, doi:10.1016/s0140-6736(00)02307-2.

46. Ibid.

47. Gernot Köhler and Norman Alcock, "An Empirical Table of Structural Violence," *Journal of Peace Research* 13, no. 4 (1976): 343–356, http://www .jstor.org/stable/422498.

48. Myrdene Anderson, *Cultural Shaping of Violence* (Purdue University Press, 2004), 227.

49. Johan Gultang, "Violence, Peace, and Peace Research," *Journal of Peace Research* 6, no. 3 (1969): 168, http://www.jstor.org/stable/422690.

50. "NAFTA's 20-Year Legacy and the Fate of the Trans-Pacific Partnership," 2014, http://www.citizen.org/documents/NAFTA-at-20.pdf.

51. Lia Kent, *The Dynamics of Transitional Justice* (Routledge, 2012), 37.

52. Verena Seufert, Navin Ramankutty, and Jonathan A. Foley, "Comparing the Yields of Organic and Conventional Agriculture," *Nature* 485, no. 7397 (2012): 229–232, doi:10.1038/nature11069.

53. Sammy Said, "Billionaires Who Could End World Hunger," *The Richest*, 2013, http://www.therichest.com/rich-list/world/billionaires-who-could -end-world-hunger/?view=all.

54. UNAIDS, "Global Fact Sheet: World Aids Day 2012," 2012, http://www. unaids.org/sites/default/files/en/media/unaids/contentassets/documents/ epidemiology/2012/gr2012/20121120_FactSheet_Global_en.pdf.

55. Gernot Köhler and Norman Alcock, "An Empirical Table of Structural Violence," *Journal of Peace Research* 13, no. 4 (1976): 349.

56. World Health Organization, "The Top 10 Causes of Death," accessed February 9, 2016, http://www.who.int/mediacentre/factsheets/fs310/en/index2 .html.

57. James Gilligan, *Violence* (Vintage Books, 1997), 196.

58. Kerry A. Dolan, "Inside the 2015 Forbes Billionaires List: Facts and Figures," *Forbes*, 2015, http://www.forbes.com/sites/kerryadolan/2015/03/02/inside -the-2015-forbes-billionaires-list-facts-and-figures/.

59. FAO Newsroom, "The World Only Needs 30 Billion Dollars a Year to Eradicate the Scourge of Hunger," accessed February 9, 2016, http://www.fao.org/ NEWSROOM/EN/news/2008/1000853/index.html.

60. Johan Galtung, "Cultural Violence," *Journal of Peace Research* 27, no. 3 (1990): 291–305.

61. Oxfam International, "An Economy for the 1%," accessed February 9, 2016, https://www.oxfam.org/en/research/economy-1.

62. Joel Kovel, *The Enemy of Nature* (Zed Books, 2002), 152–153.

63. Jad Mouawad, "Oil Companies Reluctant to Follow Obama's Green Lead," *New York Times*, 2009, http://www.nytimes.com/2009/04/08/business/energy-environment/08greenoil.html.

64. World Health Organization, "The Top 10 Causes of Death," accessed February 9, 2016, http://www.who.int/mediacentre/factsheets/fs310/en/index1.html.

65. Nick Bostrom and Milan M. Ćirković, *Global Catastrophic Risks* (Oxford University Press, 2008), 27.

66. UNAIDS, "Global Statistics: Fact Sheet 2014," 2014, http://www.unaids.org/sites/default/files/en/media/unaids/contentassets/documents/factsheet/2014/20140716_FactSheet_en.pdf.

67. Kff.org, "The Global HIV/AIDS Epidemic," 2015, http://kff.org/global-health-policy/fact-sheet/the-global-hivaids-epidemic/.

68. Ben Chu, "Bill Gates: Why Do We Care More about Baldness than Malaria?," *The Independent*, 2013, http://www.independent.co.uk/news/world/americas/bill-gates-why-do-we-care-more-about-baldness-than-malaria-8536988.html.

69. "Research and Development to Meet Health Needs in Developing Countries: Strengthening Global Financing and Coordination," *Report of the Consultative Expert Working Group on Research and Development: Financing and Coordination*, 2012, 26, http://www.who.int/phi/CEWG_Report_5_April_2012.pdf.

70. Tomaso Clavarino, "Meet the Doctors Fighting TB in South Africa," *The Independent*, 2015, http://www.independent.co.uk/life-style/health-and-families/features/tuberculosis-is-south-africas-biggest-killer-but-doctors-are-fighting-back-a6777441.html.

71. Prof. William W. Fisher III and Dr. Cyrill P. Rigamonti, "The South Africa AIDS Controversy: A Case Study in Patent Law and Policy," *The Law and Business of Patents*, 2005, 3, http://cyber.law.harvard.edu/people/tfisher/South%20Africa.pdf.

72. Sabin Russell, "New Crusade to Lower AIDS Drug Costs / Africa's Needs at Odds with Firms' Profit Motive," *Sfgate*, 1999, http://www.sfgate.com/health/article/New-Crusade-To-Lower-AIDS-Drug-Costs-Africa-s-2929307.php.

73. Johanna McGeary, "Paying for AIDS Cocktails," *Time*, 2001, http://content.time.com/time/magazine/article/0,9171,999194,00.html#ixzz0hlZGwAX5.

74. Pat Sidley, "Drug Companies Sue South African Government over Generics," *British Medical Journal* 322, no. 7284 (2001): 447, http://www.ncbi.nlm.nih.gov/pmc/articles/PMC1119675/.

75. Garry M. Leech, *Capitalism* (Zed Books, 2012), 78.

76. *Business Wire*, "Merck & Co., Inc. Statement on Brazilian Government's Decision to Issue Compulsory License for STOCRIN™," 2007, http://www.

businesswire.com/news/home/20070504005566/en/Merck-Statement
-Brazilian-Governments-Decision-Issue-Compulsory.

77. UNAIDS, "HIV Treatment Now Reaching More Than 6 Million People in Sub-Saharan Africa," accessed February 9, 2016, http://www.unaids .org/en/resources/presscentre/pressreleaseandstatementarchive/2012/ july/20120706prafricatreatment.

78. McGeary, "Paying for AIDS Cocktails."

79. Pew Charitable Trusts, "Persuading the Prescribers: Pharmaceutical Industry Marketing and Its Influence on Physicians and Patients," 2013, http://www .pewtrusts.org/en/research-and-analysis/fact-sheets/2013/11/11/persuading -the-prescribers-pharmaceutical-industry-marketing-and-its-influence-on -physicians-and-patients.

80. Ethan Rome, "Big Pharma Pockets $711 Billion in Profits by Robbing Seniors, Taxpayers," *Huffington Post*, 2013, http://www.huffingtonpost.com/ethan -rome/big-pharma-pockets-711-bi_b_3034525.html.

81. Sandro Galea, "How Many U.S. Deaths Are Caused by Poverty, Lack of Education, and Other Social Factors?" Columbia University Mailman School of Public Health, Public Health Now, 2011, https://www.mailman.columbia .edu/public-health-now/news/how-many-us-deaths-are-caused-poverty -lack-education-and-other-social-factors.

82. World Bank, "Death Rate, Crude (Per 1,000 People)," accessed February 9, 2016, http://data.worldbank.org/indicator/SP.DYN.CDRT.IN?page=3.

83. Galea, "How Many U.S. Deaths Are Caused by Poverty."

84. "The Growing Gap in Life Expectancy by Income," 2015, doi:10.17226/19015.

85. Max Ehrenfreund, "The Stunning—and Expanding—Gap in Life Expectancy between the Rich and the Poor," *Washington Post*, 2015, https://www .washingtonpost.com/news/wonk/wp/2015/09/18/the-government-is -spending-more-to-help-rich-seniors-than-poor-ones/.

86. Barry P. Bosworth and Kathleen Burke, "Differential Mortality and Retirement Benefits in the Health and Retirement Study," Brookings, accessed February 9, 2016, 10, http://www.brookings.edu/~/media/research/ files/papers/2014/04/differential-mortality-retirement-benefits-bosworth/ differential_mortality_retirement_benefits_bosworth_version_2.pdf.

87. Kate Pickett and Richard Wilkinson, "A 25-Year Gap between the Life Expectancy of Rich and Poor Londoners," *The Independent*, 2014, 24, http://www .independent.co.uk/voices/comment/a-25-year-gap-between-the-life -expectancy-of-rich-and-poor-londoners-is-a-further-indictment-of -our-9061888.html.

88. American Cancer Society, *Cancer Facts & Figures 2011* (Atlanta, 2011), 24, http://www.cancer.org/acs/groups/content/@epidemiologysurveilance/ documents/document/acspc-029771.pdf.

89. Juliet Addo et al., "Socioeconomic Status and Stroke," *Stroke* 43, no. 4 (2012): 1186–1191, doi:10.1161/strokeaha.111.639732.

90. World Health Organization, *Cardiovascular Diseases (Cvds)*, 2015, http:// www.who.int/mediacentre/factsheets/fs317/en/.

91. Peter Franks et al., "Do Changes in Traditional Coronary Heart Disease Risk Factors Over Time Explain the Association between Socio-Economic Status and Coronary Heart Disease?," *BMC Cardiovascular Disorders* 11, no. 1 (2011): 28, doi:10.1186/1471-2261-11-28.

92. UC Davis Health System, "Lower Socioeconomic Status Linked with Heart Disease Despite Improvements in Other Risk Factors," 2011, http://www .ucdmc.ucdavis.edu/publish/news/newsroom/5660.

93. Childfund International, "The Effects of Poverty on Education in the United States," 2014, https://www.childfund.org/Content/NewsDetail/2147488172/.

94. Kimberly G. Noble et al., "Family Income, Parental Education and Brain Structure in Children and Adolescents," *Nature Neuroscience* 18, no. 5 (2015): 773–778, doi:10.1038/nn.3983.

95. A. Mani et al., "Poverty Impedes Cognitive Function," *Science* 341, no. 6149 (2013): 976–980, doi:10.1126/science.1238041.

96. A. Drewnowski and P. Eichelsdoerfer, "Can Low-Income Americans Afford a Healthy Diet?," *Nutrition Today* 44, no. 6 (2010): 246–249.

97. Nancy S. Weinfeld et al., *Hunger in America 2014: National Report Prepared for Feeding America* (Westat, 2014), 119.

98. ABC News, "Fat Forecast: 42% Obese by 2030," 2012, http://abcnews.go.com/ blogs/health/2012/05/07/fat-forecast-42-of-americans-obese-by-2030/.

99. George Fink, *Stress Science: Neuroendocrinolgy* (Google Books, 2009), 595.

100. *ScienceDaily*, "Childhood Trauma Could Lead to Adult Obesity," 2014. http:// www.sciencedaily.com/releases/2014/09/140902092947.htm.

101. Brett Drake and Melissa Jonson-Reid, "Poverty and Child Maltreatment," *Handbook of Child Maltreatment* 2 (2013): 131–148, doi:10.1007/978-94-007 -7208-3_7.

102. Jordan Reese, "Stress Contributes to Increased Consumption of High Fat, High Calorie Foods, Says Award-Winning Penn Research," *Penn News*, 2008, https://news.upenn.edu/news/stress-contributes-increased-consumption- high-fat-high-calorie-foods-says-award-winning-penn-re.
    And
    S. L. Teegarden and T. L. Bale, "Decreases in Dietary Preference Produce Increased Emotionality and Risk for Dietary Relapse," *Biological Psychiatry* 61, no. 9 (2007): 1021–1029.

103. Adam Drewnowski and S. E. Specter, "Poverty and Obesity: The Role of Energy Density and Energy Costs," *American Journal of Clinical Nutrition* 79, no. 1 (2004): 6–16, http://ajcn.nutrition.org/content/79/1/6.full.

104. Robert Sapolsky, *Why Zebras Don't Get Ulcers* (W. H. Freeman, 1998).

105. Timo Heidt et al., "Chronic Variable Stress Activates Hematopoietic Stem Cells," *Nature Medicine* 20, no. 7 (2014): 754–758, doi:10.1038/nm.3589.

106. M. G. Marmot, M. J. Shipley, and Geoffrey Rose, "Inequalities in Death— Specific Explanations of a General Pattern?," *The Lancet* 323, no. 8384 (1984): 1003–1006, doi:10.1016/s0140-6736(84)92337-7.

107. Michael Marmot, "Unnatural Causes," in person (Massachusetts, n.d.), http://www.unnaturalcauses.org/assets/uploads/file/MichaelMarmot.pdf.

108. Ibid.

109. Robert Sapolsky, *Why Zebras Don't Get Ulcers* (W. H. Freeman, 1998), 374.

110. Gabor Maté, *In the Realm of Hungry Ghosts* (North Atlantic Books, 2010), 512.

111. Ibid., 36.

112. Centers for Disease Control, "Adverse Childhood Experiences (ACE) Study|Child Maltreatment|Violence Prevention|Injury Center," accessed February 9, 2016, http://www.cdc.gov/violenceprevention/acestudy/.

113. Robert F. Anda and Vincent J. Felitti, "A Free Research Publication Dealing with the Effects of Adverse Childhood Experiences on Adult Health and Well Being," *ACE Reporter* 1, no. 1 (2003), http://www.acestudy.org/yahoo_site_admin/assets/docs/ARV1N1.127150541.pdf.

114. Vanessa Sacks, David Murphey, and Kristin Moore, "Adverse Childhood Experiences," *Child Trends*, 2014, http://www.childtrends.org/wp-content/uploads/2014/07/Brief-adverse-childhood-experiences_FINAL.pdf.

115. Christopher G. Hudson, "Socioeconomic Status and Mental Illness: Tests of the Social Causation and Selection Hypotheses," *American Journal of Orthopsychiatry* 75, no. 1 (2005): 3–18, doi:10.1037/0002-9432.75.1.3.

116. Meyer H. Brenner, *Mental Illness and the Economy* (iUniverse, 1999).

117. Jim Dryden, "Poverty Linked to Childhood Depression, Changes in Brain Connectivity," Washington University School of Medicine in St. Louis, 2016, https://medicine.wustl.edu/news/poverty-linked-to-childhood-depression-changes-in-brain-connectivity/.

118. Bruce E. Levine, "What We Are Not Being Told About Suicide and Depression," *Alternet*, 2015, http://www.alternet.org/personal-health/what-we-are-not-being-told-about-suicide-and-depression.

119. Danuta Wasserman, *Suicide* (Martin Dunitz, 2001), 18.

120. Roger T. Webb et al., "National Study of Suicide in All People with a Criminal Justice History," *Archives of General Psychiatry* 68, no. 6 (2011): 591, doi:10.1001/archgenpsychiatry.2011.7.

121. Western Michigan University, "Facts about Suicide | Suicide Prevention Program," accessed February 9, 2016, https://wmich.edu/suicideprevention/basics/facts.

122. World Health Organization, "Suicide," accessed February 9, 2016, http://www.who.int/mediacentre/factsheets/fs398/en/.

123. This total is arrived at by combining the data from these two reports:

S. Rukmini, "India's New Farm Suicides Data: Myths and Facts," *The Hindu*, 2015, http://www.thehindu.com/data/indias-new-farm-suicides -data-myths-and-facts/article7461095.ece.

And

P. Sainath, "17,368 Farm Suicides in 2009," *The Hindu*, 2010, http://www .thehindu.com/opinion/columns/sainath/17368-farm-suicides-in-2009/ article995824.ece.

124. International.ucla.edu, "Rising Number of Farmer Suicides in Rural India," 2014, http://www.international.ucla.edu/institute/article/145702.

125. P. Sainath, "Maharashtra Crosses 60,000 Farm Suicides," P. Sainath website, 2014, http://psainath.org/maharashtra-crosses-60000-farm-suicides/.

126. Somini Sengupta, "On India's Farms, a Plague of Suicide," *New York Times*, 2006, http://www.nytimes.com/2006/09/19/world/asia/19india.html.

127. Vandana Shiva, "From Seeds of Suicide to Seeds of Hope: Why Are Indian Farmers Committing Suicide and How Can We Stop This Tragedy?," *Huffington Post*, 2009, http://www.huffingtonpost.com/vandana-shiva/from-seeds-of-suicide-to_b_192419.html.

128. Srijit Mishra, "Suicide Mortality Rates Across States of India, 1975–2001: A Statistical Note," *Economic and Political Weekly* 41, no. 16 (2006): 1566–1569.

129. Jonathan Kennedy and Lawrence King, "The Political Economy of Farmers' Suicides in India: Indebted Cash-Crop Farmers with Marginal Landholdings Explain State-Level Variation in Suicide Rates," *Globalization and Health* 10, no. 1 (2014): 16, doi:10.1186/1744-8603-10-16.

130. Ibid., 8.

131. James Gilligan, "Violence in Public Health and Preventive Medicine," *The Lancet* 355, no. 9217 (2000): 1802–1804, doi:10.1016/s0140-6736(00)02307-2.

132. FBI, "Hate Crimes—Overview," accessed February 9, 2016, https://www.fbi .gov/about-us/investigate/civilrights/hate_crimes/overview.

133. US Department of Justice, *Hate Crime Victimization, 2003–2011*, Office of Justice Programs, Bureau of Justice Statistics, 2013, http://www.bjs.gov/ content/pub/pdf/hcv0311.pdf.

134. Eva H. Telzer et al., "Amygdala Sensitivity to Race Is Not Present in Child-hood but Emerges over Adolescence," *Journal of Cognitive Neuroscience* 25, no. 2 (2013): 234–244, doi:10.1162/jocn_a_00311.

135. Ibid., 242.

136. Nicholas B. Dirks, *Castes of Mind* (Princeton University Press, 2001).

137. Dadabhai Naoroji, *Poverty and Un-British Rule in India* (Publications Division, Ministry of Information and Broadcasting, Govt. of India, 1962).

138. Human Rights Watch, "India: UN Finds Pervasive Abuse Against Dalits,"

2007, https://www.hrw.org/news/2007/03/12/india-un-finds-pervasive
-abuse-against-dalits.

139. *The Indian Express*, "Hate Crimes Against UK Muslims Soar After Paris Attacks," 2015, http://indianexpress.com/article/world/world-news/hate
-crimes-against-uk-muslims-soar-after-paris-attacks/.

140. Allen E. Liska, *Social Threat and Social Control* (State University of New York Press, 1992), 91.

141. David Bacon, "Globalization and NAFTA Caused Migration from Mexico," *Political Research Associates*, 2014, http://www.politicalresearch
.org/2014/10/11/globalization-and-nafta-caused-migration-from
-mexico/#sthash.xNyTpcsT.OhpD0Wd4.dpbs.

142. A. Imtiaz Hussain, *North America at the Crossroads* (Universidad Iberoamericana, 2009), 539.

143. Philip L. Martin, Susan Forbes Martin, and Patrick Weil, *Managing Migration* (Lexington Books, 2006), 168.

144. Christy Thornton and Adam Goodman, "How The Mexican Drug Trade Thrives on Free Trade," *The Nation*, 2014, http://www.thenation.com/article/how-mexican-drug-trade-thrives-free-trade/.

145. "USAID: Latin American and Caribbean Overview," *US Agency for International Development* (Washington, DC, 2013).

146. C. C. Hsieh and M. D. Pugh, "Poverty, Income Inequality, and Violent Crime: A Meta-Analysis of Recent Aggregate Data Studies," *Criminal Justice Review* 18, no. 2 (1993): 182–202, doi:10.1177/073401689301800203.

Lakshmi Iyer and Petia B. Topalova, "Poverty and Crime: Evidence From Rainfall and Trade Shocks in India," *SSRN Electronic Journal*, 2014, doi:10.2139/ssrn.2419522.

Zhilan Feng and Carlos Castillo-Chavez, "The Dynamics of Poverty and Crime," *Research Gate* 43, no. 5 (2015).

147. Fionnbarra Ó Dochartaigh and Bernadette Devlin McAliskey, *Ulster's White Negroes* (AK Press, 1994).

148. George M. Fredrickson, "Race—The Power of an Illusion, Background Readings," *Pbs.org*, 2003, http://www.pbs.org/race/000_About/002_04
-background-02-01.htm.

149. Bobby Duffy and Tom Frere-Smith, *Perception and Reality*, 2014, 38.

150. M. Steven Fish, "Why Is Terror Islamist?," *Washington Post*, 2015, https://www
.washingtonpost.com/blogs/monkey-cage/wp/2015/01/27/why-is-terror
-islamist/.

151. Ibid.

152. Barbara Crossette, "Iraq Sanctions Kill Children, U.N. Reports," *New York Times*, 1995, http://www.nytimes.com/1995/12/01/world/iraq-sanctions
-kill-children-un-reports.html.

153. Mark Siegal, "Former UN Official Says Sanctions Against Iraq Amount to 'Genocide,'" *Cornell Chronicle*, 1999, http://www.news.cornell.edu/stories/1999/09/former-un-official-says-sanctions-against-iraq-amount-genocide.

154. BBC News "UN Official Blasts Iraq Sanctions," 1998, http://news.bbc.co.uk/1/hi/world/middle_east/183499.stm.

155. Ibid.

156. Sherwood Ross, "US Sponsored Genocide Against Iraq 1990–2012 Killed 3.3 Million, Including 750,000 Children," *Global Research*, 2012, http://www.globalresearch.ca/us-sponsored-genocide-against-iraq-1990-2012-killed-3-3-million-including-750000-children/5314461.

157. ThinkProgress, "60 Minutes: CIA Official Reveals Bush, Cheney, Rice Were Personally Told Iraq Had No WMD in Fall 2002," 2006, http://thinkprogress.org/security/2006/04/23/4980/60-minutes-cia-official-reveals-bush-cheney-rice-were-personally-told-iraq-had-no-wmd-in-fall-2002/.

158. Antonia Juhasz, "Why the War in Iraq Was Fought for Big Oil," CNN, 2013, http://edition.cnn.com/2013/03/19/opinion/iraq-war-oil-juhasz/.
    And
    Samuel Wiegley, "10 Companies Profiting the Most from War," *USA Today*, 2013, http://www.usatoday.com/story/money/business/2013/03/10/10-companies-profiting-most-from-war/1970997/.

159. Jefferey R. Smith, "The Failed Reconstruction of Iraq," *The Atlantic*, 2013, http://www.theatlantic.com/international/archive/2013/03/the-failed-reconstruction-of-iraq/274041/.

160. "Roots of Iraq's Maternal and Child Health Crisis Run Deep," *The Lancet* 381 (2013), http://www.thelancet.com/pdfs/journals/lancet/PIIS0140-6736%2813%2960658-3.pdf.

161. UNAMI, *Report on the Protection of Civilians in the Armed Conflict in Iraq: 1 May–31 October 2015*, 2016, http://www.uniraq.org/images/humanrights/UNAMI-OHCHR_%20POC%20Report_FINAL_01%20May-31%20October%202015_FINAL_11Jan2016.pdf.

162. Somini Sengupta, "60 Million People Fleeing Chaotic Lands, U.N. Says," *New York Times*, 2015, http://www.nytimes.com/2015/06/18/world/60-million-people-fleeing-chaotic-lands-un-says.html.

163. Ezgi Basaran, "Former CIA Officer Says US Policies Helped Create IS," *Al-Monitor*, 2014, http://www.al-monitor.com/pulse/politics/2014/09/turkey-usa-iraq-syria-isis-fuller.html#.

164. Prof. Michel Chossudovsky, "Destroying a Country's Standard of Living: What Libya Had Achieved, What Has Been Destroyed," Global Research, 2011, http://www.globalresearch.ca/destroying-a-country-s-standard-of-living-what-libya-had-achieved-what-has-been-destroyed/26686.

165. BBC News, "Libya Violence: Islamic State Attack 'Kills 40' in Al-Qubbah," 2015, http://www.bbc.co.uk/news/world-africa-31549280.

166. Noam Chomsky, "America Paved the Way for ISIS," *Salon*, 2015, http://www.salon.com/2015/02/16/noam_chomsky_america_paved_the_way_for_isis_partner/.

167. History.com, "Origins of the Mafia—Facts & Summary," accessed February 9, 2016, http://www.history.com/topics/origins-of-the-mafia.

168. Louis Kontos, David Brotherton, and Luis Barrios, *Gangs and Society* (Columbia University Press, 2003). 99.

169. J. Trauma, "The Relationship between Socioeconomic Factors and Gang Violence in the City of Los Angeles," *The Journal of Trauma* 46, no. 2 (1999): 334–339.

170. FBI, "2011 National Gang Threat Assessment," accessed February 9, 2016, https://www.fbi.gov/stats-services/publications/2011-national-gang-threat-assessment.

171. Jonathan Glennie, "Land Grabs Have Dominated Colombia's History," *The Guardian*, 2011, http://www.theguardian.com/global-development/poverty-matters/2011/jan/31/colombia-land-grab-displaced-poor.

172. Jasmin Hristov, *Blood and Capital* (Ohio University Press, 2009), 14.

173. Ibid., 58.

174. Kate Doyle and Peter Kornbluh, "CIA and Assassinations: The Guatemala 1954 Documents," *National Security Archive*, accessed February 9, 2016, http://nsarchive.gwu.edu/NSAEBB/NSAEBB4/.

175. Stephen C. Schlesinger and Stephen Kinzer, *Bitter Fruit* (Harvard University, David Rockefeller Center for Latin American Studies, 2005).

176. Amnesty International USA, "U.S. Policy in Colombia," accessed February 9, 2016, http://www.amnestyusa.org/our-work/countries/americas/colombia/us-policy-in-colombia.

177. Dr. Steve Suppan, "Mexican Corn, NAFTA and Hunger, May 1996, FACT SHEET 3 | Institute for Agriculture and Trade Policy," *Iatp.org*, 1998, http://www.iatp.org/documents/mexican-corn-nafta-and-hunger-may-1996-fact-sheet-3.

178. Timothy A. Wise, "The Impacts of U.S. Agricultural Policies on Mexican Producers," *Global Development and Environment Institute, Tufts University*, 2010, http://www.ase.tufts.edu/gdae/Pubs/rp/AgricDumping.pdf.

179. Louis Uchitelle, "NAFTA Should Have Stopped Illegal Immigration, Right?," *New York Times*, 2007, http://www.nytimes.com/2007/02/18/weekinreview/18uchitelle.html.

180. Carmel Boullosa, *A Narco History: How the United States and Mexico Jointly Created the "Mexican Drug War"* (OR Books, 2015), 52–54.

181. Anahi Rama and Lizbeth Diaz, "Violence Against Women 'Pandemic' in

Mexico," Reuters, 2014, http://www.reuters.com/article/us-mexico-violence
-women-idUSBREA2608F20140307.

182. Franco "Bifo" Berardi, *Heroes: Mass Murder and Suicide* (Verso, 2015).

183. Niamh McIntyre, "This Theorist Believes that Capitalism Creates Mass
Murderers by Causing People to 'Malfunction,'" *Vice*, 2016, http://www.vice
.com/en_uk/read/berardi-interview.

184. Sam Becker, "10 Countries that Export the Most Weapons," *The Cheat
Sheet*, 2015, http://www.cheatsheet.com/business/the-worlds-10-largest
-arms-exporters.html/?a=viewall.

185. Thalif Deen, "Military Budgets Unexplored Source for Development
Funding,"IPS News, 2015, http://www.ipsnews.net/2015/12/military-budgets
-unexplored-source-for-development-funding/.

186. "Originally in Common Sense, 1935," reproduced in Hans Schmidt's *Mav-
erick Marine: General Smedley D. Butler and the Contradictions of American
Military History* (University Press of Kentucky, 1998), 231.

187. Milton Friedman, *Capitalism and Freedom* (University of Chicago Press,
2002), 15.

188. Robert W. McChesney, *Rich Media, Poor Democracy: Communication Politics
in Dubious Times*, (The New Press, 2015), chap. 2.

Chapter 5

1. Amy Goodman, "Dr. Martin Luther King in 1967: 'We as a Nation Must
Undergo a Radical Revolution of Values,'" *Democracy Now!*, 2013, http://
www.democracynow.org/2013/1/21/dr_martin_luther_king_in_1967.

2. Food and Agriculture Organization, "Reducing Poverty and Hunger:
The Critical Role of Financing for Food, Agriculture and Rural Develop-
ment," accessed February 24, 2016, http://www.fao.org/docrep/003/y6265e/
y6265e03.htm.
  And
  Christian Nordqvist, "How Many Calories Should I Eat a Day?," *Medical
News Today*, 2016, http://www.medicalnewstoday.com/articles/245588.php.

3. Dw.com, "European Food Waste Adds to World Hunger," 2012, http://www
.dw.de/author-european-food-waste-adds-to-world-hunger/a-15837215.

4. "To the degree that a given society that is insecure about its political, social,
economic, and uniting cultural identity, it will mask that insecurity with
a swaggering show of gendered strength," said Yvonne Howell, a Russian
professor at the University of Richmond.
  Olga Khazan, "Why Is Russia So Homophobic?," *The Atlantic*, 2013,
http://www.theatlantic.com/international/archive/2013/06/why-is-russia
-so-homophobic/276817/.

5. Bryce Covert, "Tech Executive Brags He Was Able to Hire Talented Women 'Relatively Cheap' Compared to Men," *Thinkprogress*, 2014, http://thinkprogress.org/economy/2014/09/26/3572572/tech-exec-gender-wage -gap/.

6. Carolyn Gregoire, "The Holiday Habit That's Making You Unhappy," *Huffington Post*, 2013, http://www.huffingtonpost.com/2013/12/15/psychology -materialism_n_4425982.html.

7. Lyla Mehta, *The Limits to Scarcity* (Earthscan, 2010), xvii.

8. Ibid, 7.

9. A 2001 United Nations report said that two-thirds of the estimates it analyzed fell in the range of 4 billion to 16 billion with a median of about 10 billion.

    United Nations, *World Population Monitoring 2001* (Department of Economic and Social Affairs Population Division, 2001), http://www.un.org/esa/population/publications/wpm/wpm2001.pdf.

10. Jeremy Rifkin, *The Zero Marginal Cost Society: The Internet of Things, the Collaborative Commons, and the Eclipse of Capitalism* (St. Martin's Griffin, 2015).

11. Mary Bellis, "Ever Read the History of the ENIAC Computer?," About .com Money, 2014, http://inventors.about.com/od/estartinventions/a/Eniac .htm.

12. Steve Rayner and Elizabeth L. Malone, *Human Choice and Climate Change* (Battelle Press, 1998).

13. Robert Tracinski, "7 Big Failed Environmentalist Predictions," *The Federalist*, 2015, http://thefederalist.com/2015/04/24/seven-big-failed -environmentalist-predictions/.

14. Daniel Howden, "World Oil Supplies Are Set to Run Out Faster Than Expected, Warn Scientists," *The Independent*, 2007, http://www.independent .co.uk/news/science/world-oil-supplies-are-set-to-run-out-faster-than -expected-warn-scientists-6262621.html.

    And

    Nafeez Ahmed, "Former BP Geologist: Peak Oil Is Here and It Will 'Break Economies,'" *The Guardian*, 2013, http://www.theguardian.com/environment/earth-insight/2013/dec/23/british-petroleum-geologist-peak -oil-break-economy-recession.

15. Biologicaldiversity.org, "Oil Shale and Tar Sands," accessed February 25, 2016, http://www.biologicaldiversity.org/programs/public_lands/energy/dirty_energy_development/oil_shale_and_tar_sands/.

16. Adrian Thompson and Brian Khan, "What Passing a Key CO_2 Mark Means to Climate Scientists," *Climate Central*, 2015, http://www.climatecentral.org/news/co2-400-ppm-scientists-meaning-19713.

17. Millennium Ecosystem Assessment, *Ecosystems and Human Well-Being: Synthesis* (Island Press, 2005), http://www.millenniumassessment.org/documents/document.356.aspx.pdf.

18. Jonathan Amos, "Study Highlights Global Decline," BBC News, 2005, http://news.bbc.co.uk/2/hi/science/nature/4391835.stm.

19. Center for Biological Diversity, "The Extinction Crisis," accessed February 24, 2016, http://www.biologicaldiversity.org/programs/biodiversity/elements_of_biodiversity/extinction_crisis/.

20. Elizabeth Kolbert, *The Sixth Extinction* (Henry Holt and Co., 2014).

21. Nadia Drake, "Will Humans Survive the Sixth Great Extinction?," *National Geographic*, 2015, http://news.nationalgeographic.com/2015/06/150623-sixth-extinction-kolbert-animals-conservation-science-world/.

22. C. Mora and P. F. Sale, "Ongoing Global Biodiversity Loss and the Need to Move Beyond Protected Areas: A Review of the Technical and Practical Shortcomings of Protected Areas on Land and Sea," *Marine Ecology Progress Series* 434 (2011): 251–266, doi:10.3354/meps09214.

23. Ibid., 261.

24. United Nations, "World Population Projected to Reach 9.6 Billion by 2050," United Nations Department of Economic and Social Affairs, 2013, https://www.un.org/development/desa/en/news/population/un-report-world-population-projected-to-reach-9-6-billion-by-2050.html.

25. Jonathan Amos, "Study Highlights Global Decline," BBC News, 2005, http://news.bbc.co.uk/2/hi/science/nature/4391835.stm.

26. Greenfacts.org, "How Much Forest Is There on the Planet and at What Rate Is It Disappearing?," accessed February 24, 2016, http://www.greenfacts.org/en/forests/l-3/2-extent-deforestation.htm.
    And
    Wwf.org.uk, "Crisis in Global Oceans as Populations of Marine Species Halve in Size Since 1970," 2015, http://www.wwf.org.uk/about_wwf/press_centre/?unewsid=7673.

27. Christopher Wright and Daniel Nyberg, *Climate Change, Capitalism, and Corporations* (Cambridge University Press, 2015).

28. The Conversation, "Creative Self-Destruction: The Climate Crisis and the Myth of 'Green' Capitalism," 2015, http://theconversation.com/creative-self-destruction-the-climate-crisis-and-the-myth-of-green-capitalism-47479.

29. Camilo Mora et al., "The Projected Timing of Climate Departure from Recent Variability," *Nature* 502, no. 7470 (2013): 183–187, doi:10.1038/nature12540.

30. Joby Warrick, "Why Are So Many Americans Skeptical about Climate Change? A Study Offers a Surprising Answer," *Washington Post*, 2015, https://www.washingtonpost.com/news/energy-environment/wp/2015/11/23/why-are-so-many-americans-skeptical-about-climate-change-a-study-offers-a-surprising-answer/.

31. Justin Gillis, "U.N. Says Lag in Confronting Climate Woes Will Be Costly," *New York Times*, 2014, http://www.nytimes.com/2014/01/17/

science/earth/un-says-lag-in-confronting-climate-woes-will-be-costly
.html?ref=science&_r=1.

32. Ibid.

33. Ibid.

34. Climatechange2013, "IPCC Working Group I," 2016, http://www.climate
change2013.org/.

35. *ScienceDaily*, "Poor Air Quality Kills 5.5 Million Worldwide Annually," 2016,
https://www.sciencedaily.com/releases/2016/02/160212140912.htm.

36. J. Lelieveld et al., "The Contribution of Outdoor Air Pollution Sources to
Premature Mortality on a Global Scale," *Nature* 525, no. 7569 (2015): 367–371,
doi:10.1038/nature15371.

37. Andy D. Ward et al., *Environmental Hydrology*, 3rd ed. (CRC Press, 2016).

38. D. R. Montgomery, "Soil Erosion and Agricultural Sustainability," *Proceedings of the National Academy of Sciences* 104, no. 33 (2007): 13268–13272,
doi:10.1073/pnas.0611508104.

39. Tom Paulson, "The Lowdown on Topsoil: It's Disappearing," *Seattle Pi*, 2008,
http://www.seattlepi.com/national/article/The-lowdown-on-topsoil-It-s
-disappearing-1262214.php.

40. Chris Arsenault, "Only 60 Years of Farming Left if Soil Degradation Continues," *Reuters*, 2014, http://www.reuters.com/article/us-food-soil-farming
-idUSKCN0JJ1R920141205.

41. Deepak K. Ray et al., "Yield Trends Are Insufficient to Double Global Crop
Production by 2050," *Plos ONE* 8, no. 6 (2013): e66428, doi:10.1371/journal
.pone.0066428.

42. Cbf.org, "Chesapeake Bay Foundation—Saving a National Treasure,"
accessed February 24, 2016, http://www.cbf.org/how-we-save-the-bay/issues/
dead-zones/nitrogen-phosphorus.

And

Colorado State University Extension Publications, accessed February 24,
2016, http://www.ext.colostate.edu/pubs/crops/00517.html.

And

Danielle Elliot, "Mercury Contamination in Fish Expected to Rise in
Coming Decades," CBS News, 2013, http://www.cbsnews.com/news/mer-
cury-contamination-in-fish-expected-to-rise-in-coming-decades/.

43. *National Geographic*, "Clean Water Crisis, Water Crisis Facts, Water Crisis
Resources," accessed February 24, 2016, http://environment.national
geographic.com/environment/freshwater/freshwater-crisis/.

44. Organization for Economic Cooperation and Development, *Water: The
Environmental Outlook to 2050* (Paris, 2011), http://www.oecd.org/env/
resources/49006778.pdf.

45. Steve Connor, "Lack of Fresh Water Could Hit Half the World's Population

by 2050," *The Independent*, 2013, http://www.independent.co.uk/news/science/lack-of-fresh-water-could-hit-half-the-world-s-population-by-2050-8631613.html.

46. Ibid.

47. Fiona Harvey, "Humans Damaging the Environment Faster than It Can Recover, UN Finds," *The Guardian*, 2016, https://www.theguardian.com/environment/2016/may/19/humans-damaging-the-environment-faster-than-it-can-recover-report-finds.

48. Aviva H. Rutkin, "Report Suggests Nearly Half of U.S. Jobs Are Vulnerable to Computerization," *MIT Technology Review*, 2013, https://www.technologyreview.com/s/519241/report-suggests-nearly-half-of-us-jobs-are-vulnerable-to-computerization/.

49. Alexander C. Kaufman, "Stephen Hawking Says We Should Really Be Scared of Capitalism, Not Robots," *Huffington Post*, 2015, http://www.huffingtonpost.com/entry/stephen-hawking-capitalism-robots_us_5616c20ce4b0dbb8000d9f15.

50. Daniel Tencer, "S&P: 60% of Countries Will Be Bankrupt within 50 Years," *Raw Story*, 2010, http://www.rawstory.com/2010/10/sp-60-countries-bankrupt-50-years/.

51. John T. Harvey, "It Is Impossible for the US to Default," *Forbes*, 2012, http://www.forbes.com/sites/johntharvey/2012/09/10/impossible-to-default/#41edf3d5744e.

52. World Health Organization, "Progress on Drinking Water and Sanitation," 2012, http://www.who.int/water_sanitation_health/publications/2012/jmp_report/en/.

53. A review of historical US labor statistics by sector clearly shows the pattern of machine automation replacing human labor. In the agricultural sector, almost all workflow is now done by machine. In 1949, machines did 6 percent of the cotton picking in the South. By 1972, 100 percent of the cotton picking was done by machines.

   Willis Peterson and Yoav Kislev, "The Cotton Harvester in Retrospect: Labor Displacement or Replacement?," *Journal of Economic History* 46, no. 01 (1991): 1–2, doi:10.1017/s0022050700045587.

   In 1860, 60 percent of Americans worked in agriculture, while today it is less than 3 percent.

   "Why Job Growth Is Stalled," *Fortune*, 1993, 52.

   In 1950, 33 percent of US workers worked in manufacturing, while by 2002 only 10 percent did.

   Barbara Hagenbaugh, "U.S. Manufacturing Jobs Fading Away Fast," *USA Today*, 2002, http://www.usatoday.com/money/economy/2002-12-12-manufacture_x.htm.

   The US steel industry from 1982 to 2002 increased production from 75 million tons to 120 million tons, while the number of steel workers fell from 289,000 to 74,000.

Nelson D. Schwartz, "Will 'Made in USA' Fade Away? Yes, We'll Still Have Factories, and Great Ones Too. We Just Might Not Have Many Factory Workers. Why Those Jobs Are Never Coming Back," *Archive.Fortune. Com*, 2003, 102, http://archive.fortune.com/magazines/fortune/fortune _archive/2003/11/24/353800/index.htm.

In 2003, Alliance Capital did a study of the world's largest twenty economies at that time, ranging from 1995 to 2002, finding that 31 million manufacturing jobs were lost, while production actually rose by 30 percent.

Alliance Bernstein, "Manufacturing Payrolls Declining Globally: The Untold Story," *US Weekly Economic Update*, 2003.

From 1983 to 1993, banks cut 37 percent of their human tellers, and by the year 2000, 90 percent of all bank customers used teller machines (ATMs).

Vision, "Retooling Lives," 2000, 43.

Business phone operators have almost all been replaced by computerized voice-answering systems, post office tellers are being replaced by self-service machines, and cashiers are being replaced by computerized kiosks. McDonald's, for example, has been talking about full automation of its restaurants for many years, introducing kiosks to replace the front-of-house staff, while using automated cooking tools, such as burger flippers, for the back-of-house staff.

Mike Masnick, "Mcdonald's New High-Tech Burger Flipper," *Techdirt*, 2003, http://www.techdirt.com/articles/20030801/1345236_F.shtmls.

54. Paul Mason, "Automation May Mean a Post-Work Society but We Shouldn't Be Afraid," *The Guardian*, 2016, http://www.theguardian.com/sustainable -business/2016/feb/17/automation-may-mean-a-post-work-society-but-we -shouldnt-be-afraid?CMP=fb_gu.

55. *Economia*, "More than 11 Million Jobs at High Risk of Automation," 2016, http://economia.icaew.com/news/january-2016/more-than-11-million-jobs -at-high-risk-of-automation.

And

Clive Cookson, "AI and Robots Threaten to Unleash Mass Unemployment, Scientists Warn," *Financial Times*, 2016, http://www.ft.com/intl/cms/ s/0/063c1176-d29a-11e5-969e-9d801cf5e15b.html#axzz409hmJhgY.

56. John M. Keynes, "Economic Possibilities for Our Grandchildren," 1931.

57. David Ricardo, *The Principles of Political Economy and Taxation* (J.M. Dent & Sons, 1962), 263–267.

58. Sarah Knapton, "Robots Will Take Over Most Jobs within 30 Years, Experts Warn," *The Telegraph*, 2016, http://www.telegraph.co.uk/news/science/ science-news/12155808/Robots-will-take-over-most-jobs-within-30-years -experts-warn.html.

59. Carl B. Frey and Michael A. Osborne, "The Future of Employment: How Susceptible Are Jobs to Computerisation?," 2013, http://www.oxfordmartin.ox.ac.uk/downloads/academic/The_Future_of_Employment.pdf.

60. Andy Eckardt, "Adidas Shifts Production—But Robots Get the Jobs," NBC News, 2016, http://www.nbcnews.com/business/business-news/adidas-pulls-back-asia-robots-get-jobs-n579991.

61. Hazel Sheffield, "Wendy's Replacing Workers with Machines Because of Rising Wage Cost," *The Independent*, 2016, http://www.independent.co.uk/news/business/news/wendys-mcdonalds-wages-self-service-machines-automation-a7035351.html.

62. Arthur Delaney, "Joblessness and Hopelessness: The Link Between Unemployment and Suicide," *Huffington Post*, 2011, http://www.huffingtonpost.com/2011/04/15/unemployment-and-suicide_n_849428.html.

63. Barry Schwartz, "Rethinking Work," *New York Times*, 2015, http://www.nytimes.com/2015/08/30/opinion/sunday/rethinking-work.html.

64. David Graeber, "On the Phenomenon of Bullshit Jobs," *Strike!*, 2013, http://strikemag.org/bullshit-jobs/.

65. Daniel H. Pink, *Drive: The Surprising Truth about What Motivates Us*, Amazon.Com (Riverhead Books, 2011).

66. Adam Smith, *An Inquiry into the Nature and Causes of the Wealth of Nations*, Edwin Cannan and Max Lerner, eds. (Modern Library, 1937), 319.

67. Carol S. Dweck, *Self-Theories* (Psychology Press, 1999), 41.

68. "Giving and Volunteering in the United States: Findings from a National Survey," 1992, 2.

69. Jeffrey L. Brudney and Beth Gazley, "Moving Ahead or Falling Behind? Volunteer Promotion and Data Collection," *Nonprofit Management & Leadership* 16, no. 3 (2006), https://philanthropy.iupui.edu/files/research/moving_ahead_or_falling_behind_-_volunteer_promotion_and_data_collection.pdf.

70. Lydia Saad, "Despite Economy, Charitable Donors, Volunteers Keep Giving," Gallup, 2008, http://www.gallup.com/poll/113497/despite-economy-charitable-donors-%20volunteers-keep-giving.aspx.

71. Rifkin, *The Zero Marginal Cost Society*, 133.

72. John O'Farrell, "A No-Strings Basic Income? If It Works for the Royal Family, It Can Work for Us All," *The Guardian*, 2016, http://www.theguardian.com/commentisfree/2016/jan/07/basic-income-royal-family-living-wage-economy.

73. David Crouch, "Efficiency Up, Turnover Down: Sweden Experiments with Six-Hour Working Day," *The Guardian*, 2015, http://www.theguardian.com/world/2015/sep/17/efficiency-up-turnover-down-sweden-experiments-with-six-hour-working-day.

74. John Locke, *Second Treatise of Government* (1689), Chap. V, Section 27.

75. Referred to by some as the "sharing economy," this idea has grown rapidly. See: Colleen Taylor, "Airbnb CEO: The Future Is about Access, Not Ownership," *Gigaom*, 2011, http://gigaom.com/2011/11/10/airbnb-roadmap-2011/.
    And
    A. K. Streeter, "Bike Sharing Now in 100 European Cities," *Treehugger*, 2010, http://www.treehugger.com/cars/bike-sharing-now-in-100-european -cities.html.
    And
    John Cook and Taylor Soper, "BMW Tests Car-Sharing Service in Seattle, Taking on Car2go in First U.S. Move Since Halting S.F. Pilot," *Geekwire*, 2016, http://www.geekwire.com/2016/bmws-drivenow-car-sharing-service-looks -to-take-on-car2go-in-seattle-marking-first-u-s-expansion/.

76. Paul Barter, "'Cars Are Parked 95% of the Time.' Let's Check!," *Reinventing Parking*, 2013, http://www.reinventingparking.org/2013/02/cars-are-parked- 95-of-time-lets-check.html.

77. Hedges & Company, "Vehicle Registration Data," accessed February 25, 2016, https://hedgescompany.com/automotive-market-research-statistics/ auto-mailing-lists-and-marketing.

78. Sanfrancisco.cbslocal.com, "How Uber's Autonomous Cars Will Destroy 10 Million Jobs and Reshape the Economy by 2025," 2015, http://sanfrancisco .cbslocal.com/2015/01/27/how-ubers-autonomous-cars-will-destroy-10 -million-jobs-and-reshape-the-economy-by-2025-lyft-google-zack-kanter/.

79. Big Think, "Economic Shift: The Rise of the Collaborative Commons," 2014, http://bigthink.com/think-tank/the-collaborative-commons-economy.

80. Glyn Moody, *Rebel Code* (Perseus Books, 2001).

81. Roy Rosenzweig, *Clio Wired: The Future of the Past in the Digital Age* (Columbia University Press, 2011), 79.

82. Michael A. Nielsen, *Reinventing Discovery* (Princeton University Press, 2012), 39.

83. Martin C. Libicki et al., *Byting Back* (Rand, 2007), 100.

84. Thomas Goetz, "Open Source Everywhere," *Wired*, 2003, http://www.wired .com/2003/11/opensource/.

85. Elon Musk, "All Our Patent Are Belong to You," *Tesla*, 2014, https://www .teslamotors.com/blog/all-our-patent-are-belong-you.

86. TZM Lecture Team, *The Zeitgeist Movement Defined: Realizing a New Train of Thought* (CreateSpace, 2014), 256–285.

87. Regarding component standardization and its importance, in 1801 Eli Whitney was the first to apply standardization in a high-impact way. He produced muskets, and during his time there was no way to interchange the parts of different muskets, even though they were the same overall design. If a musket part broke, the whole gun was useless. Whitney developed tools for interchangeability and after 1801, all musket parts were fully interchangeable.

While most would assume this commonsense idea to be prolific across the global industrial community today, the perpetuation of proprietary components by companies that want the consumer to repurchase any such needed component from them directly, ignoring the possibility of compatibility with other producers, creates not only great waste but also great inconvenience.

88. Dickson Despommier, *The Vertical Farm: Feeding the World in the 21st Century* (Thomas Dunne, 2010).

    And

    Hod Lipson and Melba Kurman, *Fabricated: The New World of 3D Printing* (John Wiley & Sons, 2013).

89. S. A. Smith, *The Oxford Handbook of the History of Communism* (Oxford University Press, 2014), 42.

90. Institution of Mechanical Engineers, *Feeding the 9 Billion: The Tragedy of Waste*, 2014, http://nearyou.imeche.org/docs/default-source/Devon---Somerset-Area/tim-fox-may-2014-food-waste-talk-flyer.pdf?sfvrsn=0.

91. Fabian Kretschmer and Malte E. Kollenberg, "Vertical Farming: Can Urban Agriculture Feed a Hungry World?," *Spiegel Online*, 2011, http://www.spiegel.de/international/zeitgeist/vertical-farming-can-urban-agriculture-feed-a-hungry-world-a-775754.html.

92. Mahatma Gandhi, *Soul Force* (Tara, 2004), 245.

93. Richard Sorabji, *Gandhi and the Stoics*, n.d, 124.

94. Mahatma Gandhi, *Hind Swaraj and Other Writings*, Anthony Parel, ed. (Cambridge University Press, 1997), 89.

95. Samuel Greengard, *The Internet of Things*, n.d.

96. Maged N. Kamel Boulos and Najeeb M. Al-Shorbaji, "On the Internet of Things, Smart Cities and the WHO Healthy Cities," *International Journal of Health Geographics* 13, no. 1 (2014): 10, doi:10.1186/1476-072x-13-10.

97. Ludwig von Mises, *Economic Calculation in the Socialist Commonwealth* (1920).

98. Pacific Institute, "Water, Food, and Agriculture," accessed February 25, 2016, http://pacinst.org/issues/water-food-and-agriculture/.

99. See Appendix A.

100. Ibid.

101. Ibid.

102. Martin Luther King Jr., "Where Do We Go From Here?," speech delivered at the 11th Annual SCLC Convention Atlanta, Ga., 1967, http://mlk-kpp01.stanford.edu/index.php/encyclopedia/documentsentry/where_do_we _go _from_here_delivered_at_the_11th_annual_sclc_convention/.

103. Phoebe Parke, "More Africans Have Access to Cell Phone Service than Piped Water," *CNN*, January 19, 2016, http://www.cnn.com/2016/01/19/africa/africa-afrobarometer-infrastructure-report/.

104. Peter H. Diamandis and Steven Kotler, *Abundance: The Future Is Better Than You Think* (Free Press, 2012), 108.

105. Larry Dane Brimner, *We Are One: The Story of Bayard Rustin* (Calkins Creek, 2007), 46.

Appendix A

1. This is a modified reprint with permission by The Zeitgeist Movement. For a more extensive treatment of post-scarcity economics, see: TZM Lecture Team, *The Zeitgeist Movement Defined: Realizing a New Train of Thought* (CreateSpace, 2014), 256–285.

2. The term "post-scarcity" denotes a state that eliminates access scarcity of a given resource or process, usually by means of optimized efficiency regarding production design and strategic use. Needless to say, the idea of achieving total post-scarcity—meaning an infinite, abundant amount of everything for everyone—is rightly considered an impossibility, even in the most optimistic views. Therefore, this term, as used here, really highlights a point of focus.

3. Monetary economics is rooted in viewing the world from the standpoint of shortages or inefficiencies. It is based in managing scarcity through a system of price-and-value relationships. The scarcer an item, the more it is valued.

4. Food and Agriculture Organization of the United Nations, "Globally Almost 870 Million Chronically Undernourished—New Hunger Report," accessed February 23, 2016, http://www.fao.org/news/story/en/item/161819/.

5. J. Parfitt, M. Barthel, and S. Macnaughton, "Food Waste within Food Supply Chains: Quantification and Potential for Change to 2050," *Philosophical Transactions of the Royal Society B: Biological Sciences* 365, no. 1554 (2010): 3065–3081, doi:10.1098/rstb.2010.0126.

6. Topsoil is the top layer of soil that possesses the greatest concentration of organic matter and microorganisms and from which plants obtain the overwhelming majority of their nutrients. Today, it is disappearing at an alarming rate primarily due to conventional agricultural practices such as monoculture (the practice of planting one single crop over and over again). Likewise, soil erosion is increasing rapidly with a large number of problematic effects due to inefficient farming practices.

   See: Environmental Working Group, "Losing Ground," accessed February 23, 2016, http://www.ewg.org/losingground/.

7. NewEarthDaily, accessed 23 February 23, 2016, http://newearthdaily .com/floating-vertical-farms-could-feed-the-world-with-cheap-plentiful -produce/.

8. Dickson Despommier, *The Vertical Farm: Feeding the World in the 21st Century* (Thomas Dunne Books, 2010).

9. TheFreeDictionary.com, "Hydroponics," accessed February 23, 2016, http://www.thefreedictionary.com/hydroponics.

10. TheFreeDictionary.com, "Aeroponic," accessed 23 February 2016, http://www.thefreedictionary.com/aeroponic.

11. Growing Power Inc., "Aquaponics," accessed February 23, 2016, http://www.growingpower.org/aquaponics.

12. Jake Cox, "What Is Vertical Farming?," *On Earth*, 2009, http://www.onearth.org/blog/what-is-vertical-farming.

13. *AENews*, "Waste to Energy," accessed February 23, 2016, http://www.alternative-energy-news.info/technology/garbage-energy.

14. Rachel Oliver, "All About: Food and Fossil Fuels," CNN, 2008, http://edition.cnn.com/2008/WORLD/asiapcf/03/16/eco.food.miles/.

15. "Feeding 9 Billion: Vertical Farming—Singapore [video]," *Off Grid World*, 2013, http://www.offgridworld.com/feeding-9-billion-vertical-farming-singapore-video/.

16. Martha Irvine, "'Mega' Indoor Vertical Farm: Chicago Suburb New Home to Nation's Largest Such Facility," *Huffington Post*, 2013, http://www.huffingtonpost.com/2013/03/28/mega-indoor-vertical-farm_n_2971328.html.

17. Aquaponics is a food-production system that combines conventional aquaculture (raising aquatic animals such as snails, fish, crayfish, or prawns in tanks) with hydroponics (cultivating plants in water) in a symbiotic environment.

18. *Green Futures Magazine*, "World's Largest Vertical Farm Is Certified Organic," 2013, http://www.forumforthefuture.org/greenfutures/articles/world%E2%80%99s-largest-vertical-farm-certified-organic.

19. It is worth noting that all major nutritional requirements are technically available in the genre of plant production. Contrary to popular belief, animal products are not required for a high-quality human diet. The six major classes of nutrients (carbohydrates, fats, dietary fiber, minerals, proteins, and vitamins), omitting water, can all be found in plants.

20. Renee Cho, "Vertical Farms: From Vision to Reality," *State of the Planet*, 2011, http://blogs.ei.columbia.edu/2011/10/13/vertical-farms-from-vision-to-reality/.

21. Bina Venkataraman, "Country, the City Version: Farms in the Sky Gain New Interest," *New York Times*, 2008, http://www.nytimes.com/2008/07/15/science/15farm.html?_r=0.

22. Generally, in New York City the average length of a north-to-south block is 1/20th of a mile, or 264 feet. An east-to-west block is about 1/5th of a mile, or 1,056 feet. So, a square block would be $264 \times 1,056 = 278,784$ square feet, which is equal to 6.4 acres.

23. United States Census Bureau, 2013, http://www.census.gov/.

24. The City of Los Angeles is 498.3 square miles. That converts to 318,912 acres.

25. Seventy-eight buildings, occupying 6.4 acres each, equals 499.2 acres used total; 499.2 acres is 0.15 percent of the total acreage of Los Angeles (318,912).

26. Worldometers, "World Population Clock: 7.4 Billion People (2016)," accessed February 23, 2016, http://www.worldometers.info/world-population/.

27. 7.2 billion (total population) divided by 50,000 (production capacity of one thirty-story vertical farm) equals 144,000 needed structures.

28. 6.4 (acres used per farm) multiplied by 144,000 (vertical farms) = 921,600 acres.

29. James Owen, "Farming Claims Almost Half Earth's Land, New Maps Show," *National Geographic*, 2005, http://news.nationalgeographic.com/news/2005/12/1209_051209_crops_map.html.

30. 921,600 (acres needed to place vertical farms) is 0.006581% of 13,981,811,200 (total acres of land on Earth used for traditional agriculture, both crops and livestock).

31. 6.4 acres (which is what has been determined as enough space to feed 50,000 people) goes into 4,408,320,000 (total land used currently for only crop cultivation on Earth) 688,800,000 times. 688,800,000, which represents the number of possible facilities where each can produce enough food to feed 50,000 people, translate into an output capacity of 34,440,000,000,000 people who can be fed. (688,800,000 × 50,000 = 34,440,000,000,000.)

32. Philip Thornton, Mario Herrero, and Polly Ericksen,"Livestock Xchange," *ILRI*, no. 3 (2011), http://cgspace.cgiar.org/bitstream/handle/10568/10601/IssueBrief3.pdf.

33. FAO Newsroom, "Livestock a Major Threat to Environment," 2006, http://www.fao.org/newsroom/en/News/2006/1000448/index.html.

34. *National Geographic*, "Big-Fish Stocks Fall 90 Percent Since 1950, Study Says," 2003, http://news.nationalgeographic.com/news/2003/05/0515_030515_fishdecline.html.

35. BBC News, "World's First Lab-Grown Burger Is Eaten in London," 2013, http://www.bbc.co.uk/news/science-environment-23576143.

36. Merriam-Webster.com, "Definition of Freshwater," accessed February 23, 2016, http://www.merriam-webster.com/dictionary/freshwater.

37. World Health Organization, "Health Through Safe Drinking Water and Basic Sanitation," accessed February 23, 2016, http://www.who.int/water_sanitation_health/mdg1/en/.

38. National Geographic, "Clean Water Crisis, Water Crisis Facts, Water Crisis Resources," accessed February 23, 2016, http://environment.nationalgeographic.com/environment/freshwater/freshwater-crisis/.

39. Jon Clift and Amanda Cuthbert, *Use Less—Save More* (Chelsea Green Publishing, 2007).

40. Peter Brabeck-Letmathe and Asit K. Biswas, "Water: A Global Crisis," *The Diplomat*, 2015, http://thediplomat.com/2015/06/water-a-global-crisis/.

41. Cecilia Tortajada and Asit K. Biswas, "Water Quality: An Ignored Global Crisis," *Bloomberg Business*, 2013, http://www.bloomberg.com/bw/articles/2013-03-21/water-quality-an-ignored-global-crisis.

42. Eetd.lbl.gov, "Uvwaterworks: From the Lab to the Marketplace—Ten Years Later," accessed February 24, 2016, http://eetd.lbl.gov/l2m2/waterworks.html.

43. "Ultraviolet Disinfection," *Tech Brief*, 2000, http://www.nesc.wvu.edu/pdf/dw/publications/ontap/2009_tb/ultraviolet_dwfsom53.pdf.

44. Trojanuv.com, "UV Disinfection & Water Treatment Solutions," accessed February 23, 2016, http://www.trojanuv.com/uvresources?resource=403.

45. Water Footprint Network, "Securing Fresh Water for Everyone," accessed February 23, 2016, http://www.waterfootprint.org/?page=cal/waterfootprintcalculator_national.

46. Ibid.

47. Mark Fischetti, "Which Nations Consume the Most Water?," *Scientific American*, 2012, http://www.scientificamerican.com/article.cfm?id=water-in-water-out.

48. Worldometers, "Water Consumption Statistics," accessed February 23, 2016, http://www.worldometers.info/water/.

49. 9 trillion 972 billion divided by 3 billion.

50. NYC.gov, "Catskill-Delaware Water Ultraviolet Disinfection Facility," accessed February 25, 2016, http://www.nyc.gov/html/dep/html/dep_projects/cp_catskill_delaware_uv_plant.shtml.

51. Jules Dofour, "The Worldwide Network of US Military Bases," *Global Research*, 2015, http://www.globalresearch.ca/the-worldwide-network-of-us-military-bases/5564.

52. IDA, "Desalination—An Overview," 2013, http://www.idadesal.org/desalination-101/desalination-overview/.

53. Ibid.

54. Jennifer Newton, "Flow Electrodes May Enable Large-Scale Sea Water Desalination," *Chemistry World*, 2013, http://www.rsc.org/chemistry-world/2013/03/sea-water-desalination-capacitive-deionisation.

55. Jim Lozier, "Advancements in Desalination," *Summer Seminar*, 2013, http://www.weat.org/sanantonio/files/06%20-%20Summer%20Seminar%202013%20-%20Jim%20Lozier%20-%20Adv%20in%20Desal.pdf.

56. Steve Lancaster, *Green Australia* (Wakefield Press, 2012).

57. Only Melbourne, "Wonthaggi Desalination Plant," accessed February 23, 2016, http://www.onlymelbourne.com.au/melbourne_details.php?id=31996#.UljSCWRDp94.

58. 9 trillion 972 million divided by 150 million.

59. Bob MacNeal, "Essays: The Coastline Paradox," *Grokearth.Blogspot.com*, 2012, http://grokearth.blogspot.com/2012/04/coastline-paradox.html.

60. Water.org, "Global Water Crisis: Water and Sanitation Facts," accessed February 23, 2016, http://water.org/water-crisis/water-facts/water/.

61. An advanced technology called the "Slingshot," invented by Dean Kamen, is a small-scale water-purification system that can produce clean water from almost any source, including sea water, by means of vapor-compression distillation. It requires no filters and can even operate using cow dung as fuel.

62. Renewableenergyworld.com, "Renewable Energy Overview," accessed February 23, 2016, http://www.renewableenergyworld.com/rea/tech/home.

63. Phys.org, "Fukushima Nuke Pollution in Sea 'Was World's Worst'," 2011, http://phys.org/news/2011-10-fukushima-nuke-pollution-sea-world.html.

64. Energyzone.net, "Energyzone Resources and Information," accessed February 23, 2016, http://www.energyzone.net/aboutenergy/renewable_energy.asp.

65. World Bank, "Energy," accessed February 23, 2016, http://web.worldbank.org/WBSITE/EXTERNAL/TOPICS/EXTENERGY2/0,,contentMDK:22855502~pagePK:210058~piPK:210062~theSitePK:4114200,00.html.

66. Geothermal power in this context isn't to be confused with small-scale geothermal heating/cooling processes that utilize heat from a few feet below the Earth's surface (i.e., geothermal heat pumps).

67. Geothermal.marin.org, "Geothermal Education Office," accessed February 23, 2016, http://geothermal.marin.org/pwrheat.html#Q1.
And
"Back to Basics Video: What Is Geothermal Energy Anyway?," accessed February 23, 2016, http://www.renewableenergyworld.com/rea/video/view/back-to-basics-video-what-is-geothermal-energy-anyway.

68. Massachusetts Institute of Technology, *The Future of Geothermal Energy, Impact of Enhanced Geothermal Systems (EGS) on the United States in the 21st Century* (Massachusetts Institute of Technology, 2006), http://geothermal.inel.gov/publications/future_of_geothermal_energy.pdf.

69. US Energy Information Administration. "EIA Projects World Energy Consumption Will Increase 56% by 2040," 2013, http://www.eia.gov/todayinenergy/detail.cfm?id=12251.

70. Gemini Unni Skoglund, "Geothermal Energy Could Provide All the Energy the World Will Ever Need," *Renewable Energy World.Com*, 2010, http://www.renewableenergyworld.com/rea/news/article/2010/09/geothermal-energy-is-the-solution-for-the-future.

71. Energy.gov, "Geothermal Energy at the U.S. Department of Energy," accessed February 23, 2016, http://www1.eere.energy.gov/geothermal/faqs.html.

72. Think GeoEnergy, "Geothermal Energy News," accessed February 23, 2016, http://thinkgeoenergy.com/archives/1733.

73. Katherine Harmon, "How Does Geothermal Drilling Trigger Earthquakes?,"

Scientific American, 2009, http://www.scientificamerican.com/article
.cfm?id=geothermal-drilling-earthquakes&page=2.

74. Southern Methodist University, "First Google.Org-Funded Geothermal
    Mapping Report Confirms Vast Coast-to-Coast Clean Energy Source," 2011,
    http://www.smu.edu/News/2011/geothermal-24oct2011.

75. *National Geographic*, "Plate Tectonics, Tectonic Plates Information, Facts,
    News, Photos," accessed February 23, 2016, http://science.nationalgeographic
    .com/science/earth/the-dynamic-earth/plate-tectonics-article/.

76. Ibid.

77. Global Energy Network Institute, "Global Renewable Energy Resources,"
    accessed February 23, 2016, http://www.geni.org/globalenergy/library/
    renewable-energy-resources/geothermal.shtml.

78. Geo-energy.org, "Geothermal Energy Association," accessed February 23,
    2016, http://geo-energy.org/geo_basics_environment.aspx.

79. 3,626 m^2 / 404 m^2 = 8.975 square meters.

    It is worth noting that geothermal and all other renewables addressed in
    this text inherently combine the extraction or harnessing location *with* the
    processing and power distribution location. All hydrocarbon sources, on
    the other hand, require both extraction (e.g., coal) and processing/power
    production facilities (i.e., refineries/power plants), almost always in separate
    locations. As per the current example, the mining land required for coal
    extraction is omitted from the equation. In short, renewables take up sub-
    stantially less land and have an exceptionally lower environmental impact
    in this regard.

80. Bruce Linwood, "Streaming Back: What to Look for in a Webcam for Pri-
    vate Video Chats," *Daily Ethiopia*, accessed February 23, 2016, http://www
    .dailyethiopia.com/index.php?aid=1498.

81. 8,760 (hrs in a year) × 1000 (MWh) = 8,760,000 Mwh/yr.

82. 0.55 zettajoules converts to about 153 billion MWh.

83. 153 billion MWh (total global use) / 8,760,000 MWh (geothermal plant
    capacity) = 17,465 geothermal plants.

84. World Coal Association, "Resources," accessed February 23, 2016, http://
    www.worldcoal.org/resources/frequently-asked-questions/.

85. 17,465 / 9 = 1,940.5.

86. World Coal Association, "Coal & Electricity," 2015, http://www.worldcoal
    .org/coal/uses-of-coal/coal-electricity/.

87. Ryan Wiser and Mark Bolinger, *Annual Report on U.S. Wind Power Instal-
    lation, Cost, and Performance Trends: 2007*, US Department of Energy, 2008,
    http://www.nrel.gov/docs/fy08osti/43025.pdf.

88. Cristina L. Archer and Mark Z. Jacobson, "Evaluation of Global Wind
    Power," Stanford.Edu, 2005, http://www.stanford.edu/group/efmh/winds/
    global_winds.html.

89. *Business Insider*, "The Earth Has Enough Wind Energy Potential to Power All of Civilization," 2012, http://www.businessinsider.com/the-earth-has-enough-wind-energy-potential-to-power-all-of-civilization-2012-9.

90. 8,760 (hrs in a year) × 1,320 (MW) = 11,563,200 MWh/year.

91. 13,231 × 9,000 acres = 119,079,000.

92. 119,079,000 acres is 0.32 percent of 36,794,240,000 acres (total land on Earth).

93. Marc Schwartz et al., *Assessment of Offshore Wind Energy Resources for the United States*, National Renewable Energy Laboratory, 2010, http://www.nrel.gov/docs/fy10osti/45889.pdf.

94. *Business Insider*, "The Earth Has Enough Wind Energy Potential to Power All of Civilization," 2012, http://www.businessinsider.com/the-earth-has-enough-wind-energy-potential-to-power-all-of-civilization-2012-9.

95. TheFreeDictionary.com, "Solar Energy," accessed February 23, 2016, http://encyclopedia2.thefreedictionary.com/solar+energy.

96. Emma Fitzpatrick, "World's Biggest Solar Thermal Power Plant Fires Up for First Time," *Renew Economy*, 2013, http://reneweconomy.com.au/2013/worlds-biggest-solar-thermal-power-plant-fires-first-time-89135.

97. National Renewable Energy Laboratory, "Concentrating Solar Power Projects—Ivanpah Solar Electric Generating System," 2014, http://www.nrel.gov/csp/solarpaces/project_detail.cfm/projectID=62.

98. 153 billion MWh / 1,079,232MWh = 141,767 plants @ 3,500 acres = 496,184,500 acres. 496,184,500 acres is 1.43 % of 36,794,240,000 (total land).

99. Dave Levitan, "Is Anything Stopping a Truly Massive Build-Out of Desert Solar Power?," *Scientific American*, 2013, http://www.scientificamerican.com/article.cfm?id=challenges-for-desert-solar-power.

100. Chris Clarke, "Solar Plant Generates Power for Six Hours After Sunset," *KCET*, 2013, http://www.kcet.org/news/rewire/solar/concentrating-solar/solar-plant-generates-power-for-six-hours-after-sunset.html.

101. Worldwatch Institute, "Use and Capacity of Global Hydropower Increases," 2013, http://www.worldwatch.org/node/9527.

102. According to Michael Bernitsas, a professor at the University of Michigan Department of Naval Architecture and Marine Engineering: "[I]f we could harness 0.1 percent of the energy in the ocean, we could support the energy needs of 15 billion people." Jasper Copping, "Ocean Currents Can Power the World, Say Scientists," *Telegraph*, 2008, http://www.telegraph.co.uk/earth/energy/renewableenergy/3535012/Ocean-currents-can-power-the-world-say-scientists.html.
And
Ocean Energy Council, "Examining the Future of Ocean Thermal Energy Conversion," 2014, http://www.oceanenergycouncil.com/examining-future-ocean-thermal-energy-conversion/.

103. Gunnar Mork et al., "Assessng the Global Wave Energy Potential," *Proceedings*

of OMAE2010 6, no. 11 (2011), http://www.oceanor.no/related/59149/paper_
OMAW_2010_20473_final.pdf.

104. Ei.lehigh.edu, "Energy—Student Resources: Tidal Energy," accessed February 23, 2016, http://ei.lehigh.edu/learners/energy/tidal2.html.

105. Lunar Energy, "Facts and Figures," accessed February 23, 2016, http://www.lunarenergy.co.uk/factsFigures.htm.

106. European Ocean Energy Association, *Conference on Marine Renewable Energies Towards a European Atlantic Strategy*, accessed February 23, 2016, http://www.crpm.org/pub/agenda/1384_nathalie_rousseau.pdf.

107. Ottmar Edenhofer, Ramón Pichs Madruga, and Y. Sokona, *Renewable Energy Sources and Climate Change Mitigation* (Cambridge University Press, 2012), 505–506.

108. European Ocean Energy Association, *Ocean Energy: Position Paper for IPCC*, accessed February 23, 2016, https://www.citethisforme.com/cite/report.

109. Ibid.

110. Nicole C. Moore, "'Fish Technology' Draws Renewable Energy from Slow Water Currents," *Michigan News*, 2008, http://ns.umich.edu/new/releases/6842.

111. Ibid.

112. Water & Wastewater International, "Norway's Osmotic Power a Salty Solution to the World's Energy Needs?," accessed February 24, 2016, http://www.waterworld.com/articles/wwi/print/volume-28/issue-2/regional-spotlight-europe/norway-s-osmotic-power-a-salty.html.

113. Richard Webb, "First Osmosis Power Plant Goes on Stream in Norway," *New Scientist*, 2009, http://www.newscientist.com/article/dn18204-first-osmosis-power-plant-goes-on-stream-in-norway.html#.UmCJ-WRDp94.

114. *MarketWatch*, "Osmotic Power Play: Energy Recovery Teams with GS Engineering & Construction Corp to Develop Highly Available Renewable Energy Source," 2013, http://www.marketwatch.com/story/osmotic-power-play-energy-recovery-teams-with-gs-engineering-construction-corp-to-develop-highly-available-renewable-energy-source-2013-10-15?reflink=MW_news_stmp.

115. Edenhofer, *Renewable Energy Sources and Climate Change Mitigation*, 507.

116. Daniel Cusick, "Ocean Thermal Power Will Debut Off China's Coast," *Scientific American*, 2013, http://www.scientificamerican.com/article.cfm?id=ocean-thermal-power-will-debut-off-chinas-coast.

117. Duane Shimogawa, "100-MW OTEC Project Planned for West Oahu," *Pacific Business News*, 2012, http://www.bizjournals.com/pacific/print-edition/2012/10/05/100-mw-otec-project-planned-for-west.html?page=all.

118. Kiki Von Gilnow, "Ocean Thermal Energy Conversion Could Power All of Hawaii's Big Island," *Huffington Post*, 2013, http://www.huffingtonpost.

com/2013/09/16/ocean-thermal-energy-conversion-hawaii_n_3937367
.html.

119. International Energy Agency, *Renewable Energy Essentials: Hydropower*, OECD/IEA, 2010, http://www.iea.org/publications/freepublications/ publication/Hydropower_Essentials.pdf.

120. US Energy Information Administration, "How Much Electricity Does an American Home Use?," 2015, http://www.eia.gov/tools/faqs/faq .cfm?id=97&t=3.

121. Statisticbrain.com, "Total Number of U.S. Households—Statistic Brain," 2014, http://www.statisticbrain.com/u-s-household-statistics/.

122. While the current state of CPV solar efficiency, as of 2013, is 44.7 percent. Soitec, "Soitec—World Record Solar Cell with 44.7% Efficiency," accessed February 23, 2016, http://www.soitec.com/en/news/press-releases/ world-record-solar-cell-1373/. With consumer available products averaging only about 18 percent [SRoeCo Solar (new), "Solar Panel Efficiency Comparison," 2013, http://sroeco.com/solar/most-efficient-solar-panels], more advanced methods are suggesting upward of 80 percent. [Ryan Whitwam, "New Nano-Material Could Boost Solar Panel Efficiency as High as 80% | Extremetech," *Extremetech*, 2013, http://www.extremetech.com/ extreme/168811-new-nano-material-could-boost-solar-panel-efficiency-as -high-as-80]. Likewise, battery storage for household use has been advancing via emerging *graphene super capacitors* [Darren Quick, "Graphene-Based Supercapacitor a Step Closer to Commerical Reality," *Gizmag*, 2013, http://www.gizmag.com/graphene-based-supercapacitor/28579/], which can charge faster, last many times longer than conventional batteries, are less polluting, and take up less space. Another advancing battery technology is termed the LMB, as developed by Donald Sadoway and MIT.

123. It is worth mentioning once again that all business establishments perpetuate themselves mostly by the markets they have created *prior*. A new invention that can interfere with the existing income infrastructure of a given business is often subject to influences that slow or even suppress that income-interfering technology. While many see this kind of behavior as a form of "corruption," the truth is that the very mechanism of bringing a given good to the market is subject to imposed financial limitations, which achieve the same goal. For example, if the new good cannot be considered profitable during the course of its development, regardless of its true merit, it will be hindered. The extremely slow pace of renewable energies on the whole, even though the principle of most means has been understood for hundreds of years, is a direct result of monetary investment or lack thereof. The more efficient a technology, the less profit will be realized in the long term.

124. Wholesale Solar, "Off Grid Intertie Home Power Solar Electric System

Minimum System Size Calculation," accessed February 23, 2016, http://www.
wholesalesolar.com/StartHere/OFFGRIDBallparkCost.html.

125. "Free Power Wind Turbines," accessed February 23, 2016, http://www.
     freepowerwindturbines.com/honeywell_wind_turbine.html.

126. US Department of Energy, "Geothermal Heat Pumps," accessed February
     23, 2016, http://energy.gov/energysaver/articles/geothermal-heat-pumps.

127. TheFreeDictionary.com, "Piezoelectric," accessed February 23, 2016, http://
     www.thefreedictionary.com/piezoelectric.

128. Jorge Chapa, "Energy-Generating Floors to Power Tokyo Subways," *Inhabitat*,
     2008, http://inhabitat.com/tokyo-subway-stations-get-piezoelectric-floors/.

129. A.K. Streeter, "Six Sidewalks That Work While You Walk," *Treehugger*,
     2010, http://www.treehugger.com/clean-technology/six-sidewalks-that-
     work-while-you-walk.html.

130. Ovidiu Sandru, "Israel Highway Equipped with Pilot Piezoelectric Gen-
     erator System," *The Green Optimistic*, 2009, http://www.greenoptimistic
     .com/2009/10/06/israel-piezoelectric-highway/#.UmHNTmRDp94.

131. Timon Singh, "New Piezoelectric Railways Harvest Energy from Passing
     Trains," *Inhabitat*, 2010, http://inhabitat.com/new-piezoelectric-railways
     -harvest-energy-from-passing-trains/.

132. Maurice Picow, "Under Highway Piezoelectric 'Generators' Could Provide
     Power to Propel Electric Cars," *Green Prophet*, 2010, http://www.greenprophet
     .com/2010/09/piezoelectric-generators-electric-cars/.

133. Tessa Henderson, "Piezoelectric Kinetic Energy Harvester for Mobile Phones,"
     Energy Harvesting Journal, 2010, http://www.energyharvestingjournal
     .com/articles/piezoelectric-kinetic-energy-harvester-for-mobile-phones
     -00002142.asp?sessionid=1.
         And
         Laura Shin, "Charge Your Phone by Typing on It," *Zdnet*, 2011, http://
     www.smartplanet.com/blog/science-scope/charge-your-phone-by-typing
     -on-it/8797.

134. *Gizmag*, "Harvesting Energy from Vehicle Air Flow Using Piezoelectrics,"
     accessed February 23, 2016, http://www.gizmag.com/harnessing-vehicle
     -air-flow-energy/13414.

135. Futuristic News.com, "Future Transportation—P-Eco Electric Concept
     Vehicle Powered by Piezoelectricity," accessed February 23, 2016, http://
     psipunk.com/p-eco-electric-concept-vehicle-powered-by-piezoelectricity/.

Appendix B

1. This is a modified reprint with permission of The Zeitgeist Movement. For
   a more extensive treatment of post-scarcity economics, see: TZM Lecture

Team, *The Zeitgeist Movement Defined: Realizing a New Train of Thought* (CreateSpace, 2014).

2. "Fixed automation," also known as "hard automation," refers to an automated production facility in which the sequence of processing operations is fixed by the equipment configuration. It is fast but has less variation in output-design capacity. Flexible automation can create more variation, but the disadvantage is the time required to reprogram and change over the production equipment. These terms are common to the manufacturing and robotics industry when it comes to plant design.